D0354279

MARIA
MENEGHINI
CALLAS

Michael Scott

Northeastern University Press
BOSTON

To Nicholas J. Hamer

Library of Congress Cataloging-in-Publication Data
Scott, Michael.
Maria Meneghini Callas / Michael Scott.
p.   cm.
Includes bibliographical references and index.
ISBN 1-55553-146-6 (alk. paper)
1. Callas, Maria, 1923–1977. 2. Sopranos (Singers)—Biography.
I. Title.
ML420.C18s35   1992
782.1′092—dc20   92-17103
[B]   MN

Printed and bound by The Maple Press in York, Pennsylvania.
The paper is Maple Antique, an acid-free sheet.

MANUFACTURED IN THE UNITED STATES OF AMERICA

96 95 94 93 92   5 4 3 2

Music Advisor to Northeastern University Press
GUNTHER SCHULLER

CONTENTS

ACKNOWLEDGMENTS

Of all those to whom I owe so much Callas herself must come first. Not that I knew her well, as did my friend John Ardoin: my acquaintance with her was of the slightest, but I did have the advantage of seeing her in opera on many occasions: at Covent Garden, London; La Scala, Milan; Epidavros; the Paris Opéra and even in Dallas. But if John only saw her once in the 1950s, in a concert she gave in Detroit in 1958, he came to know her extremely well after her operatic career was over, and I cannot sufficiently express my deep gratitude to him for putting at my disposal so much of the material he has accumulated.

It is a pleasure to mention many others who have helped me unstintingly: Richard Bebb, who might feel out of place in a work on Callas, since he questions her worth as an actress; Kathleen Begley, of the Bank of England library, for providing foreign exchange rates during Callas's career; Matthew Epstein, who introduced me to a number of books on Callas; Arthur Germond, who let me poach freely on his preserves to compile the Chronology of Callas's performances; Robert Roberts for copying out the embellishments Callas used in *La Sonnambula* at La Scala in 1955 (see p. 150) and for providing a key to my notational references (see p. vii); Mary Tzambiras who translated the Greek reviews. I am extremely grateful to all those whom I have quoted. Only lack of space forbids me mentioning them here.

I am also grateful to many friends who have obliged me in countless ways: Stephen and Mary Banks; John Bird; the late Edward Bridgewater; Jack Buckley; Karen Christenfeld; the late Gerald Fitzgerald; Peter Fleming; Giorgio and Erika Galliano; Michael Hartnall; Jack Henderson; Joel Honig; Pamela Jones; Vivian Liff; Guthrie Luke; Liz Measures; Andy Miller; Claudio and Alison Painelli; Umberto and Muffie Pergola; Joel Pritkin; John Ransley; Patric Schmid; my sister, Edith Scott; my brother, John Scott and my sister-in-law, Koby; Robert and Jill Slotover; Don White; and the late Michael Zaccaria. Anyone else whom I may inadvertently have omitted, I thank all the same.

I owe a special debt to Diana Cagli who, during my research, invited me to her villa near Lucca to relax; Randolph Mickelson who enabled me to do my Venice research while staying in his Grand Canal apartment; Geoffrey, Paula and Romola Nuttall who have endured my frequent visits to London; and to Michael Aspinall, to whom I owe so much for his counsel and erudition, I only hope he approves of the finished result.

Finally, I should like to thank Gina Guandalini for kindly supplying all the photographs for the book, as well as giving me the benefit of her encyclopaedic knowledge.

NOTE: RATES OF EXCHANGE

The following approximate rates of exchange apply:
1947–49: £1 sterling = US $4.02 = Italian Lire 2,300 = French Francs 480.
1949–56: £1 = $2.80 = Lire 1,750 = Francs 980.
1957–63: £1 = $2.80 = Lire 1,750 = Francs 13.75 = Greek Drachmae 84.50.

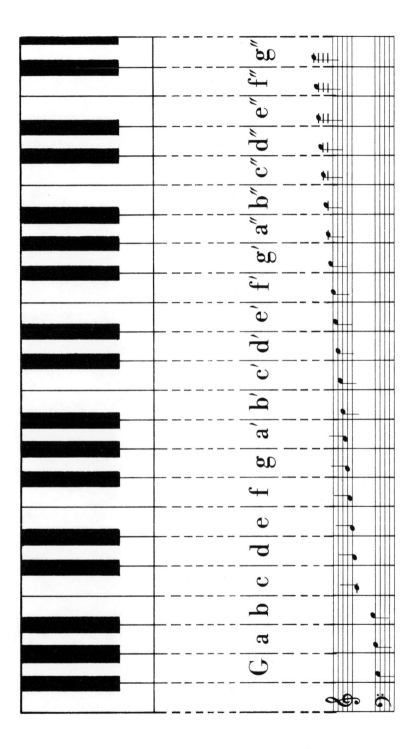

PRELUDE

CALLAS IS ONE of the three greatest opera singers of this century. In her heyday her voice was more responsive to music than any singer's had been since the days of Caruso and Chaliapin. Her talent although profound was simple, and there was nothing in the least mysterious or abstruse about it. Callas's records prove how great a singer she was. Whether she was also a great actress is today irrelevant, for only the smallest part of her histrionics survives: two films of Act II of *Tosca*; and it is not Tosca, the last part she undertook in the theatre, that makes her unique. In verismo opera there was not sufficient scope for a musical talent so profound. Significantly, *Turandot* was the most modern work that she sang, though as soon as she could she dropped it from her repertory. Indeed, she was the first famous opera singer who never sang a contemporary opera.[1]

Callas realized instinctively, as the music abundantly illustrates, that operas from the age of bel canto, in the first half of the nineteenth century, by Rossini, Bellini, Donizetti and the young Verdi, show singers off to the best advantage. They were written in an age when singers were opera's *raison d'être*, long before stage directors had much more to do than wheel the scenery on and off, and even conductors were seated directly behind the prompt box, with their backs to the orchestra players to enable them to attend primarily to the singers. Yet Callas sought assistance in rediscovering this music by accepting the authority of well-seasoned conductors, like Serafin, and by attracting stage directors from the world of the cinema, like Visconti, to help her revitalize a forgotten repertory; by her time it was impossible even for a singer with her highly developed instincts not to need guidance in this repertory.

As well as professional collaborators Callas had the support of her husband, Giovanni Battista Meneghini. He was the first person of substance she met when she arrived in Verona in 1947 at the time of her Italian début; and in the course of the next few years he sold his share of his family business and invested his time and money solely in her career. He gave her, for the first time, the financial security without which, in the early days of her career, she might have suffered want. During the time they lived together, from 1947 to 1959, she sang more than 475 operatic performances, and she styled herself Maria Meneghini Callas. After they were separated she had his name struck off her records: not only from the few she was still to make, but also from all those which she had been so insistent should bear his name on in the first place.

In 1959 Callas left Meneghini and ran off with Onassis, after which, during the final six years of her career, she managed only 48 operatic performances. But this should not suggest that Onassis caused the end of her career. Closer examination reveals a dramatic falling off in the number she gave between 1956 and 1959. In fact, she did not leave Meneghini for Onassis until her career was virtually over. She had devoted herself to her art so completely that she had no conception of life without it. Onassis would save her, or so she thought. At first he probably flattered himself into believing that it was he who had seduced her away from opera, which he never liked. Only later did he realize that without it she was like a rudderless boat at sea. It was then that he scuppered her, turned to bigger fish and launched off with a President's widow.

There was a contradiction between the depth of Callas's extraordinary musicianship and the narrowness of her intellect. There was no reconciling the two; and what she said, particularly in her latter days, so often bears little relationship with what had actually happened. A number of stories, of which she was responsible, have been parroted about without much scrutiny. In 1944, in New York, she was allegedly offered a contract at the Met which she turned down; but the Met archives disprove it. In 1957 the Director of the San Francisco Opera dismissed her; but, in fact, he was driven to it, for less than two weeks before the season was to begin she wanted to give up half her contract on grounds of ill-health. Callas needed time to recover from a recording, which she had only agreed to make long after signing with the San Francisco Opera and because of the large fee she was offered. At the end of 1958 when Bing fired her from the Met she led off for hours in a tirade against him; yet, Meneghini admits, they had planned it all beforehand; deliberately keeping Bing dallying so that he would eventually lose his temper. There are other stories which call for closer scrutiny: the case of the Norma walk-out at the Rome Opera, for example. She was obliged, so she said, to withdraw at the

end of Act I when she had only sung 'Casta Diva'. She claimed she
was suffering from a virus, and certainly she had told the management
when she arrived in Rome six days beforehand that she was unwell
and that they should have an understudy ready; yet, that being so,
we may wonder why she risked her health only two nights earlier,
singing 'Casta Diva' on Eurovision.

Much of what she said in the 1960s and 1970s, when she was
interviewed so often, but sang so little, was only a rationalization or
justification. By that time the cosmetic image in the media of Callas
is irrelevant to her story as a singer; just as colour photographs of her
on CDs and record sleeves bear little resemblance to Maria Meneghini
Callas in her prime. In the later 1950s we can hear on her records not
only how her voice is deteriorating at a prodigious rate but how she
increasingly mistakes artfulness for artistry. It was as if, as Harold
Rosenthal puts it: 'One were witnessing an artificial performance by
Callas imitating Callas'[2] – how could it have been otherwise when she
had to be so careful before emitting every note?

In her youth Callas had been pitched into becoming a singer; during
the war she was locked up in Greece and it is doubtful whether she
had much opportunity for anything else. She had been born in New
York, and when her parents separated her mother took her back to
Athens. At first she was alienated from her background not only by
her inability to speak Greek but also by her acute myopia, which
prevented her seeing anything more than a few feet away. These
factors, plus the difficult conditions during the war, encouraged her to
seek expression through music and to accomplish this she developed
her singing technique so consummately that the profundity of her
instincts were fully revealed. The only language she really spoke was
music. Even her beauty was too imperfect for the cinema, and could
only make its effect in the spaces of an opera house. It is indicative that
her one spoken movie was not a success; as an actress she could only
communicate through music. It was Callas's extraordinary musical
gifts, most evident in her early years, that stamp her as one of this
century's supremely great singers: and in the age of recording she will
continue to be so.

I

BEFORE CALLAS

AN AUTOBIOGRAPHY WILL often begin with details of the subject's birth as told by a parent or friend and it may be imprecise or inaccurate, either deliberately or accidentally; but a mother's biography, it might be thought, would at least have got natal details right. It is therefore a matter of some surprise that the very first sentences in Evangelia Callas's *My daughter Maria Callas* should be incorrect: 'My daughter Maria began life in a storm – symbolically, it would seem, for she has been a storm centre for most of her adult years. The day she was born, the fourth of December 1923, there was a snow storm such as I had never seen before.'[1] But Maria's birth certificate states that she was, in fact, born on December 2nd and New York meteorological reports show that the weather, although cold, was dry, there was no snow, indeed, no precipitation at all. According to Callas's memoirs published in 1957 the second was in fact the date on her passport but she preferred the fourth; partly because it was St Barbara's day (the patron saint of artillery) but also because her mother had told her so and 'I have to believe what my mother says'.[2]

The Callas family's name was originally Kalogeropoulos. They had emigrated from Greece that year and arrived in New York by boat on August 3rd, the day after President Harding died. Father George, a chemist, was born in 1886; mother Evangelia, who was then five months pregnant, was born in 1898; and sister Yacinthy was born in 1917. According to Evangelia her family was from quite a different class than George's: '[they] had estates, orchards and olive groves',[3] whereas he was only an apothecary, a fact she was constantly upbraiding him with. Nevertheless in Greece they enjoyed a high standard of living and it is difficult to understand why they should have left. In their home town, Meligala, in the Peloponnisos, they were big fish in a small pond: George Kalogeropoulos had the only successful chemist's business for miles around, and the family lived in a comfortable house complete with staff. Certainly Evangelia did not want to go to America. Perhaps they went because '[George] wished to punish his wife for her endless whining about what he clearly believed to be his masculine rights',[4] his extra-marital adventures; or maybe, through his business, he had formed a liaison with the wife of some eminent local figure who had come to learn of it and was set on making his life as uncomfortable as possible.

The Kalogeropoulos's arrived in New York during a period of booming affluence, but they had at once to face the first problem: the English language. They moved across the East River from Manhattan to 87 Sixth Avenue, Astoria, Long Island, little Athens, as it was known then, where lived a community of Greek immigrants. George soon found that learning sufficient English took him a lot longer than he had anticipated, and it was six years before he could open his own business. Meanwhile he had to scrape a living as a laboratory assistant and teach Greek in a local school. Throughout this time he endured Evangelia's constant carping; she could not forgive him for leaving Greece. It was not until 1929, when Callas was five, that George finally secured a licence to open his own drugstore, but by then he was broke and had to borrow more than ten thousand dollars from a friend. He styled it 'The Splendid Pharmacy' – something of a euphemism, since it was located in Hell's Kitchen, hardly a salubrious part of New York; the precise address was 483 Ninth Avenue, at 37th Street. Much of the neighbourhood was then Greek so George needed to speak only a little English. Here he ran the familiar New York drugstore. He had a back shop workroom where, as at Meligala, he would mix and grind his own preparations.

In the early 1920s George and his family were a part of a vast influx of non English-speaking immigrants anxious to establish themselves in the New World. Soon after they arrived George simplified their name, reducing it to Kalos, and their Christian names too were simplified: Evangelia became Litza, Yacinthy Jackie, only George remained George. At the beginning of December the birth of Litza's child was expected. Leonidas Lantzounis, a Greek orthopaedist living in New York who had known George years before in Meligala, arranged for the baby to be born at the Flower Hospital, Manhattan, on Fifth Avenue at 105th Street. Litza was convinced she was going to have a boy. Every Greek mother spends her pregnancy determined to have a boy, it would, she felt, compensate her for the loss from meningitis, only the previous year in Meligala, of three-year-old Vassily. However, it was not to be; another daughter was born. She was a large baby weighing more than 5½ kilos (twelve pounds).

George took Jackie to see her and she remembers 'a wispy corona of jet-black hair so unlike the rest of us'.[5] The names on her birth certificate, presumably chosen by George, since he registered her, are Sophie Cecelia (sic) Kalos.[6] It took Litza the rest of her hospital stay to be able to accept another little girl. Perhaps, had the baby been a boy, then the relationship between George and Litza might not have deteriorated so quickly.

By the time Litza had left hospital she was reconciled to her new daughter, though she still continued her feud with George. The baby was baptized at the Greek Orthodox Cathedral, the Holy Trinity, 319 East 74th Street, on February 26th 1926. On this occasion Litza prefixed the names Maria Anna to those under which George had registered her, so in her early days in New York she came to be called Mary. Jackie remembers teaching her sister to walk and how she loved having children's stories read to her. On Sundays their father would take them out and years later Callas had not forgotten how she would stop by an icecream vendor and wait expectantly until her father bought her one.[7] Perhaps the biggest fun the little girls had was with Litza's pianola. Jackie would insert into it rolls of operatic paraphrases while Mary, when she had grown sufficiently, would work the pedals with her hands. As Jackie states, 'we were raised to the sounds of grand opera and . . . mother's incessant nagging'.[8]

Indeed, every time George wanted to play Greek folk songs on the gramophone Litza would be so scornful that eventually, for the sake of a quiet life, he would let her substitute an aria of Bellini or Puccini. In typical Greek fashion the children were completely under her sway, and for a long time they came to accept their mother's judgments of their father: he was stupid, a liar and he had no idea how to behave. From their earliest days the children were brought up to the background of constant domestic strife: as a baby Mary would, Jackie tells, 'cling to me in desperation'.[9] Litza had complete control over them. She kept them apart from other children, taking them to school in the mornings and bringing them back home in the afternoons. One day, before Mary had started school, Litza took her to collect Jackie. As soon as Mary caught sight of her sister she rushed precipitately into the street in front of a car which, being unable to swerve, dragged her along in front of it. This accident may have been due as much to short-sightedness as childish impulse; she was obliged to wear glasses from the age of five. She was rushed to hospital but apart from shock and a few cuts she was no more than badly shaken, and that night she returned home. As Jackie recalls,[10] over the years details of this incident became increasingly exaggerated by Litza.

George's drugstore had been open barely four months when, in October 1929, the great slump began. Within a year the depression had swept *The Splendid Pharmacy* away. People may always need drugs and medicine, but these were only a part of its stock-in-trade; much of its business came from ice-cream, cakes, soft drinks, and other comestibles, which the ever-increasing number of unemployed soon had to learn to live without. At first Litza seemed to completely ignore what was going on, all her time being taken up with her girls: she arranged for them to have piano lessons and Italian lessons and she took them away for a holiday with cousins at Tarpon Springs, Florida. No doubt her lack of fluent English accounts for her inability to comprehend the black news emanating from Wall Street. It took her some time to realize that George's business was crumbling, and she would go round to the drugstore, incessantly nagging him. He would do his best to ignore her until finally 'she [went] to the dangerous medicines cupboard, grabbed a handful of pills and swallowed them';[11] then she had to be rushed to hospital to have her stomach pumped. But the experience did not make her more understanding; according to Lantzounis, 'after George lost the drugstore, [Litza's] mind turned. He put her in Bellevue as crazy and probably she was crazy!'[12] She spent a month in the notorious asylum before she returned home. From this time husband and wife, although still living under the same roof, went their separate ways.

George became a travelling salesman for a drug company. Financial circumstances were certainly hard and during the next few years the family moved through a catalogue of addresses: 240 West 34th Street; 465 Columbus Avenue; 64 West 135 Street; 520 West 139 Street; 609 West 137 Street; 569 West 192 Street and 561 West 180 Street.[13] It seems likely they did a moonlight flit from most of these, that way they would at least avoid paying more than the minimum rent. During that time Mary was a pupil at six different schools: P.S.228M, P.S.9, P.S.43, P.S.192M, P.S.189 and P.S.164. It was not until after they had moved to Washington Heights, Jackie relates,[14] that George devised a treatment for gingivitis, the financial results of which enabled them to stay there until Mary left New York.

School records indicate that Mary was an able child: 'She received As, B+s and Bs in all her work for the entire period from 1929 through 1937.'[15] During the depression the family had little money and Litza would frequently take the girls down-town to the Public

Library on Fifth Avenue at 42nd Street. There they would borrow
records and familiarize themselves with operas. It is these expeditions,
and the glamour with which Litza imbued opera, that account for
much of Mary's early musical proficency; she started to play the
piano when she was only eight and had already shown an interest
in singing. Years later Callas laments how her mother had made her
practise and she did not 'have a wonderful childhood',[16] but Litza was
determined that the family's straitened circumstances would have no
effect on her girls. Opera was, in Jackie's words, 'a simple extension
of Mother's golden world'.[17] In those days, once a week '[she would]
transport . . . us beyond the cheap flock wallpaper . . . of a Chinese
noodle house and . . . [turn it] into . . . a Renaissance palace'.[18]

A neighbour chanced to overhear Mary singing and told Litza she
should have voice lessons too. From this time Litza became obsessed
with Mary's voice. The family would listen to the Metropolitan's
Saturday afternoon broadcasts. On one such occasion Mary heard
Lily Pons in *Lucia*[19] and she was quick to point out her faulty
intonation; she would, she maintained, sing it accurately when she
undertook it. At the end of 1934 Litza got Mary, then eleven, to take
part in a children's radio contest in which there were not only young
singers but other young musicians and even young comedians. So it
was that Callas 'made what could be called her first public appearance
[on WOR radio station] . . . on a nationwide amateur hour',[20] '[s]he
was dressed in a simple straight dress with her hair cut short and [a
fringe on] her forehead'.[21] Accompanied at the piano by her sister
she sang Yradier's popular, 'La paloma', and a number Jeannette
MacDonald included in the film *San Francisco*, 'A Heart that is
Free'. Callas mentions this contest in 'Person to Person' with Ed
Murrow: 'the Master of Ceremonies was Jack Benny, and he was
quite furious that I had not won first prize'.[22] This was won by an
accordion player, whilst Mary took second prize, a Bulova watch. As
a result of her success Litza tells of her entering other competitions,
and she took 'prizes for singing in school and, I seem to remember,
in church and Sunday School too',[23] but this is the only radio contest
that Callas, her mother or her sister refer to.[24]

In the mid-1930s Mary began, Jackie recalls, 'singing, singing,
singing'.[25] She sang a small role in a school production of Gilbert and
Sullivan's *Mikado* at P.S.164 and Litza made her costume. We may
imagine the effect this had on her mother, who became possessed with
the idea that Mary should have singing lessons somehow or other. But
even in those days '[they] cost ten dollars an hour, a fortune at that

time',[26] so eventually Litza determined that '[she w]ould take Mary to Greece to have her voice trained'.[27] By the autumn of 1936 she had finally persuaded her husband that they should go; perhaps, when he had thought about it sufficiently, it made sense, and he agreed to pay their fares. It must certainly have been a pleasure to be rid of Litza so painlessly and he was content that his daughters should go along too. Mary was thrilled at the idea of journeying to the country she had never yet been to but which her mother had been talking about for as long as she could remember. Jackie went over by boat in December 1936 and Litza and Mary followed in February 1937.

Litza tells of their travelling on an Italian liner tourist class and one day Mary sang 'La paloma' and the Bach-Gounod 'Ave Maria' in the lounge. As a result she was invited to sing at the church service on Sunday, but she declined. Nevertheless she agreed to sing at a party the Captain gave in first class, accompanying herself. She offered the Habañera from *Carmen* as an encore, and on the final phrase when Carmen throws José a rose from her hair, she created quite an effect 'pull[ing] a carnation from a vase [on] the piano and toss[ing] it to the Captain'.[28] We can imagine when the boat finally reached Greece and the thirteen-year-old disembarked, the initial impression created by the port of Patras hardly warranted Litza's elaborate build-up. Mary must have thought it 'the dingiest place [she] had ever seen . . . run-down [and] filthy'.[29] In those days Greece was still poor whereas, in spite of the slump, America was a rich country, almost its antithesis. When they reached down-town Athens they were greeted by a large contingent of Dimitroades, Litza's family, and although Mary then 'spoke only broken Greek'[30] Litza 'introduced [her] as a person of consequence embarking on a brilliant career'.[31]

To that end no sooner had they arrived than Litza marshalled her family and 'her campaign . . . got under way in earnest'.[32] She had Mary sing to them. Her brother, Efthemios, who had contacts in the Conservatory, agreed to help and promised that when Mary had had time to acclimatize herself he would do what he could to secure her an audition. At first Litza and her daughters stayed with her mother before renting an apartment, but after a few months George became unwell and no further money arrived from New York, so the Dimitroadis family were called on to help. All the while Litza was looking for opportunities to secure Mary's future. She had her sing to almost anyone who looked as if he might have contacts in Athens's musical life. She even got her singing in a Perama taverna, on which occasion John Kambanis, a tenor at the Athens opera, heard

her. He advised her to go to his teacher, Maria Trivella, whom he felt
sure would be able to help her. With this incentive Litza's brother
managed to persuade Stefanos Trivella, her brother-in-law, to effect
an introduction. One day in September 1937 it was at last arranged
that Mary would give an audition to Trivella.

Although not yet fourteen Mary sang like a budding prima donna,
without any apparent nerves. But, years after, she claims that though
she appeared extremely calm '[yet a] painful sensation of panic would
overcome me in the middle of a difficult passage and it seemed to me
that I was about to choke'.[33] Nevertheless Trivella was impressed,
'But this is talent!',[34] she declared, and at once agreed to teach her.
It was arranged that Mary would join the National Conservatory.
The Director, Kalomiras, decided to award her a scholarship[35] and
so as to enable her to secure it her mother upped her age to sixteen.
Trivella also agreed to teach her Greek. Mary at once plunged into
work, practising for hours on end and on occasion she even forgot to
eat – 'which,' as her mother says, 'for [her] was miraculous'.[36] We get
an intimation of her remarkable single-mindedness from the rigorous
schedule she undertook during the next six months. At the same time
music, Jackie tells, seems to have 'unleashed a sense of rivalry that
made her need to come out on top in whatever she was doing'.[37]

At the beginning of 1938 Litza took her girls to their first
opera, Verdi's *La Traviata* at the Palas Theatre. That spring,
on April 11th, Mary made her first concert appearance at the
Parnassos Hall, styling herself Marianna Kalogeropoulou. As
Trivella remembers, 'after nearly a year of daily one-hour lessons,
I found her voice developing superbly and decided to let her
sing in our annual "show-case" recital'.[38] This included sixteen
different singers in songs and arias of Mozart, Tosti, Rossini, Verdi,
Chaminade, Beethoven, Gounod, del Acqua, Massenet, Leoncavallo,
Alabieff, Grieg, Puccini, Ponchielli, Rachmaninoff, Johann Strauss
and Schubert, all piano accompanied. Marianna was the eighth and
last soloist. Her contribution was sung in Greek, as were most of her
Greek appearances, and included an aria from Weber's *Der Freischütz*,
the cavatina 'Plus grand dans son obscurité' from Gounod's *La Reine
de Saba*, 'Two nights' by Psaroudas, a critic as well as composer, and
with Kambanis, the tenor who had recommended her to Trivella, she
concluded the programme with a duet from Puccini's *Tosca*.

During the next year she remained a pupil at the National
Conservatory. In the mornings she would be among the first students
to arrive and at night one of the last to leave. As she herself recalls, 'I

used to listen to [the other] pupils singing all sorts of repertory: light operas, heavy operas, arias for mezzo-sopranos, tenors'.[39] Her mother tells of her refusing 'to leave her piano for meals [and] she would put the plate in her lap [while she went] on working'.[40] At this time she first began steadily to put on weight, she ate carelessly and irregularly. Psychiatry might ascribe her excessive weight to a lack of love: she had no boy-friends and she felt lonely. But even if this explanation was right similar feelings of deprivation would not be enough to produce another Callas, Callas is scarcely the first woman to have become fat. Perhaps she did feel unattractive and unloved yet it is indicative that then, at the very beginning of her career, her looks took second place to her voice. A less modish explanation for her putting on weight comes from her complete commitment to her art and being totally taken up with becoming a singer – everything else, how often she ate and how much she weighed, was then of incidental importance.

At any rate her weight did not seem to have had any deleterious effect on her dramatic talent and she very much impressed George Karakandas, the drama coach. Next year she had developed sufficiently to undertake her first role in the theatre: on April 2nd 1939 she sang Santuzza in Mascagni's *Cavalleria Rusticana* at the Olympia Theatre. 'It was a simple affair: plain backdrop, the boys in black trousers and white shirts and the girls in simple skirts and blouses.'[41] She is mentioned in Psaroudas's review that appeared in *Elefteron Vima*. For this performance she won first prize 'but,' as her mother admits, 'it never occurred to either of us that this was her "operatic début"'.[42] In the course of May and June she took part in other recitals. On May 22nd, once again at Parnassos Hall and again piano accompanied, she opened the programme with the Barcarolle from *Les Contes d'Hoffmann* with Anita Bourdacou. After contributions by eight other singers, she sang 'Ocean! Thou mighty monster' from Weber's *Oberon*, 'Ritorna vincitor' from *Aida*, and another song by Psaroudas, 'I will not forget you'. There followed three arias by the tenor Kambanis, and they then brought the evening to a conclusion with the duet, 'O terra addio', from *Aida*. The next night, at the same hall, in an assorted programme, embracing pianists and violinists, she finished the evening repeating the aria from *Oberon* and adding 'Dis-moi que je suis belle', the Air du Miroir from Massenet's *Thaïs*. Psaroudas praised 'her excellent singing of Rezia's exacting aria, although she lacked something in the Mirror air, nevertheless her voice is rich and responsive'.[43] More than twenty years later, in March 1961, Callas recorded the Air du Miroir in French with the Orchestre de la RTF under Georges Prêtre; presumably it was to have been included in an album she was making at that time, *Maria Callas Sings Great Arias from French Opera*, but for whatever reasons it was not published.

On June 25th Marianna appeared in an extract from Act III of Verdi's *Un Ballo in Maschera* and the second scene of *Cavalleria Rusticana*. The programme included other singers in selections from *Faust*, *Werther*, *Madama Butterfly*, *La Gioconda*, *Aida* and *Lucia di Lammermoor*, piano accompaniment was provided by Elli Nikolaidi, and Karakandas was in charge of staging. It was at this time Litza and her two daughters moved to a spacious apartment on Patission, 'a beautiful avenue . . . that comes out at Concord Square'.[44] It was on the top floor with six rooms and a balcony. Mother and daughters were still there in 1945 when Marianna returned to New York. Meanwhile Europe was on the brink of war. Already, in April 1939, Mussolini had invaded Albania and King Zog had been forced to flee. The Greeks watched uneasily yet they were not at once dragged in and peace persisted throughout the next eighteen months. That spring Marianna remained at the National Conservatory and it was during the summer of 1939, 'on a humid afternoon',[45] as Elvira de Hidalgo remembers, that she came to audition for her.

De Hidalgo (1888–1980) had been a successful coloratura soprano, though never in the same class as Tetrazzini or Galli-Curci. One of a clutch of Spaniards, including Josefina Huguet, Maria Galvany, Maria Barrientos and Graziella Pareto, she made the biggest impression at the beginning of her career. She was only nineteen when, in 1908, she made her first appearance as Rosina at the San Carlo, Naples. The following year at Monte Carlo she replaced Selma Kurz in Gunsbourg's stellar production of Rossini's *Il Barbiere* with Titta Ruffo, Dmitri Smirnov, Antonio Pini-Corsi and Chaliapin. In 1910 Gatti-Casazza brought her to the Metropolitan, New York and she sang two Rosinas, one Amina in *La Sonnambula* and an aria in a Sunday evening concert. Her youth and charm were appreciated but, Henderson remarked acidly, 'old frequenters of the Met [do not consider] the institution as a nursery for little girls'.[46] In 1911 and 1912 she reappeared at Monte Carlo as Linda in Donizetti's *Linda di Chamounix*, afterwards adding Amina, Elda in the world première of Nerini's *L'Epreuve dernière* and Gilda in *Rigoletto*. However, by the time she came again, in 1919, she preferred less altitudinous parts: Mimì in *La Bohème* and Nedda in *Pagliacci*. Meanwhile she toured with Battistini's company appearing as Zerlina in *Don Giovanni*, Adina and Linda, and she also sang at La Scala,

Milan, the Costanzi, Rome and at other theatres roles like Filina in Thomas's *Mignon*, Dinorah, Lakmé, Maria in Donizetti's *La Figlia del Reggimento* and Lucia. In 1922 at the Colón, Buenos Aires she undertook Violetta. Two years later she came to Covent Garden as Gilda in one of the British National Opera Company seasons. At the end of 1924 she travelled once again to the Met for Gilda and Rosina then later the same season journeyed to Chicago for a couple of Rosinas and a Lakmé before returning to the Met the last time for a solitary Lucia. By 1930 her career had slumped to fringe appearances in Lisbon, Helsinki, Corfu and Athens. It was at Athens that she first took up teaching, later she taught in Ankara and Milan. In Ankara one of her pupils was Leyla Gencer, a soprano widely deemed to have copied Callas, warts and all, but perhaps that is doing Gencer a disservice for the telling influence was more likely to have been de Hidalgo. At first she was very proud that Callas was her pupil but, as time passed, and Callas's reputation grew to swamp hers, she would decline even to mention her.

In 1957, when de Hidalgo was teaching in Milan, Callas saw a lot of her. She describes her as an unforgettable and superlative Rosina (although she could never have seen her Rosina), 'an illustrious artist. The elect woman who . . . gave me her whole heart . . . was witness to my whole life in Athens. She could say more about me than any other person, because . . . [we] had contact and familiarity'.[47] She goes on in the same vein for a paragraph. But whether she really felt so much for de Hidalgo is questionable; it seems more likely she was using her as a stick with which to beat her mother. Litza herself maintains that '[Marianna] did not love de Hidalgo as she had loved Trivella'.[48] It seems more likely that she determined to study with de Hidalgo because of her reputation in florid music. Although with Trivella she had sung arias and duets from *Aida, Tosca* and *Cavalleria Rusticana* she became increasingly preoccupied with acquiring a technique that would enable her to surmount any musical difficulty. As she herself says: 'A singer conquers these difficulties just as an instrumentalist must, beginning first with slow scales and arpeggios, then gradually building up speed and flexibility.'[49] Without this basic skill she knew she could never hope to realise her ambitions. By 1948, at the time of Callas's first appearance in Bellini's operas, even the very word coloratura smacked of decadence, whereas she knew instinctively that a mastery of ornamentation is essential to all singers; florid singing may be antique but it remains a vital part of the singer's art. For this reason she determined to leave Trivella and study with a mistress of coloratura. It also explains why, at her audition for de Hidalgo, she sang one of the few pieces she knew that contained any florid music, 'Ocean! Thou mighty monster' from Weber's *Oberon*.

As Marianna began to sing de Hidalgo closed her eyes and listened: 'I heard a violent cascade of sound . . . dramatic and moving. I had been secretly looking and waiting for that voice for some time. It was as if it were an appointment with destiny.'[50] The Greek soprano Arda Mandikian, another pupil of de Hidalgo, describes Marianna: 'She was a fat, tall girl with beautiful eyes and great self-assurance. Judging by her appearance, I didn't think she would be able to sing. But when she opened her mouth . . . my mouth fell open too. It was an amazing voice.'[51] De Hidalgo lost no time accepting Marianna as a pupil and at once arranged to have her enter the Athens Conservatory. From their first meeting Marianna's dedication was whole-hearted and she learned at a prodigious rate, taking daily lessons. Mandikian confirms her amazing facility: 'arias she was given . . . would be ready after one or two lessons.'[52] Callas herself later remembered how 'I started going to [de Hidalgo's] classes from morning to night, from ten o'clock . . . till we went to lunch or had a sandwich there, and then on through to eight . . . at night – it would have been inconceivable to stay at home, I shouldn't have known what to do there'.[53]

It was on February 23rd 1940, at the Odeon Concert Hall, that Marianna, with Mandikian, sang an extract from Bellini's *Norma* in public for the very first time: the Act II duet, 'Mira, o Norma . . . Si, fino all'ore estreme'. Thereafter, on April 3rd, this duet was included with two others from *Aida* and *La Gioconda* in a radio broadcast. Later, on June 16th, she appeared in the title role of Puccini's *Suor Angelica*. Her sister, Jackie, who sang Rose in an extract from Delibes's *Lakmé* at the beginning of that evening, remembers how 'although there was no scenery they did manage to dress the cast as nuns'.[54] Callas herself says: 'The plan at first was that I should only study and not sing professionally [but] this did not last long',[55] and on October 21st she had her first engagement with the Lyric Theatre company singing songs in a production of Shakespeare's *The Merchant of Venice* with Alexis Minotis as Shylock (eighteen years later he would direct Callas in the Dallas production of *Medea*). These were the first performances she ever earned money for and she would remain with it throughout her Greek years. Meanwhile Hitler, on September 1st 1939, turned his eyes eastward and the Germans marched into Poland. The Second World War had begun. Following his example Mussolini, ensconced in Albania, began to make bellicose gestures in the direction of Greece. He sent the Prime Minister an ultimatum demanding that Italy be at once permitted to occupy strategic positions. The Greeks declined and so on October 28th 1940, the day following the fifth and last performance of *The Merchant of Venice*, the Italian army marched southwards into Greece. Nevertheless, although the Greek army was much smaller, it had no difficulty driving the Italians back into Albania.

For the next few months there was a period of phoney peace. On January 21st 1941 Marianna began a series of appearances with the Lyric Theatre company at the Palas Cinema as Beatrice in Suppé's *Boccaccio*. This was her professional operatic début, although the part was not a large one: 'she was one of four girls who sang and danced in a barrel.'[56] It was in the spring of 1941 that the Germans swept southwards into the Balkans and hostilities were resumed; now, with Teutonic reinforcements behind them, the Italians managed to occupy Greece. When news reached Athens of the Luftwaffe's devastating raid on Salonika on April 6th, Jackie's fiancé, Milton Embericos, urged mother and daughters, reversing the Biblical pattern, to flee to Egypt. But they only managed to reach Piraeus before they learned that the Germans had sunk the *Elli*, a Greek battleship, so Litza dug her heels in and flatly refused to leave.

They returned to Athens and in the days before the invasion, like everyone else, they went out and bought up what they could; not only provisions of all kind but almost anything else that could still be bought across the counter. By the time enemy troops had arrived the shops were completely empty. On April 27th the Italians entered Athens closely followed by the Germans; although the Italians claimed to be the occupying forces it was not long before it became all too apparent that the Germans were really in command. Public offices were closed and theatres, schools and universities were obliged to impose a six o'clock curfew. Nevertheless, despite the closure of the Conservatory, Marianna continued to take her daily lessons with de Hidalgo. Every day she would go to de Hidalgo's house walking through deserted streets, stepping off the pavement so as to let enemy soldiers pass by and picking her way over bodies lying in the gutter. Memories of the occupation remained with her always: 'No one who has never experienced starvation can know what a . . . comfortable existence means . . . I can never spend money needlessly and will suffer . . . at the waste of food, even if it is only a crust . . .'[57]

Abroad news was dismal, too. South of Greece the fighting in Crete resulted in the British being driven from the island. During the next few months a Greek officer, aware of the Kalogeropoulos's long stay in America, brought to their apartment a couple of escaped British officers – there, so he reasoned, at least they would be understood. He begged that they be hidden somewhere and, despite the fact that had they been discovered then Litza and her daughters would have been shot as well, they agreed. The men stayed some weeks cooped up in a bedroom. Only during the blackout were they allowed to come out and listen to the BBC; at such times Marianna would go to the piano and start singing so as to cover the noise of the radio. Eventually mother and daughters, in a mood of braggadocio, disguised the British servicemen in mufti and risked taking them out in the streets; luckily they were not caught. Some time later Greek soldiers came and took them away again.

That summer a semblance of normal life began to return. The curfew, although not completely lifted, was not so strictly enforced and theatres were allowed to reopen. During July at the Park Summer Theatre, Marianna undertook further performances of Beatrice in *Boccaccio*. The repertory, during 1941/2, embraced a considerable selection of works, including Mozart's *Entführung*, Puccini's *Madama Butterfly*, Lehár's *Die lustige Witwe*, *Giuditta* and *Das Land des Lächelns*, and Johann Strauss's *Der Zigeunerbaron*. Although no record has yet come to light that Marianna sang in any of these, it would be interesting to know if she ever appeared in a comprimario role or, indeed, sang in the chorus. We know that 'she began her career as a member of the chorus until spotted by the discerning director-general [of the Greek National Opera] Kostis Bastias'.[58]

The end of 1941 proved a particularly dire time for Athenians; not only was it one of the coldest winters for years, it was also no longer possible to rely on food imports. The Germans may have driven the British expeditionary force from the Balkans, but this did not prevent a British naval blockade. There was little home produce for the city's inhabitants, and not only were a large number of inhabitants shot but many others starved to death. Litza tells of her going off into the country in search of food, but Jackie admits that they were luckier than most: 'Without Milton we would have starved. The small amount of money my father sent us from America was blocked by the war, and never arrived.'[59] Milton was from the Embericos shipping family, 'one of the wealthiest and most prominent in Greece',[60] and he would frequently bring them food and money. Not only did they survive the war with no visible means of support, save for Marianna's very modest salary of about 3,000 drachmas, which she earned only when she was singing; they also continued to live in the same large apartment and even kept a maid. Photographs of Marianna taken during the war certainly do not suggest that she ever had to endure a starvation diet.

Meanwhile Marianna continued her studies with de Hidalgo. Her next engagement was on August 27th 1942 when she sang Tosca for the first time, at an open-air amphitheatre at Klafthmonos Square. These performances, despite the difficult circumstances of life under the occupation, were enthusiastically received. Lalauni, in the *Giornale di Roma*, a newspaper for the Italian forces, acclaimed her: 'La Kalogeropoulos is truly miraculous with her beautiful voice, trained in the school of the celebrated singer . . . de Hidalgo. Her performance was full of feeling, beauty and grace. As a singer she brings together all the qualities called for and she has certainly a great future.'[61] After six Toscas sung in Greek, on September 8th she undertook the first of another dozen performances in the original – this marks the first time she ever sang in Italian. De Hidalgo had insisted she learn Italian, 'sooner or later you will go to Italy . . . and in order to interpret and express well, you must know the precise meaning of every word'.[62] Marianna found a teacher and took a bet with her, as she herself later relates, 'that in three months I would be able to converse in Italian';[63] and, in what was to prove typical fashion, she won. Yet her mother tells how 'the Italians, who love *Tosca*, loved her too, but much of the applause was also for Delendas. Even in Athens [she] had not yet achieved real fame.'[64]

Marianna was only eighteen and such a success by so young a singer was bound to cause friction and jealousy among the rest of the company. She did not refrain from rejoicing in her new-found acclaim and by so doing she made herself an easy target for resentment. Yet her overweening self-confidence, like many another aspect of the outer woman, was not genuine: at her early age such confidence could only be a reflection of her mother's. Indeed her mother proudly remembers an 'unrehearsed curtain-raiser to this . . . *Tosca*'.[65] Apparently the production had been planned for the soprano Remoundou. She, however, became indisposed but when Marianna was announced instead, so determined was she that the upstart should not sing she sent her husband to the theatre with instructions to block her way on to the stage. A pitched battle broke out, '[Marianna] flew at him and scratched his face'.[66] She earned a black eye, but she gave as good as she got, forced him to one side and went on to sing.

In Greece she felt herself a foreigner. It was only many years later, when Callas was trying to slough off Meneghini, that she adopted Greek citizenship; but that was not for more than a generation, and by then her career was over. And the Italians, too, particularly from this time onwards, were for her not enemies but lovers of the very art that was her whole life. Italian servicemen came increasingly to be among her friends and this only quickened the antipathy shown her by Greeks. It was during the occupation that Litza invited an Italian officer, Colonel Bonalti, 'a charming, cultivated man and a fine pianist',[67] to their apartment to hear Marianna sing, after which he came often. He played accompaniments for her, brought her gifts and even shared his rations with her. Litza's preoccupation with her daughter's career made her completely unaware of the bad feeling her friendliness with the occupying forces created.

After the success of Marianna's Tosca the Italians invited her to sing in Salonika in October 1942, in a special concert for the Italian forces to commemorate the 150th birthday of Rossini.[68] It seems likely that she sang 'Bel raggio' from Semiramide and 'Selva opaca' from Guglielmo Tell. This time her mother determined on going with her. She went to Major di Stasio, an Italian officer in charge of arrangements, to insist that as Marianna was only eighteen she should be chaperoned, so eventually room was found for them both. At the concert she was joined by tenor Delendas and two sopranos, Mireille Flery and Tani Anaslanthiadou. For the occasion payment was in food: cheese, ham, tomato paste, sardines, spaghetti, chocolate, and so on.

Throughout 1943 the occupation continued. That year Marianna took part in Kalomiras's 'O Protomastoras, on eleven occasions between February 21st and March 16th. Although a twentieth-century opera it was by no means modern, its first performance having taken place in March 1916, eight years before Turandot. Kalomiras was Director of the Conservatory, which no doubt explains its appearance in the repertory. She sang a comprimario part in an intermezzo with six other singers. On February 28th, the day after one of the performances, she took part in a concert at the Sporting Cinema at New Smyrna 'to endow school meals for poor children'.[69] On April 22nd at the Italian Institute she sang with Mandikian in Pergolesi's Stabat Mater. An engagement such as this, so to speak, in the bosom of the enemy, followed from the influence of di Stasio, the Italian officer who had arranged the Salonika concert the previous year. Marianna had formed a romantic attachment with him but, as we shall see, it is difficult to say which mattered more to her, the relationship itself or the opportunities the relationship opened up for her. On July 17th she sang in the first of three more performances of *Tosca* at the Summer Theatre at Klafthmonos Square and on the day of the second, the 21st, she also sang in a concert at the open-air Theatre at Kosta Mousouri. She shared the programme with violinist Nicos Dikeos: he played in the second half, she sang in the first half. Marianna's programme included 'Care selve' from Handel's *Atalanta*, the Rondo Finale from Rossini's *La Cenerentola*, 'Io son l'umile ancella' from Cilea's *Adriana Lecouvreur*, one of Leonora's arias from *Il Trovatore* and two Greek songs: Lavda's 'They are marrying off my love' and Palandios's 'Kimitiri'.

Apropos of the aria from *Adriana Lecouvreur*: the Italian lyric-dramatic soprano Augusta Oltrabella (1897–1981), in an interview with Lanfranco Rasponi, published in *Opera News*, tells how in the war she went to Athens to sing for Italian troops in performances of *Adriana Lecouvreur* and in some concerts. There she met de Hidalgo, an old acquaintance, who pressed her into taking Marianna as one of her supporting artists. Oltrabella asked to hear her, 'and to my amazement, an enormous whale of flesh arrived, charmless, terribly nearsighted, looking desperately poor, with torn shoes. She revealed stunning coloratura. . . . In that she was truly sensational, but the rest of the voice was simply manufactured.'[70] Oltrabella's memory of Marianna may have become, after nearly forty years, somewhat distorted – or maybe Rasponi, sometime publicity agent for Callas's great competitor Renata Tebaldi, vents his admitted dislike of Callas in retelling Oltrabella's tale; yet the fact that she should have remembered Marianna's 'stunning coloratura' seems very plausible in the light of many selections in her concert programmes. Knowing, too, how highly competitive Marianna always was, it is easy to believe that her inclusion of an excerpt from *Adriana Lecouvreur* in her recital was the result of having heard Oltrabella sing the role. And we know that Marianna did appear in at least one concert for Italian troops at Salonika at the end of August that year.

Meanwhile the Second World War was moving to a dénouement and on July 10th the Anglo-American front shifted from North Africa to Sicily. On the 25th Mussolini was forced to resign. In Greece Italian troops, who had never had much taste for hostilities, would have at once laid down their arms had not the Germans immediately 'surrounded their barracks, shot any resisters and shipped the rest of them out, either to forced labour or concentration camps'.[71] With the Italians gone the Germans were now unambiguously in command. Jackie conjectures what Marianna must have felt when her first real romance with di Stasio had ended so abruptly. '[I]t must have been a terrible time for her. That she was able to go on performing showed how much the theatrical life had already replaced the world of real emotions for her.'[72] Notwithstanding the precipitate departure of di Stasio, she continued to do what she knew she could: she sang. For her, in those days, the world beyond, blocked by the occupying powers, was of secondary importance. Even at this stage of her career real emotions for Marianna were what she found and expressed in her art.

On September 26th, at the Olympia Theatre, she appeared in concert to help raise funds for scholarships for needy students. The programme was a hotch-potch of pianists, singers and orchestra. She sang, piano accompanied, 'Abscheulicher' from Beethoven's *Fidelio*, 'Et incarnatus est' from Mozart's Mass in C minor, 'Dis-moi que je suis belle' from *Thaïs*, 'Ritorna vincitor' from *Aida*, a song of Turina and again the Lavda song. Her final appearance that year took place at the Kotopouli-Rex Theatre on December 12th, in a benefit for tuberculosis victims. The programme included five other singers and a concert pianist: in the first part she sang 'Abscheulicher' and 'Bel raggio' from *Semiramide*, then, after the interval, an aria from *Il Trovatore* and Turina's 'Tamare'.

It was not until another four months had passed that she sang in public again. On April 22nd 1944 her career took a major step forward when, again at the Olympia, she undertook the role of Martha in Eugen d'Albert's *Tiefland* on eight occasions. Leonidas Zoras, the conductor of the Athens performances of *Tiefland*, had known the opera for some time and had been waiting for an opportunity to mount it. Although German, it may be said to represent the quintessence of verismo, with a plot even more lurid than Verga's *Cavalleria Rusticana*. It must have excited Callas dramatically: 'I feel that I must sing a dramatic part to satisfy my temperament',[73] she told Matz in 1956. Although by that time she would be better known for reviving operas from the bel canto period, she always acknowledged the significance of verismo. After *Tiefland* Herzog, in *Deutsche Nachrichten*, acclaimed her: 'What other singers must learn, she possesses naturally: the dramatic instinct, the intensity of her acting, and her freedom of interpretation.'[74] And no fewer than seven other reviews[75] testify to her dramatic prowess. Though verismo operas have fallen out of critical favour in recent years, at the time of the last war in Greece, away from the mainstream, they were still vital and meaningful works. Indicatively, it was in Greece that she gave her only performances of Santuzza and Martha. Tosca too she sang in Athens twenty-one times in 1942 and 1943 but in Italy between 1947 and 1959, in her great years, she would sing it only six times. In 1957 she dismissed it slightingly: '[It] occupies the last place in my scale of preferences.'[76] It was not until 1964, when she possessed only a remnant of her former voice, that Zeffirelli revived it for her and she undertook it eighteen times.

The conductor Zoras describes rehearsing *Tiefland* with Marianna. 'The electricity was cut off. We would sit in the theatre at night with oil lamps, and every ten minutes or so the lights would go out, then they would come on again . . . Her patience was fantastic, always trying to reach perfection. Her Martha was so successful the Germans wanted to put it on in Vienna. At the time they were very helpful . . . but when they made this proposition, we didn't want to because we should have been accused of collaborating. So everyone found an excuse and we didn't go.'[77] Sebastiano, the baritone lead, was Evanglios Mangliveras then 'past his prime but still greatly admired'.[78] More than thirty years Marianna's senior, he provided her with a considerable amount of advice and assistance during rehearsals. He was captivated by her youth and extraordinary intuitive talent and, the Italian major having passed on to other climes, for a time at least they were lovers. But Nikolaidi, the *répétiteuse*, although affirming 'that [Marianna] sang at her best and Martha was a big success for her [nevertheless insists] the lessons Mangliveras gave her were the beginning of her downfall, because he encouraged her to force. De Hidalgo warned her about it, but she wouldn't listen. I think the wobble that she later developed was a direct result of this.'[79] Whether it was because of de Hidalgo's wise counsel or simply because Marianna felt there was nothing else that she could learn from Mangliveras, she was not slow in bringing their relationship to a conclusion. 'He was too old, she said.'[80] Later he appeared in *Fidelio* with her but when, thereafter, he became fatally ill and wanted to see her, as Mandikian recalls, 'she refused. She behaved very badly toward him . . . she was very strange that way.'[81]

On May 6th, before performances of *Tiefland* were finished Marianna appeared for the second time as Santuzza in *Cavalleria Rusticana*, this time at the Olympia. Newspapers were enthusiastic:

'[Her] Santuzza was of impulsive temperament. Her dramatic soprano showed itself to be both effortless and sensitive in her broad sweeping operatic manner, and tears in the voice were certainly evident.'[82] Nevertheless Nikolaidi thought that though 'she always sang beautifully yet her voice was hardening'.[83] On May 21st, at the Olympia, in a concert programme to raise money for indigent artists and featuring several other members of the company, including Delendas and Mangliveras, she undertook for the first time 'Casta Diva'. That her musical progress was continuing steadily becomes apparent on July 30th when she appeared once more in *'O Proto-mastoras*, but this time she moved up from a comprimario role to undertake the soprano lead, Smaragda. But even her mother, after praising her ecstatically, cannot avoid mentioning how the 'opera . . . nearly broke her voice'.[84]

Her most significant achievement in Greece took place on August 14th, at the Amphitheatre of Herodes Atticus, when she sang the first of a number of performances of Leonore in Beethoven's *Fidelio*, with Delendas as Florestan and Mangliveras as Pizarro. Also in the cast as Jacquino was the young tenor Giorgios Kokolios. Seven years later, in 1951, he would be the only Greek colleague from Marianna's early years to appear with her in Italy; Callas procured his engagement at the Florence May Festival. Photographs suggest that the *Fidelio* production was more professional-looking than anything else Athens managed during the war, with set designs by Oscar Walleck from the German Opera in Prague. Although sung in Greek, the Germans were behind it, which seems odd, for *Fidelio* is nothing if not a political opera and could hardly have been construed as being anything other than a call for freedom. But by this time (the Germans would have left Athens in another two months) perhaps they did not care. What they wanted was to put the best complexion on German art. Callas later remembered how she was engaged as Leonore because the soprano who was to have sung it was 'too busy to learn it [and] since rehearsals had to commence immediately, I was asked if I could replace her. Naturally I accepted for I knew the part thoroughly. I'm telling you this to show you that my one weapon is always to be prepared.'[85] This is confirmed by Nikolaidi: 'when she came on the first day of rehearsals I gave her the score and told her that I would go through her part the next day from start to finish. But when she arrived I found that she knew it all in detail, phrase by phrase . . . She had learned it all in one day . . . This is talent. It was not just a question of having a voice, it was also the love of hard work ... Talent means a strength which impels you to study.'[86]

In *Fidelio* Beethoven is only incidentally concerned with the voice. It is not so much that the vocal range of Leonore is excessive, but that the tessitura is undoubtedly more suited to the horn player, who accompanies her, than it is to Leonore herself. We hear this at the beginning of the cabaletta, 'Ich folg' dem innern Triebe', which has never yet been recorded by a voice sufficiently responsive at either end of its range. It is regrettable that in her great years Callas did not make a recording of this scene, as she did in 1953 of Donna Anna's Act II aria from *Don Giovanni*, 'Non mi dir', in which she realizes the florid writing with illuminating accuracy. One Athens critic refers disparagingly to her singing of 'Abscheulicher', 'as if it were a piece of Italian bel canto';[87] but that, of course, is precisely what Beethoven was attempting to write. The weight of opinion confirms that her singing was of an extraordinary accomplishment 'in the severest Beethoven style'.[88] A German critic makes some telling observations about 'her exceptional flexibility, [and] sonority of tone',[89] and a Greek writes 'though her voice is still not perfect and she has much to learn [yet] her musicality and beauty of voice'[90] were notable. We can at least derive a measure of the effect of her Leonore from these reviews, even if she may have have indulged in, as Nikolaidi describes, 'forcing [and] excessive temperament [for although] she was very good yet there were moments when she shouted'.[91] We shall note this again, in *Norma* in Mexico City in 1950, of which a recording survives, in which she seems to be trying too hard. Nevertheless, of all her Athens undertakings, reviews suggest, none was more memorable than this. At the time she was not an established artist so she felt she had to prove her worth. As her mother relates, 'sometimes her high notes would turn shrill [but in *Fidelio*] I can only remember [her] singing as I had never heard her sing before, [and] as I had not known she could sing'.[92]

In October Marianna had another engagement at Salonika, but this time for Greeks, not for Italians. Then, on the 12th, the German army withdrew and Athens was at last free. However, the after-effect was, as Jackie describes, '[a] sudden void'.[93] For the Kalogeropoulos ladies things were no different than for many other Athenians. Nature, however, abhors a vacuum, and in no time another conflagration had begun: civil war. It stemmed from the Greek resistance group who were largely communist-inspired. Elsewhere in Eastern Europe, with the Red Army behind them, similar groups had easily been able to topple the returning monarchist cliques that had dominated the pre-war Balkans, in Romania, Bulgaria, Albania and Yugoslavia; but in Greece circumstances were different.

At this time theatres were shut, but Litza eventually managed to procure Marianna a job with the mail department at British Command Headquarters. To get there each day, while the internecine strife went on, she had to go a tidy distance and make 'the trip on foot'.[94] On December 3rd a demonstration by communists in Constitution Square resulted in the police opening fire. The next day, the 4th, the day Marianna believed was her birthday, her 21st, in fact, fighting broke out in the street below and she was obliged to stay indoors. Life proved even more difficult than it had under the occupation. There was nothing to eat save for 'a box of very old beans',[95] and when eventually she did risk going out she tells of the terrifying ordeal she went through and how she had to 'run desperately through the midst of that devastation until under fire she arrived safe and sound at British Headquarters'.[96] These circumstances made so vivid an impression on her that she never forgot them. Eventually the communists were routed, for it was the British army, not the Red army, as in the rest of the Balkans, that had played an important part in the retreat of the German army. By February 1945 the government of George II was restored.

After all the fighting there was a vast amount of rebuilding to do, including improving relations between the various groups of people in Athens. Within a month, on March 14th, the Olympia Theatre reopened again with Marianna as Martha in a revival of d'Albert's *Tiefland*. While performances were going on, she took part on the 20th in a Musical Afternoon at the Olympia for British troops, on this occasion singing in English. Her selection included the traditional setting of the Willow Song and Landon Ronald's 'Love, I have won you'. Ronald, a conductor of repute, once a famous song composer and accompanist, made records with Patti and Melba. His songs require the most polished vocalism to reveal a distinct, albeit faded, charm – not at all appropriate material for Marianna's talents, one would think. She finished the programme with Vaughan Williams's song cycle 'On Wenlock Edge'.

After this engagement the next five months were a fallow period for Marianna, largely the result of her alienating her colleagues during the war. In those days she had certainly worked hard and had achieved a great deal but, constantly pressurized by her mother, she could not comprehend the value of a little *politesse* in her progress. She had never been slow to show how she looked down on her colleagues, and that she should have been justified in doing so only added salt to their wounds. Now that peace was declared she had to reckon with those jealous artists who had not found work in the interim, not for political reasons but because of their voices, or lack of them. They were only too anxious to be rid of someone who had managed to achieve so much, even during the occupation, and it was easy to accuse her of collaboration. Her contract was not renewed. Furious and frustrated, she was obliged to consider going abroad. De Hidalgo urged her to go to Italy but as she was an American citizen by birth she decided to return to New York. Indeed, she had been told that if she did not return now she was twenty-one she might lose her citizenship.

The American Embassy in Athens advertised that Americans who wished would be granted places on the first boat out from Piraeus to New York. A letter from Marianna's father arrived, he urged her to come over and sent her $100. 'That clinched it',[97] she remembers. Although she was able to get her passage paid in advance by the U.S. government she still needed some more money. To raise it her mother determined she should undertake a solo recital, the first she ever sang, on August 3rd at the Kotopouli-Rex Theatre. Her programme included one of Zerlina's arias from *Don Giovanni*, 'Bel raggio' from *Semiramide*, 'Ritorna vincitor' from *Aida*, an aria, one of Leonora's, again unspecified, from *Il Trovatore*, 'Ocean! Thou mighty monster' from *Oberon*, some Spanish songs and two Greek songs by Kariotakis and Poniridis, at the piano was Alice Lykoudi. Her mother used her dressmaking skill to contrive Marianna's apparel and so, inevitably, she remembers it in detail: 'She wore a white dress and a black velvet bolero jacket trimmed with sequins; with her black hair and her fair white skin and her enormous eyes she seemed to me all that a budding operatic star should be.'[98] The programme was advertised in the fashion of half a century ago, as a 'farewell concert' prior to embarking for America.

Before departing for the U.S. she made her last appearances with the Athens Opera as Laura in some performances of Millöcker's *Der Bettelstudent*, beginning on September 5th. These came to an end when she was granted passage to New York. On the 14th she embarked on the *Stockholm*. She claims her 'mother and sister refused to accompany me to Piraeus',[99] but her mother says it was 'Marianna [who] refused to let us come . . . with her'.[100] She boasts that some friends who were there to see her off counselled her to take good care of her money, but she told them she had none. Since it was lunch-time the banks were shut and they could give her nothing, so she left for New York 'alone without a cent',[101] one wonders what had become of the proceeds from the concert she had given specially to undertake the journey.

One day towards the end of the month the boat arrived in New York, and there to greet her was her father. Not having forwarded his address in the letter he wrote to Athens he had, nevertheless, been anxiously scanning Greek-language newspapers in the hope of finding someone he knew who might, peace being restored, be coming over to New York and could give him news of his family. Great was his surprise when he saw his daughter's name on the passenger list of the *Stockholm*, and he came down to the docks to meet her. When he had last seen her she was only thirteen so he was not quite sure what she would look like. He scrutinized the passengers as they came down the gang plank, but he had no difficulty recognizing her. She remembers: 'I really don't know how to describe the limitless relief with which I drew myself to him, hugging and kissing him as though he had been raised from the dead, and crying on his shoulder from joy.'[102] Although, by the time they arrived at his apartment, in 157th Street, and she found he was living with 'the woman upstairs, [she was] certainly not ready to share his affections with that Papajohn woman'.[103] It is a comment on her extreme self-centredness that she should have felt cheated because her father had not lived like a monk in the eight years since her mother had left him.

But New York was sufficiently distracting. In those days, after the war to someone who had just come across from occupied Europe, it must have seemed like heaven, or, at the very least, a hamburger heaven. At first, as Dr Lantzounis remembers 'eating seemed to be [Marianna's] full-time occupation. She was always hungry'.[104] Now she could eat, it seemed to her, whatever she fancied and whenever she felt like it, which was quite often and quite a lot! Although she herself was later convinced that she was fat, at that time she weighed only eighty kilos (176 pounds) and she was five feet nine inches. To begin with she spent her time doing up her bedroom, and she bought herself new clothes and 'elegant shoes'.[105] But after a few weeks she began to feel sufficiently recovered to carry out her assault on the musical citadel singing for opera companies, teachers and agents.

In December she auditioned at the Metropolitan, about it legends run riot. The story she often told[106] is that she was offered Madama Butterfly but declined, excusing herself on the grounds she was too fat, and that she refused the role of Leonore in *Fidelio* because it was to be sung in English. However, the Met records tell a different story. A card dating from the first audition reads 'exceptional voice. Ought to be heard on stage.' Two weeks later she was, but this time she seems to have made less of an impression, and she was certainly not offered anything. 'Good material. Needs work on her voice.'[107] So it was everywhere she went, she was fobbed off with one excuse or another. Nicola Moscona, a Greek bass, who had heard her in Athens and promised his help should she come to New York, declined to bother Toscanini on her behalf. Giovanni Martinelli, one of the leading Italian tenors in the generation after Caruso, recommended that she should take further lessons. Romano Romani, a repetiteur and minor composer, an opera of whose had once been sung at Covent Garden with his pupil Rosa Ponselle, could suggest nothing. Gaetano Merola, Director of the San Francisco Opera, told her she should go to Italy.

It was at the pharmacy, where her father worked, that she met a soprano, Louise Taylor, who gave singing lessons. In the next few weeks she would spend three or four hours a day working on her voice. At Taylor's studio she was introduced to Eddie Bagarozy, who heard her and was impressed enough to have her sing for his wife, Louise Caselotti, another soprano who was also teaching at that time. Caselotti remembers how 'Marianna – we all called her then – sang "Casta Diva" . . . The voice was professional material but the high notes weren't good. They needed work and [she] was fully aware of that.'[108] She worked single-mindedly with her customary fervour, endeavouring to put her voice in perfect order. She subjected it in the kind of rigorous practice an instrumentalist might undertake and '[she] would get furious if she couldn't reach the high notes she aimed for'.[109] She would commence work at eleven in the morning and continue with only an hour's break until midnight, then she would walk the five blocks home from Riverside Drive, no matter how inclement the weather.

Although she received no real encouragement at any of her auditions, the schedule of work she set herself suggests the total dedication that burned within her. Stassinopoulos considers, in the light of Marianna's experience, that 'she would have had to be superhuman not to begin doubting the wisdom of her decision'[110] to take up a career as a singer. But it is precisely her superhuman commitment to her career that makes Callas Callas. It is impossible to believe that she could ever have doubted her ultimate success; she worked ceaselessly on honing her instrument, so that it became for her consummately expressive. At her best, in the early 1950s, she was a great singer because her prodigious technical skill enabled her voice to reveal every nuance she desired to effect, articulating easily the most formidably intricate music. This makes her unique among sopranos this century.

On Christmas Eve 1946 Litza arrived in New York. She came over by boat to Marseilles and then by train to Cherbourg before embarking on the *Queen Elizabeth*. Since Marianna had arrived in New York she had written to her regularly and at length but, according to Litza,[111] it was not so much what she said as what she didn't that spoke volumes. Although she had been very glad to get away from her mother that was more than a year ago and her failure to secure any work caused her gradually to change her attitude. She needed a strong ally at her elbow, and distance lent Litza enchantment, so Marianna had Lantzounis loan Litza the fare for the boat passage.

Meanwhile, during the last months of 1946, Bagarozy, who had become preoccupied with the idea of starting a new opera company in the U.S., came a stage nearer realizing his dream. He met Ottavio Scotto, an Italian impresario, who had been married to Claudia Muzio, a famous diva of a quarter of a century before. Impressed by this pedigree Bagarozy entrusted the business management to Scotto. The end of the Second World War heralded a new era of prosperity so, reasoned Bagarozy, there would be a revival in opera's fortunes, and he decided to launch a new company, the United States Opera Company. It would commence operations in Chicago with *Turandot*. At that time *Turandot* was still a fairly new opera, only twenty years old, but it had not been heard in Chicago since 1938. The cast was to be headed by Calas, as her name was then spelled. Timur would be sung by Nicola Rossi-Lemeni but the rest of the company were mature artists. Liù was Mafalda Favero, who had undertaken it at Covent Garden with Eva Turner in 1937, and Galliano Masini, who had appeared opposite Turner in Chicago, was Calaf. It was to be conducted by Sergio Failoni and the production would be brought over from Italy. The company also included Cloe Elmo, Luigi Infantino, Géori Boué, Max Lorenz, and Hilde and Anny Konetzni, for it was announced that the repertory would also include French and German works.

Although events seven years later, when the Chicago Lyric Theater was founded, would prove Bagarozy right, he lacked the requisite skill and his company was built on shifting sand. He supposed that European artists, in the difficult post-war circumstances, would be anxious to come over for next to nothing, and he was content to put the management into the hands of Scotto. But, as Rossi-Lemeni remembers, '[Scotto] was a scoundrel. He disposed of the entire amount that he had received for the season before it had even started.'[112] The first night was originally announced for January 6th 1947, then it was postponed until the 27th and finally, when the American Guild of Musical Artists demanded a deposit so that the chorus and orchestra soloists were sure of being paid, the United States Opera Company just fizzled out. Bankrupt before it had even begun, the European artists were stranded in America. On February 6th several of them appeared in Chicago in a concert with Ottavio Marini, another conductor, at the piano, and with $6,000 that was raised they managed to return home. Some of them, however, sang elsewhere in the States: Elmo and Lorenz went to the Met, and Infantino to the New York City Opera.

The constant postponements had meant that Calas and Rossi-Lemeni had not left New York. Rossi-Lemeni went looking for other work and that spring he sang for Giovanni Zenatello. Zenatello, the famous tenor, was founder of the opera seasons in the Arena of Verona, his home town and, in his capacity as Artistic Director, was looking for singers for the summer season. After booking Rossi-Lemeni for Alvise in *La Gioconda* he had some discussion with him as to the rest of the cast, the title-role was a problem, he said. He had considered Zinka Milanov, the Met's leading lyric-dramatic soprano, and Herva Nelli, who would sing Desdemona in a concert performance of *Otello* under Toscanini in December that year. Rossi-Lemeni immediately suggested Calas and it was agreed that he would bring her round to sing for him at his Central Park West apartment. So, with Caselotti at the piano, Calas sang 'Suicidio' from *La Gioconda*. One story has it that Zenatello became so enthusiastic that '[he] rushed to the piano, turned the pages of the score to the passionate duet between Enzo and Gioconda, and despite his seventy years, he began singing it . . . with a passion and intensity he had forgotten he possessed'.[113] But Enzo and Gioconda are not lovers and their duet is not passionate but furious: Enzo is busy calling Gioconda names – 'furibonda jena' ('a raging hyena')! Zenatello may have booked Calas there and then, but his doing so seems to have been based on mundane considerations; Milanov and Nelli wanted too much money, whereas Calas was happy to accept 40,000 Lire a performance. As Meneghini observed, 'he saw she was down and out so he offered her a hangman's contract'.[114] Zenatello had a reputation as a shrewd businessman: sixteen years earlier he had discovered Pons and had her audition for Gatti-Casazza who brought her over to the Met for '$450 a week, of which his share was more than a trifle'.[115] After Pons created a furore the following year her fee went up dramatically, but Zenatello continued to earn the same percentage and in order to extricate herself she was obliged to take him to court.

When Calas signed her Verona contract, she perhaps recalled de Hidalgo's advice, that she should go to Italy. Well, this was one way of getting there, but she needed money and her parents were unable to assist her, so she borrowed a thousand dollars from her godfather, Dr Lantzounis. Before the departure of Calas and Rossi-Lemeni Bagarozy got them to sign contracts for a ten-year period from June 13th 1947. He was to be their personal representative and accordingly would be entitled to ten per cent of all their earnings. In return he would do his best to promote their careers. Events had proved that as a company manager he could be outsmarted, but his skill in perceiving that both of them were worth signing up shows that at least he could tell which singer's bandwagons were worth jumping on! His wife went along with them to Italy, where she would look for work herself as a soprano – and, no doubt, make quite certain that Calas and Rossi-Lemeni would be punctual in paying their percentages.

II

1947–1948

MORE THAN TWO years had passed since VE day and this was the first complete opera season held at Verona since the war. The *Rossia*, the Russian cargo boat that brought Callas[1] from New York, docked in Naples on June 27th. It was certainly no luxury liner, Rossi-Lemeni remembers 'the accommodations were terrible. There was no service to speak of, and we were constantly scolded if we arrived a minute late for a meal. At the end . . . the Russians asked everyone to sign a document saying what a wonderful crossing we'd had. Maria . . . exploded. "It's a filthy ship and we've been treated like soldiers"'[2] and she refused. With Caselotti and Rossi-Lemeni she immediately undertook the journey to Verona. The weather was stiflingly hot, the train overcrowded, and with a deal of difficulty they managed to find a single seat which they used in turn. The next day they arrived in Verona. That evening Gaetano Pomari, one of the directors of the festival, invited Caselotti with members of the cast to dinner at the Ristorante Pedavena, which he also managed, in the piazza near the Arena. There she met Giovanni Battista Meneghini.

Meneghini was fifty-one, a typical provincial Italian who would converse by choice in his native Veronese. A bachelor and a prosperous brick manufacturer, he enjoyed the reputation of being a ladies' man. At the end of the war the Germans had occupied his house and left it uninhabitable, so he had been obliged to move into a small apartment over the Ristorante Pedavena, which he shared with Pomari. Next to it were rooms Pomari was using as the festival offices and since Meneghini was an ardent opera lover he inevitably met a large number of singers who came to Verona. On one occasion he asked, half in jest, whether he might be given a special assignment, perhaps to look after some ballerinas. Then he hastily added that ballerinas were not really his type and that he preferred the Titianesque. 'You are a distinguished man . . .' he was told, '[a] major representative of Verona's industries . . . You should . . . accompany the prima donnas . . . This season . . . there are two. One is Renata Tebaldi, a splendid girl . . . However, she doesn't strike me as your type. The other one, though, may be more fitting for you. She's Greek, but . . . grew up in America.'³

It happened some days later that Meneghini arrived back at Verona very late. He had been at Trento, more than sixty miles away, all day on business. He was tired out and on the point of making his way upstairs to bed when Pomari spotted him and obliged him to join the company of musicians. When he tried to order something, he was told the kitchen was shut. A young woman on the other side of the table immediately offered him her veal escalope. So it was that Meneghini met Callas for the first time. He soon forgot her, however, becoming involved in a heated altercation with Caselotti, who was seated next to him, as to the respective virtues of Italy and the United States. He told her: 'I am convinced that even one decomposed brick from the foundations of a Venetian palazzo is worth more than all your skyscrapers.'⁴ He decided the best way to settle the argument would be to organize an excursion to Venice the next day. In the meantime he persuaded Caselotti, with Rossi-Lemeni and Callas, to come at once and see the main square in Verona, the Piazza dei Signori. It was not until they got up to go that he had his first close look at Callas. He noticed how overweight she was. He was 'moved to pity' by her swollen legs and her standing apart, self-consciously, 'her eyes lowered.'⁵

Next morning he came round to the hotel with his car ready to leave for Venice. Rossi-Lemeni and Caselotti joined him, but Callas sent down a message to say she was sorry she could not come. However, Rossi-Lemeni went up to her room and tried to persuade her: '"I don't want to meet him", she declared. "I don't need anybody's help. I don't want him to get the idea that he can take advantage of me because of his money." I assured her Meneghini was a gentleman.'⁶ Eventually she changed her mind, and got into the car. On the way she scarcely spoke a word. The party reached Venice and took a vaporetto disembarking at Harry's Bar, that way they would come into Piazza San Marco without seeing it first. When Callas clapped eyes on it, she could hardly contain herself. All her reserve was at once swept aside. Turning to Meneghini she said: 'You were right . . . Something like this is worth a trip from America. Who knows when I might have had another chance to see anything comparable.'⁷ She communicated her enjoyment so completely that he was touched. 'Anyone who delights in beauty in that fashion, he said to himself, must have special sensibilities which sooner or later will burst forth.'[8]

Meneghini took his guests to dinner in the Piazza San Marco and Callas sat next to him. In the course of the evening she gradually opened up, telling him of her experiences in America, her relations with her father and mother, how uncertain her career was. 'She didn't have the enthusiasm characteristic of young people. She was sad and pessimistic. Her words were cold and bitter.'[9] She also explained why she had not wanted to come in the first place. She didn't have anything to wear and was ashamed to appear wearing the same blouse as the evening before. 'I would have bought something . . . but I don't have any money.'[10] However Callas's mother describes the shopping trip she had taken her daughter on before she left New York. She claims that with the money Dr Lantzounis had given her she bought 'a fine wardrobe, almost a trousseau, of evening and daytime dresses, hats, coats, underwear, shoes and two or three suits'.[11] A number of photographs of her taken on board the boat survive and they do suggest that she did have at least more than one blouse. Later on, as we shall see, she claimed Bagarozy had embezzled the money. Meneghini listened to her and did his best to reassure her, promising he would help her. When they finally got back to Verona it was after two in the morning. He kissed her, bid her good night, and the next day lost no time in writing to confirm his offer of assistance.

The rehearsal schedule for *La Gioconda* began straight away. Callas worked every day with Ferruccio Cusinati, a voice teacher as well as chorus master at the Arena. She would divide her time between the Arena and Cusinati's studio in Via Valverde. She prepared much of her repertory with him rather than Serafin. As she herself later stated: 'It is not true that my husband asked . . . Serafin to coach me in my roles and that it was he who taught them to me. My teacher was . . . Cusinati.'[12] It was not until two weeks before *La Gioconda* was to open that she first sang for Serafin at a rehearsal held at the Teatro Adelaide Ristori. At the *prova generale* at the Arena, during Act II she had an accident, because she was short-sighted and did not wear spectacles. '(S)he didn't see an open trapdoor which led to the subterranean basement beneath the ancient amphitheatre, and . . . stumbled into it. The fall could have been fatal . . .'[13] 'Fortunately, there was a wooden chute, otherwise [she] could have cracked [her] head on th[e] rocks,'[14] as it was 'she survived with only a bruise and a badly sprained ankle'.[15] Notwithstanding the pain and shock she suffered 'instead of having it bandaged [she] chose to continue the rehearsal',[16] and on first night she was hardly able to drag herself around the huge stage.

It was on August 2nd that Callas made her Italian bow as Gioconda at the Arena. This was her first public appearance in two years; finally she was able to concentrate wholly on her singing once more. Only when she got back to the Accademia Hotel that night did she realize how painful her ankle was, so Meneghini insisted on staying by her bed until dawn. It was then that she became aware of another, more personal dimension beginning to open up in her life. 'I remember the gratitude and tenderness I felt . . . for Titta [as she called Battista Meneghini] [for] stay[ing] . . . to help . . . and comfort me.'[17]

Reports of Callas's performance in the newspapers next day are neither particularly fulsome nor very illuminating. The *Corriere della Sera* expends only a line or two on the singers and does not distinguish her contribution from that of the Enzo, Richard Tucker. Desmond Shawe-Taylor and the Earl of Harewood went to one or other of the five performances. What Shawe-Taylor writes, years later, is in the same vein as the Italian reviews: 'Striking as Callas certainly was, her success was shared with that of . . . Tucker.'[18] Lord Harewood, later Director of the English National Opera then a young opera buff, heard one of the later performances and for him 'the things that were wonderful were the scale of her singing, the scale of the whole voice, the edge, the way in which she dominated everything'.[19] The Laura, Elena Nicolai, years after remembers that her 'musicality had something special'.[20] Nevertheless, in Meneghini's words, 'it was not a triumph . . . She had a nice success . . . [but] that was it. No one proclaimed a miracle. If they had, offers for engagements would have arrived immediately . . . (but) Maria did not receive a single offer of work.'[21] In view of their subsequent close relationship it is interesting that Serafin took no part in immediately assisting Callas to secure her next engagement. He wrote to Meneghini that he thought her 'just a competent singer, like so many others,' and that in spite of 'excellent vocal gifts . . . she didn't possess "an Italianate voice"'.[22]

It was at a reception given to honour the singers at Castelvecchio, during the run of performances, that Callas saw Tebaldi for the first time, at Verona Tebaldi was singing Margherita in *Faust*, but they did not meet. By then Tebaldi was already an established singer in Italy. A couple of years older than Callas, she had made her début at Rovigo in 1944 as Elena in *Mefistofele*. In 1946 she appeared at La Scala, at the first concert given there since the war, conducted by Toscanini. After the five *La Giocondas* were over Meneghini relates how Callas turned over ten per cent of her fee to Caselotti. Notwithstanding the fact that she had therefore earned only 180,000 Lire, and had no other engagements yet, with the surety of Meneghini's assistance, she elected to stay in Italy. As she herself later told: 'If [Meneghini] had wished, I would have abandoned my career without regret.'[23] In view of her total commitment to her career we may wonder how true that was. Even from her earliest days, she was married to her career; but then, as we shall see, her career came to mean a great deal to Meneghini, too.

He tells in detail the story of his concern to help her realize her ambitions. To this end he supported her, playing two roles: husband and father. When she went to renew her passport at the U.S. consulate in Venice and was told that first she must repay the U.S. government the $1,000 that had been advanced her in Athens, so that she could get to New York, he immediately paid up. Needless to say the niggardly size of her Verona fee soon made it necessary for him to pay for her room at the Accademia Hotel, and he also paid for her to go on studying repertory with Cusinati. At the same time he began to take an active part in endeavouring to secure her future engagements and, during the next few months, he it was who continued to provide her financial support.

One can imagine how bewildered he must have felt in the world of opera for the first time, he had known nothing about it from the inside before he met Callas. There had been, so he tells, some discussion with the Liceo, Barcelona as to her singing in *Norma* and *La Forza del Destino*[24] that November, but this never came to anything. So he decided the best thing would be to jump in at the deep end, and accordingly he got a friend to secure a letter of introduction to La Scala, Milan, so that Callas might audition for the Artistic Director, Mario Labroca, a composer whose creative reputation was used as a kind of icing on the artistic direction of La Scala. Labroca summoned Callas to Milan and after hearing her sing 'Casta Diva' from *Norma* and 'Ma dall'arido stelo divulsa' from *Un Ballo in Maschera*, he spoke to her about rectifying some vocal faults, talking vaguely of how she might be able to undertake the role of Amelia in a revival of *Un Ballo in Maschera* that La Scala was planning the following April. But to Meneghini, when asked for his candid opinion, he replied brusquely: 'There's nothing for her here . . . absolutely nothing.'[25] Over dinner, at Savini's in the Arcade, Meneghini told Callas, as tactfully as he could, what Labroca had said. To his surprise she seemed to take it philosophically.

Meanwhile Nino Cattozzo, who had just been appointed Director of the Fenice, Venice, determined to begin his first season, at the end of December, with a new production of Wagner's *Tristano e Isotta*. These were the last years in which Wagner's music dramas would still be given in Italian in Italy. At that time, directly following the last war, artists' contracts were not made years in advance, as they are now, but only months beforehand, sometimes less. Cattozzo, who had been at Verona in August and had heard Callas's Gioconda, suggested her to Serafin and it was agreed that he should find out if she knew the role of Isotta. Accordingly he telephoned the Ristorante Pedavena and asked to speak to Meneghini, whom he had known for some years, but Meneghini and Callas were out so he left a message asking that she return the call if she knew the role. The message was left with Angelina Pomari, a sister of the restaurant proprietor but, perhaps because she was also a soprano with Wagnerian aspirations, she failed to pass it on.

At that time, anxious to find work, Callas and Meneghini had gone off to Milan to do a tour of agencies. They went to one of the Milan agencies, ALCI, and spoke to its President, Lidiuno Bonardi, 'an amiable old bandit'.[26] All he could suggest was a solitary Gioconda later that month at Vigevano, a small town about twenty miles south-west of Milan, and for this she was offered 20,000 Lire, even less than she had earned in Verona and barely enough to pay for a hotel and the rail fare. Meneghini was so incensed that, without waiting to know what Callas's wishes were, taking her by the hand he stalked out of Bonardi's office flinging the door open; it hit Cattozzo, who was just about to walk in, full in the face. Bonardi immediately jumped up and escorted the Director of the Fenice to the most comfortable seat, applying a handkerchief to his bloody nose. Meneghini hastened to apologize. When Cattozzo had recovered he announced that he had come looking for an Isotta.

'Why don't you give the part to Callas?' [Meneghini] suggested.

'What do you mean?' [Cattozzo] asked, surprised. 'Callas knows the part?'

'Certainly,' Meneghini assured him.[27]

Cattozzo then revealed the message he had left with Angelina Pomari, and that he had assumed that as Callas did not phone him back she did not know the part. She hastily reassured him. As soon as Serafin arrived in Milan, she went round to sing it for him. He welcomed her and then asked her which passages she would like to audition; as a matter of fact she did not know any of the role, but she replied: 'You choose, maestro'.[28] They went through various excerpts, all of which she 'sight-read . . . with confidence and extraordinary accuracy'.[29] Serafin was more than satisfied, and 'wanted to congratulate (her)'.[30] 'But,' as she tells herself, 'I couldn't keep from confessing the truth to him.'[31] Altogether four months elapsed between the Verona Giocondas in August and the Venice Isottas in December. During this time she continued her studies with Cusinati with renewed vigour, working even harder on Isotta than she had on Gioconda. When she had had time to learn the role Serafin invited her to Rome to go over it with him. She felt metamorphosed by his new-found interest, after his reservations about her in Verona, and on October 28th she left Verona by train to spend a week with him studying Isotta.

Callas was in Rome twelve days, her first separation from Meneghini since meeting him. She wrote him a copious number of letters, on some days up to three. She describes how on the morning of her arrival it was raining, and since the hotel Serafin had recommended was full, she had been obliged to traipse the streets in the wet going to at least a half-a-dozen others before she managed to secure what she deemed a bargain: a room without bath for 900 Lire a night! Her preoccupation with money was understandable then, though it would remain a feature of her personality all her life. Notwithstanding the fact that this was her first visit to the eternal city she has little to say about it, beyond a brief comment on its being 'splendid [and] beautiful'.[32] Her correspondence certainly does not read as one might have expected of a young woman. When she complains of leg trouble and how painful it had been climbing on to a bus to visit Serafin, we might have guessed she was sixty-four not twenty-four. Her enforced parting from Meneghini crops up in the letters like a leitmotif. The lasting impression is her lack of self-confidence and total dependence on him. This is no doubt what he intends by including so many of her letters in his biography, but even if they have been somewhat cut about, it is hard to believe that she has much else but him on her mind, apart, that is, from her singing. At that stage there is certainly not much in them to indicate the diva: though when she details her work with Serafin, she casts her sentences in a more assertive mould. 'I have been in good voice, and the more I sing . . . the better it gets. Isotta is a very dramatic part and I love it.'[33] In Rome she met Serafin's wife, Elena Rakowska, for the first time. An ebullient Pole, herself a Wagnerienne, she took an immediate liking to the young Greek-American, though Serafin, in his usual fashion, did not get too carried away. Rakowska's enthusiasm was, we shall see, to prove significant for Callas.

Long before Serafin arrived in Venice Callas had mastered Isotta. She made her début at the Fenice on December 30th; Barbieri was Brangania and she remembers how '[Callas] sang it . . . lyrically and in utterly different fashion from the German style'.[34] For *Il Gazzettino* 'her beautiful, very warm voice was both brilliant and lyrical where appropriate, especially in the upper range'.[35] and *Il Gazzettino-Sera* acclaimed her 'splendid high notes [and] tenderness' and in the death scene her 'limpid phrasing and spontaneous musicality'.[36] Meneghini must have been exhilarated; he had backed a horse with some pedigree. Serafin was pleased and needless to say Rakowska was full of praises: 'I knew it would be a triumph.'[37] Cattozzo too was delighted. Straight after another three Isottas he engaged her for five Turandots. This she already knew in anticipation of her abortive Chicago début. Bagarozy's wife, Caselotti, was still in Italy when Callas undertook Turandot at the Fenice on January 29th 1948. She too had been looking for work as a singer; Meneghini had tried to help her but without success.[38] She was highly critical of Callas's singing and after the performance was over went round to tell her as much. They had a quarrel that brought their friendship to an abrupt end: 'What matters is *that* you sing, not how you sing',[39] Callas declared hotly. Stassinopoulos thinks that Caselotti's problem was one of sour grapes, yet although Callas sang Turandot twenty-four times in the first two years of her career she was quick to drop it. She later declared that she knew it to have been a voice-wrecker.[40]

The notion that Wagnerian roles are inevitably the most taxing is untrue. Callas herself points out that 'Wagner could never hurt your voice if you know how to sing well'.[41] Several reasons contributed to her giving up Wagner roles: after the Second World War in Italy Wagner came to be increasingly performed in the original, and Callas did not sing in German. Then too, she never enjoyed the kind of surpassing strength that a Flagstad or a Nilsson possessed. Although Wagner's vocal writing is not unsympathetic in the way of many verismo composers, yet having to combat the orchestra in full flood, inevitably it lacks opportunities for the expressive range and refined variety of bel canto.

Of the Fenice performances, one thing stuck out firmly in Callas's memory: '[T]he fee, not without some effort, was raised from 40,000 Lire, as it was at Verona, to 50,000 a performance.'[42] She fails to add, however, that she did not pay Bagarozy his percentage, of which we shall hear more later. Tebaldi was in Venice at the same time singing Violetta, also under Serafin, and Callas remembers that one night she came round to congratulate her. Tebaldi told her: 'If I had to perform such an exhausting part [as Isotta] they would have to scrape me up with a spoon!'.[43] It was in a broadcast of the second performance, on January 3rd 1948, that Francesco Siciliani, later Director of the Comunale, Florence, first heard her. At the time he was still working at the San Carlo, Naples, and he called the Fenice to enquire who she was. Harewood, too, remembers 'twiddling the radio one winter evening and [catching] the last act of *Tristano* . . . from Venice. [T]he voice of the soprano seemed familiar, though [at first] I could not put a name to her.'[44]

On the rebound other engagements came in northern Italy and until the next autumn she was busy travelling round the lesser Italian houses. In March she proceeded to Udine, in the north-east, near the Yugoslavian border, where on the 11th she undertook the first of a couple of Turandots. Meneghini describes the public clamour for her, the enthusiasm of her colleagues for her voice, and he also notes how proud she was that her restaurant bill was less than the other singers'. She tells how journalists cross-questioned her, asking her all sorts of questions about her life and her work. But, perhaps indicatively, she felt most complimented when one of them told her how beautiful she looked. 'In short', she writes, hardly believing it, 'I was received very warmly.'[45]

In April she travelled south-east to Trieste then, only three years after the Second World War, still a free city and not yet reunited with Italy. There, on the 17th, she appeared in another new role, Leonora in Verdi's *La Forza del Destino*, which she was to repeat three times. Her fee had now risen another 10,000 Lire to 60,000. *Il Lavoratore* acclaimed her: '[S]he demonstrated that she is an actress of the first class, conscientiously prepared and very sure in the upper range.'[46] The baritone in these performances was Benvenuto Franci. Callas wrote Meneghini telling him how '[Franci] . . . paid me many many compliments. [He] said no one in Italy sings Verdi like me.'[47] Franci had studied with Antonio Cotogni (1831–1918), a famous baritone, whose other pupils included stellar names like Jean de Reszke, Gigli, Giacomo Lauri Volpi and Mariano Stabile. Franci was then at the end of a career stretching back more than 30 years. In 1921 he had made his first records with one of Caruso's predecessors, also a Neapolitan, Fernando de Lucia.

On May 12th Callas appeared at Genoa as Isotta in the first of three performances of *Tristano e Isotta;* again the opera was conducted by Serafin, and the rest of the cast included Nicolai, Lorenz, Raimondo

Torres and Rossi-Lemeni. Her fee was now 75,000 Lire. This was the last season that Genoa had to make do with opera in the cramped circumstances of the Grattacielo, a cinema called upon to deputize for the Carlo Felice, severely damaged in the Second World War. In later years Callas recalls the performances, she describes how the company was of 'no mean size. Imagine all those colossuses moving about a tiny, tiny little theatre . . . I remember that when Isotta orders Brangania to run to the prow of the boat and tells Tristano she wants to speak to him, I didn't manage to keep a straight face. In fact, there was not enough room and she could only move at most six or seven feet. In order to allow sufficient time for the stage action, she kept pirouetting about, provoking our amusement. Still, it was a stupendous performance and the Genoese didn't forget it.'[48] That that was a true estimate of the performance, at least as far as she was concerned, is apparent from an enthusiastic review she earned from Borselli in the *Corriere del Popolo*: 'her Isotta was a great interpretation. Her magnificent figure brought to the part an added appeal and irresistible grandeur. But the greatest fascination, the most moving quality was that projected by her voice, a majestic splendid instrument, vibrant and warm, smooth and equalized in every register – the ideal voice for Isotta.'[49] As Rossi-Lemeni remembers, 'Isotta marked a stage in her career; everyone there immediately realized Callas was somebody.'[50]

She then proceeded southwards to Rome, to make three appearances as Turandot, from July 4th, at the Baths of Caracalla under de Fabritiis. Here Masini sang Calaf, he was to have sung in the Chicago performances. Her fee continued to rise and she was now receiving 90,000 Lire a performance. On the 27th she appeared at Verona again for the first of another four Turandots under Antonino Votto. Years later he recalls these performances: 'From the podium, where I was, and the spot where she sang her first line, "In questa reggia", there was a distance of about 130 to 160 feet, she couldn't see, but she sensed exactly when I gave the downbeat. A musical sensibility of the first class – even beyond the first class. When I started with her she was already precise, already perfect . . . she already had a well defined musical personality. I remember she had this habit of singing in rehearsal, even with piano, in full voice. This was disturbing for her colleagues for it obliged them also to sing out. They liked to save themselves, but they are wrong, for the rehearsal is a track on which the singer practises running; if you have a mile to accomplish, then you don't practise it running only half a mile.'[51]

How Votto's logic would have struck Patti, the greatest soprano three quarters of a century before Callas, would be interesting to know, for not only did Patti not sing at all at rehearsals, she did not even go to them! She would send Maurice Strakosch, her brother-in-law, and he would tell the other singers what she would do. It is interesting that Patti and Callas should both have been remarkable musicians, perhaps the two most outstanding among sopranos on record. Conductors like Serafin, de Sabata, Votto and Bernstein spoke fulsomely about Callas and Patti was highly praised by Rossini and Verdi. The divas' different attitude to rehearsals is a reflection of their different historical backgrounds. Their careers reflect two particular stages in the development of Italian opera.

Patti was the first great singer to maintain her popularity through her career with essentially the same repertory that she had learned in her teens. Though, when she first undertook them in the 1860s, many of her roles were new, by the 1890s she was still singing Rosina, Lucia and Violetta. She had begun to sing in public at the age of eight in 1851 and an echo of the remarkable spontaneity of her art survives on records she made more than half a century later, in 1905 and 1906. Having been a child prodigy, the daughter of two busy opera singers, her style and interpretations were authentic and, in one of the most exhaustive careers ever, she established them as 'traditional' all the way from South America to Imperial Russia. By 1885, when she was surrounded by younger artists, she could see no point in attending rehearsals. She knew precisely what she was going to do, and if her colleagues needed to know then Strakosch could tell them, that was enough.

But for Callas rehearsals were obligatory. She was working in the dark, for she never ventured any contemporary opera. When she sang roles like Lucia or Violetta they were not merely old, they were antiques. She was attempting to recreate the music of the age of bel canto more than a century after the works were written, by which time performance practice had inevitably become corrupted. By Callas's day a score represented no more than a ground plan of the music. Though it might have seemed impossible for her to reconceive the manners of an age long past, yet by the assiduity of her musicianship she shows us how much more there is in these operas than anyone else had ever realized. It may seem that she is able by some alchemy to transform black and white notes into colour; yet if we follow any of her assumptions with the score, we appreciate how much her skill is the product of concentration and sheer hard work.

III

1948–1949

B EFORE CALLAS UNDERTOOK Norma for the first time she
was busy with Turandot and Aida. Straight after four Turandots in
Verona she sang another two at Genoa, at the first of which, on August
11th, she appeared opposite Mario del Monaco for the first time. After
this she proceeded to Turin where, on September 18th, she added
Aida to her repertory, undertaking it four times. Her emolument had
now risen to 100,000 Lire a performance. *La Stampa* acclaimed '[her]
splendidly exuberant and secure use of her voice'[1]. *L'Unità di Torino*
wrote of 'her easy emission, tossing off excellent high notes with a
. . . secure mastery of vocal means'[2]. She repeated Aida, commencing
on October 19th, three times at the Sociale, Rovigo. The *Gazzettino*
acclaimed her: 'She is the best dramatic soprano heard here for many
a year.'[3] At the second performance, on the 21st, after 'O patria mia',
Tebaldi was seen applauding vigorously and, the next day, in the same
theatre, Tebaldi undertook Maddalena in *Andrea Chénier*. On the
24th, a Saturday matinée, Callas sang Aida again and that evening
Tebaldi repeated Maddalena. Which gives us some idea of the vocal
profligacy at that time for Rovigo, situated in the Po valley, is even today
a town of fewer than 50,000 inhabitants. During the season Callas tells
how she and Tebaldi 'became, I may say, dearest friends. We were
often together, and we exchanged advice about clothes, hairdos, and
even about repertory'.[4] About clothes, maybe, but as to repertory they
had no roles in common at that time; it was not for more than another
year, in 1950, that Tebaldi would venture her first Aida at La Scala.

It was on November 30th that Callas sang Norma at the Comunale,
Florence. Its Artistic Director was Siciliani. A composer as well as
director, his career vindicates the Italian preference for professional
musicians as administrators. He was Artistic Director of the San
Carlo, Naples until 1948, when he came to Florence, then in 1958
he moved to La Scala. More recently he was Music Director of RAI,
and he only finally retired in 1990 as President of the Accademia di

Santa Cecilia Orchestra, Rome. One of the most remarkable men in the Italian musical world after the Second World War, he has been consistently undervalued. 'Shy and reserved, he was rather uncommunicative, though his musical and cultural background was on a level far superior to that of most theatre directors.'⁵ Older men, especially musicians, always influenced Callas, sometimes unduly, and it was natural for her to seek father figures, for her childhood had been dominated by her mother. In her first years in Italy she had two paternal influences: Meneghini and Serafin. The public has come to believe in the greatness of Serafin, and to question Meneghini's motives, while other important figures in her life, like Siciliani, have been overlooked. He was less than a decade her senior, and in such company a mere boy. One supposes she felt him to be her contemporary and not worth any special regard. Yet a number of his distinguished revivals involved Callas. He it was who not only introduced her to Norma and Violetta in *La Traviata* but he revived *I Vespri Siciliani*, *Armida* and *Medea* for her, and not all of these were conducted by Serafin. It was Meneghini who perceptively observed: 'If Serafin was the first conductor to appreciate Callas's potential, Siciliani was the first artistic director to utilise her gifts intelligently, looking for roles which would show her off.'⁶

Siciliani was planning his inaugural season when he remembered the broadcast of *Tristano* he had heard with Callas from Venice. He asked Serafin to arrange for him to hear her, so it was that, with Serafin at the piano, she sang scenes from *La Gioconda*, *Turandot* and *Aida*. 'Parts of the voice', Siciliani recalls, 'were beautiful, others [were not] . . . She had worked with de Hidalgo, which struck me as strange, for de Hidalgo was a coloratura. She told me she could sing florid music too, though she regarded herself as a dramatic soprano, then to my amazement she sang the Mad Scene from *Puritani*. It was overwhelming, the kind of singing one read about in books, a real dramatic coloratura.'⁷ Siciliani had scheduled *Madama Butterfly* to open the season but changed his mind on the spot and determined to present *Norma*, the first time the opera had been heard at the Comunale since 1935.

Norma represented the first quintessentially Callas role that she undertook. In the course of the next seventeen years she would sing it eighty-eight times, considerably more than any other role. Even then, Frangini in *La Nazione*, wrote: 'She has a powerful voice, one that is steady and attractive in timbre, penetrating in loud passages and sweet in more delicate moments. Her technique

is secure and perfectly controlled.'[8] Rigacci in *Il Pomeriggio* thought
that she has 'unusual flexibility all through the range, markedly so
in delicate nuances. Therefore Norma appears almost an entirely
different character from the one we are accustomed to hearing;
softer, more feminine – a Norma that does not strike so much as
moves us.'[9]

She sang only two performances for she was troubled by acute
abdominal indisposition. As soon as she returned to Verona she
went into the Borgo Trento Hospital where she was operated on
for appendicitis. Within a few days she began to recover. However
hospitals are not very cheerful places. As soon as she had recovered
from the post-operative shock, she had Meneghini stay on a folding
bed in her room, although they were not yet married. After ten
days she was well enough to return home. She had been obliged
to relinquish performances of Aida in Florence, which were to have
begun on December 23rd, but she was soon well enough to continue
with her schedule. She went to Venice, to the Fenice, on January 8th
1949, to undertake another Wagner role for the first time, Brunilde in
La Walchiria, conducted by Serafin.

That winter in Italy there was a serious 'flu epidemic and one of
its victims was the lyric soprano Margherita Carosio. News of her
indisposition and inability to perform the role of Elvira in Bellini's
I Puritani, the next opera in the Fenice season, reached Serafin the
next day. He got into a huddle with Cattozzo and phoned singers
and agents in an endeavour to find a replacement, but without success.
During the afternoon Callas called round at the Hotel Regina to see
Serafin. Rakowska was there with her daughter, Vittoria, they told
her of his predicament, and how he was at the theatre even then
but they expected him soon. Callas decided to wait, and to fill in
the time she went to the piano and started idly leafing through a
score of *I Puritani* that lay on it, singing some passages. She recalled
years later: 'Rakowska sat up, "As soon as Tullio arrives", she said,
"sing that for him." Thinking that she was joking, I said yes.'[10] But
Serafin did not return and at length Callas said she would come back
at a more convenient time. Later that night at the Fenice hotel, Callas
received a telephone call from Serafin, who told her to get dressed
and come round to his hotel at once. After he had prevailed over
her objections she went and there found him with his wife, his
daughter and Cattozzo. They had come to a conclusion: Serafin
had been complaining about his inability to find anyone suitable
when Rakowska told him about Callas's singing that afternoon. He

immediately remembered the audition she had done for Siciliani in
Florence, so he called her over and they worked through the entire
score. At length, turning to her, he proposed that she undertake
Elvira.

"'Isn't it possible to find anyone else?", [Callas] demanded.

"We've tried everyone. There's nobody left", Serafin told her.

Callas was silent, then she said: "All right, give me a score to look
over and I'll see if I can. Tomorrow evening I'll be able to give you
my reply."'[11]

She took the score back to her hotel, and in bed she began to leaf
through it, propping it against a pillow. Although there were only
ten days left before first night and she still had another three
Brunildes to sing, she decided she could do it. And Meneghini
managed to secure her a fee of 130,000 Lire a performance.

Callas appeared as Elvira in *I Puritani* at the Fenice on January
19th. Of all the many roles she undertook it is doubtful if any had
a more far-reaching effect. In those days, when vocal specialization
had reached its apogee, the notion of any one singer embracing
music as divergent in its vocal demands as Wagner's Brunilde and
Bellini's Elvira in the same career would have been cause enough for
surprise; but to attempt to essay them both in the same season seemed
like *folie de grandeur*. A Milan newspaper snorted contemptuously:
'[W]e hear that Serafin has agreed to conduct *I Puritani* . . . with a
dramatic soprano . . . Three cheers for those old-timers without any
artistic sense who amuse themselves mangling opera. When can we
expect a new edition of *La Traviata* with Gino Bechi's Violetta?'[12]
The morning after the first performance of *I Puritani* Pugliese in the
Gazzettino[13] spent a large part of his review telling us more in fact
about the decadence of critical standards than anything about Callas:
'her vocal devices', he complained, 'her trills, scales, embellishments
were only a technical accomplishment; not, as Bellini demands,
expressive.' Though he does not seem too sure, '[for] whenever
her part became more lyrical, especially in the dizzying expressive
climaxes, she had moments of great, intense musicality.' But he
obviously had a notion, perhaps based on Carosio's singing, that
it 'should have been more restrained, more intimate, so that the
angel-like character would be the result of a crystal clear Bellini
style'. In particular he objected to her use of portamento, nor did
he care for her 'rippling' effect, as he describes it; presumably he
was referring to the clarity of her downward scales in the Mad Scene,
such phenomenal accuracy was then nothing if not novel.

After three Elviras she went down to the other end of Italy and, on January 28th, sang the first of two Brunildes at the Massimo, Palermo. A letter to Meneghini, written on the day of the première,[14] shows her in an assertive and more confident mood and she rails against the circumstances surrounding the Sicilian performances. She describes the dress rehearsal: there were thirty stage hands who were in everyone's way; her headpiece had not been made and her shield and spear were not ready either. The orchestra was the anithesis of those she had appeared with before: at the dress rehearsal the players had no discipline, the conductor made no effect, and she was apprehensive as to what would happen at the première. In fact, it proved little short of a fiasco, as she later writes.[15] Although she was supposed never to have read critics, she was highly indignant with the critic of *L'Ora*, firstly for devoting so much space to the Siglinde then, after admitting that as Brunilde she sang with intensity and that 'her voice was beautiful and its timbre attractive', he complained 'she was not a sufficiently barbaric Valkyrie'.[16] 'What an imbecile . . . I will never again set foot in Sicily. It seems I am too musical and too ladylike on stage to be appreciated here.'[17] But in two years she was back as Norma.

After four appearances at the San Carlo, Naples as Turandot, beginning February 12th, she made her bow at the Teatro dell' Opera, Rome on the 26th. She sang, what transpired to be the only time on stage, Kundry in *Parsifal*. Adriano Belli in *Il Quotidiano* writes: 'She seems today a more complete singer. She has security of vocal production, perfect equalization of registers, and a fine upper extension, which victoriously surmounted every difficulty.'[18] The critic was comparing her with her performance the previous summer as Turandot at the Baths of Caracalla: again we note how she enjoyed a more complete success in a Wagner role. It had been during the run of performances of *Turandot* that Visconti, the theatre and film director, had become aware of Callas's name for the first time, but it was not until *Parsifal* that he went to the Rome Opera and saw her. 'I remember . . . a tiny Circassian stool on her head, which kept falling over her nose, but she kept on singing. I said to myself, that woman needs someone to design her costumes, someone who'll give her hats which don't fall on her nose when she's singing.'[19] Serafin was conducting and it was after this performance that he counselled Callas to remember the length of Wagner acts: 'No matter how much you fascinate the public with your voice, they still have time to look you over and cut your costume to pieces. So your appearance on stage must be harmonious with the music.'[20] The performances were directed by Hans Duhan, a Viennese baritone, but Callas remembers how '[Serafin] used to do the staging . . . When . . . I was supposed to kiss [Hans Beirer, the Parsifal] on the mouth . . . I was ashamed to; and Beirer . . . was, too. So Serafin came up on stage, saying "You women are all afraid, but I am a man, and I will show you how," and he kissed him right on the mouth.'[21]

Between the third and last *Parsifal* she went up to Turin and on March 7th sang in a RAI concert for the first time: the Mad Scene from *I Puritani*, 'O patria mia' from *Aida*, 'Casta Diva' from *Norma* and the Morte di Isotta. After Rome she returned to Verona and it was there, during a pause in engagements, that she invited her sister to visit her. Jackie tells of how 'amazingly fat'[22] she had become. She describes a meal of 'soup, pasta, fish, meat, salad, ice-cream [and] fruit', and how Meneghini 'seemed to take a sort of strange pride in her capacity to digest large quantities of food'.[23] According to Jackie it was she who encouraged Callas to persuade Pia Meneghini, Battista's sister, to get him to propose. But the sisters soon fell out. If Maria was jealous of Jackie's svelte figure and good looks, then Jackie was jealous of Maria's rapidly advancing career. At first Jackie had hoped Maria would invite her to go with her when she was to sing in Buenos Aires that May, but there was soon little love lost between them. Jackie records how irritated Maria became when one of Meneghini's friends thought she was her younger sister and, jokingly, he announced that 'as [Meneghini] was getting married maybe [he] should too and who better than [to] the beautiful sister of [Meneghini's] fiancée'.[24] After fifteen days Jackie felt it time to return to Athens.

According to Meneghini[25] Callas and he had first decided on marriage in 1948. But as soon as his brothers realized that she was no mere passing infatuation they joined together and did all in their power to thwart it. He was the eldest son and when his father had retired he succeeded him as managing director of a small brickmaking business, in which all his brothers worked. He had always wanted to settle down in the usual way but for a long time he found himself married to the business instead. It was not until the end of the Second World War, when the firm had grown considerably, that he met Callas, and the possibility of his getting married arose. It was precipitated by Callas's imminent departure for Buenos Aires; Meneghini determined that they could brook no further delay. Callas's faith was Greek Orthodox, so they received papal dispensation and the marriage could go ahead. Every kind of obstacle was placed in their path by members of his family and it was not until the very day of her departure that it eventually took place. The civil ceremony was at three in the afternoon of April 21st at the Town Hall of Zevio, near Verona, after which, at five the same day, they were married at Meneghini's local church in Verona, the Chiesa dei Fillippini, in a side chapel which, although consecrated, was not actually in the church. It was an extremely private ceremony, apart from the priest and his assistant, the only others present were a friend, Mario Orlandi, and a relative of Meneghini's, his brother-in-law Dr Giovanni Cazzarolli. 'I was dressed in blue, with black lace over my head',[26] Callas remembers.

At midnight she set sail from Genoa aboard the *Argentina*. Rossi-Lemeni was on the boat and he remembers how she 'was crying like a child when she left Meneghini . . . It was perhaps the only moment when I saw Callas really moved, really sincere, really caring for somebody. She was . . . desperate leaving Meneghini. [He] was not only her husband, he was her father, brother, the security she found after rather a difficult life that she had had as a child and a young woman.'[27] During her travels she kept up a busy correspondence with him writing regularly. 'With the passing of each day her feeling of melancholy became increasingly more oppressive, and Maria suffered greatly . . . Her letters were overflowing with love, devotion and tenderness, but also with sadness, pain and anxiety.'[28] 'All she did was eat, sleep, sprawl in her bunk, and talk about her husband: how tender he was, how he spread flowers about her bed.'[29] She caught 'flu after they crossed the equator and was unwell for the next five days, though she tells how 'I used to go to [Serafin's] rehearsals [whether she was in the operas or not]. I was short-sighted and could not always see well [but] I used to go and listen. It was fascinating!'[30] Even after she arrived in Buenos Aires she had still not completely recovered. In her letters she is appreciative of such august figures as Rakowska and Serafin, and she is unreservedly effusive to Meneghini, but the effect of her continued indisposition comes out in her attitude to some of the other singers. She casts them in the role of villains, whether she knew them or not.

The Colón was the first of the sextet of the world's greatest opera houses in which Callas sang (the other five being La Scala, Covent Garden, the Metropolitan, the Vienna Staatsoper and the Paris Opéra). Although she was to undertake all the performances of Turandot and Norma, she would manage only a solitary Aida and Delia Rigal sang the rest. Callas went to one of Rigal's Aidas and seems only too happy to tell Meneghini of how '[Rigal] cracked on the high note [a c''] at the end of "O patria mia". God understands . . . Poor Rigal!'[31] She is also dismissive of those who did not offer her any competition: 'a certain Menkes',[32] who eventually did not sing, and 'some Argentine soprano [Arizmendi] who isn't bad',[33] she sang Liù. She has plenty of spleen for del Monaco too, who to judge from a recording of Act II of *Turandot*, seems in good form; '[he] has been very unpleasant to me . . . if I ever get an opportunity to block him when something important comes his way, I'll do it willingly'.[34] And she goes on lamenting how she has never treated any of her colleagues the way they have treated her. We should remember that these statements were part of her confidential correspondence, and never intended for publication. It has been implied that Meneghini poisoned her relationship with her colleagues, but these letters suggest that if he did then his seed was sown on very fertile ground.

Just as the beauties of Rome made little appeal to her, so she has next to nothing to say of Buenos Aires. She finds time only to note its being 'full of enormous cars', 'elegant stores and spacious avenues'[35] and, of course, there are the usual complaints about how 'living here is very expensive'.[36] Unfortunately we never hear the other side of the story; how much she was earning, presumably the reason she went there in the first place. As her mother tells, 'she was not allowed to take the money . . . out of the country [so] she bought a fabulous collection of furs.'[37] She made her début in the first of four appearances as Turandot on May 20th with del Monaco. Arnosi writes, 'she has a voice of considerable range and size, though its production is somewhat uneven, but she adds to it phrasing and an effective stage presence'.[38]

Turandot was the only operatic role Callas ever sang that was younger than she was herself (it was first performed on April 25th 1926). It was the nearest she came to contemporary music. At the present time there are at least two living sopranos who contrive a surpassing effect in the role, both of them Eastern Europeans: the Bulgarian Ghena Dimitrova and the Hungarian Eva Marton. They come from countries still locked in the past, where an opera singer's career not only has the glamour of a boxer's but requires something of his horse-power. Turandot is the perfect vehicle for ample-sized dramatic soprano voices with steady, steely and brilliant tones rising to c''. It requires little in the way of subtlety or vocal refinement and no great demands are made on the art of legato and portamento, or on the expressive articulation of ornaments. It is not to be compared with

Norma, a role which calls for dramatic accents for far longer stretches and a complete mastery of fioritura through every dynamic shading from pianissimo to fortissimo.

Part of one of Callas's Buenos Aires Turandots survives: a recording of the Riddle Scene beginning with 'In questa reggia'. Although it does not put the best complexion on her voice, it sounds of ample proportions, even if it does not project as surely as del Monaco's; certainly his *c'* makes a big impact and he seems to sell the note surely, to judge from audience reaction. However, Callas manages the lower passages, which pass back and forth across the break into chest register, far more effectively than the average Turandot. 'In questa reggia' is interesting, but the music is simply not capable of showing her off to particular advantage; she has a whole battery of effects at her disposal which she cannot employ effectively. Occasionally, however, her subtlety is apparent. On the phrase 'O principi, che a lunghi carovane' how sensitively she responds to the caravan-like rhythm Puccini suggests in the accompaniment. Too often, however, one is conscious of her singing too strenuously; she should have remembered that it is not necessary to be effortful to be effective. Still, we should not confuse her liberal use of vibrato with her characteristic wobble which developed later.

The critic Arnosi is more enthusiastic about her second role, Norma, which she sang four times commencing on June 17th. 'She was much better than in *Turandot*.' He went on about her wide range and ample tone but what really impressed him was her ability with florid music. 'This made her singing of "Casta Diva" especially notable, although at certain dramatic points she seemed to lack sufficient power but her phrasing was unforgettably expressive and her style impeccable as was her dramatic mastery.'[39] On July 2nd she ventured a solitary Aida. Roberto Turrò of *Opera News* thought: 'Though she possesses a voice of great range that allows her to sing with agility and power, some of her tones are dry and in general lack quality, except in piannissimi, which are of amazing beauty.'[40] Her last appearance at the Colón was at a concert on Independence Day, July 9th, at which she sang 'Casta Diva' and Act III of *Turandot*. Thereafter she took a ten-week vacation, the longest lacuna in her schedule for two years.

She had been away from Italy almost three months and in her absence Meneghini had secured 'a cosy apartment'[41] which he had had built directly above his firm's offices behind the Verona arena at Via San Fermo 21. He describes it as 'beautiful . . . spacious and well-lit'.[42]

Zeffirelli, however, remembers its style as more reminiscent of 'a poor man's Zsa Zsa Gabor: everything gilded, imitation rococo curtains, three different kinds of flowered wallpaper ... golden mirrors and shocking pink curtains'.[43] For the décor Meneghini had employed a firm of interior decorators, but they had their work cut out coping with Callas. She had her own idea of what should be in the apartment and how it should look. As soon as she could she left the Accademia Hotel, where she and Meneghini were then living, and moved in with a housekeeper. She would hang and rehang the various works of art Meneghini had bought; move and re-move the furniture. She loved attending to such mundane household matters as keeping a box of tools and meticulously labelling all the drawers. She also liked to play the role of housewife: she would cut recipes out of newspapers, and stick them in a scrapbook. Although she was rapidly putting on weight, Meneghini says, she was content to watch him, and would rarely eat anything herself. In his opinion her weight problem was due to a 'glandular disorder'.[44] However, as her sister tells,[45] at other times these roles seem to have been reversed: she ate and Meneghini just watched. The apartment was on top of his business, literally, and his family continued their hostility, so after another year passed they decided to move to a palazzo in Via Leoncino. There they stayed until 1955 when they bought an apartment in Milan.

On September 18th Callas resumed her career with her only performance in oratorio, singing Erodiade in Alessandro Stradella's San Giovanni Battista at the Chiesa di San Pietro, Perugia; for this her services had been secured by Siciliani while she was in Florence the previous December. On October 31st she appeared in a public concert in Italy for the first time, at the Nuovo, Verona, when her programme included six arias. Four she had sung in March that year for RAI, from Norma, Tristano, Aida, and I Puritani, and she added the Shadow Song, 'Ombra leggera' from Meyerbeer's Dinorah and 'Ah! fors' è lui' and 'Sempre libera' from La Traviata. Meneghini makes a point of telling how Callas sang for nothing, since it was promoted by a friend of his who 'was going through a difficult time with his business and needed to make money'.[46] Yet one wonders if this was not an attempt at self-promotion. At all events it failed and the theatre was no more than half full, despite the fact that Memo Benassi, a leading Italian tragedian, was also on the bill. It would take a good few more years before Callas's presence invariably meant a sold-out house. A week later she recorded the arias from Norma, Tristano and I Puritani at the RAI auditorium, Turin for Cetra, an Italian record company. By this time the days of her having to hawk herself around auditioning were already over, and directors came to seek her out. When Vitale from the Rome Opera begged her to come and sing Norma and Turandot, she agreed to Norma but she told him that she would not undertake Turandot again and suggested *Tristano* instead. They also discussed Refice's *Cecilia*, but for whatever reason, possibly because she did 'not like modern operas',[47] nothing came of it. On November 24th she was announced to sing in Turin another RAI concert. This time the programme was to include Act II of *Tosca* and Act IV of *Manon Lescaut*, which would have been her only performance of the latter work, except for the commercial recording, but the broadcast never took place.[48]

The earliest complete opera recording of Callas's to survive is from December 20 1949, the first of three performances (the only ones she ever gave) of Abigaille in Verdi's *Nabucco* at the San Carlo, Naples. Her contribution sounds out clearly enough although, unfortunately, the microphone is orientated in the direction of the orchestra and the principals are not infrequently submerged by it. Gui's conducting is to some extent distorted by the imbalance but it is alive and has appropriate slancio. Callas was not fond of him: 'Gui is happy working with me. But I'm not with him. He's always talking about himself.'[49] Listening to the recording we notice at once how much more at home she is as Abigaille than as Turandot. She demonstrates how Abigaille's music, though extremely difficult and abounding in fioritura across the widest range, is not taxing, when sung easily it is only a soprano without sufficient technique who will find it hazardous. Notwithstanding the orchestra's predominance, we hear the great effect she makes. Had she attempted it as forcibly as the recording of *Turandot* from Buenos Aires suggests, then it would have been impossible for her to manage the dramatic and florid passages equally adeptly and manipulate her voice with such alacrity and accuracy. As we can also hear on the Cetra 78s, at this stage of her career, when she was only twenty-six, her singing has a ring, a brilliant head resonance throughout her entire range that she would quickly lose. Abigaille's music corruscates through the widest intervals. In Act II, at the end of the recitative, 'Ben io t'invenni', before her aria, 'Anch'io dischiuso', she reveals how forward is her vocal placement and how responsive her instrument. We note her eloquent shaping of the phrase 'chi del perduto incanto mi torna' and in the cabaletta, 'Salgo già', she nips nimbly through a passage of ascending trills, rising from c', e' and g' to c'' and then cascades back down two octaves.

The demands Callas made of herself caused her to work ceaselessly to render her voice supremely responsive, so satisfying her musicianship. In her youth she had the physical strength to manage this: Rossi-Lemeni recalls how in those days, unlike most singers, '[she] would tuck away a huge steak and a plate full of vegetables [directly before going on stage]. Her colleagues could not understand how she could move, much less sing.'[50] We note how she supports her uppermost tones more highly in the head than she was to do only three or four years later. The result is that the tone is not only more brilliant, it is also more covered; and for an instrument of ample proportions this is a safer, less exposed way of managing it. We note the optional piano g' at the end of the recitative immediately before the Act III duet, 'Donna che sei?'; this is steadier than it would become in only a few years. At the end of the same duet she exultantly leaps into head voice to e'' flat, supporting it fully and marking the upward interval with a sweeping portamento.

Throughout we notice a basic hallmark of her singing: the peculiar responsiveness of her voice. It was her utter dedication and single-minded commitment to the music which accounts for this, not her 'upper palate [being] shaped like a Gothic arch, [rather than a] Romanesque arch'[51] as Walter Legge amusingly claims to have observed – one imagines him, Jonah-like, gazing up, his head between the jaws! Physical absurdities like this have also been put forward in an attempt to explain away the surpassing art of Caruso and Chaliapin. Callas was certainly phenomenal artistically, but not so physically. In such fashion is unique talent belittled, as if her greatness were an aberration of nature rather than the product of hard work. Her art was certainly exceptional, but not freakish. At the height of her powers a surpassing technique enabled her to manage the most difficult and elaborate passages, all the way from the bottom to the top of her voice, with complete security. It was her technical skill which allowed her, albeit briefly, to realize the music as consummately as her artistry demanded. Callas's Abigaille proves incontrovertibly that in music so demanding no singer can hope to express her artistry fully, and in doing so reveal the composer's intentions, until her instrument is sufficiently finely tuned.

IV

1950

C ALLAS BEGAN 1950, a busy year, by singing Norma on January 13th, her fifth role at the Fenice, Venice. Pugliese in *Il Gazzettino* speaks of 'the wealth of trills'[1] that she lavished on the part, from which we may assume that previous Normas had been somewhat sparing with them. After three performances she proceeded to Brescia, almost halfway between Verona and Milan, where she undertook Aida on February 2nd. That month she sang more than twice a week, juxtaposing appearances at the Grande, Brescia with the commencement of a run of performances as Isotta, the last time she would sing this role, at the Rome Opera, under Serafin's direction, on February 6th; then, on the 23rd, she added Norma. The schedule was tight:

Brescia: Aida,   February 2nd,
Rome: Isotta,   February 6th,
Brescia: Aida,   February 7th,
Rome: Isotta,   February 9th,
Rome: Isotta,   February 19th,
Rome: Norma, February 23rd,
Rome: Isotta,   February 25th,
Rome: Norma, February 26th,
Rome: Isotta,   February 28th,
Rome: Norma, March 2nd,
Rome: Norma, March 4th,
Rome: Norma, March 7th.

As she remembers, 'I began shuttling by train between Brescia and Rome . . . [and] I saw no reason for me to withdraw from my contract at Brescia for such a footling reason [as the Rome commitment], although Serafin was against my undertaking such a tour de force.'[2] However at Brescia during the second performance 'after the famous aria "O patria mia", at the moment when the audience would have begun to applaud, a voice from the gallery, in Brescian dialect, called out – "Quiet, the aria isn't over yet."[3] This was sufficient to deprive her of any applause, and she must have regretted that she had not taken Serafin's advice.

The *Normas* in Rome created a tremendous impression. In later years Visconti recalls not missing even one of them. He tells of one night during the run of performances when Serafin invited him to his house to meet Callas, and how despite her protestations she was eventually coaxed into singing 'Ah! fors' è lui'. 'It was really moving, I had never heard anything like it before, even though when I was young I often went to La Scala . . . Serafin's house was not large and the chandelier started shaking!'[4] At this stage of her career the size of her voice is much commented upon, and there are no complaints over its unsteadiness even in the most exposed passages. Of the Rome *Norma Il Giornale d'Italia* praised '[her] particularly unlimited vocal possibilities . . . especially in the upper register, and her expressive temperament', but in those days the critical conception of Norma was out of temper with hers: 'It does not seem to us, however, that such a voice and such a character suit the stylistic needs of Norma, which in the recitatives requires vocal consistency in the middle range which cannot be replaced by mere intelligence.'[5] Here we see how the most remarkable singing can be too novel and foreign-sounding for critics, who need time to get previous conceptions out of their ears. Until the 1950s they were accustomed to hearing the music of Norma sung by sopranos like Gina Cigna, Iva Pacetti and Maria Caniglia, as though it belonged to the verismo school with rich, not to say raucous singing in the middle voice and head voice, coloratura skimped or cut, and the drama conveyed by emphatic, exaggerated declamation.

From Rome Callas proceeded to Turin and on March 13th sang in a Martini-Rossi concert for the first time; her programme included arias from *Oberon, La Traviata, Il Trovatore* and *Dinorah*. Then three days later in Sicily, at the Massimo Bellini, Catania, she began a series of four Normas.

It was on April 12th that Callas made her bow at La Scala as Aida in lieu of an indisposed Tebaldi, at a gala honoured by the presence of Luigi Einaudi, President of Italy. She repeated it twice, but the Milanese were not about to capitulate. Tebaldi had already sung six performances and created a sensation. 'All [they] heard,' as Zeffirelli, who was present, recalls, 'was the unevenness, the changes of register . . . which she thought helped reveal . . . the character of the barbarian princess.'[6] Although by this time she had sung nearly as many Aidas as Normas, in the next three seasons the number of Aidas she sang would drop dramatically, and after 1953 she would not sing it again, By then the message had got through even to her. In the *Corriere Lombardo* Celli, later one of her most redoubtable supporters, writes a fair, well-considered appraisal (at least, based on the evidence of a recording of her Aida from Mexico City made six weeks later). 'She obviously possesses temperament and fine musicianship, but her scale is uneven. She seems to improvise differently from note to note the method and technique of her voice production. She does not have clear diction and she also forces her high notes, thereby imperilling the security of her intonation.'[7]

She had been determined to breach the wall into La Scala but Aida was for her too blunt a weapon for the assault, and she only succeeded in alienating Antonio Ghiringhelli, the theatre's Sovrintendente. 'He was an extraordinary man with a deep love of the theatre. Not a musician but a self-made man whose origins had been rather humble.'[8] For some reason he took an instant dislike to Callas, perhaps because she too had a humble background or, maybe, because she was one of Serafin's protégées; was it a coincidence that Serafin had last conducted at La Scala in the year of Ghiringhelli's appointment? Certainly Callas did not treat the Scala deferentially, and the theatre has long enjoyed, back to the days of Stendhal, a unique reputation. After having waited such a long time perhaps it was only natural that she should have feigned indifference. Though she did have a plausible excuse, it seems disingenuous: 'Sure, it's a magnificent theatre. But me, I'm myopic. For me theatres all look alike. La Scala is La Scala, but I'm Callas, and I'm myopic. Ecco!'[9]

At the San Carlo, Naples, Callas sang four more Aidas and then departed for Mexico City. She left without Meneghini but with the mezzo soprano Giulietta Simionato, with whom she was to sing for the first time. They quickly became friends. In those days the air trip took them via New York, where Callas was expecting her mother to meet her but, in a letter to Meneghini, she expresses her 'sad surprise'[10] at not finding her. In fact, Litza was in hospital. Her parents' apartment was empty when they arrived and Simionato was dying of thirst, so Callas went to the fridge to fix her a drink. She found a bottle of 7-Up but Simionato had scarcely drunk it when she became violently ill. It had a strange taste, and she thought it was kerosene. In haste Callas managed to phone her father to ask him what she should do. He told her to give Simionato some milk and quickly take her to hospital. It was only later, when Callas visited her mother, that she discovered it was she who had substituted insecticide for 7-Up and left it unmarked in the fridge. Luckily the hospital gave Simionato a purgative and she recovered quickly; but it was not for many years that Callas eventually admitted to her what the bottle contained.

Callas's relations with her mother were always complicated. They had not met for three years, since she had left New York. From the time she came to Italy she had turned her back on her difficult early years in New York and Athens, which she did not care to be reminded of. Her mother relates that Callas was guilty of distorting the evidence in her description of her early life, but Litza never seems to have properly appreciated how much Callas wished to forget. Litza was not unintelligent, but she was totally self-preoccupied. She would make no compromises with her husband, and was determined on separation. Meneghini could never understand the relationship between Callas and her mother, for he was a typical Italian, as he himself says, 'a mamma's boy'.[11] He put what he felt to be the best interpretation on it; after Callas's success in Venice as Isotta in December 1947 he spontaneously sent Litza a telegram to advise her of her daughter's triumph. When he told Callas, 'she had tears in her eyes and thanked me repeatedly'.[12] After which, he goes on, she endeavoured to adopt something of his attitude. Perhaps it was at his suggestion that she arranged to meet her mother as she passed through New York, and it was her way of expressing affection when she wrote to her offering to pay all her expenses so that she could come down to Mexico and hear her, certainly it is untypical to find Callas paying out without complaining! When she finally met her mother again, visiting her in hospital where she was being treated for acute iritis, she gave her the round trip air ticket to Mexico, telling her to come as soon as she was fit to travel. She wrote to Meneghini: 'She is certainly not well and her eye infection creates real problems. She continues to worry and her children are always on her mind . . . Like all good mothers she thinks only of her children.'[13] But no sooner had she realized that her mother was only waiting to get out of hospital, and that she intended coming not only to Mexico but returning with her to Italy, she protested: 'She wants to come and live with us. God forgive me, Battista, but at this moment I want to be alone a little only with you. Nobody has the right to compromise my happiness. How can I possibly explain this to my mother?'[14] By this time, May 19th, Callas was in Mexico City and the opera was beginning to make demands of her, so she had to hold her fire.

She arrived in Mexico City with Simionato on the morning of

May 14th where they were met by the Administrator of the Opera, Caraza-Campos. Her contract had been arranged by Bonardi who had told them that she would sing up to five roles: Norma, Aida, Tosca, Leonora in *Il Trovatore* and Violetta in *La Traviata*. But it was characteristic of Callas that no sooner were they in the car than she told them that it would not be possible for her to sing Violetta. It was enough that this would be the first time that she sang Leonora. 'I do not sing *La Traviata*', she declared[15] offering Elvira in *I Puritani* instead, but they were not interested.

Everyone in Mexico had been eagerly awaiting her arrival since Siepi first spoke enthusiastically about her. '[She] has sung Norma, Turandot, Brunilde and Elvira ... She has a tremendous range – she goes up to high E flat with a dramatic colour that makes people wild.'[16] Diaz Du-Pond, assistant to the Administrator, came to a rehearsal of *Norma*. No sooner was the first duet over than he rushed to a telephone and told Caraza-Campos to come round at once. He likened Callas to famous Normas of the past, Ponselle and Arangi Lombardi. Caraza-Campos came and brought a score of *I Puritani* and asked Callas to sing the Mad Scene with an *e''* flat, but she declined: '[If] [you] want ... my E flat, [you] must sign me for *I Puritani*.'[17]

Callas was to make her début as Norma on May 23rd but on the 19th she wrote to Meneghini that they 'had not had even one rehearsal with the orchestra and chorus. It's enough to make me crazy ... and the tenor ... Baum has not arrived yet.'[18] But when he did he barely knew the score, as is apparent from the recording of the performance. At rehearsal he had had the score in his hand but, at the première, this did not prevent his hanging on to every high note at the end of ensembles, and being wildly acclaimed. Callas felt aggrieved, for she did not receive much applause after 'Casta Diva'. She told Diaz DuPond that she was not surprised at the cool reception: 'people do not like my voice at first, they have to get used to it.'[19] But when he told her how much they loved high notes, she interpolated into the Act I finale a sustained full-throated *d''*. Baum's reaction is not on record.

Norma shows off her voice at its most youthful. In Mexico City it sounds more brilliant in the upper reaches, where she seems inclined to linger longer. Throughout soloists, chorus and orchestra reveal the need for rehearsal, and whenever Callas sings she leads and conductor, Picco, does his best to follow. In 'Casta Diva', for example, he plays the introduction lethargically but speeds up substantially as soon as she enters. Her singing is impressive throughout, though her interpretation is much cruder than it was to become. She takes 'Ah! bello a me ritorna' at a spanking lick. There is a particular brilliance about the a'' before she begins 'Ah! si fa core' then, after Adalgisa's entrance in the duet, a perfect c'', rarely a good note for Callas. Nevertheless her florid singing is not as accurate nor is she as musical in the dramatic fioritura of 'Oh non tremare' (the trio at the end of Act I), as she was to be in later years. Occasionally she felt inclined to expend all and make an effect, perhaps to spite Baum, for although she does manage a brilliant d'', she overreaches herself and grabs it too soon. At the beginning of Act II, when Norma is about to take the lives of her children, the obtrusive tears make us aware of her youth (she was then only twenty-six). As in *Nabucco*, the previous year, we note how effulgent she is at certain moments: on the phrase 'Pei figli suoi, t'imploro', before she commences the duet, 'Deh! con te', or the pair of splendid ringing c''s in the recitative with Clotilde, 'Ei tornerà'. Later, however, in Act III, in 'Qual cor tradesti' and 'Deh! non volerli vittime', she seems unable to mirror the cumulative effect of this scene in the way she was to do with such notable eloquence in later years. And we notice how Baum brings out the worst in her, at the end of 'In mia man', she joins him hanging on to a b'' flat an inordinate time. He gets the better of her; yet, as she shows when they sang together again in *Il Trovatore*, she did not easily forget.

After another *Norma* came *Aida*, also with Simionato and Baum, it had its first performance on May 30th. Caraza-Campos invited Callas and Simionato to his home after the prova generale. He was keen to hear Callas's e'' flat. He proposed that she should, like Angela Peralta, a Mexican soprano of the last century, interpolate one at the end of the Triumphal Scene. At this Callas expressed some surprise and said it would not be possible without the agreement of her colleagues. But on the way back to the hotel Simionato urged her to try it. Callas did not reply but during the performance she became so enraged by Baum, who was up to his usual antics, that she summoned Diaz Du-Pond, and requested him to go 'to Simionato and Robert Weede [who was singing Amonasro] and ask them if they would mind if I give a high E flat.'[20] They did not mind, and when she took it, she recalls, 'the public went crazy and Baum split with envy'.[21] He swore that he would never sing with her again and that she would never secure an engagement at the Metropolitan, where he was a regular member of the company. Nevertheless singers' memories are notoriously short. He appeared again in *Aida* with her at Covent Garden in 1953, though then she did not interpolate an e'' flat and, in *Norma* in her début season at the Met in 1956, he sang Pollione, but only in the last two performances. By that time he had to be content playing second fiddle to del Monaco.

After another two *Aidas* the season finished with a couple of *Toscas* and then she made her début as Leonora in *Il Trovatore*. A recording gives us an idea of how mature Callas's art was then even when undertaking a role for the first time. She demonstrates something that had been forgotten by her time: Leonora has a deal of florid music in it, more, in fact, than Gilda or Violetta. In those days this usually got short shrift; what was not cut was simplified or taken too slowly. But from her entrance she chooses perfect tempi: the opening measures of the Act I aria, 'Tacea la notte', are delivered expansively with all manner of rubato, but her rhythmic control is such as to leave no doubt as to the shape as well as breadth of the phrases. In the cabaletta she infuses new life into *Il Trovatore*; she launches into 'Di tale amor' at a prodigious speed, faster than any other Leonora would dare, or dream possible, faster, indeed, than she herself ever ventures again. She executes the most intricate passages with stunning accuracy. Her voice is the epitome of limpidity. And, at the end, after a traditional cut, she suddenly and unexpectedly, takes a powerful and thrilling e'' flat. In the concerted music we can not fail to notice how incisive is her articulation when compared with the rough and ready attack of Baum and Leonard Warren. They seem almost desperate in their attempts to keep pace with her, but she easily outflanks them. They hang on to high notes: Baum yelling and sagging in pitch, and Warren quivering and quavering every time the music gets fast. Years later, after her career was over, Callas comments: 'high notes . . . must be measured; if you hold them too long, the public will tire of them and you will have spoiled your effect . . . Being a bad colleague means holding on to a note longer than the other singer.'[22] By that time she had obviously quite forgotten her halcyon days, when she was prepared to hang on to any number of high notes longer than her colleagues. We are not surprised that at the next *Il Trovatore* Warren refused to sing the Act IV duet with her,[23] and he cancelled the third performance, claiming he was unwell. He'd had quite enough.

Nevertheless her singing of Leonora's music is superlative. The Act IV aria, 'D'amor sull'ali rosee', she takes expansively and at what is for her a perfect tempo. She is not tempted to produce too plangent a tone, as she does in *Aida*, nor does she contrive too forceful a style, as in *Turandot*, so undermining her vocal repose. She herself told Harewood: '[I]n *Il Trovatore* Leonora never really sings all the time that loud.'[24] Nor does she, throughout she is sure and composed, perhaps because the competition has been vanquished: di Luna is off-stage and Manrico has been imprisoned (not inappropriately, in Baum's case!). In those days Callas's voice was immediately responsive. Her singing is an exercise in shaping and colouring long phrases with subtle use of rubato and perfectly drawn portamenti; each differently weighted according to the dynamics, the interval accomplished, and the speed of the music. The trills, an integral part of this piece, are all not only forwardly placed, clearly defined and correctly resolved, but each of them is coloured differently, according to the weight of vocal registration she applies. As in *Nabucco* she accomplishes this through her perfect vocal facility. There is a superb d'' flat, cleanly attacked, which Verdi has written but is rarely sung. Her delivery is so musically authoritative and so vocally secure that she is able to make the maximum effect with phrasing of extraordinary breadth. The conductor, the otherwise unheard-of Guido Picco, is content to follow her, so demonstrating that she needed no Serafin or Karajan to make her mark on this music. 'Always rhythmically strict as regards measures, she treats the rhythm within each measure with individual freedom – nothing is dragged, nothing is rushed, and yet everything is animated right down to the softest vibrations of tone.'[25] It is no exaggeration to say that her singing here has an expressive variety not found on records of any other soprano since Patti; and appropriately, that last quotation is from Hanslick on Patti.

Callas brings this aria to a conclusion with a device which she accomplishes in characteristic fashion: a cadenza not only fluently executed but musically phrased. She asked Janine Reiss, the pianist and *répétiteuse*, when she was studying the air, 'Comme autrefois' from Bizet's *Les Pêcheurs de perles*: 'I would like you to explain to me how the cadenza is constructed, rhythmically and harmonically, because one can only sing it well if one knows how it is written.'[26] When we think of all the singers who have sung cadenzas, we wonder how many, or how few, have ever attempted to make music out of them. In 1950 she did not have to consider, as she would have to do so soon, making adjustments to accommodate her failing powers, and she did not fulminate against the practice of adding ornaments. But, in later years, when she heard recordings of these Mexico City performances, she would disclaim them: 'Don't listen to them – they're awful! I was singing like a wildcat'.[27] She must have been astounded by them, and embarrassed by the recollections they stirred up, but it is precisely her vocal fecundity in her youth that makes her singing so remarkable.

She was always a supreme musician; but it was at the beginning of her career, inevitably, that her voice was most perfectly responsive. After she had slimmed and become preoccupied with histrionic ambitions, her singing began to lose not only its size and range, but also its unique responsiveness. Now, however, that her recordings are all that is left to us, it is to the early years of her career that we turn for the perfect demonstrations of her skills as a musical executant.

When Callas next sang Leonora, seven months later in Naples, we note immediately how Serafin, like so many great maestri since Toscanini, is anxious to get a move on, obliging her to hurry the music, so robbing her singing of breadth and repose. In only one respect is she superior in Naples: her declamation of recitatives shows a surer command of Italian – not, we may note, a musical improvement. Callas was wont to admit that Serafin's influence over her was very great, but a comparison between her singing in Mexico and Naples causes us to question just how beneficial it may have been. Legge, in his obituary of Callas,[28] makes great play of Serafin's not ranking her among his three greatest opera singers. According to Legge, Serafin stated 'In my long lifetime there have been three miracles – Caruso, Ponselle and Ruffo. Apart from these there have been several wonderful singers.' But, in fact, what Serafin was talking about was voices, not singers. Caruso could have come under either heading but Ponselle and Ruffo, though gifted with phenomenal voices, are not unique artists like Chaliapin or Battistini, both of whom Serafin had also conducted. Like them Callas was an individualist, had she not existed her art would have been unimaginable. We might remember, even if Legge chooses not to, how in a fit of pique, after Serafin had recorded *La Traviata* with Antonietta Stella, Callas cut him out of her career for more than three years. Perhaps it is not surprising that she fails to secure a place in his singers' trinity! More than musicianship, of which quality she had plenty herself, she could hardly have helped feeling unsure of herself when tackling a predominantly forgotten repertory. Elderly musicians like Serafin, she reasoned instinctively, must be custodians of at least a remnant of performance practice. However, as we hear, when we listen to the rest of the cast in Naples, Serafin has to work with journeymen, and he is obviously preoccupied having to keep singers, chorus and orchestra together. Circumstances do not allow him giving Callas the opportunity for full musical expression whereas, in Mexico City, she is able to take advantage of the chaos and have her own way.

During Callas's first Mexico City season the high altitude adversely affected her health, as it had done Caruso's more than thirty years previously. It certainly aggravated the mother/daughter relationship. Meneghini tells of Callas 'struggling with two conflicting emotions: the desire to help her mother, and the fear of once again being the victim of her will. [Her] depression, her difficulties, her nervousness and her insomnia that she attributes in her letters to the weather, the lack of organization, the malice of her colleagues . . . were provoked by family problems she could not resolve'.[29] When she flew to Madrid, where Meneghini joined her, her mother remained at the hotel surrounded by fresh flowers brought in daily, and wearing the mink her daughter bought her. Callas paid her hotel bill in advance, settled all her medical expenses and gave her $1,500. Neither of them could have known it then, but this was the last time they were ever to meet.

Back in Verona it took Callas some while for her to recover from the altitude of Mexico City, and her mother. She laments: 'I never felt well: I continually felt the effect of influenza. I suffered from nausea and from aches in my bones.'[30] She took a long break and did not resume engagements until she sang Tosca on September 22nd and 24th at the Nuovo, Salsomaggiore and the Duse, Bologna, after which she returned to Milan. At this time Toscanini was planning to conduct a special production of Verdi's *Macbeth* to be given in Busseto by an ensemble from La Scala to mark the 50th anniversary of Verdi's death. News reached Callas through an admirer that Toscanini had been told she was an ideal choice for Lady Macbeth and wished to hear her. Accordingly she went to his Milan residence on the afternoon of the 27th and sang some of Lady Macbeth's music. Afterwards, turning to her, he said: 'You are the woman whom I have been looking for a long time. Your voice is perfect. I will do *Macbeth* with you.'[31] In his biography of Callas Meneghini adopts a typical posture and spends a whole chapter[32] dilating on the Toscanini/Callas meeting in detail. Although the portrait he paints of the maestro is, albeit unintentionally, not very flattering, by the 1950s Toscanini's legend was calculated to make a profound impression upon almost anyone. Within seconds of meeting him Callas was, Meneghini relates, completely in his thrall; we have only to remember her preoccupation with antique music to appreciate her disposition to mummy worship.

We get an idea of what his *Macbeth* might have sounded like from records Toscanini has left of other mid-period Verdi operas: *La Traviata* made in 1946 or *Un Ballo in Maschera* made in 1954. At the time he was in his ninth decade and he had been conducting more than sixty years. Hardly surprisingly, his reputation was legendary. Today it is possible to see his career more clearly with the added perspective of history. We should be careful not to underrate his achievements. There is no doubt that at the beginning of this century he created a revolution in orchestral playing, particularly in Italy, a country only recently united, where a lack of consensus too often bordered on anarchy. For more than a half a century he was at the forefront of the movement dedicated to textual accuracy. In his early years there was undoubtedly a case for his removing the more idiosyncratic stylistic aberrations which, throughout the last century, each generation of performers had imposed unwittingly on the works of its predecessors, before the gramophone brought performing practice within common lore. But by 1921, when Toscanini made his first records, these victories were already won. It is a great pity that he went on working too long, unlike Callas. Where length is concerned his career is comparable with Patti's; yet whereas hers only just reached the age of recording, today we have not only his records but also the films he made in the late 1940s and early 1950s. In these we are enthralled by his extraordinary concentration and the lucidity of his stick technique, but we cannot help noticing how, by this time, it is as if singers, orchestra players and audiences are spellbound by him. There is something uncomfortably strait-jacketed about his performances. For his greatness had long become a part of history, and his authority, aggrandized by the media, as Joseph Horowitz details,[33] succeeds in alienating the music from its performing tradition. It is as if he were Verdi or Puccini. These days, with so much music of the past coming to be revived, we are obliged to blame him for the fact that we are lost in a desert, with little idea of performing tradition, forever trying to determine what Toscanini had pitched out with the bathwater.

The Toscanini *Macbeth* project was still-born: as his biographer, Harvey Sachs, relates, on March 1st 1951 he suffered a stroke. Callas did not sing Lady Macbeth for another two years; she had to wait for the opening of the 1952/3 season at La Scala, when it was conducted by de Sabata. On October 2nd she appeared at the Rome Opera as Aida and then journeyed to the Verdi, Pisa for a couple of *Toscas* on the 7th and 8th. At these Masini was Cavaradossi. Meneghini tells how the company was in financial difficulties. It proved impossible to pay the cast before the second act had begun, and Masini 'shut himself in his dressing-room declining to sing unless he was paid'[34] so Meneghini paid him. Meanwhile the saga with Litza was continuing. Callas's health had never been perfect and she was frequently indisposed and obliged to take to her bed. Meneghini discovered the reason when he found a letter from her mother and got it translated. In fact, it proved to be but one of a stream that she had been deluging Callas with. All of them were complaining about something. They began by criticizing Callas's father, for making her life in New York unendurable then, when Callas refused to be drawn, she started criticizing Meneghini too; he was rich and, she claimed, she was in need of money. Callas could not cope with her mother, the only way she felt secure was by refusing to have anything more to do with her. So, in a burst of childish pique (we should remember she was not yet twenty-seven) she sent her a letter: 'I can give you nothing. Money is not like flowers, growing in gardens . . . I bark for my living. You are a young woman [her mother was fifty-two], and you can work. If you can't earn enough to live on throw yourself out of the window.'[35]

Callas returned to Rome on October 19th, this time to the Eliseo, as Fiorilla in Rossini's *Il Turco in Italia*, which she sang four times. Gianandrea Gavazzeni, the conductor at the Eliseo, and again in 1955 when the opera was revived at La Scala, remembers the performances. 'They were part of a season promoted by the Associazione Amfiparnasso. This was my first encounter with Callas, who was then still fat. She was already quite famous, but for Kundry, Isotta, Norma, Turandot and Elvira in *Puritani*. The sets and costumes were by Mino Maccari an artist with a very humorous gift and the stage director was Gerardo Guerrieri. *Turco* was a revelation of Callas as a buffa. I soon learned the capacity she had for artistic discipline. We had a long period of study and rehearsal . . . where she rose to a remarkable musical level. When she began rehearsals she had mastered the technical difficulties. She knew the opera. Together we worked out the cadenzas, all the conventions we created anew. We also discussed the psychology of the characters, and we discussed the cuts. She was so studious, and never tired of rehearsing. When the other singers would be through for the day, she would want to remain behind to go over some point, to convince herself she had made the right decisions. She adapted her big voice to the needs of a comic role. This was one of her great gifts: the ability to adapt. The voice was very equal in scale, with a great diversity of colours but with a binding legato. The agility was there, and we worked diligently on the recitatives so as to catch the comic character of Fiorilla. All this, usually at the service of tragic and dramatic gifts, caused a great surprise and she had such a success. People still speak of her Fiorilla.'[36]

It was during these performances that La Scala was planning its first production of Gian-Carlo Menotti's *Il Console* to be given in

January 1951. Menotti[37] tells of the difficulty he had had trying to find a singer to undertake the title-role. Ghiringhelli had assured him: 'Find a soprano who pleases you and I'll be glad to give her a contract.' It was Wally Toscanini who first mentioned Callas: 'she's fat, ugly and half-blind but with a remarkable voice and stage presence', and she urged Menotti to go and see Callas. He thereupon took the train to Rome, and 'heard her in *Turco* – instantly I realised she was an extraordinary singer and went to speak to her ... I asked her if she would be interested in doing the *Console* at La Scala.' He telephoned Ghiringhelli and told him he had found a singer – 'Her name is Callas.' Ghiringhelli started to rant and rave: 'Oh! my God, never, never, never'. Menotti protested, 'you promised me I could have whomever I wanted and de Sabata was present at our meeting. You can't go back on your word.' Ghiringhelli equivocated: 'Well, I promised any singer you chose would be acceptable, but I will only have Callas in this theatre as a guest artist.' Menotti went back to tell her, as circumspectly as he could. He remembers how surprised and indignant she became: 'Mr Menotti,' she said, 'unless I go back as a regular artist I will never put my foot in that theatre again.' However, according to Meneghini, 'Callas did not think her voice suited Menotti's music'.[38] It seems likely that she only let Menotti think she would undertake it, perhaps because she hoped to use it as a way of getting herself on to the La Scala roster of artists. When this failed she took no further interest in it.

After Fiorilla in *Il Turco in Italia* Callas's last engagement in 1950 was as Kundry in a concert performance of Wagner's *Parsifal* for the RAI in Rome on December 20th and 21st. This was, in fact, the last time she was ever to sing a Wagner role. Callas came at the tail end of the Italian Wagner tradition. Just as the very word opera, like so many musical words, is of Italian origin so, even as recently as 1950 in Italy, foreign works were still given in translation, even Wagner, for opera was still a popular entertainment, especially in the provinces. As with the opera then, so with the cinema now; today most foreign films in Italy are dubbed in Italian, scarcely ever sub-titled. When Domingo, an 'Italian' tenor of our day, recorded Lohengrin and Tannhäuser he created something of a furore. But in the early years of this century there would have been nothing remarkable about his singing them, save that he undertook them in the original. Caruso sang Lohengrin in 1901 in Buenos Aires, while Giuseppe Borgatti, who created Andrea Chénier, and also appeared in *Mefistofele, Lucia, Aida, Tosca, Pagliacci* and *La Gioconda*, made a prodigious reputation with Tristano, Sigfrido and Parsifal throughout Italy. And there were many eminent 'Italian' Wagnerians: Cobelli, Elmo, Caniglia, Bertana, Stignani, Pertile and Pasero. In 1928 at La Scala, however, Frida Leider undertook Brünnhilde in the original, although the rest of the cast sang in Italian, and by the outbreak of the Second World War polyglot performances of Wagner had become the rule. By this time it was not so much the music as the librettos that had lost their vitality; it no longer seemed essential to understand them. After the war it became increasingly the norm in Italy to give Wagner in German, Massenet's *Manon* or *Werther* in French, and in the present day even English and Russian operas are given in the original.

We are extremely lucky that a recording of Callas's RAI *Parsifal* survives, for there is in it much to tell us of an age-old dispute between many knowledgeable critics. It was Shaw who commended Wagner for being with Handel 'beyond all comparison [one of] the most skilled and considerate writers of dramatic vocal music . . . The secret of healthy vocal writing lies in keeping the normal plane of the music, and therefore the bulk of the singer's work in the middle of the voice.' Unfortunately, he goes on, in badly produced or inadequately trained voices it is the middle voice which usually weakens quickest. 'There is, therefore, a constant temptation to composers to use the upper fifth of the voice almost exclusively; and this is exactly what Verdi did without remorse.'[39] The point is well taken. Verdi did write high-lying and taxing music, most particularly for the baritone voice; but Wagner created new problems by conceiving the vocal line in a symphonic framework, although he can hardly be blamed for unleashing the sheer power of today's orchestra.

In Italy, in the first half of this century, the Italian language and its lyrical musical tradition ensured that Wagner's operas be given with what he himself had always demanded of singers: a beautiful cantabile line. Permanent testimony to this is provided by records of Wagner arias by de Lucia, Borgatti and Pertile. As Callas herself observes 'Wagner could never hurt your voice, if you know how to sing well'.[40] She sings in simple, unaffected, flowing style, the voice effortlessly poised, bel canto, if the term means anything. It is a tradition that goes back to the turn of the century, it can be heard – just, on Mapleson cylinders of Lillian Nordica, Milka Ternina and de Reszke,[41] whose style, although they are singing in German, prefers lyrical values and knows nothing of Julius Kniese's Sprechgesang. Callas sings Kundry so as to show that Wagner's music does perfectly suit a correctly produced voice. Though the tessitura is low, the weight of orchestration does not make it impossible for her and she accomplishes it easily. In one of Kundry's brief appearances in Act I she sings a G, on the last syllable of 'dormire'. This has the same high vocal placement which she always used in those days, keeping her tone limpid and emphasizing its natural brilliance. The note only just falls within her compass yet, like other great singers (Battistini and Chaliapin, for example) who sing from a high placement even at the bottom of their ranges, she makes no attempt at any readjustment; this would merely have impeded the perfection of her legato. As Kundry Callas bases her art on legato; with it she shapes the music and at the same time it enables her to articulate the text eloquently. We shall have many occasions to note this again.

Callas's Kundry sounds a young woman. She never takes her chest register up ostentatiously to g and even a' flat, so piling on the pressure, as she does in *La Gioconda*. In Kundry's Act II aria, 'Ho visto il figlio', her singing actually sounds, *mirabile dictu*, beautiful. Towards the end, as she suddenly accelerates, how responsive is her voice. By so doing she reverses the usual problem, and it is the orchestra that has suddenly to speed up and keep pace with her. In the last measures we note a feature of her singing she executes consummately: how delicately and expertly she observes two wide upward portamenti: from G sharp to g' on the words 'gioia' and 'sentisti'. Those who always believed Wagner's music could be sung as eloquently as it is played by the orchestra alone, as in recordings Stokowski and the Philadelphia made of Wagner paraphrases, are infinitely grateful that Callas's Kundry survives. Altogether it is not difficult when listening to her to believe Kundry a siren. We feel confident Shaw would have been delighted and recognized in this recording the Perfect Wagnerian.

V

1951

IN THE EARLY 1950s Callas's schedule was hectic, and it was scarcely surprising that she was not able to undertake every commitment she entered into. At the beginning of January 1951 she was to have undertaken Elisabetta in Verdi's *Don Carlo* in Rome under Serafin's direction. But, as she tells us, 'my health became so bad I could not even swallow a sip of water. Battista then . . . forced me to return to Verona and . . . I took to my bed with jaundice'.[1] However she was determined not to give up her next undertaking, so she got out of bed to prepare her first Violetta in *La Traviata*, on the 6th, at the Comunale, Florence. Her fee had now reached 300,000 Lire. By her own account, at the dress rehearsal she had an argument with Serafin, who was also conducting. He complained about her 'dressing too casually, and because [she] did not behave as a prima donna should'.[2] But we should not take her Uriah Heap-like attitude too literally, for she tells this in 1957 when, she had, albeit briefly, fallen out with him. She sang Violetta three times and created a furore. The young Zeffirelli was there and he has not forgotten how 'the audience went wild',[3] 'it was sensational vocally and musically'.[4] *La Nazione* described the performance 'entirely dominated by the personality of Callas . . . She created a poetic, sweet and ardent Violetta, who not for an instant lacked musicality of the highest school.'[5]

From Florence she departed for the San Carlo, Naples where, on the 27th, the 50th anniversary of Verdi's death, she sang Leonora in *Il Trovatore*, the first of three performances, again with Serafin conducting. She enjoyed a great success, but Lauri Volpi's Manrico was booed. As a recording testifies, his strident high c's in 'Di quella pira' are very flat, but he persists in yelling them and the uproar in the audience is inevitable. By all accounts the same thing happened again the second night. He then withdrew and addressed a furious letter to the Neapolitan press. In it he goes out of his way to extol Callas's Leonora, but it was not she who was booed. It was as if he could not bear to have to admit to himself so obvious a failure, although by this time he was fifty-eight.

After Naples Callas proceeded to the Massimo, Palermo, where on February 9th she undertook the first of three performances of *Norma*. Whilst there she received another call from La Scala: Ghiringhelli's hostility may not have abated but he was beginning to feel the pinch. The Toscanini *Macbeth* had not taken place, nor was she invited to undertake Magda Sorel in *Il Console*, but he was too perceptive not to realize the way the wind was blowing. He offered her another Aida, this time replacing Constantina Araujo, a Brazilian soprano, but she declined. Now she had more cards in her hand and she was not prepared just to stand in again. She repeated what she had told Menotti; she would only come if she were on the season's roster of artists. Though she would not sing Aida at La Scala, on her way back from Palermo, on February 28th, she stopped off for a solitary performance of it at the Cilea, Reggio Calabria.

On March 12th she appeared in Turin in her second Martini-Rossi concert, for which she selected a vocally comprehensive programme: Agata's aria from Weber's *Il Franco Cacciatore*; Filina's Polacca, 'Io son Titania', from Thomas's *Mignon*; 'Ma dall'arido stelo divulsa' from *Un Ballo in Maschera* and Proch's Variazioni. Unfortunately, no recording of Agata's aria survives. This is sad, she had sung this at her very first appearance in concert in Athens in April 1939, and she would not undertake it again. Amelia's aria, compared with later recordings, is more expansively phrased, her tone fuller in forte passages, in the recitative particularly, and it has none of that curdled quality it was to take on later, after she had lost weight. Nevertheless it is not as finished a performance, though she lingers longer on top notes and finishes the cadenza an octave up. Unfortunately, the two other pieces, both incomplete and in poor sound, are far more telling: the *Mignon* Polacca and Proch's Variazioni. Still, something can be gleaned from them.

In choosing such pieces Callas was going back to her student days, but these performances do not evoke memories of de Hidalgo so much as Tetrazzini. Records show that Tetrazzini was the last coloratura in the grand tradition who sang florid music with the accuracy, brilliance and sweep that Callas was to bring back to this music. The Italian diva left more than one record of both 'Io son Titania' and the Proch Variazioni. Her voice does not possess the exceptional range and power that Callas's does, at least, in the days of this broadcast, and she did not undertake any Wagner heroines. The nearest she got to them was when she appeared in a private concert in Rome before Queen Margherita and sang 'some of tragic Isolde's [presumably Isotta's] songs.'[6] However, in her salad days in South America she did manage Aida, Leonora in *Il Trovatore* and Leonora in *La Forza del Destino*.

A comparison between the Proch and Thomas recordings as sung by Tetrazzini and Callas is not inappropriate, for they are both sonically primitive. At once we note characteristic features of Tetrazzini's art: as well as her ease of execution, there is her impeccable attack, swagger and splendidly firm rhythm, the key to her inimitability. Though she was a mistress of mechanics there is nothing at all mechanical sounding about her singing. She contrives much of her effect by taking the florid music at what today seems a prodigious speed. It is true that Callas sings it at a more expansive tempo, but the scale of her voice introduces another proportion, one that, in itself, creates an effect. As the aria from *Un Ballo in Maschera* demonstrates, before she had lost weight she took music at a more expansive tempo. There is a relationship between the speed of the music and the size of a singer's voice, or there ought to be. One of the unfortunate side effects of Callas's fame is the number of light-weight sopranos who since her time have come to adopt her slow tempi; ostensibly so as to reveal the weight of their art but in actuality to cover up for their insufficiency of alacrity in florid passages. We should not suppose that Tetrazzini's speeds inevitably trivialize; on the contrary her mastery of rhythm shows her to have been a complete musician. Even in a piece without any fioritura, like Violetta's 'Addio del passato' too often staled by pallid and sentimental performance, her interpretation is musically telling; she even includes both verses, without any ornamentation, and the repetition is affecting, not tiresome. Her tone is so limpid that she lets the registration of her voice itself freely colour the rise and fall of the vocal line. We shall see Callas's instrument creates the same spontaneous musical effect in her interpretation of Elena in Verdi's *I Vespri Siciliani* at the 1951 May Festival in Florence.

Before she was to appear in Florence Callas travelled to Cagliari, appearing on two occasions at the Massimo as Violetta; then, at the Verdi, Trieste, she sang in concert with Tito Schipa and Dolores Wilson. It was on May 26th that she undertook the first four performances of Elena in *I Vespri Siciliani*; it was the second that was in fact broadcast. Like *Norma* this was another major revival and again it was presented by Siciliani. It was directed by Graf and conducted by Erich Kleiber, making his first visit to Italy to conduct opera. By Meneghini's account[7], Callas and Kleiber's relationship did not get off to a good start. She failed to appear at one rehearsal and he rebuked her, but it had not been included on her schedule and she was highly indignant and threatened to withdraw. When Kleiber understood he apologised, and from then on they became friends yet, as the broadcast indicates, they still seem unable to agree about tempi, and a battle is fought over Elena's Act V Bolero. In those far-off days in 1951 cuts were still frequently made; not only on account of the length of the work, to keep it within time bounds imposed by the budget, but also so as to suit modern taste. Kleiber's cuts include a sizeable part of Elena's opening scene, exacting music but which Callas would have been able to despatch easily. Even so there can be no doubt she created a striking impression. Harewood tells how he saw her in it for the first time since *La Gioconda* in Verona in 1947. 'She had put on a lot of weight and . . . was now a very large lady indeed: but . . . the vocal qualities had not changed, although I found them better integrated than before. The technique and assurance seemed to have grown enormously, and what had formerly been an obvious aptitude for operatic tragedy had turned into nothing less than a sovereign dramatic authority.'[8] 'She has an astonishing technique, to which she owes her quite unusual versatility . . . Her dramatic flare was very much in evidence in the smooth cavatina and exhortatory cabaletta with which she roused the Sicilians against the French in Act I, and the smouldering fury of "Il vostro fato e in vostra mano" was extraordinarily vivid. At this performance, her voice showed a tendency to lose quality in forte passages [apart from a ringing top E at the end of the "Bolero"], but her soft singing in Acts II and IV was exquisite, and the long crystal clear chromatic scale with which she ended her Act IV solo, made a brilliant effect.'[9]

Elena is written predominantly in the middle and lower part of the voice but, in concerted passages rises frequently to b'' flat and b'' natural and an occasional c'', where she must dominate other soloists, chorus and orchestra. Callas moulds persuasively the cantabile measures of Elena's Act I aria, 'Deh! tu calma, Dio possente', she shows her ability to find music anew in a work which in her day had virtually no performing tradition. How telling her enunciation is as she launches into the cabaletta, 'Coraggio, su coraggio', she almost takes off as she hurtles through it. There are two duets for Elena and the tenor Arrigo: in the first, in Act I, she accomplishes some remarkable pianissimo singing, on the phrase 'Tu dal l'eccelse sfere', and two slow downward runs, cast in the minor mode commencing on b'' flat, demonstrate her wide breath-span.

The Act IV andante, 'Arrigo! ah parli a un core', is one of her most distinguished pieces of singing. How responsive is her voice and how complete her rhythmic control. She reminds us how rhythmic mastery is, or was, a basic feature of the art of great performing musicians: we may think of Patti, Battistini, Paderewski, Chaliapin, Caruso, Rachmaninoff, Kreisler, Cortot and many other famous singers and instrumentalists. But since the Second World War it has become steadily compromised by the declining vitality of classical music. Rhythm, we should not forget, is the heart beat of music, it will not stay vital for long without it. Nowadays the increasing influence, directly and indirectly, of Afro-American popular music has led, in the interpretation of classical music, to a semantic confusion between rhythm and beat. Whereas 'beat' is certainly rhythmic, the performer is locked into it. Rhythm, on the other hand, does not just beat time. If we listen to Callas in this andante, as she repeats the words, 'Io t'amo', the first time she marks the notes a little ahead of time, but so discreetly as not to need any accommodation from the accompaniment, the second time, she is at one with it. This is what Garcia calls 'an exquisite feeling for rhythm, an imperturbable poise'.[10]

In Florence her vocal responsiveness is constantly apparent. In this same excerpt when she descends into chest register, on phrase endings '. . . era doverti' and '. . . poser tra noi' on *d* and *c* sharp, so easily produced is her voice that these are managed with the lightest touch, as if she were just flicking an organ stop, and the consequent colouring of the line is communicated spontaneously, one of those effects that Tetrazzini shows herself mistress of. At the end comes the cadenza: it begins on *e* flat, ascends to *c''*, and then back down a long chromatic run of more than two octaves. Each note is, as Harewood mentions, crystal clear, until she reaches *G* but then, the last note, an *F* sharp, is merely a grovel. That we can tell on which note her voice gives out proves how perfect her support was then, again it suggests that hers was naturally a high soprano, we shall have occasion to discuss this more fully later. Verdi does offer an alternative, simplified cadenza, which only descends to *c* sharp (Mazzoleni, who sang Elena in *I Vespri Siciliani* at La Scala in 1909, recorded it), but Callas never essayed it. She makes a feint at the more elaborate cadenza even when she recorded it in 1964, though by then she is quite unable to support the uppermost tones, and the bottom degenerates into a hoarse whisper.

We hear the remarkable extent of her compass in the Act V solo, the Bolero or Siciliana when, in the last bars, she interpolates *e''*.

Harewood uses the word 'ringing' to describe it, which conveys something of the brilliance of her singing in the performance he heard although, in the broadcast, the note is for a few fleeting moments flawed. Nevertheless we should not make too much of the fallibility of her execution of top or bottom notes. We might remember that in the days long before pirate recordings Caruso and Tetrazzini both dropped clangers: Caruso did on many occasions in the theatre and Tetrazzini does on more than one record. What should concern us more is the quality of Callas's singing; and here she gives a model demonstration. She takes the Bolero more slowly than usual, but she adopts a wide dynamic range and she sings it well within her means. The long-phrased breath spans do not deleteriously affect her deft marking of the rhythm or her stately phrasing. As she herself was always stressing, everything she sang was in the score, and so it is too, but the point is how much she sings, and how well she sings it. In this aria she provides an excellent opportunity to clarify these points: the clean semitone trills, each precisely responsive to the varying dynamic level indicated and, as we noted in the excerpt from Act IV above, those same grace notes, each deployed so as to be rhythmically responsive and yet not disturb the vocal line. The delicately accented g's, the perfectly even runs embracing c'' and a. This was not Callas's first sight of the music, but it is only the second performance she ever sang in public. It is a classic.

Meanwhile at La Scala events were moving to a climax and Ghiringhelli decided to accept the inevitable. After the first night of *I Vespri Siciliani* he sent Callas a congratulatory telegram and announced that he would himself be coming to Florence to discuss her engagement at La Scala. Meneghini tells what difficulty he had in arranging this, Callas seemed to be in no hurry and was always busy and unable to see him. He finally secured a meeting on June 2nd. He came backstage after her third Elena, paying 'her many compliments and invit[ing] her to open the [1951/2] season at La Scala'[11] also as Elena, in addition he offered her Norma, Constanza in *Il Serraglio* and Elisabetta in *Don Carlo*. Callas thanked him, but she insisted on his including Violetta. The situation was one to relish: the mountain had come to Mahomet. By all accounts Ghiringhelli's knowledge of opera would not have covered the back of a postage stamp, but he was the quintessential politician, sensitive to the winds of change. He had been content to adopt a contemptuous mode until audience reaction made it abundantly obvious that Callas was on the verge of a great career, then he quickly did an abrupt about turn. On June 23rd he confirmed his offer in writing, to which she replied expressing satisfaction with the details, only reminding him again about *La Traviata*.

Four days after the last *I Vespri Siciliani* on June 9th Callas appeared as Euridice in Haydn's *Orfeo ed Euridice*, again under Kleiber in Florence, but this time at the more intimate Pergola. *Orfeo ed Euridice* was certainly not the most modern opera Callas had undertaken, yet, as the world première in London in 1791 had been suddenly cancelled, these performances represented the first staging of the work. So it was that the only opera in which Callas ever created a role was by Haydn! The part of Euridice is not especially taxing: as written it does not ascend above *c″*; although we may wonder whether, bearing in mind her fondness for interpolating high notes in those days, she was content to leave her part unembellished. The most brilliant piece in it is an isolated aria for the Blessed Spirit; revived in the 1960s this aria was poached by the Euridice, Joan Sutherland. Of the Florence première Newell Jenkins, in *Musical America*, is somewhat critical, perhaps because he himself was a conductor of classical operas. He claims that '[t]he Euridice of Maria Meneghini Callas had more to do with the *Sicilian Vespers* ... than with the classic style of Haydn. Her voice was rich and beautiful, but was often uneven and sometimes tired. She sang the death aria in the second act with rare insight and fine phrasing ... [although] the role was too heavy for her.'[12] Too light for her, surely – this must be a misprint. Taubmann, on the *New York Times*, was at the next night's performance, and particularly praised the way 'she could manage the classic florid style with assurance. She has full control of voice in soft singing and she did coloratura passages with delicacy and accuracy.'[13]

On June 11th, the day after her second Euridice, she brought her Florence engagements to a conclusion with a recital at the Grand Hotel accompanied at the piano by Bruno Bartoletti. She sang six pieces: 'Casta Diva', Dinorah's 'Ombra leggera', 'O patria mia', Proch's Variazioni, Filina's Polacca from *Mignon*, and 'Ah! fors è lui' and 'Sempre libera' from *La Traviata*. No recording of this survives but we may be sure that, save possibly for the Aida, in those days she would have managed so daunting a programme to considerable effect. This is what Rock Ferris in the *Musical Courier* suggests: 'Well fitted for the "heavy" roles, she seems just as much at home ... in *Mignon* or *Dinorah* ... Her high E's [sic] and F's [sic] are taken full voice, and there seemed no feat which she could not achieve. The audience included many American singers and Rudolf Bing [Director of the Metropolitan] cheered her efforts'.[14] Nevertheless Bing was unimpressed. Years later he attempts to excuse his failure to have snapped her up: 'She was monstrously fat, and awkward', and to Bonardi, the ALCI agent, he declared, '[she] has still a lot to learn before she can be a star at the Met'.[15] But the notion that Callas's unique importance depended on how she looked rather than how she sang is more a reflection on his judgment than on her skill. Here we get an indication of how Bing's ignorance of singing was to prove a greater liability at the Metropolitan in the years of his sovereignty than Ghiringhelli's was at La Scala.

On July 3rd Callas made her Mexico City rentrée as Aida, this time with Oralia Dominguez, del Monaco and Giuseppe Taddei. Diaz du-Pond recalls taking Callas and del Monaco to Caraza-Campos's office and how he immediately set about persuading the tenor to let Callas sing the e'' flat again in the Triumphal scene. Del Monaco raised no objections. In fact, he determined to venture the note himself (an octave lower, of course), although it would have to be in falsetto. As a recording shows Callas produces an even more spectacular e'' flat than she had in 1950, but if del Monaco attempted one no trace of it can be detected.

Aida follows Norma, Violetta and Lucia as Callas's most frequently sung role. By the time she left Mexico in 1951 she had in fact sung it more than any other part, save for Turandot, more even than Norma, much more than Violetta, while she would not sing Lucia for the first time until the following year. As in Turandot, so in Aida, the tessitura of the role often lies uncomfortably for her. The breaks in her registers become obtrusive and throughout she sings too strenuously. If we compare her Mexico City performances we note that in only a year, between 1950 and 1951, the higher, more exposed, passages become less secure. This should not surprise us. For in that time she had sung several roles of a higher range for the first time: Leonora, Fiorilla, Violetta and Elena, in which she took the head voice to e'' flat and even e'' natural. Inevitably the equalization of her scale had suffered and inconsistencies have become more obtrusive.

Callas's interpretation of Aida is full of effects more appropriate to the verismo style. Her attack in dramatic moments is certainly vehement and, although then still at her vocal peak, she frequently sings too strenuously. Her tone often curdles and she sounds obsessively competitive. This does not mean that she was careless or unmusical, for in appropriate parts of *Aida* she displays her characteristic finish. For example, on the opening phrases of the duet 'Là, tra foreste vergini', her voice has a limpidity which enables her to use tempo rubato, sparingly and with such disciplined skill. In the 1950 Rome performance, where she is given her head by the conductor, Vincenzo Bellezza, who conducted many famous singers from Caruso to Kraus, she accomplishes miracles of pianissimo shadings, singing dolcissimo, as the score directs, and with a great deal of refined tempo rubato. There are innumerable occasions in her Aida, as in so many of her interpretations, in which she tellingly renders the subtlest, and what may seem the least significant, markings in the score. If we listen attentively we note how her perfect legato enables her to suggest by musical means even the exclamation marks and commas of the text.

On July 15th in Mexico City, after three Aidas, Callas took part in a Verdi broadcast. Untypically for those days she sang two arias with a similar tessitura: 'Pace, pace mio Dio' from *La Forza del Destino* and 'Morro, ma prima in grazia' from *Un Ballo in Maschera*. That season, perhaps to be sure to keep her mother out of the way, she invited her father to join her. Diaz du-Pond remembers how proud he was to hear his daughter in opera for the first time. She undertook four Violettas beginning on July 17th, this was, according to Diaz du-Pond, 'the first television broadcast [in Mexico] I can remember'.[16] About her Violetta critics almost passed out in panegyrics: '[S]he is a beauty of majestic and distinguished comportment [she wore her own costumes which she had had made that January for performances in Florence]; she has the maximum degree of grace for acting, elegance for dressing; and temperament . . . and above all, a voice for singing,' etc.[17] 'One has to hear her . . . achieve the perfection of coloratura . . . in those passages [where she] achieves the incredible in precision, intonation and beauty' etc. etc.[18] With her were Cesare Valletti and Taddei, the latter replaced at the fourth and last performance by Carlo Morelli, brother of a celebrated pre-war Otello, Renato Zanelli.

After the Mexico City season Callas returned to Europe and a period of relaxation spent at home in Verona. Her operatic activities were resumed that September with a visit to Brazil. She was to open the season at the Municipal, São Paulo in *Aida*. But, as she tells, 'my legs were swollen . . . and [I was] not in good health'.[19] At length, after the dress rehearsal of *Aida*, she was obliged to withdraw. Her first appearance took place on the 7th, as Norma under Serafin's direction, the cast included Barbieri, Mirto Picchi and Rossi-Lemeni. Two days later, again under Serafin, she sang Violetta with di Stefano and Tito Gobbi. A recollection of that Violetta remained vivid in Gobbi's memory for thirty years: 'I cannot believe that anyone else in the whole history of [*La Traviata*] ever sang that first act as Callas sang it . . . Later perhaps she looked the part more convincingly, later she may have added certain refinements to her characterization of the role, but I find it impossible to describe the electrifying brilliance of the coloratura, the beauty, the sheer magic of that sound which she poured out then. And with it – perfect diction, colour, inflection and above all feeling. It was something one hears only once in a lifetime. Indeed, one is fortunate to hear it once!'.[20] Rakowska, Serafin's wife, was also present and she confirms the effect Callas's singing had. She chastised her husband for 'not having the courage to tell the public . . . "this evening you will hear ['Sempre libera'] sung in the original key"'.[21] In those days Violetta was performed by singers, like Tebaldi and Stella, who had neither range nor technique to cope with the florid measures; how 'Sempre libera' was sung or in what key it was in was not considered important.

From São Paulo Callas proceeded to Rio de Janeiro. On September 12th she appeared at the Municipal as Norma. There were two performances. With her were Nicolai and Christoff, and only the Pollione, Picchi, had sung in São Paulo. Then, again under Votto, on the 24th she added Tosca, with Gianni Poggi and Paolo Silveri, and finally a couple of La Traviatas, on the 28th and 30th, with Poggi and Antonio Salsedo. The Brazilian season was under the direction of Barreto Pinto, a member of one of Brazil's richest families. Meneghini describes him as 'almost repellent: small, toothless, his head was set down in his shoulders, and he gave an impression of being dirty'.[22] He seems to have been the biggest prima donna amongst his divas, quite often he would make last minute decisions on a caprice. The performances of La Traviata were scheduled to be conducted by Votto. The opera was about to begin when a couple of Votto's friends arrived, but the house was totally sold out. The only places he could find them were at the back of Pinto's box. Unfortunately Pinto turned up and demanded to know what they were doing. They endeavoured to explain but he gave them no opportunity, and when Votto tried to he was cut short: 'You're dismissed, clear off!'[23] Pinto then ordered a deputy to conduct in his stead.

He had organized the Brazil season around Tebaldi and Callas, who shared Violetta and Tosca. The competition between the two was then at its height. How much was due to their own rivalry and how much to their fans is now difficult to determine. As can be heard easily enough today they were radically different, and it seems hard to believe that there could ever have been any real friction between them. Nevertheless, reading various interviews that Callas gave suggests that, for whatever reasons, she felt that Tebaldi resented her and was for ever trying to steal a march on her. In that Brazil season a gala had been arranged for the Red Cross at the Municipal, Rio, on September 14th. By Meneghini's account[24] it was agreed that only one aria would be sung by each singer. According to Callas[25] this proposition had actually been made by Tebaldi, so Callas only sang 'Sempre libera' but Tebaldi, after she had finished 'Ave Maria' from *Otello*, offered two encores: 'La mamma morta' from *Andrea Chénier* and Tosca's 'Vissi d'arte'. Callas tells how 'I was very surprised, but I merely attached to Renata's action the same weight one would have done to a child's whim. Only later . . . did I come to realize that my close colleague and dear friend had changed her attitude towards me. She didn't hide her bitterness every time she spoke to me.'[26] In fact Callas was indulging in a little forgetfulness. Her programme included not only 'Sempre libera', but it began with 'Ah fors' è lui' and she also sang Aida's 'O patria mia', which made her contribution quite as lengthy as Tebaldi's. As we saw with the offer she claimed she received from the Metropolitan in 1946, she would repeat a fiction so many times that eventually she came to believe it herself!

The only Brazilian performance of which a recording survives is of a solitary Tosca Callas undertook in Rio on September 24th. As we hear, she sings it extravagantly. Tosca is not so exposed a role as Aida but, at this stage, at least, it was not suited to her. Though she would undertake it increasingly towards the end of her career this was only because, by then, its comparatively modest vocal demands still made it possible for her, and over the years she refined her theatrical interpretation considerably. Nevertheless, like other Puccini's heroines, Manon Lescaut, Mimì and Butterfly, it calls above all for a beautiful voice. So it was perhaps not coincidental that it should have been during this performance that, as she recalls, 'a regrettable incident occurred. I had just finished the Act II aria ["Vissi d'arte"] when I heard someone call out over the applause the name of another singer, Elisabetta Barbato [a local soprano], and I felt there was some bad feeling in a part of the audience.'[27]

According to Callas,[28] the day after Tosca she was summoned to Pinto's office and told that she would not be needed to sing subsequent performances: these consisted of another *Tosca* and two *La Traviatas*. But when she insisted on being paid, Pinto finally let her sing the *Traviatas* but not *Tosca*, though he warned her that 'no one will come to hear you'.[29] However at *La Traviata*, as we noted above from the difficulty Votto had in getting seats for his friends, the house was full. When Callas came to secure her cheque after the last performance, Pinto, according to her, 'spoke these precise words to me: "With that catastrophe, I shouldn't even have to pay you"'.[30] At which she grabbed the nearest heavy object from his desk, a bronze inkstand and paper holder, and was only restrained from throwing it in the nick of time. Meneghini's memory differs somewhat and begins on the morning of an announced second *Tosca* on October 3rd, after the performances of *La Traviata* were over. According to him the Meneghinis were passing the theatre and looked up at a poster and noted, to their great surprise, that Callas's name was not on it; he does not mention that Tebaldi's name must have replaced hers, for she it was who sang.[31] Callas immediately stormed into Pinto's office demanding to know why she had been replaced. '"Because the other evening you were terrible," he replied.'[32] Then it was that she picked up the inkstand. When it was loosened from her grip, Pinto announced he was going to call the police. At this she could not contain herself, leaping on him she struck him a ferocious blow practically incapacitating him. Meneghini quickly seized her by the arm and hurried her back to the hotel. Sometime later a messenger came up to their room bringing 'an envelope with her cachet as stipulated in her contract for performances which she had not yet sung',[33] and plane tickets. Within a few hours they were on their way back to Italy. Meneghini is usually accurate about dates and numbers of performances, and was probably working from a diary. On this occasion he states that Callas had originally been contracted for eight performances, but that was the number she in fact sang and, by his account, she was to have undertaken at least one more Tosca.

From Rio the Meneghinis travelled home via New York, where they stopped off briefly to meet Dario Soria, President of the Cetra-Soria record company. After some discussion details were settled and Callas signed a contract to start making recordings the following year of four complete operas: *La Gioconda, La Traviata, Manon Lescaut* and *Mefistofele*. They then proceeded to Italy for a brief vacation. Hardly were they back in Verona when Ghiringhelli came to see them, he had brought the Scala contract for Callas to sign. But before doing so she raised the subject of *La Traviata* again and a great deal of wrangling went on while Ghiringelli did his best to talk her out of it. Eventually she signed, after he had offered her the opening night as well as promising 'to produce *La Traviata*'.[34]

Meanwhile, on October 18th at the Donizetti, Bergamo, Tebaldi had begun a series of three performances of *La Traviata*. They were conducted by Carlo Maria Giulini, who was conducting an opera for the first time. As Giulini remembers, 'Tebaldi had a bad cold and so for the second performance', on October 20th, Callas was called in to deputize for her. 'I was asked if I knew her. I said yes, I had heard her in Rome the year previously in Rossini's *Il Turco* . . . She was very fat but the voice was there – the musicality, the intelligence . . . Callas's voice was very special [like] a stringed instrument – a violin, viola, 'cello. The first time you hear these instruments, the feeling is a little strange, but after a few minutes you get used to it – the sound itself is a musical quality [and] after a few moments you are fascinated, enraptured . . . If melodrama is the ideal unity of the trilogy of words, music and action it is impossible to imagine an artist in whom these three elements were more together than Callas.'[35]

VI

1951–1952

AFTER SPENDING NOVEMBER at the Massimo, Catania, where she sang four Elviras in *I Puritani* in the middle of a run of four *Normas*, Callas reappeared in Milan on December 7th 1951, the feast of St Ambrose the patron saint of Milan, to open the La Scala season as Elena in *I Vespri Siciliani* under Victor de Sabata, the theatre's Artistic Director. As she remembers 'I had never faced so difficult a test in all my life. But the welcome given me by the Milan public was sufficient to remove my doubts.'[1] By this time her cachet had grown to 350,000 Lire a performance. Except that the cast included Eugene Conley, in place of Kokolios, the principals were the same as those who had been at Florence that spring. Until this year the Scala season had opened with established classics, like *Otello* and *Il Trovatore*, but in the Age of Callas the repertory would become markedly less familiar. In 1952 it would open with Verdi's *Macbeth*, in 1953 Catalani's *La Wally*[2], in 1954 Spontini's *La Vestale* and in 1955 Bellini's *Norma*.

The next day Visconti cabled Callas: 'All my warmest congratulations after having heard you with the greatest pleasure on the radio yesterday evening.'[3] Between the sixth and seventh performances of *I Vespri Siciliani* Callas departed for Parma where, on December 29th, she appeared at the Regio in a solitary *La Traviata*. In that theatre, where the audience is notoriously critical, she enjoyed a signal triumph. The *Gazzetta di Parma* hailed her 'an interpreter of Violetta the likes of which we have not heard before . . . [She] was continually cheered and acclaimed, during and between the acts, with a fervour that has not been heard in the theatre in many years.'[4] Legge and Elisabeth Schwarzkopf were there and she recalls how 'the house was already seething with anticipation when we took our seats. To our amazement the back of the orchestra was lined with policemen, firemen and nurses, anticipating things to come.'[5] No sooner had the Act I prelude begun, with de Fabritiis, the conductor, taking a few measures on the fast side, than hissing broke out. Savarese, the baritone, got a frog in his throat and did not risk a solo bow. Schwarzkopf goes on: 'Even Maria had a moment's opaqueness on a top note. Still, we all witnessed a major victory for [her]. As everyone knows, there is no victory in Italy like being acclaimed in Parma in a Verdi role!'5 Afterwards, as she makes a point of telling, she went backstage to tell Callas that she would never sing Violetta again. Considering that when she had ventured it in English at Covent Garden only a few years before it was to 'divided opinions' and she was thought 'miscast' and 'vocally . . . cold'6 this could have been no great sacrifice.

In spite of the fact that Callas often met Ghiringhelli at La Scala, she had heard no more from him about the production of *La Traviata* he had promised her that season. But she had not forgotten it, and at the beginning of 1952 she told Meneghini it was time to raise the subject again. 'Ghiringhelli thinks he can play me around with *La Traviata*, but he'll regret it. If he doesn't reassure me unequivocally, I shan't sing Norma in a couple of weeks. Write to him using precisely those words.'7 Meneghini did but Ghiringhelli tried delaying tactics. Callas then told him she would cancel Norma, so he quickly rushed off a special delivery letter assuring the Meneghinis that 'every problem with Madame Callas will always be solved with the utmost cordiality'8. At a meeting in his office they got him with his back to the wall, he gave in and made a costly compromise. Though, for whatever reasons, he would not put on *La Traviata* that year he promised, 'next season we shall mount a new production especially for you. But for performances not given this year, I will, nevertheless, pay you your regular cachet.'9 Without further ado he dipped his hand into the desk drawer, drew forth a cheque book and wrote out Callas's full fee for four performances: 1,400,000 Lire. The occasion remained vivid in Meneghini's memory, and no doubt it went some way to assuage Callas's wrath, for Ghiringhelli heard no more about *La Traviata* though it was not staged for another three seasons.

On January 9th 1952, when Callas had sung her seventh and last La Scala Elena, she returned to the Comunale, Florence as Elvira in *I Puritani*, with Conley, Carlo Tagliabue and Rossi-Lemeni. Jenkins, in contrast with his reaction to her Euridice the previous year, was now completely won over; despite the slight regard in which Bellini's operas were then held, he shows an almost bobbysoxer appreciation of Callas. In *Musical America* he writes: 'One can only deal in superlatives in describing Miss Callas's singing: her velvet tone, her exciting phrasing, her hair-raising coloratura, her stage presence, her majesty of bearing, her fine acting.'[10] She attempted to juxtapose performances of *I Puritani* in Florence with rehearsals for Norma, her next role that season at La Scala, but the schedule proved too demanding so, after her second Elvira, the role was undertaken by Virginia Zeani.

On January 16th she began nine performances of *Norma*. In *Musical America* Jenkins sounded off in the same vein about her Norma as he had done about her Elvira in *I Puritani*: 'She never rushed and she never dragged. Her tones came out round and full, with a legato like that of a stringed instrument. Her agility was breathtaking. Hers is not a light voice, but she negotiated the most difficult coloratura without batting an eye . . .' But he did notice that 'there was occasionally a slight tendency to shrillness and hardness on the high notes, although her pitch was faultless. It is to be hoped that this defect resulted from fatigue, for it would be sad to hear so superb an instrument lose any of its sheen.'[11] Meanwhile the Legges were in Milan, Schwarzkopf was singing the Marschallin in *Der Rosenkavalier*, which Karajan both conducted and directed, and at one of the performances Legge brought the Meneghinis backstage. They all went through the usual courtesies while, as Legge recalls, 'Karajan couldn't take his eyes off a huge emerald [Callas] was wearing'.[12] Obviously Legge did not take his eyes off Karajan, Callas or the emerald! Callas was now leading prima donna in Italy's leading theatre.

The Oroveso, Rossi-Lemeni, discusses her in those days. 'I can say one thing. How very humble she was . . . She was always afraid she had sung badly, that it wasn't as good as she wanted; her ambition was such that she was never satisfied with herself. She would ask me, I was very flattered by this, how to open each act on stage. She thought I had a good instinct for the stage and she would always discuss this with me. She was very simple in those days. She had an incredible amount of energy in her singing, in supporting her voice, in projecting the sound and making it musically perfect. Music was her instrument. But then she was very insecure and uncertain over the characterisation of a role, later on, of course, she came to work with good stage directors. I remember in the last scene of *Norma*, how she sang the final ensemble. Even though it was bel canto she was extremely realistic. I cannot say that I ever saw her cry yet she left the impression that there were tears in her voice. Her singing had a remarkable intensity. It was an extraordinary instrument – all the fioritura, the cadenzas, the embellishments, all of them were musically perfect. Yet, in those days, her presence was not magnetic. The magnetism that she gained little by little came as much from the press and people around her. In those days she was a great musician, a great instrumentalist. Although she remained a wonderful Norma, even after she became beautiful and slimmed, yet her voice was no longer a great instrument. Nor was she any more the monumental Norma I remember from the Scala production in 1952. In those days it was her voice that was perfect.'[13]

On February 8th she undertook a concert for the Circolo della Stampa. She sang 'Ah! fors' è lui' and 'Sempre libera' and followed it with the Mad Scene from *I Puritani*. At the piano was Antonio Tonini, an assistant conductor and principal repetiteur at La Scala, a highly significant figure in Callas's background. On the 18th, at the RAI auditorium Turin, she appeared in another Martini-Rossi concert with tenor Lauri Volpi under the direction of de Fabritiis. Of this, a recording survives; she sings 'Anch' io dischiuso' from *Nabucco*, 'Vieni t' affretta' from *Macbeth*, the first part of the Lucia Mad Scene and the Bell Song from Delibes's *Lakmé*. This is the most remarkable selection. With music many coloratura sopranos have reduced to a vocalise, she creates a quite extraordinary effect. As she narrates the story she supports her voice aloft in the longest-breathed legato, bringing to her singing a considerable range of dynamics. Each note is cleanly and clearly marked and throughout she makes expressive shadings. In both verses, at the end of the phrases 'La magica squilletta dell 'incantator' ('The magic bells of the enchanter') and 'la squilla dell'Indian incantator' ('The bell of the Indian enchanter'), which occur immediately before she imitates the bells, she subtly anticipates them by finding a matching timbre to suit the word 'incantator'. It is the definition of exquisite singing. In such fashion Callas demonstrates just how much more music there is in this than the average coloratura is able to suggest.

After three *La Traviatas* at the Massimo Bellini, Catania beginning on March 12th, at the première of which 'she encored "Amami, Alfredo"',[14] on April 2nd she reappeared at La Scala as Constanza in *Il Ratto dal Serraglio* (as *Die Entführung aus dem Serail* was known in Italian). This was Callas's only Mozart role. In 1952 Mozart operas were not yet a part of the mainstream at La Scala. In the first quarter of this century only *Le Nozze di Figaro*, in 1905, and *Il Flauto Magico*, in 1923, were performed, between 1925 and the beginning of the Second World War *Figaro* was revived on three occasions and *Don Giovanni* twice. But it was not until 1941, and the Axis pact, that

Viorica Ursuleac came from Vienna to appear as Fiordiligi in the first performance of *Così fan tutte* since 1814. Another decade passed and on this occasion *Il Serraglio* was given the first time. In Italy opera kept its vitality until the second quarter of this century and the classics did not begin to form a significant part of the repertory until a decade after *Turandot* in 1926. By then popular operas were no longer being composed in sufficient bulk to satisfy the musical appetite, which was quickened by the invention of the gramophone and the radio. Short of any new modern masterpieces, the public inevitably became satiated with the standard repertory and began to turn to works of the past for novelty.

Callas was offered other Mozart roles, though not in Italy. In 1950 when she was in Mexico City Bonardi wrote to tell her that Bing wanted her to sing the Queen of the Night. She told Meneghini: 'He's crazy'.[15] Nevertheless, by the spring of 1955, when plans were under way for her Metropolitan début, at first they agreed on Lucia and the Queen of the Night. But, as Bing tells, 'she refused to sing *The Magic Flute* in English, even though I agreed to take the second-act aria down a whole tone for her'.[16] By the 1950s singers had forgotten that composers allowed for transposition; a device permitting them to show off the music and their voices to the best effect. They had become ashamed to employ it and generally tried to conceal the fact. But, by 1961, when Sutherland sang the Queen of the Night at Covent Garden, she was not coy about admitting that she transposed the Act I aria down a semitone and the Act II aria down a whole tone. Callas essayed Constanza in *Il Serraglio* four times. Reviews, while applauding her, are not particularly revealing, but unfortunately there was no broadcast from La Scala, though she has left a couple of short souvenirs of her Constanza: the Act II aria, 'Tutte le torture', which she sang in a Martini-Rossi concert in 1954, and at a rehearsal for a recital in Dallas in 1957.

Following the last *Norma* at La Scala on April 14th, given after the *Serraglio*s, Callas left for the Comunale, Florence where she sang three performances of Rossini's *Armida* beginning on April 26th. This was the first revival of *Armida* in the twentieth century. It was composed in 1817 during Rossini's Neapolitan sojourn, the title-role being written, as so often, for Isabella Colbran, whom he later married. Colbran was a pupil of one of the last castrati, Crescentini. She enjoyed an enormous vogue in Naples, and at the San Carlo headed a troupe of consummate virtuosi including Pisaroni, David, Garcia I, Nozzari and Galli. We get an idea of her remarkable facility from the elaborate vocal ornamentation Rossini composed for her. One of the most demanding pieces is the air and variations, 'D'amore al dolce impero', from Act II. A critic of the *Giornale delle Due Sicilie* describes Colbran's singing of it: 'She proves herself superior to any other singer in some variations in which she embellishes a delightful tune of Rossini's with all the graces of the art of song, now running through chains of triplets of extraordinary and . . . insuperable difficulty, now giving a vocal imitation of the most difficult arpeggios of stringed instruments, and finally, with superb nonchalance, executing a formidable ascending and descending scale of two octaves.'[17] The same music in the Florence revival is singled out by Andrew Porter: '[Callas's] presence is imperious, her coloratura not piping and pretty, but powerful and dramatic . . . [She] sailed up a two-octave chromatic scale and cascaded back down again [in "D'amore al dolce impero"] and the effect was electrifying.'[18]

Callas remembers, 'I had to learn [Armida] in five days'[19] sandwiched, as it was, between performances of *Norma* at La Scala and of *I Puritani* in Rome. The press, as usual, were bidden to the *prova generale*. At her first entrance, borne aloft, she had a piece of recitative to sing, but it was not untypical of her that she had forgotten the words, and the prompt was not ready so she had to be carried back off and the orchestra played the entrance music again. At the première her overwhelming mastery created a sensation, though the opera was ruthlessly cut and sung by the rest of the cast in an alien, unstylish fashion. As a recording reveals, Serafin, who was conducting, fails to put in any appoggiaturas and at the end of truncated codas, he leaves Callas hanging on to interpolated high notes.

Callas's vocal prowess not only enables her to sing the music accurately, but it also enables her to provide the necessary dynamic range and colour her tone, so restoring the opera's dramatic vitality. Her singing is brilliant at the top, powerful in the middle and weighty at the bottom. Her Armida, even today, when we have grown accustomed to Rossini revivals, is a prodigious achievement. She contrives an effect in today's terms equivalent to that which Colbran must have done in 1817 – how appropriate that Armida should be a witch. And how unlike the 1988 revival at Aix-en-Provence. This was uncut and the performance sung, at least by the rest of the cast, more accurately than it had been in 1952. Nevertheless, listening to it was like being at an excavation: the mummy may have been in perfect condition but the dust of ages was all too obviously sticking to it.

On May 2nd Callas commenced a run of performances at the
Rome opera as Elvira in *I Puritani*, once again with Lauri Volpi. In
between whiles, on the 4th, she dashed back to Florence to conclude
her assignment in Rossini's *Armida*. 'This all-purpose soprano, a
prototype of the legendary singers of old, makes a buxom Elvira . . .
Her tone is not uniformly beautiful . . . Her bel canto style is liable
to sudden bursts and protuberances which disappear entirely in
passages of agility, so that her descending scales are like rippling
water. Add to this her proudly confident sense of the stage and
you have one of the singing heroines of the twentieth century.'[20]
After her last Elvira in Rome on May 11th she departed for Mexico
City.

Her third and last Mexico City season commenced on May 29th
with Elvira in *I Puritani*. She sang in each opera twice, this season
her fee was $1,000. She was joined by di Stefano. Although they had
already appeared together once before, in *La Traviata* at São Paulo,
that had been literally thrown together. As di Stefano tells, at the first
rehearsal of *I Puritani* 'we sang the same phrase, I had such a surprise
– such fire! I had never heard anything like it from any other soprano.
She gave the same passion a man could. What was astonishing was the
coloratura. I had never heard it sung like that before.'[21] It was with this
rehearsal that their musical partnership could be said to have begun.
At the end of Act I Callas turned to Du-Pond and said, 'Carlos, this
is the tenor we are looking for, for the records . . . I have planned to
do'.[22]

Callas's next role in Mexico City was Violetta, on June 3rd, again
with di Stefano. She undertook it sixty-three times between 1951
and 1958. It is in 1952 in Mexico City, as a recording testifies,
that she sings her most brilliant and exuberant Violetta, surpassing
both her achievement the previous year, also in Mexico City, and
those of later years. In 1971, in her Master Classes, she said 'there
are only certain moments in Violetta's music when you should sing
out; the rest are mezzoforte and piano . . . When you are young,
the tendency is to give and give, especially because you want to
please the public, which likes long notes. But with the years, you
learn to underplay such things, and the drama then increases.'[23]
Well, when she said it she may have meant it, but by that time
she was forty-seven, and her career a long time over; she had not
sung in the theatre for six years and in *La Traviata* for more than
twelve. In her youth she not only liked holding on to notes, she
also liked interpolating high ones. The notion that the public

has no taste because it likes 'long notes' sounds like a bit of the fox and sour grapes! She seems to have forgotten that vocal brilliance is a part of the operatic convention, in itself dramatic; indeed, in that 1952 *La Traviata*, when she let her musical instincts guide her (and they were almost never wrong), she seems well aware of this.

Putting to one side Callas's latter-day plaint this performance undoubtedly contains some of her finest singing. In her youthful days the element of competition played an important part in the effect she created. It is indicative how vocally fresh she is, as di Stefano recalls, '[we] did [it] without rehearsal'.[24] Here it is in Act I that she surpasses herself. By Callas's day Violetta had become a role simply to make a dramatic effect in. How accurately it was sung was a matter of indifference and Act I was thought inferior to the rest; the tendency was to dismiss it as so much vocal frippery. This is in marked contrast to the impression that the opera made on Chorley, the great Victorian critic, when he heard it first in 1856: '[T]he music of the first act pleased . . . because it is almost the solitary act of gay music from the composer's pen . . . In the other two there is little or nothing worth the trouble of singing.'[25]

Three days after her second Mexico City *La Traviata*, on June 10th, Callas undertook Donizetti's *Lucia di Lammermoor* for the first time. 'I wanted to try [it] out abroad', she stated, 'before taking it into my repertory.'[26] Diaz Du-Pond remembers vividly: 'I am sure that the emotion and the tears that Maria shed in her dressing room after her first Mad Scene and after being called to the curtain sixteen times, a record, in the history of the Bellas Artes [Theatre], was never repeated.'[27] A recording enables us still to hear something of the effect this performance created. At the end of the Mad Scene, when the music culminates on an *e''* flat (although this is not a perfect note), we are not surprised it is the audience that has the mad scene. It is unlikely that celebrated Lucias from the past historic, before the gramophone, like Persiani or Patti, could have created such a sensation. They never undertook Norma and even Lilli Lehmann, who did manage both parts, did not sing them at the same time in her career. Since Callas's day a number of successful Lucias have ventured Norma, Sutherland, Scotto and Sills, although they barely suggested the monumental or tragic elements in Bellini's opera. None of them juxtaposed performances of Norma, Lucia and Cherubini's Medea, as Callas did. In 1953 she would sing Norma on April 18th in Rome, Lucia on April 21st in Catania and Medea on May 7th in

Florence! In Mexico City so great was the demand to hear her that she was coaxed into singing a third performance, for which she was paid an increased fee, on the 26th and 'the house was sold out in two hours'.[28]

Before it, on the 17th and 21st, she sang Gilda, for the only time. This is the first role in which she is self-evidently play-acting. Whereas her art was extended by her assumption of Lucia, which developed her powers of imbuing florid singing with dark colours and articulating the fioritura with a sweeping virtuosity, the contrivance of her Gilda anticipates the cautious vocal manoeuvring that became a part of her stock-in-trade, ever more so after she had slimmed. Callas built her reputation about operas like *Norma*, *Lucia* and *La Traviata*, all a century or so old; and in this respect she differs from the greatest singers of the first half of this century. Caruso created Loris in Giordano's *Fedora*, Maurizio in Cilea's *Adriana Lecouvreur* and Dick Johnson in Puccini's *La Fanciulla del West*, and the bulk of his repertory was, when he first undertook it, less than fifty years old. So too was Chaliapin's: of his popular successes only Basilio in *Il Barbiere* might in his day have been styled antique. He created Massenet's Don Quichotte (1910), and his staple repertory included Boris Godounov (1874), Mefistofele (1868) and Méphistophélès (1859). By Callas's time it was not the music so much as the librettos that had dated. It was hardly likely that they could ever again be uttered with anything approaching the effect they had had on contemporary audiences. We are not surprised that as her career proceeded, so her art began increasingly to lack spontaneity. Visconti remembers Toscanini commenting at a rehearsal at La Scala of *La Vestale* in 1954: 'I find this Callas woman very good, a beautiful voice and an interesting artist, but her diction is unintelligible.'[29] This may seem rather startling but Callas, as we can hear in *Rigoletto*, often relied on a loud-mouthed prompter. On the opening words of the Act II scena, 'Tutte le feste', we hear what happens when, after vociferating loudly until then, he seems to have dropped off. Not for a second is there any hesitation in her musical memory, she simply makes up the words.

Inevitably, the revival of interest in early-nineteenth-century operas which Callas had such an important part in recreating, depended on the music rather than the text. One should not suppose, however, that this prejudiced her dramatic powers, only, as recordings confirm, the music was her first guide. As she told Harewood: 'The main thing I believe is not the [words] . . . I try to find the truth in the music.'[30]

By the 1950s how could it have been otherwise? If we listen to her as Lady Macbeth at La Scala or Violetta in Mexico City in the letter-reading scenes, we cannot fail to notice how amateurish she sounds without the music's setting of the words to guide her. It is not until she worked on Violetta at La Scala with Visconti that she would come to read the letter more persuasively. In her great days, though her enunciation is never unclear through technical failings (a frequent fault among today's singers), she does not, indeed, she could not, make a perfect marriage between word and music, for the librettos have lost the dramatic topicality they possessed at the beginning of this century, in the days of Caruso and Chaliapin.

Although Callas's Norma and Lucia sound to the manner born, she adapts her means for Gilda, suiting her voice throughout its entire range. She has the technical prowess to accomplish this. Despite the wide tessitura, Gilda presents her with no problems, she keeps her voice young sounding and does not carry her chest register up too high as she often does in Gioconda. We note the rhythmic accuracy of her attack in the allegro vivace passage, when she calls for Giovanna before the Act I duet with the Duke, 'E il sol dell'anima'. 'Caro nome' she sings at what is for her a typical tempo, though most Gildas, if they took it so slowly, would run out of breath long before they got to the end of phrases. How precisely she shows the difference between 'Caro no-me', as it is written, and 'Caro no me', as it often becomes without a proper conception of legato. Particularly affecting is her beautifully phrased, impeccable rendering of groups of falling sixths, rising from g' and a'' flat to b'' flat. She takes a similarly expansive tempo in Act II, in her treatment of 'Tutte le feste'. Especially eloquent is her realization of the characterful significance of the passage of triplets directly before the scene sweeps on to a fortissimo climax at Rigoletto's entrance. She contrives a lachrymose effect taking these in one breath, articulating clearly the middle note of each group, yet she avoids breaking the phrases – easier said than sung! In the duet 'Piangi! piangi, fanciulla', how freely and firmly she accelerates the tempo, marking the accented e' flats again so as to give them an appropriate doleful quality. At the end she leaps upwards using portamento and accomplishes the interval precisely from a' flat to b'' flat. She does it so skilfully that we hardly notice where she draws breath. Recordings testify to her ability to create a unique effect even in a role for which she must have been unfitting theatrically.

On June 28th Callas sang Tosca, her last opera in her last season
in Mexico City. Di Stefano, who appeared opposite her that year in
all her roles, compares her Tosca with her Violetta. 'When she sang
Violetta, because she was a dramatic coloratura, she was fantastic
. . . [but] she didn't have the right kind of voice for Tosca and
so she had some difficulty.'[31] In *Opera News* Robert Lawrence,
a pedagogue and conductor, writes of the overall impression she
made that season. 'There seems to be no general admiration . . . for
the basic timbre of her voice. It is her method, her virtuosity that
commands plaudits . . . the current debate centres around the extent
of this virtuosity. As to communicative power, her interpretations
are intelligently planned, sincerely carried out, but perhaps lacking
in spontaneity. Great emotional summits, such as "Amami Alfredo"
in *Traviata*, miss the expressive impact. Miss Callas is at her best in
archaic pieces like *Puritani*, which demand her marvellously equalized
scales and superb control of the legato line. She is less successful in
the standard repertory.'[32] Callas repeated Tosca on July 1st, 'her final
performance in Mexico City . . . At the end . . . the orchestra played
"Las Golondrinas" a Mexican farewell song, and there were tears in
[her] eyes and also in many eyes in the audience.'[33] The following year
when Du-Pond came to La Scala in the hope of getting her to return,
at dinner at the Biffi Scala, after a performance, Callas told him, 'Tell
Don Antonio (Caraza-Campos) that if he wants me to go again to
Mexico City, I want $3,600 a performance'.[34] Needless to say they
could never have afforded such a sum. She obviously felt that three
times in Mexico City was enough.

That summer at the Verona Arena she sang four Violettas and
two Giocondas; this was the first time she had undertaken Gioconda
since her Italian début five years previously. In that time her fee had
risen fifteen times to 600,000 Lire a night. Dragadze in *Opera* writes
that she 'did not seem as much at home in [Gioconda] as in her usual
roles'.[35] Claudia Cassidy, the *Chicago Tribune* critic, was on a visit
and heard her for the first time. She writes more critically than she would
after Callas had sung in Chicago and she had become an abject fan.
'She has three voices, a truly beautiful mezza voce of opulence and
warmth, some faked, rather hollow chest tones, and a puzzling top
voice. They tell me she sings high E and F in dazzling coloratura, and
it may be that to do this she has sacrificed her dramatic tones. For
her Gioconda had trouble with high C, which was wobbly, forced
and shrill. The report is that she will not sing the role again. That
would be wise.'[36] It is indicative that Callas's wobble should first

have become obtrusive in *La Gioconda*. It was during that summer that she broke two-and-a-half months' silence with her first complete opera recording for Cetra, made in Turin; and this, pace Cassidy, was Ponchielli's *Gioconda*.

The recording is not subject to the innumerable cuts that were made in most nineteenth-century operas by the 1950s; which confirms that, although first performed in 1876, *La Gioconda* is a direct antecedent of verismo, for its style had not become antiquated; notwithstanding its indebtedness to the architecture of Grand Opera, and its sheer scale. In the first generation after its composition, before the influence of the gramophone, performance practice inevitably took time to catch up with changes in musical style. Two of Gioconda's early exponents at the Met were Christine Nilsson and Lillian Nordica, both of whom, like Callas, had a florid wing to their repertories; though it is doubtful whether either anticipated much of the verismo style brought to the role by Cigna or Milanov.

Callas endeavours to sing Gioconda in verismo style and yet employ her customary exactitude – demands impossible for her, always the assiduous musician, to reconcile. From Gioconda's first appearance in Act I, 'Vieni! guidata sei da me', the tessitura traverses the widest range in only two bars: from f to e', then a sharp to a' sharp and back to f again. Here Callas uses eloquent piano singing, as Gioconda tells her mother that they must wait before going into church, 'L'ora non giunse ancor del vespro santo', contrasting with her forte as she rounds on Barnaba, 'Al diavol vanne colla tua chitarra!' ('Go to the devil, you and your guitar!'). It is typical of her to accept the music's demands. Later in the act, when she begs Alvise to spare her mother's life, in the agitato passage beginning 'Pietà, pietà', she sings the music passionately and accurately at either end of her range. There are a number of typical touches: she takes the trouble to mark the phrase 'Mi chiaman la Gioconda' as it is written, 'con eleganza', and how rhythmically responsive is her pianissimo delivery of the first phrases of the sextet, 'O madre mia, ti guarda'. Nevertheless, singing so intensely at the extremes of her compass makes it impossible for her to reconcile the different registers, and on the famous sustained b'' flat on the last phrase of Act I we cannot help noticing the wobble.

In the Act II duet, 'L'amo come il fugor', it is worth comparing Callas in duet with Barbieri, and Cigna with Elmo on a 78 record. Cigna sounds rough and ready yet her rendering has more vocal thrust, and if she sings with less precision the music scarcely needs it. Callas does, of course, make some memorable effects: in Act IV in 'Suicidio!', for example, she plays on her vocal registers like an organist, and there is nothing in the least coarse or haphazard about her singing. Even at the end of her great days, seven years later, when she ventures a second recording of *Gioconda* for EMI, she can still make an unparalleled effect.

VII

1952

CALLAS RESUMED HER operatic activities in the autumn of 1952 with her first visit to London. The Earl of Harewood, who was a member of the Board of Governors at Covent Garden, had 'talked about her to David Webster [General Administrator] . . . [and] was delighted . . . to learn that negotiations immediately started to get her to sing'.[1] This was the third major opera house that she had sung in, after the Colón, Buenos Aires and La Scala, Milan. She made her début there as Norma on November 8th 1952; the first time the opera had been given since Ponselle had sung the title-role in 1929.

Norma was then something of a *rara avis*. In those days opera that exalted the voice seemed decadent to critics, who would repeat the complaints about Bellini's lack of concern for orchestration, and his 'big-guitar'-like accompaniments, neglecting to note how consummately *Norma* is written for singers. This is indicative of how far opera had come away from its moorings. Throughout the nineteenth and into the twentieth century *Norma* had proved to be one of the relatively few operas to survive the test of time. Pasta had sung it at His Majesty's, London in June 1833, within eighteen months of its La Scala première. Grisi, who had created Adalgisa, undertook Norma at Covent Garden almost every season from 1847 to 1861. Throughout the 1860s and 1870s Vilda, Fricci, Tietjens, Parepa and Cepada all sang it. Performances then got a little thin on the ground and, save for a solitary evening in 1890 in the unfashionable autumn season, it was not until 1899 that it was revived for Lilli Lehmann, the great Wagnerian; had not the Master expressly excluded it from his strictures on Italian opera? She also undertook it at its première at the Metropolitan, New York, the first time in German in 1890 then, the following year, in Italian. In this century at La Scala, Milan it has been given with Burzio, Russ, Scacciati and Caniglia. At the Met in the 1930s and 1940s it was revived with Cigna and Milanov but it is with Ponselle's performances there in 1927, and at Covent Garden, that Callas's are most often compared.

A comparison between Ponselle and Callas is interesting. Both were born in the United States, both daughters of immigrants. In other respects, however, they differ markedly. Whereas Ponselle was the first great American diva since Clara Louise Kellogg to have studied and made her reputation at home without previously going to Europe, Callas did not appear in the United States until she was almost thirty-one. Her voice was then at its perihelion, if not already a little past it. Ponselle was only twenty-one when she began her career in November 1918 at the Metropolitan. At that time the First World War was making it difficult to procure the best European singers, so she made her début as Leonora in Verdi's *La Forza del Destino* opposite Caruso in the first week of the season. Talk about jumping in at the deep end! Indeed it would be hard to find another famous singer whose career began more auspiciously. She remained a member of that company for more than eighteen years, until her last Carmen at Cleveland in 1937. She sang at Covent Garden, her first appearance outside the U.S., in 1929 and returned during the next two seasons on a total of 21 occasions. In 1933 she made her only visit to continental Europe, as Giulia in two performances of Spontini's *La Vestale* at the first Maggio Musicale in Florence. Altogether in nineteen years she appeared in twenty-three roles 388 times, whereas in the eighteen years between Callas's Italian début at Verona as Gioconda in 1947 and her last Covent Garden Tosca in 1965, she appeared in thirty-seven roles 525 times; at most recent count, for details of her early seasons are still incomplete. During those years she sang in more than twenty Italian cities, as well as Buenos Aires, Mexico City, São Paulo, Rio de Janeiro, London, Chicago, Berlin, Vienna, New York, Philadelphia, Cologne, Edinburgh, Lisbon, Dallas, Epidavros and Paris.

Yet there are some similarities between Ponselle and Callas. Both singers abandoned their careers at a relatively early age. In 1965, when Callas made her last operatic appearance, she was forty-one and her voice only a shadow of what it had once been. With Ponselle it was not that her voice had gone but that its range, through the years, had been undergoing a downward shift. As early as 1927, when she was thirty, it had already been her custom to make substantial transpositions in Norma.[2] A live recording of *La Traviata* confirms that she took 'Ah, fors' è lui' down a semitone and 'Sempre libera' a full tone, both transpositions familiar from the practice of Lucrezia Bori. By the mid-1930s when she sang Carmen, she did not find it necessary to make upward transpositions as many other sopranos, like Calvé and Farrar, did. In the 1930s Ponselle broadcast selections with unambitious tessitura from *Cavalleria Rusticana*, Tchaikovsky's *Jeanne d'Arc*, *Semiramide* (without any altitudinous ornaments), *Otello*, *Adriana Lecouvreur* (which she vainly endeavoured to get the Met to mount for her in 1937) and even *Samson et Dalila*. Recordings indicate that by this time her voice had come to assume almost a contralto hue, the chest register being of compelling size and power. Like her Italian contemporaries, Arangi Lombardi, Cobelli and Stignani, she could just reach *c''* but the note never fell easily within her reach, as we hear in a 1923 recording of 'O patria mia', where it develops a flaw. Yet, notwithstanding the difference in the pitch of Ponselle's and Callas's instruments, it was no coincidence that in her best years Callas's singing had something of the characteristic quality of Ponselle's. Ponselle is one of the few sopranos Callas is known to have admired. She came to sing a number of Ponselle's roles: the Leonoras in *Il Trovatore* and *La Forza del Destino*, Gioconda, Giulia in *La Vestale*, Violetta, Maddalena in *Andrea Chénier*, Elisabetta in *Don Carlo* and Norma. In Callas's youthful days in New York she no doubt heard some of those Ponselle broadcasts and was perhaps, albeit unconsciously, trying to imitate her; or does this indicate, *vide* Legge, that the shape of the roof of Ponselle's mouth was also gothic?

A relatively large number of recordings of Callas's Norma survive. As well as a fragment from Buenos Aires in 1949 there are complete (or nearly) broadcasts from Mexico City in 1950, London in 1952, Trieste in 1953, the RAI, Rome and La Scala, Milan in 1955, and various excerpts from different performances in Paris in 1965. There are also two commercial recordings, neither of which represents her at her best: in the first, made in 1954, her voice is not as steady as it still could be at that time and the tone has some of that disagreeably overwrought quality we have already noted in *Aida* and *La Gioconda*. She takes her chest register to unheard-of heights, a flaw rarely apparent in any live recordings. She does not attempt the *d''* in the finale to Act II, which she still included as late as 1957 at Covent Garden. Curiously, just before 'Ah! bello a me ritorna' she omits a short unaccompanied vocalise modulating from E flat, the key of the recitative, into F for the cabaletta. Perhaps, recording the opera as they did, in higgledy-piggledy fashion she, or Legge, forgot it.

Her best recordings of Norma are from Covent Garden in 1952 and La Scala in 1955. The London performance conducted by Gui is typical of his work, not remarkable for subtlety or fine taste perhaps, but nevertheless an imposing large-scale conception. His direction is superior to Votto's at La Scala; we have only to listen to the orchestra's statement of the melody immediately before the singers' entrance in the Act IV duet, 'In mia man alfin tu sei'. Callas is at the top of her form, her voice limpid and her performance on a scale to match the direction. She uses slightly less vibrato than in 1950, and we are not here referring to her characteristic wobble, at this stage of her career barely discernible in Bellini's music. As in Mexico City she brings the opening recitative, 'Sediziose voci', to a conclusion with a secure and steady a'' flat. The 1952 Norma includes one of her best renderings of 'Casta Diva' although, even here, she takes a minute or so to relax sufficiently, before the voice is completely composed and she can execute the climactic b'' flats with the smoothness at which she is clearly aiming. Garcia points out that this aria 'though to a certain extent . . . it retains the gravity of the legato [style], yet it continually changes in character by borrowing from the florid style, presenting alternately, sustained notes and brilliant passages'.[3] In 1952 Callas was to realize this perfectly in the cabaletta, 'Ah! bello a me ritorna', when she sweeps up from d to a'' in one breath with the most adept use of portamento, and then lets her voice fall again in a passage of descending semiquavers (sixteen notes), like some articulate 'cello. No such effect is attempted before on records of Boninsegna, Russ, Ponselle or Raisa, yet if we consult the score we see how phrase markings seem to ask for it. In such fashion she reveals the music.

The audience acclaimed her on her first visit to Covent Garden, so we might feel surprised at the lack of enthusiasm in the press, yet it is worth remembering that the art of the greatest singers has no precedent. They are not the consummation of a tradition, rather they represent something new and different which suddenly appears breaking all the rules. Caruso, when he arrived at the Metropolitan in 1903, had some difficulty establishing himself. Klein, a seasoned critic, wrote: 'I fell in love with the voice, but was disappointed in the artist.'[4] Nor was Chaliapin appreciated when he made his bow there in 1907. Henderson, whose judgments are usually confirmed by recorded evidence, was outraged at his stagecraft, calling it 'cheap claptrap'.[5] It does not seem so curious then, that on that first occasion in London, when Callas's voice was known only from two 78s, the critics were not unduly enthusiastic. Two of the most reputable were Philip Hope-Wallace on the *Manchester Guardian* and Ernest Newman on *The Sunday Times*. Hope-Wallace was certainly no slouch when it came to appreciating a singer, yet he spends three quarters of his space on the opera, the conductor and the rest of the cast before considering Callas. In his opinion 'she looks most impressive ... she dominated the stage with her deportment and with acting as vigorous and vivid as any Tosca. She enunciates with dramatic power. Her phrasing was memorable, arresting even perhaps exaggerated; though she is a most musicianly singer. Yet the flawless vocal emission which is the cardinal quality called for in this exposed and perilous role was not vouchsafed. The voice is uneven. Some things, such as the gliding runs in the first scene and the attacked high notes in the second, were dazzling and amazed the audience. There were some beautiful soft phrases. But the voice did not ride the big final ensemble as it should. Much of the proper resonance was "boxed in" and uncomfortable and though the performance she gave was impressive, I myself cannot feel that she is more than a plausible Norma. The classical dimension was wanting.'[6] This characterizes much of the criticism: that *Norma* is a Classical opera, not a Romantic one.

Newman, who was, by this time, rather long in the tooth, also spends most of his space on the opera.[7] He suggests that by then, 1952, we may have 'gained something in operatic sensitivity since Bellini's day'. One wonders what, though he does at least go on to ask whether 'we have not also lost something'. His finding anything agreeable in a singer's opera, in view of his generally supercilious attitude, reads like a death-bed conversion. He compounds this by going on to quote from Liszt – by then presumably he had forgotten his almost legendary antipathy to him, which he expresses succinctly in his biography of Liszt. He refers to Liszt's having heard *Norma*, he claims, in '1837 ... at La Scala'. But *Norma* was not mounted that year so we must presume that he got his biographical facts a little out of order and the occasion was the following year when Liszt, in company with Comtesse d'Agoult, journeyed to Milan spending some time there before returning to Geneva. He also has Lilli Lehmann describe *Norma* as 'ten times as exacting as *Fidelio*'. It would be interesting to know what he was quoting from. She did say, we know, that Norma was more difficult than all three Brünnhildes,[8] but that is not quite the same thing. When he finally gets round to Callas what he has to say scarcely tallies with the evidence of the off-the-air recording. 'I found [Callas] a trifle inadequate for much

of the time: her voice was magnificently lustrous and flexible above
the stave but somewhat colourless and ineffective within it; and of
course it is within this lower range that dramatic psychology must
look for its full expression. Her general bearing was dignified, but
her gestures did not go much beyond two or three conventional arm
movements. All in all, while grateful to her for much beautiful singing,
I could not quite accept her as the Norma of my dreams, or, I venture
to think, of Bellini's or Lilli Lehmann's. If I may coin a word, she was
slightly sub-Normal.'

We get a better idea of the workings of the critical mentality in those
days from the reviews of Stignani's Adalgisa. Newman writes '[she]
has all the refinement of style we have come to associate with that fine
artist'. Hope-Wallace tells of her singing 'with great classical beauty
. . . a lovely voice, perfectly placed'. Stignani had previously appeared
at Covent Garden twice before the Second World War and she had
returned earlier that year making a great impression undertaking
that quintessentially Italian mezzo part, Azucena, in company with
a collection of indifferent singers. It could hardly have been difficult
for her to have merely huffed and puffed and blown the opera house
down. That she should have been cast as Adalgisa by 1952 indicates
that opera was then still in one of its dark ages, the corruption of which
was not clearly perceived at that time. Singers were out of tune with
florid music as, indeed, were most critics, and they praised Stignani's
performance ecstatically. Of course, recordings can distort the truth
and it would be unwise, for example, to attempt to deduce much
about the size of a singer's voice from them; but the florid intervals
are etched indelibly. Rosenthal, in *Two Centuries of Opera at Covent
Garden*, assures us that Stignani's 'classically poised bel canto singing
was a constant joy'.[9] Well, maybe it seemed so forty years ago, when
singing standards were low, especially where accuracy of execution is
concerned, but listening to her today her voice sounds old and blowsy.
In comparison with Callas's instrumentally accurate execution, hers is
merely an approximation.

In the Act I duet 'Ah si, fa core' we note how Callas's vocal
responsiveness enables her to execute bracketed dotted semiquavers
(sixteenth notes) accurately and not disturb her legato, as Stignani
does, lumping along after her. Towards the end Stignani omits a c''
at the beginning of a downward run, and even in 1929, when she
recorded the Act II duet 'Mira, o Norma' with Arangi Lombardi, it
is transposed down a tone, from F into E flat. In the age of verismo
Adalgisa was bracketed with heroic mezzo-soprano roles like Azucena

and Amneris (singers like Stignani, Castagna and Minghini-Cattaneo sang them all) yet, a glance at the score of *Norma* confirms that, sung in the keys it was composed in, it should be undertaken by a soprano. Adalgisa was created by one of the most successful nineteenth century sopranos, Grisi, who later became a famous Norma. It is indicative that in those 1952 *Norma*s it was not Stignani, a mezzo soprano, who later became a celebrated Norma but the Clotilde, the soprano Sutherland.

At the end of Act II in the andante marcato trio, 'Oh! di qual sei tu vittima', we note again how assiduously Callas observes every marking in the score. This music is essentially vocal and it lies comfortably in the soprano voice: how expertly it is written! Although the line is exposed and calls for absolute accuracy of execution, it ranges for the most part over less than an octave. In Act III the weight of Callas's voice in 1952 is very apparent, as she moulds the phrases 'Teneri, teneri figli, essi, pur dianzi delizia mia'. Yet there is a distinct and awkward register break when she negotiates tessitura, between *e'* and *g'* at the top of the stave, from middle into head voice. In the ensuing duet 'Deh! con te', which is transposed down from C into B flat, she begins gracefully and her exact execution of note values affords a contrast to Stignani. There is a world of difference between that lady's matronly plodding in the opening phrases of 'Mira, o Norma' and Callas's enunciation of the first words, 'Ah! perchè, perchè'. We note how precisely and effortlessly produced is Callas's tone when Norma and Adalgisa duet in thirds. We can follow her easily when her voice is set against the background of Stignani's woolly tones, so revealing the virtues of accurate execution. In 1952, as we can hear, Callas's performance has not yet the total integrity it would acquire in the next three years, although some of her singing in her more youthful days does create an even more musical effect. The phrase 'Si, Norma', for example, she sings in a beautifully poised mezza voce of which her voice is not capable by 1955.

Callas describes 'the moment I stepped on to the [Covent Garden] stage [and] I thought that my heart had suddenly stopped beating. I had been preceded in London by sensational publicity, and I was terrified by the idea of being unable to live up to expectations.'[10] However she kept her doubts and fears to herself. John Pritchard, then assistant conductor, remembers how at a rehearsal in the last act she 'pulled her ocelot coat around her, walked up on to the stage and heaved the mallet as she went to strike the gong. As she approached it the chorus shrank back and I had the distinct feeling that so did the gong too. She approached it with a kind of manic fury. I am certain no gong had ever been struck like it before, it was the complete follow through of which a golf player pro would be proud.'[11] On the first night, notwithstanding critical caveats, the public's approval was instantaneous and the vociferous reception obliged Callas and Stignani, as Harewood remembers,[12] to encore the Act I duet.

One day during the season the Harewoods[13] invited the Meneghinis out to lunch at the Musicians' Club in South Audley Street. There Callas was introduced to Renée Gilly, a daughter of the famous baritone Dinh Gilly; she was a mezzo soprano 'of formidable presence' who had sung at the Paris Opéra in the 1930s and 1940s. Harewood recalls Mme Gilly 'demanded to be introduced in order to compliment the diva'. Callas removed her spectacles and 'gaz[ed] in a generalised sort of way [while Mme Gilly] lectured her in an admittedly complimentary fashion'. After she swept on Harewood couldn't help asking Callas why she had taken her glasses off; he knew she could see nothing without them. But that was exactly why, she laughed: 'She seemed so ferocious it was the only protection I had'. After lunch, it was mild for the time of year, Lady Harewood proposed that they go shopping but Callas, who was clad in a short-sleeved dress, shook her head. Looking down at her figure, she said: 'Oh! I don't know that I'm going to feel up to it really: lugging all this round London, I don't think I'm going to want to do that.' On another day, November 17th, the Italian Embassy gave a reception for the cast. It had been agreed the principals would all sing an aria but, in the event, Harewood recalls, 'Callas, the Greek, was the only one who turned up. She did indeed sing for her supper – the first act aria from *La Traviata* which was magnificent if inordinately big-scale in the relatively small space.'[13]

Little more than two weeks after her last Covent Garden Norma Callas was back in Milan to open the La Scala season on December 7th; and this year Meneghini had secured her a fee of 500,000 Lire a performance. The opera selected was Verdi's *Macbeth* conducted by de Sabata. These were the only five performances of Lady Macbeth that Callas would ever sing. Great were the lamentations when she failed to appear in productions arranged for her in San Francisco in 1957, at the Metropolitan in 1959 and Covent Garden in 1960. But all of these would have been too late, which was probably why they never happened: wisely, we may feel, she realized that the condition of her voice made it impossible for her to have equalled the effect she made at La Scala. As Norma she had had competition from the shades of Ponselle and Lilli Lehmann, but her Lady Macbeth had virtually no precedent. Perhaps the only great singer who ever undertook Lady Macbeth before Callas, and left her mark on it, was the mezzo soprano Pauline Viardot. She appeared in the original edition of Verdi's *Macbeth* in Dublin in 1859 then in the British provinces. She was thirty-eight and, reviews indicate, much past her best. In fact, her career was virtually over after only another three years, though she lived on until 1910. A facsimile of a letter from her to Luigi Arditi, who conducted these performances, appears in his memoirs[14] and from it we learn how she coped with Verdi's Lady Macbeth. The Act I aria, 'Vieni t' affretta!', and cabaletta, 'Or tutti sorgete', she transposed down a minor third. As she herself wrote, 'the [Act II] cabaletta "Trionfai" is not sung' (in 1865 Verdi would replace this with 'La luce langue'), and the Brindisi and Act IV Sleepwalking Scene were both down a tone. After she had retired from the stage Viardot taught singing in Paris and Baden-Baden, and her influence in Germany, especially, remained a potent factor well into this century.

It is interesting to note that a number of the first revivals of Verdi's *Macbeth* took place in Germany between the wars, and that Lady Macbeth was sung on those occasions by mezzo sopranos, even contraltos, among them Sigrid Onegin. Bing saw Onegin's Lady Macbeth in the early 1930s, and forty years later he had not forgotten her: 'Onegin's was one of the most individual and beautiful voices I have ever heard ... [Her Lady Macbeth] was ... such a great hit ... a startling performance ... and temperamentally the character ... came naturally to her.'[15] She was a pupil of de Ranieri who had studied with Viardot, so we can call her one of Viardot's 'grandpupils'. There were also revivals with Gertrud Runge and Elisabeth Hongen, and recordings show that they both inherited some of Viardot's, transpositions. Even in 1959 the noted French critic René Leibowitz[16] mistakenly assumed Lady Macbeth to be a mezzo, not a soprano, part.

Callas's Lady Macbeth needed no such transpositions. A recording reveals that it was a complete triumph, though it is extremely interesting to read some of the unenthusiastic reviews. Most of these would appear to have been the result of a vociferous contingent in the gallery. After the Sleepwalking scene, as she herself tells, 'I distinctly heard two or three whistles amid the applause. It wasn't the usual whistling ... it was obvious that the disrupter was using a real whistle.' Like the vegetables heaved on to the stage after one of her Scala *La Traviata*s in 1956, we agree, this must have been the result of 'a prearranged plan [requiring] careful preparation'.[17]

Of all the many roles she sang, probably Lady Macbeth most

suited her voice and temperament; it was enough that she was herself. Unlike Norma or Medea, Callas had no children, and in the last years of her life, in the mid-1970s, when she had lost her voice, her husband and Onassis, was she not herself almost sleep-walking? At her first entrance we hear her reading the letter but, as we have noted above, we must wait for her to start singing before she makes an effect. She had already included the Act I aria 'Vieni t' affretta!' in a broadcast that January, and she would often sing it in concert in later years, but this is the finest performance she ever gave of it, both vocally and musically. The degree of freedom and perfect discipline within the phrasing, based upon de Sabata's tempi, lend the music the contours of grandeur; over the opening phrases, appropriately, is the word 'grandioso'. Here, unlike her Gilda, Callas's art sounds spontaneous. De Sabata lends the music a broad sweep to underlie her phenomenal vocalization. Her voice is so responsive that she can follow every one of his subtle promptings and yet, at the same time, express a characterization completely her own.

Throughout her performance there are so many exceptional features. In the Act I aria how precisely she makes us feel the difference between a dotted semiquaver (sixteenth note) on the words 'a te promettono' and the triplet at the end of the succeeding phrase, 'le profetesse il trono', and how nimbly the trills are all executed. In the cabaletta, 'Or tutti sorgete', with what precision she articulates the awkwardly written passage of upward semiquavers (sixteenth notes) on the words 'i mortali'. In the duet with Macbeth that follows how perfectly poised and accurate is her execution of the two octave downward run from b'' flat immediately before Duncan's entrance, and how diligently she observes markings in the score, 'sempre sotto voce,' 'leggere' etc. Although she is interpreting a baleful role, her voice is always fresh and responsive as Lady Macbeth is egging Macbeth on in the murder scene. She emits a suppressed laugh at the end of the phrase, 'Ma dimmi, altra voce non parti d'udire?' as she asks, ironically, whether he thought he heard another voice. She accomplishes this where a sustained marking is written over a rest, yet without disturbing the perfect support of her legato as she accommodates it. In the passage beginning 'combatte, delira, trema, delira' how effortlessly she plays with the rhythm, and does so so subtly and with such great discipline. Garcia II tells how his father and Paganini would accomplish similar effects. 'While the orchestra maintained the tempo regularly they, on their part, would abandon themselves to their inspiration and rejoin with the bass only at the moment the harmony changed. This requires an exquisite feeling . . . an imperturbable poise.'[18]

At the end of Act II, in the second verse of the Brindisi, her voice is so limpidly produced that she can realize the score's direction to sing 'con forza' by amplifying her tone and marking the rhythm, not by pushing and yelling, as any other singer might do. The Sleepwalking Scene has been criticized,[19] but on de Sabata's account, for he takes it faster than the score suggests. But his is a notable conception. There is a peculiar frenetic quality about it: the way he underlines the rhythm, so making it suggest haunted palpitations, and how exquisite is the string playing. We note again how Callas suits her tone so acutely to the musical directions: 'sempre sotto voce', 'cupo' and 'un fil di voce'. Although Lady Macbeth is a dramatic role, she is not tempted to abuse her chest register. It is in this scene particularly that her voice is in impeccable condition. Her perfect support enables her to contrive an eerie, other-world quality, so lyrically and there is no trace of that wobble which in less than two years was to wreak itself irrevocably upon her voice. If I were obliged to select just one of Callas's performances for the proverbial desert island, this would be it, for here she is supported by a great conductor. Though she may not have known Shakespeare's play, her interpretative genius (and it is no exaggeration to call it so) communicates the sense of whole speeches in a few bars of recitative. It was de Sabata who said: 'If the public could understand as we do how deeply and utterly musical she is, it would be stunned.'[20] In describing Callas's Lady Macbeth the epithet 'Shakespearian' is for once no glib cliché.

VIII

1953

I T WAS ON January 17th 1953 that Callas went to Florence and with Legge made her first EMI recording. Meanwhile at La Scala, the day after Christmas 1952, she ventured *La Gioconda* on the first of six occasions. Abbiati in *Corriere della Sera* thought that although 'passionate and delicate [she was] slightly diminished by . . . too much that she is bestowing upon opera audiences'.[1] Dragadze, in *Opera*, complained that '[she] . . . was not up to her usual standard in this role as her voice sounds tired, especially in the heavy spinto passages'.[2] The Enzo was di Stefano and he tells how 'Maria was having trouble in the last act . . . she told me [how] unhappy she was about it'.[3] Doubtless singing such a part five times in nine days was excessive but the point was not so much the number of performances she sang as the basic unsuitability of the tessitura to her voice. At any rate she got the message and never ventured Gioconda on stage again. On the first night Toscanini was in Milan and gave a dinner party to which she was invited. There it was that Biki, the couturier, met her the first time. She remembers how 'big and clumsy she was and how badly dressed: she wore some extraordinary plastic earrings.'[4] Between the fifth and sixth performances, on January 8th, she took time off from La Scala for a couple of *La Traviatas* at the Fenice, Venice, with Albanese and Savarese under Angelo Questa and, a week later, on the 15th, these were followed by another three performances at the Rome Opera, supported by the same singers, but this time under Gabriele Santini. It was during the Rome run that Callas agreed to record *La Traviata* with this ensemble for Cetra that September.

Her EMI recording contract began with 'a series of tests of [Donna Anna's Act II aria from *Don Giovanni*] "Non mi dir". [so that Legge could] get the psychological feel of working with her, sensing how receptive she would be to criticism, and to find placings to give at least a decent sound.'[5] It was never intended to be issued and remained unpublished until 1985, when it was first published in France in an album entitled *Les Introuvables du chant mozartien*. In view of what Callas subsequently recorded it seems a strange choice. Who knows? Maybe Legge was toying with recording *Don Giovanni*, with Gobbi, Callas and Schwarzkopf. We are grateful for just this aria: we can hardly think of any other piece she could have sung in those days we should have more wanted to hear.

Save for Constanza, at La Scala the previous year, she never undertook any Mozart role, although a record made in 1964 does include four arias. But in it she sounds as if she were sight reading; by that time her operatic career was practically over. In this recording, however, she opens up another vista of her art: Callas the great Mozartian. She is on record expressing disapproval of the way Mozart's music is customarily sung: 'with too much delicacy, as though the singer were on tip-toes . . . his music should be performed with the same . . . bel canto approach one would use in *Trovatore* . . . Mozart . . . was a master of bel canto, and a necessity of bel canto is a full, sustained tone and . . . legato. [S]ing Mozart as [if] he were Verdi.'[6] Which is precisely what she does. Her singing causes us to reexamine the music: the most remarkable thing about it is its sense of style. She reminds us that problems of style are not, as is commonly supposed, historic but musical. There is nothing in the least contrived or arty-sounding about it, in the manner of many Mozartians. Her voice is easily produced, her tone perfectly supported, and her phrasing a model. She demonstrates this by her use of upward portamento, always discreetly employed. She chooses appropriate colours within a modest frame so as to suit the text. We notice here a characteristic of her art: how, although completely unselfconsciously, her voice seems to echo the timbre of the wind instruments in the orchestra, as is appropriate in classical music. She executes all the exacting fioritura impeccably and seems hardly to breathe through the spacious phrasing. Especially remarkable is the breadth of the leisurely rallentando before she embarks on the allegretto, 'Forse un giorno'. Altogether her singing admits of no technical problems; this aria, one of the most demanding ever written, appears not to cost her the slightest effort. Not only does she sing it more easily than Lilli Lehmann, no mean feat, her recording has hitherto been *non pareil*, but she also sings it more persuasively: she communicates that she is appealing to Ottavio, not about to throttle him.

On January 25th she sang her first Lucia in Italy, for Siciliani, at the Comunale, Florence. The cast also included Lauri Volpi, Bastianini and Raffaele Arié conducted by Ghione. While the four performances were going on she commenced a complete recording of Lucia in the same theatre. This would be among the first releases of Angel records to be published in the U.S. in January 1954. In 1952, as a result of a breakdown in an agreement which had lasted half a century, RCA and EMI went their separate ways. Until that time what had been issued in the States on the Victor label appeared in Europe on the HMV label. EMI therefore determined, so as to market its records in the United States, to launch a new company, Angel, though the name is an old one, the trademark dates back to the earliest days of recording. The prime figures in this were Soria and Legge. Soria, an Italian who had come to live in New York before the Second World War, had previously been in partnership with the Italian record company Cetra (in the U.S. this was known as Cetra-Soria), and in such fashion he had acquired the necessary business experience for the U.S. market. For Angel to create the right effect in America it was necessary to come into the market place with a big bang so it was decided to lead off in 1953 with records of a number of artists of international acclaim. Callas was one of the most important of these. Her contractual relations with Cetra were of course well known to Soria, so it was not so difficult for EMI to tempt her with a more attractive as well as, no doubt, more lucrative contract.

Walter Legge had been busy in the world of music since 1932 when, as an HMV employee, he started the Hugo Wolf Society, a series of recordings devoted to Wolf's Lieder with Gerhardt, McCormack, Hüsch, Janssen, Kipnis and many others. Society Recordings, so-called, were a device he invented whereby HMV would 'collect subscriptions in advance . . . and make the records . . . when the requested number of subscribers had been enlisted'.[7] Among the most successful he supervised was that devoted to Beethoven's piano music played by Schnabel. By the beginning of the Second World War Legge had produced a quantity of Beecham's recordings: including a complete *Die Zauberflöte*; symphonies of Haydn, Mozart, Beethoven, Schubert and Brahms; violin concertos of Prokofiev and Sibelius with Szigeti and Heifetz, and a host of incidental pieces. In 1938, as a result of Beecham's influence, he had been engaged at Covent Garden as Assistant Artistic Director. He returned again a generation later, when he was invited to join the board. By then his reputation had increased substantially, for EMI he recorded Karajan, Schwarzkopf (whom he came to marry), Hotter, Lipatti, Fischer, Furtwängler, Flagstad, Dobrowen, Klemperer, Gedda, Gieseking, Fischer-Dieskau, Christoff and many others. He founded the Philharmonia Orchestra, which remained for a generation one of the finest in the world. By the 1950s Legge had become one of the important figures in the musical establishment. His taste was reflected in London's concert life: the Philharmonia played oratorios of Bach, Mendelssohn, Verdi and Brahms; operas of Mozart in concert form, usually to coincide with recordings; symphonies of Beethoven, Schubert, Bruckner, Brahms and Mahler; and a stream of celebrated conductors appeared with the orchestra. He presented *Liederabende* with many famous singers. By means of recordings Legge's influence was felt across Europe and in America. His cultural affections could be described as German-orientated (he spoke the language fluently), and his love for Wolf's Lieder, especially, remained important all his life.

However, the resurgence of interest in older Italian opera, which Callas was responsible for quickening, was outside Legge's cultural sympathies. He claims to have heard her first on her Cetra 78 recordings, which were issued in Italy first in May 1950. He states that, as a result, in 1951 'at the earliest opportunity',[8] he went to the Rome opera to hear her Norma but, in fact, she did not sing there that year, although she had appeared as Norma in February 1950. If he went there then it took another two and a half years, until July 21st 1952, before she signed an EMI contract and three were to elapse before she recorded Lucia. The excuse that he 'had to threaten to resign from EMI to get them to sign Callas',[9] is hard to believe when in 1950 he recorded *Le Nozze di Figaro* and *Die Zauberflöte* under Karajan with the Vienna Philharmonic. Karajan may have been better known then than Callas, but the notion that either of these operas would have sold more than a popular Italian work, like *Tosca* or *Cavalleria Rusticana*, both of which Legge was to record with Callas in 1953, is difficult to credit. We should not forget also that between 1950 and 1952 Decca/London were busy recording not only *Tosca*, but also *La Bohème*, *Madama Butterfly* and *Aida* with Tebaldi.

Had Legge been more interested in Italian opera he might have signed Callas up before she recorded *Gioconda* for Cetra, as well as making fuller use of her unique talents. He did not bother himself with many of the operas that she was busy singing on stage for the first time in years, failing to see in them indicators of the way taste was changing. Between 1952 and 1957, as well as standard German operas and operettas, he recorded a bevy of untypical works, ancient and modern, with Schwarzkopf; some of these, like Cornelius's *Der Barbier von Bagdad* or Orff's *Die Kluge*, were every bit as unfamiliar as Callas's repertory then was. Over the years we cannot help noticing how, compared with Legge's German opera recordings, EMI's La Scala company is too often Callas et al. It was enough for Legge that he recorded her in time-honoured chestnuts, a number of which she never undertook in the theatre and which she was vocally unsuited for. It is true that she did record Fiorilla in Rossini's *Il Turco in Italia* before it was given at La Scala, but not without some hard bargaining and after he secured her to sing Leonora in *La Forza del Destino*. Perhaps, instead of being made almost sea-sick over her tremulousness in *La Forza del Destino*, as he makes a point of telling us,[10] he might have attended more assiduously to his own business: the second-rate ensemble he offers alongside her.

The Legge method, if it can be so designated, is most closely identified with his wife, Schwarzkopf, who shows off to advantage the success of his infinitely painstaking and rigorous approach. As he envisaged it, a recording is a document that represents an artist's work formally and it should be tampered with, as often as may be necessary, to make it as nearly perfect as possible. In such fashion he assisted in transforming Schwarzkopf from a soubrette into a fully-fledged lyric soprano of international renown. Some singers benefited from this procedure, but Callas was not one. This kind of cerebration produced from her too much of the letter and not enough of the spirit of a work; a weakness also exploited by Karajan, as we shall see. Her prodigious musical skill is evident the very first time she ever undertakes an opera; listen to her first performances of *Il Trovatore*, *Lucia* and *Rigoletto*, all from Mexico City. Not only did her voice tire but, as many of her EMI recordings show, when Legge, as it were, came between her and the music, he only succeeds in depriving her art of spontaneity.

Had Legge been more in tune with Italian opera, had he shown the same measure of sympathy with Callas's art that he showed Schwarzkopf's, then we should not have had to make do with hardly hi-fi live recordings of *I Vespri Siciliani*, *Armida*, *Macbeth* and *Anna Bolena*, and it is indicative that he left *Medea* to the Italian firm Ricordi. Siciliani had engaged Callas for her first Norma in 1948, even before Decca/London had started FFrr LP recordings and threatened to outflank EMI with Tebaldi. Had Legge taken his cue from him, who knows what we might have today: perhaps Callas as Rossini's Semiramide; or Donizetti's Lucrezia Borgia; or Wagner's Isotta with, maybe, del Monaco as Tristano; or in Meyerbeer's *Gli Ugonotti* she might have pulled off the ultimate hat trick and sung the Queen, Valentina and Urbano in the same set. Why not? Christoff sings Boris, Varlaam and Pimen in not one but two recordings of *Boris Godounov*! What a pity it was that EMI did not have a more powerful Italian wing, run by someone like Siciliani who knew and cared for 'Italian' opera.

Callas has left a number of souvenirs of her Lucia. There is her first performance from Mexico City in 1952, the very first time she ever sang it, the first EMI recording made in Florence in 1953, the visit of La Scala to Berlin in 1955, performances from the San Carlo, Naples and the Metropolitan, New York, both in 1956, a RAI broadcast in 1957 and the second EMI recording in 1959. Then there is the first part of the Mad Scene from a 1952 RAI concert, the complete Mad Scene from her second performance of *Lucia* in Mexico City in 1952, and most of the La Scala performance of 1954. Of these three stand out: the first from Mexico City, although it is not until the second performance that she gets complete control over the climactic e'' flats in the Mad Scene. The second is the first EMI recording. The third is that from La Scala, the première of Karajan's production, unfortunately not only not in good sound but incomplete. Nevertheless, so far as one can hear, her singing sounds as fine as it was at La Scala for Medea a month previously, notwithstanding the fact that she had lost sixteen kilos (thirty-six pounds) since she had made the EMI recording the previous February.

The cast of the EMI recording includes di Stefano, who had replaced Lauri Volpi in the third Florence performance on February 5th, Gobbi in place of Bastianini as Enrico, and Arié, who also sang in Florence, as Bide-the-Bent. As can be seen from photographs, Callas was then at her heaviest. Gobbi remembers one lunch-time during the recording sessions Serafin rebuked her for letting 'her weight . . . become a problem. She protested . . . she was not so heavy. [She went to a weighing machine but] after the shock of reading what [it] recorded, she gave me her handbag and her coat and kicked off her shoes . . . [Still] the result was . . . dismaying, and she became rather silent.'[11]

A voice reflects a physique, so it is not surprising that her singing should have had more body in those days. In the Act I aria, 'Regnava nel silenzio', it is fully supported and she coasts through the music effortlessly. As we shall see, not only would the instrument lose its warmth and become thin and acidulous, but the altitudinous passages would to her no longer come easily. This ease in her vocal production enables her to suffuse her tone with a fittingly plangent quality, as we can hear in the Act II duet 'Soffriva del pianto'. In the Sextet she manages a wider range of dynamics than in any of her later

Lucias. In the Mad Scene she has worked some refinement since Mexico the previous year, her singing is neater, more accurate, and she deploys slightly less weight of tone; but it is more self-conscious, less spontaneous, in the Legge style, although it remains outstanding.

The sensation this recording created when it was issued may be said to have led directly to a revival of interest in florid singing; an ancient art and not mere singer's vanity, as was once supposed. By the first half of this century the growth and development of opera, its increasing preoccupation with the orchestra, meant that singers inevitably were no longer placed first. It had been forgotten that they provide a unique function: that of marrying words and music. Other aspects of their art too are peculiar to them and untranslatable, among them florid singing. Newman dismisses it scathingly: 'Ornaments were only evidences of the bad taste of the singers and the tyranny imposed by them upon audiences, and . . . while the vulgar among the listeners may have delighted in them, to the genuinely musical ear they must have been intolerable.'[12] By this century it had been forgotten that florid singing is part of a basic vocal grammar much older than opera. Although changing fashion in the West has led to its being outmoded, in the Middle East at sunrise muezzins on mosques are still today, after hundreds of years, delivering roulades and fioriture. Coloratura, as it was superciliously styled, the decadent twitterings of Pons and Pagliughi, may have become fit only for birds; indeed, Wagner consigned coloratura to one, quite literally, in *Siegfried*, but in so doing he reminds us that instrumental music derives from vocal music. It is no coincidence that in modern times mordents, staccati, gruppetti, even ad libitum cadenzas, called 'scat', should feature in Afro-American popular music.

Callas's Lucia created a furore, not only because she sang the florid music with an accuracy unequalled since the days of Tetrazzini, but also because she undertook it with stunning weight of tone and breadth of phrasing, so bringing to it a dramatic perspective. In the cadenza to the Mad Scene, the sudden intrusion of the flute sounds as if she were cavorting with a tin whistle; Richard Bonynge remembers 'the size of her voice and what she could do with it!'[13] She made out of Lucia something *sui generis*, even surpassing her achievement as Norma: its tragic dimension, records suggest, had never been divined before. As with Rossini's Armida, she not only looked back on Lucia from a distance of more than a century and sang the ornamental passages with unheard-of accuracy, but she imbued the music with all the dramatic weight of later composer's works yet, without in any way forcing the boundaries of Donizetti's style, by so doing she enables us to put a proper value on his art. We remember an incident Flaubert describes in *Madame Bovary*, when the heroine went to a performance of *Lucie de Lammermoor* in Rouen and was moved to tears by unhappy Lucie's fate. It no longer seems so ludicrous.

From Florence Callas returned to La Scala and sang her last Gioconda. It was at this time, provoked by repeated comments from all manner of people, from Serafin to her sister Jackie, that she began to lose weight, having reached a colossal ninety-two kilos (202 pounds). Though she never self-consciously decided to do so, the idea of becoming a beauty was in itself enough to strengthen her desire to slim. There was nothing cerebral about her, as Rescigno says: 'she was not a philosophical or a metaphysical performer . . . [but] an instinctive performer . . . Maria was not born a beautiful woman . . . [she] was fat, obese [yet] she transformed herself into possibly the most beautiful artist on the stage.'[14] This change in her figure was reflected in a change in her marital relations. In her first years in Italy, as we have seen, Meneghini was the architect of her career; he had provided the financial backing as well as the emotional security necessary to enable her to wait for La Scala to capitulate. Gradually, however, as her career developed and he grew older, she began to travel to non-Italian-speaking countries, where he spoke not a word. By then he was completely at sea; all that was left him was to stoke the fires of her discontent.

At La Scala, on February 23rd, she sang her third role that season, Leonora in *Il Trovatore*. Dragadze in *Opera* praised her, 'Callas again passed a difficult test and showed once more her remarkable artistic intelligence, her exceptional gifts as a singer, and the fact that she possesses a vocal technique second to none. Her handling of the dramatic content of her part was a masterpiece of artistry.'[15] After another two Leonoras she interpolated a couple of Lucias at Genoa, again with di Stefano, and then returned to La Scala, bringing her second season to a conclusion with two more Leonoras. Meanwhile, negotiations had been going on for her to undertake Violetta in the final weeks of the season at the Metropolitan, New York. She would sing three performances at $600 each. Bing believed she had accepted but 'then we received a letter to the effect that our failure to procure a visa for her husband . . . made it impossible for her to come to New York'.[16] This was in the days of the McCarran act, when a visitor could procure a visa only if he could prove that there was some need for him in his home country, usually by a letter from an employer.

However, Meneghini had liquidified his business assets in order to devote himself fully to his wife's career, and as a result he had no employment. Although he was fifty-seven and a man of considerable financial substance, U.S. immigration would not give him a visa. So Callas did not come to the Met that year and New York opera lovers were denied the opportunity of hearing her in her palmy days.

On March 24th, before Callas's last Leonora at La Scala she took part in another EMI recording: Bellini's *I Puritani*. This was the first to be made under the imprimatur of La Scala, Milan with its orchestra and chorus. Many of the series would also be recorded in the theatre but since *I Puritani* was scheduled during the season, sessions took place in Milan at the Basilica of Santa Euphemia. Serafin again conducts and the ensemble includes di Stefano, Panerai and Rossi-Lemeni. Like *Lucia*, the opera is considerably cut, but in *I Puritani* most of the cuts are in order to make it easier to find a suitable tenor. Originally this opera was a vehicle for the great virtuoso Rubini, who created Arturo, but by Callas's day changes in tenor voice production, brought about by the Verdi and verismo repertory, necessitated so many cuts that eventually *I Puritani* became in effect a soprano vehicle. It was revived for Barrientos at the Met in 1918 and for Carosio at La Scala in 1942. It was in lieu of Carosio, as we noted above, that Callas first sang it.

Bellini is justly renowned for writing eloquently for the voice; his tessitura is always expressive and never makes unnecessary demands of the singer. Callas sings Elvira easily and effortlessly, as she had also for the most part in Mexico City the previous year but, whereas there the performance barely hung together, here Serafin contrives a cogent reading. From her first entry she is in perfect voice. In the Act I Polacca, 'Son vergin vezzosa', her singing is at its best: limpid, steady, easy and accurate. Her delicate, unobtrusive, yet firm marking of the rhythm is admirable. Towards the end a pair of nimble chromatic runs down and up an octave, in which one can hear every note, are followed by repeated staccato a''s. In these, so limpid is her tone that she reminds us of the difference between staccato and marcato; between merely attenuating a note and marking it obtrusively. Few singers are aware of the difference or, at least, make us aware that there is one.

In the Finale of Act I, 'Ah vieni al tempio', where Bellini has written 'declamato con tutto lo slancio d'un core innocente contento', Callas's voice matches the music perfectly. She sings lightly, and even when she descends into chest voice on *e* and *d* she accomplishes it easily. She demonstrates that legato is the basic characteristic of Bellini's vocal writing. She reminds us 'it is legato you should pursue. [Like] a violin – it has to be more or less intense according to the words, according to the psychological situation.'[17] Evident in this ensemble, as we noted before in the *Norma* finale, is Bellini's use of triplets to suggest a doleful character. Towards the end Callas sings one of the few decorative passages she introduces into *I Puritani*, a traditional interpolation which, in all probability, she had learned from Serafin: she carries the line up to c'' and d'', echoing the strings in the accompaniment.

The Act II Mad Scene was one of the first records she made on 78s for Cetra in November 1949, more than three years before. By 1953 her florid singing is more adept, the tone noticeably lighter: as she herself states 'a voice must be put into a zone where it will not be too large in sound, but nonetheless penetrating'.[18] Photographs taken at the recording session suggest that she had barely commenced her slimming regime. The whole scene is a most eloquent piece of vocal writing and displays a correctly produced voice to the best advantage. Much of its effect is contrived by the use of portamento. In recent times no characteristic feature of singing has been more misunderstood. It is an ancient grace and forms a basis of eighteenth-century vocal music. As with Caruso's, Callas's many recordings show that it calls for exquisite reproduction. Not surprisingly in an age as little concerned with the art of singing as modern times, portamento has been either ignored or dismissed disparagingly: critics styled it 'scooping' when she used it in *Norma* at Covent Garden in 1953[19]. It is certainly true that one cannot hope to sing portamento correctly unless the voice is perfectly placed and fully supported, otherwise it will degenerate into so much scooping and sliding. But without it singing remains musically inexpressive. Only through a mastery of it is the singer able to fulfil simultaneously the basic lyrical functions: making music and words tell simultaneously. Like so much of Bellini's music, the *Puritani* Mad Scene is an exercise in portamento. From the first phrase of the recitative we hear how it assists in joining the syllables, so making the phrasing explicit: 'O rende-temi la spe-me-o lascia-te, lasciatemi mori-re'. In her three recordings (1949, 1953 and 1957) Callas gives a lesson in communicating intensity of expression through her masterly execution of this device, singing it lightly or very markedly, according to the width of the interval and the duration of the notes.

On April 1st she was to have travelled to London to sing at the Royal Festival Hall the soprano part in Verdi's Requiem, but a 'flu epidemic had broken out in Milan and British immigration would not allow her to enter the country; as we shall see, this was one of three occasions in which she almost sang in it. So from Milan she went to Rome where, on April 9th, she undertook the first of four performances of *Norma* with Corelli, then at the beginning of his career. On this occasion, for the first time, as Jolly in *Opera* reports, '[Callas] sang "Casta Diva" in the original G major – which even by the first edition had become F – but in spite of this tour de force she did not fully come into her own until the admirably concerted first duet with Barbieri, [with] the . . . pathos of some of her notes and boldly-handled triplets and ritenuti [seemingly suspended in air] . . .'[20] On April 21st, three days after her fourth and last Norma in Rome, she sang the first of two Lucias at Catania.

On May 7th she undertook another novelty for Siciliani at the Florence Festival: Cherubini's *Medea*. It had not been heard in Italy since it was revived at La Scala in 1909 with Mazzoleni. When Siciliani[21] had decided to present it, Cherubini was a Florentine, he told Italo Montemezzi, the composer, who threw his hands up in horror, remembering Mazzoleni's Medea. Although Mazzoleni's repertory was adventurous her vibrant singing and flamboyant style owed much to verismo and were hardly suited to *Norma*, records suggest, let alone classical opera like *Medea*. *Medea* was conducted by Gui and Callas and he did not get on well: 'She felt [the] Greek tragedy so intensely that [during rehearsal] she had violent clashes . . . with [him] over the proper interpretation of certain passages.'[22] Nevertheless, as a recording shows, his conducting is the finest of all those who worked with her in this opera. She gave three performances of it. By now we are used to reading of the sensation that each of her revivals created and her Medea earned a paean of praise. Menotti went to one of the rehearsals and he recalls, 'how she just stood still and when the stage director [André Bersacq] tried to move her about she told him, "I'm sorry, move the other members of the cast around me, I stand still." She had an extraordinary sensitivity which, in a few years time, after she had worked with Visconti, would blossom into something quite incandescent.'[23]

Pugliese in *Il Gazzettino* wrote that '[she] has surmounted a challenge that maybe no other singer today would even be able to attempt.'[24] Dragadze, in *Opera*, acclaimed her: 'deeply immersed in the role in its dual aspect of frenzied threats and compulsive pleading, she played no tricks either of voice or mannerism. She had learned the strenuous part in a few weeks, and yet she has never to my mind given a more even or more sung-in interpretation.'[25] Celli in *Corriere Lombardo* was 'astonish[ed]. [She is] a great singer and a tragic actress of remarkable power, she brought to the sorceress a sinister quality of voice ferociously intense in the lower range, and ... penetrating in the upper range. She also had tones that were heartrending for Medea the lover and touching for Medea the mother ... [S]he went beyond the notes, directly to the monumental character of the legend.'[26] Confalonieri in *La Patria* praised 'the sheer intensity of her singing [and] her voice, which though rather rebellious by normal standards, was perfectly suited to Cherubini's remarkable declamation'.[27] Unlike her Gioconda or Aida, there was no cavilling about Callas's vocal prowess as Medea.

IX

1953–1954

FROM FLORENCE CALLAS proceeded to Rome to undertake Lucia in the first of three performances at the Teatro dell' Opera. But before this, on May 16th, she appeared in a concert at Palazzo Pio. She sang 'D' amor sull' ali rosee' from *Il Trovatore*, 'Pace, pace mio Dio' from *La Forza del Destino* and 'Ombra leggera' from *Dinorah*. Jolly went to *Lucia* at the Opera and, although she did not care for the production, 'it needs a lot of gingering up', nevertheless she found it memorable for Guelfi's impressive voice and for Callas's simplicity. 'To hear all the low notes of this part was a rare, unforgettable experience. She phrased beautifully, with the sweetness of her piano tone much in evidence and a whiteness at the beginning to fix the innocence of her characterization. [It was] . . . almost unbelievable to those who had seen her [only a week before in Florence] as Medea.'[1] Gavazzeni was the conductor and he remembers 'during rehearsals certain unexpectedly expressive qualities in her fioritura . . . I tried to capture some of these in the orchestral echoes of the same phrases. Callas's intuition in this was an invariable stimulus to me, and from then on my interpretation of Lucia was not the same.'[2]

She returned to London to appear at Covent Garden in the Coronation season as Aida, in three performances beginning on June 4th with Simionato and Baum. Sutherland was the Priestess and John Barbirolli conducted. By 1953 Callas's repertory was developing in such a way as to make her Aida, like Turandot and Gioconda, a thing of the past. The warts it revealed were all too evident. Shawe-Taylor in *The New Statesman* writes: 'She is at her worst in *Aida*, gulping through "Ritorna vincitor", very unsteady at the climax [the ascent to high C] in "O patria mia", and hardly attaining beauty before "La, tra foreste vergine" – which is really too late. [Although] as a rule her sense of line is superb.'[3] Porter in *Opera* could not help noting how '[she] often sacrificed a smooth line, and disconcertingly changed vocal colour. She has . . . a tendency on sustained high B flats or C's to develop a rapid trill, through the full semitone below the note.' Yet he found much to admire. 'How beautifully she caressed the phrases [in the final duet] starting "Vedi? di morte l'angelo" touching gently the notes marked staccato, ravishing the ear with the downward portamento from the high B flat [a steady, sweet one here].'[4]

On June 15th she repeated Norma, undertaking it four times in all. As she had in Rome that April, she sang 'Casta Diva' in the higher key of G major. Porter thought 'it seemed to lie better for her voice there; the opening phrases were beautifully placed. The B,B,B,B sempre crescendo *al* ff C, did not sound nice – but then neither had they done in the lower key. [She] was in far better voice than she was for Aida; the tone was even, rounder, more consistently brilliant with fewer of those disconcerting little shifts into an edgy timbre.'[5] Whatever reservations the London critics may have expressed over her Aida, and to a lesser extent over Norma, when she sang Leonora in *Il Trovatore* on June 26th (repeating it twice) she earned unanimous golden opinions. *The Times* considered the opera should have been styled *Leonora*: 'Callas sang and acted everyone off the stage. That she could dispense roulades and fioritura was a foregone conclusion after Norma, but she was also able to make a vivid and touching figure of Leonora, whether transported by tempests of the heart, or racked with anguish outside the Aliaferia Palace, or calmy sinking into death. She is not an artist given to gesturing but ... when she moves an arm the audience sits forward, gripped by the stimulus of a dynamic personality in action. The beauty of her vocal line, its plasticity, and its strength, and the easy richness with which she unfolds long phrases, were memorably shown in "Tacea la notte", and especially in the last melody she sings, "Prima che d'altri vivere", when her voice soared up the scale of E flat with a breathtaking blend of tension and effortlessness.'[6] Producer John Copley was then working backstage and he can not forget 'the way she sang the cadenza in "D'amor sull' ali rosee". It was the first time I had ever heard a cadenza, or any of the scales and arpeggios, that made it mean something. Instead of a lot of top notes, à la Milanov, Callas linked them together phrasing them so that it was completely expressive ... It was not just the clarity and separation of the notes which was exemplary but she actually sang it as if it really meant something.'[7]

On July 23rd back in Verona she appeared for the last time in *Aida*, in a production of G.W. Pabst, a celebrated director who had made the film *Don Quixote* twenty years before with Chaliapin in the title-role. Visconti went to Verona and was 'enchanted by a marvellously oriental *Aida* with Maria.'[8] In between the fourth and last performances Callas returned to Milan and, on August 3rd and 4th, she recorded Santuzza in Mascagni's *Cavalleria Rusticana*, a role she had not undertaken since her early days in Greece and would not again. Although at La Scala in the 1954/55 season she would be announced to sing it under Bernstein, in the event performances did not take place. Although Serafin's conducting is very slow (though not as slow as Mascagni's) it is eloquent and preserves much of the traditional rubati that save such music from the trivial treatment it too often gets.

In recent times the role of Santuzza, like Carmen, has become the province of mezzo sopranos, or, at least, so they were called before many of them took to jacking up their voices. But in the years following its composition it was a soprano vehicle. It was created by Gemma Bellincioni, who in her youth had sung roles in Callas's repertory, like Elvira in *I Puritani* and Lucia, and Emma Calvé was another noted Santuzza, a famous Carmen who also undertook Lucie and Lakmé. Both of them were renowned as dramatic sopranos at a time when an appreciable proportion of the operatic repertory was still vital. They were deemed dramatic in their histrionic approach. In those days, when the drama still told, the term did not refer, as it does today, solely to the size of a singer's voice. We may recall, in the period between the wars, the impressive chest registers of noted soprano Santuzzas, like Arangi Lombardi, Cobelli, Bruna Rasa and Pacetti. Callas, as we hear on many of her recordings, often sounds least effective in the lower middle range; which may account for her attempting to patch over the weak spot in dramatic music, like *La Gioconda*, by taking the chest register up much too high, to *g* and even *a'* flat. Legge relates that he discovered, at the end of her career in 1962, '[when] trying to record . . . "Mon coeur s'ouvre à ta voix," the lower register needed more consistent power than she could sustain',[9] yet her Santuzza is not troubled by the tessitura. Throughout we note the effect of her exploiting her registers so as to create the widest range of colour in the music. One example will suffice: at the beginning of the opera, as Santuzza laments to Mamma Lucia her being excommunicated, 'sono scommunicata'. The first six of the seven syllables are all set on *e*, appropriately she casts this very much in chest register then, gradually she lightens the tone, shifting imperceptibly into middle voice before rising to *a'*. In such fashion there is no awkward break in her registers as she finishes the phrase.

Marianna in 1942, rehearsing for *Tosca* at the Summer Theatre, Klafthmonos Square, Athens.

Callas in December 1949 at the San Carlo, Naples, as Abigaille in *Nabucco*.

Callas in April 1952 at La Scala, Milan, as Constanza in Mozart's *Il Ratto del Serraglio* with, left to right, Nerio Bernardi (Selim), Ghiringhelli (the Sovrintendente of La Scala) and Salvatore Baccaloni (Osmin).

In January 1950 at the Fenice, Venice, as Norma.

Callas in January 1952 at the Comunal Florence, as Elvira in *I Puritani* – she was he at her stoutest, yet she still looks beautiful.

In December 1952 at La Scala, Milan, as Lady Macbeth in Verdi's *Macbeth* with, left to right, the conductor Victor de Sabata, Violetta Elvin (Ecate) and Enzo Mascherini (Macbeth).

In April 1952 at the Comunale, Florence, as Rossini's Armida.

In January 1953 at the Comunale, Florence, as Donizetti's Lucia with Valiano Natali (Arturo).

Callas in May 1953 at the Comunale, Florence, Medea, with Carlos Guichandut as Giasone.

In March 1955 at La Scala, Milan, as Amina in Visconti's production of *La Sonnambula*.

In April 1955 at La Scala as Fiorilla in Rossini's *Il Turco in Italia*. Zeffirelli was both producer and designer.

Callas as Violetta in *La Traviata* in Visconti's La Scala production, May 1955, with a clutch of cocottes.

Callas in March 1956 at the San Carlo, Naples, as Donizetti's Lucia with Gianni Raimondi as Edgardo.

Callas as Giordano's Fedora at La Scala, May 1956.

La Scala, June 1957. Callas in Gluck's *Ifigenia in Tauride*, another Visconti production.

Callas as Donizetti's Anna Bolena at La Scala, April 1958. This was yet another Visconti production and one of Callas's great nights, as conductor Gavazzeni recalls.

Remarkable is her rendering of 'Voi lo sapete', in which Santuzza tells Mamma Lucia tearfully the tale of how Turiddu has deserted her for Lola. She imbues it with a characteristic vocal plangency, singing it in verismo style, but she remembers it is the singer's business to indulge her listeners and not herself, by so doing she renders the music with such precision that she makes something almost classical out of it. Towards the end of the first part there is an impeccably attacked fortissimo a'', and the same perfection in her delivery of the piano f' sharp at the beginning of the phrase 'Priva dell'onor mio'. We notice how her effects are never made at the expense of the music. On g, on the word 'piango' ('I weep'), she contrives a lachrymose effect not by gasping or by an uneasy lurch in the line, she makes almost an acciaccatura from the register break an octave below. Throughout we admire her fearless accuracy. In the postlude there is the same unaffected poise with which she launches a perfect seventh from b' to a'' on the phrase 'Io son dannata'.

Back in Verona again on August 8th Callas sang Aida for the last time. By then she had reduced by 11 lbs (five kilos). Two days later, in Milan once more, she commenced another La Scala recording, this time of Puccini's *Tosca* and made in the theatre, for the company was then on vacation. It has been ecstatically praised. Legge, who superintended it, states in his obituary of Callas: 'the supreme Callas recording was her first Tosca, after nearly twenty-five years still unique in the history of recorded Italian opera'.[10] But this is Legge indulging in self-advertisement; if we had only this recording how little of Callas's art would have survived! Tosca is not an ideal part for her. It does not reveal as much of her unique skills as Rosina in *Il Barbiere*, and certainly not as much as the Bellini, Donizetti or early Verdi roles she sang; indeed, it tells us less even than her Kundry in *Parsifal*. The role is typical of verismo: not demanding in point of range, dynamics or alacrity of execution. What it does require is dramatic talent married to an ample-sized, beautiful voice to mirror the lyricism of the orchestral writing. At one of her rare performances of Tosca in her heyday, at the Metropolitan, Menotti heard her: 'I was expecting a great interpretation . . . but curiously though she was marvellous in *Norma*, *Sonnambula* and *Medea*, I thought her Tosca rather conventional and disappointing.'[11] Sandro Sequi, the opera director, explains why it was not her role: 'Realism was foreign to [Callas] . . . Opera is the least realistic of theatre forms. [She] was wasted in verismo roles, even Tosca, no matter how brilliantly she could act . . . Verismo made her smaller than she was. Her greater genius was revealed in *Norma, Sonnambula* and *Lucia*.'[12] Oltrabella confirms: 'Verismo was not for her because, despite what everyone says, she was an actress in the expression of the music . . . [and] in verismo the music is often secondary.'[13]

Even so the EMI recording is certainly a first-class account of the opera. Apart from Callas there is Gobbi. Whereas his Figaro is taxed by the roulades, Puccini perfectly suits him. The part calls for a baleful vocal characterisation and Gobbi draws a vivid portrait with the broadest strokes; from his first entrance, in Act I in the Chiesa Sant' Andrea della Valle, when he rebukes the choristers, 'Un tal baccano in chiesa' ('What an uproar in church!'), he creates a notable effect. Di Stefano, too, sings persuasively, Cavaradossi showing him off to much better advantage than either Arturo or Edgardo, and he makes something attractive out of both his arias. But, as di Stefano says, 'the miracle of that Tosca was de Sabata . . . It was a joy to hear the sound that the orchestra under him gave . . . [and working for him was] very rewarding – he used to send kisses every time he got the right response. He served us with his orchestra – we were not just three singers, with de Sabata we were four.'[14] Indeed, what we miss so much in the Rio de Janeiro and Mexico City performances is a distinguished accompaniment, which is precisely why *Tosca* is not a singers' opera. In fact, accompaniment is altogether too mean a word to describe the stellar contribution of the Scala orchestra under de Sabata: in the operas of Rossini, Donizetti, Bellini or the young Verdi the orchestra does not signify to the same extent. When this recording was made the gramophone had been keeping the Puccini style alive in the half-century since *Tosca*'s première, the Scala orchestra players still had it in their blood, for Puccini had been dead less than thirty years.

In the summer of 1953 Callas finished her operatic engagements with a solitary Leonora in *Il Trovatore* at the Verona arena on August 15th. Save for the Cetra recording of *La Traviata*, made in September, she did not sing again until she undertook four performances of *Norma* in Trieste, beginning on November 19th. During that time she shed a further fifteen lbs (seven kilos), now she weighed only 173 lbs (eighty kilos). *Norma* reveals a performance unremarkable in its dramatic purpose, Votto's direction being only routine, and throughout she sounds underpowered, although her singing is eloquent. Indeed, it is doubtful if she ever sings 'Casta Diva' more easily; the climactic runs to *b''* flat betray none of her typical stridency or insecurity. Possibly to make it easier for Nicolai, the Adalgisa, or perhaps because Votto preferred the lower keys, in this performance she transposes 'Casta Diva' and 'Mira, o Norma' back down again to F and E flat respectively. So the only *Normas* she would appear to have undertaken in the higher keys were those earlier in 1953, in Rome and London, neither of which unfortunately was broadcast and no recordings survive.

The 1953/54 season at La Scala began with Catalani's *La Wally* on December 7th with Tebaldi. Ghiringhelli had persuaded Callas to give Tebaldi the honour, she had been appearing since the theatre regularly since it reopened in 1946. Callas and Meneghini came to opening night, and he thought '[Tebaldi] sang truly well, even though the opera did not set the stars spinning'.[15] Callas explained how she 'went to La Scala to applaud my colleague with warmth, as she certainly deserved: I smiled at her often, to make my intentions understood. I expected a sign or a salute from her that would have authorised me to visit her in her dressing room, but that sign was not forthcoming.'[16] Although when Callas sang three nights later Tebaldi returned the compliment, Meneghini was quick to notice that she had left before the end. Tebaldi remained at La Scala through the rest of that season but, save for Leonora in *La Forza del Destino* in April 1955, she did not return again until December 1959, after Callas had left. As we see from the above quotation, from Callas's memoirs published in *Oggi*, she goes out of her way to show how friendly she was to Tebaldi. There is something not entirely convincing about her protestations. However, her style may have been totally an invention of the journalist. As Tebaldi herself says, 'the rivalry was from newspapers and fans . . . Maria had a completely different voice from mine'.[17]

Callas had been scheduled to appear in the next opera in the Scala season Scarlatti's *Il Mitridate Eupatore*, which was to be conducted by de Sabata. Echoes of the furore she had created as Cherubini's *Medea* in Florence reached Milan, and prompted a change in operas. Then, less than two weeks before first night, de Sabata was stricken with a heart attack and Ghiringhelli hastily called in Leonard Bernstein. Only a month previously he had created a sensation throughout Italy in a concert tour, culminating in an appearance at La Scala at which he both played the piano and conducted the orchestra. At first, however, he was reluctant to accept Ghiringhelli's offer. Rumours had reached him that Callas was a difficult personality. But a meeting was arranged between them and as soon as they had met and got to know each other, as Callas says, 'he put all uncertainties aside'.[18]

Medea is a bastard. In the original 1797 edition the opera has spoken dialogue, but the version Callas sings is with recitatives by Franz Lachner added for a revival (in German) in Munich in 1855. As well as Bavaria, in the last century *Medea* was mounted occasionally elsewhere. In London in 1865 Colonel Mapleson, a noted impresario, staged it at Her Majesty's and later at Covent Garden, where it was sung by the celebrated Hungarian soprano Theresa Tietjens. Although it was performed with recitatives, these were not by Lachner. It might prove diverting to dredge this version up, for they were the work of its conductor, Arditi, he of such famous showpieces as 'Il bacio', 'Parla', 'Leggero invisibile' and 'Se saran rose'. Leonard Bernstein was also a successful composer of light music, and both he and Arditi belong to the once familiar tradition of composer/conductor. Like Arditi, Bernstein proved an imaginative writer of vocal ornamentation, as we shall have occasion to note when discussing embellishments he composed for Callas in the Scala production of *La Sonnambula* in March 1955. It is a great pity that those farsighted enough to get him to write them then did not also have time to engage him to compose recitatives for *Medea*. They could not have failed to prove more satisfying than those of the journeyman-like Lachner.

Margherita Wallmann who directed the Scala production of *Medea*, describes Callas: 'At that time, she had just begun to lose weight . . . [and] her figure was still powerful. She looked like one of the caryatides on the Acropolis . . . For Medea, her physique was an advantage, which gave the character a quality of antiquity. Her portrayal lost this special kind of presence when she became too thin.'[19] Medea is the role which most reveals Callas's art *sui generis*. Although Norma, Lucia and Violetta benefit from her interpretation, they can still survive an indifferent performance and even Rossini's Armida a leggero soprano can make a whistle-stop through, as Anderson proves, but nobody else has ever made a hit in *Medea*. A score of it reveals nothing prodigiously difficult and several latter-day singers have managed to get through it: Farrell, Gorr, Bumbry, Jones, Olivero, Caballé and Plowright, yet it has resisted their interpretations. No one who saw Callas as Medea will have forgotten that her acting was a response to her musical assumption: with every one of her undertakings, as the lasting success of her records proves, it is the music that speaks through her singing. Her voice, alone among those who have attempted the role, was sufficiently responsive to realize what Cherubini intended. Her prodigious variety of vocal colour, the incisiveness of her articulation, her consummate execution of the often awkwardly written tessitura, enables her to make *Medea* at least seem a work of major importance.

In recordings that survive from Florence and La Scala in 1953 especially, and also later in Dallas in 1958, Callas gives a lesson in the art of singing. In the uncomfortably written Act I aria, 'Dei tuoi figli', 'a killer',[20] as she called it, she demonstrates the perfection of her legato. So perfectly supported is her voice that we are hardly aware of her subtle use of portamento, which she employs in a classical fashion, only very occasionally making it obvious, so as to create some special effect. On the phrase 'per tanto amor che volli a te' it is the perfection of her legato that enables her to enunciate each note in the groups of dotted-semiquavers (sixteenth notes) and demi-semiquavers (thirty-second notes) cleanly and precisely whilst still maintaining a smooth line. Throughout Medea her technique is always at the service of the music. Like a great instrumentalist she reveals her acute rhythmic sense, how it organizes, shapes and disciplines her singing, enabling her to recreate the music fresh minted. She accomplishes this so completely that when we first hear Medea we hardly have time to notice that what preoccupies us is the art of the singer, not the song. It is scarcely surprising that all the other singers who took it up with such alacrity soon dropped it. Just as Callas's Santuzza demonstrates that verismo need not be a synonym for vulgarity, so her Medea will surprise anyone who supposed classical opera was bloodless.

She undertook five performances of *Medea* that season at La Scala, interpolating between the second and third, beginning on December 16th, three performances of *Il Trovatore* in Rome. William Weaver in *Opera* praised her: 'Callas, considerably slimmer, distinguished herself above all in "D'amor sull'ali rosee" which was movingly sung with beautifully timed trills.'[21] On January 18th 1954 she appeared in her second role that season at La Scala, in *Lucia di Lammermoor*, a new production conducted and directed by Karajan. Zeffirelli calls him 'the cleverest of all directors who used Callas. He didn't even try to direct her, he just arranged everything about her. She did the Mad Scene with a follow-spot like a ballerina. He left the music to her ... She was the perfect illustration of the music – no director taught her ... She knew the trick of achieving the maximum with the minimum effort.'[22]

A recording of the broadcast of the La Scala *Lucia* is not in good sound or complete; nevertheless, it represents Callas's Lucia in the best light. The performance benefits from the stylistic authenticity of the orchestral playing coupled with Karajan's virtuoso mastery; Callas has no difficulties with the *e″* flats, though she had lost some thirty-eight pounds (seventeen kilos) since her EMI recording in February 1953. She herself recalls 'that season at La Scala marked two of my greatest successes: the first in *Medea* and the second in *Lucia*'.[23] They would repeat *Lucia* with Karajan and an ensemble from La Scala, though not with the orchestra, regrettably, in Berlin at the end of September the following the year and in Vienna in June 1956. After seven *Lucia*s at La Scala she proceeded to the Fenice, Venice where, commencing on February 13th, she undertook another three *Lucia*s, under Questa's direction with Infantino, Bastianini and Giorgio Tozzi, and then three *Medea*s under Gui in Bersacq's production borrowed from Florence, with Renato Gavarini, Gabriella Tucci, Tozzi and Miriam Pirazzini. On March 10th, at the Carlo Fenice, Genoa, she gave three performances of *Tosca*, the first time she had sung it since Mexico City in 1952, the cast also included Mario Ortica and Guelfi under Ghione, these would be her last *Tosca*s in Italy.

In February 1954 came the first legal dispute[24] in which Callas was involved. She eventually won the case after more than five years. It concerned the use of her name, without her permission, in an advertisement by the Pantanella company, makers of flour and pasta. In it a photograph of a letter appeared stating that: 'In my capacity as the doctor treating Maria Meneghini Callas, I certify that the marvellous results obtained in the diet undertaken by Signora Callas were due in large part to her eating the physiological pasta produced in Rome's Pantanella Mills.' It was signed by Dr Cazzarolli, who was Meneghini's brother-in-law and a friend of long standing. He had been best man at their wedding. When Callas saw it, she claims, she was flabbergasted. She was soon besieged by telephone callers wanting more information about the 'physiological' pasta. She insisted on a public retraction and apology. The Pantanella company equivocated, so she was obliged to serve them with a writ. However the company had ties with the Vatican, its president was a nephew of Pius XII, various backstage attempts were made to encourage her to abandon the action, but she persisted. The Pope expressed a desire to meet the Meneghinis and, after Callas ignored an invitation to a public ceremony, at length they were summoned to the Vatican and ushered into a private audience. The Pope spoke to her, 'You are Greek, and grew up in America. Yet the way you speak Italian one would say you are from Verona,' and he went on to congratulate her on her singing of Kundry in *Parsifal*, which he had heard on the radio. He then said how sorry he was that she had not sung it in German, but Callas was quick to disagree: 'to understand the depth of the music, it is also indispensable to understand the words.'

The discussion continued some while but she stood her ground – she was not accustomed to giving way. Meneghini became increasingly agitated and did his best to change the topic of conversation. He remembers how the Pope 'fixed his gaze on me [and then] said, "I read the newspapers from cover to cover. Nothing escapes me. Not even your legal fight with the Pantanella company . . . We should be grateful if you come to a speedy agreement, in a manner in which the Pope could be left in peace."' Meneghini assured him they would do their best to settle the matter at once, but no sooner had they got outside than Callas told him: 'This has nothing to do with the Pope . . . I don't intend that they should go unpunished as a favour to him.' So for the next three years the case dragged on. Eventually the Pantanella company was ordered to pay legal expenses and damages and publish a letter of retraction. They appealed about the letter but accepted the rest of the judgment. Meneghini managed to talk Callas into conceding them the public apology. In October 1958, however, the Pope died. As soon as she heard the news Callas insisted that there was no further need to grant the Pantanella company any favours, and she demanded their apology. It was not until the following summer that the court of appeals in Rome confirmed the decision, and Pantanella and Dr Cazzarolli were obliged to publish the letter, as well as pay damages and settle legal expenses in full. But by that time the Meneghinis were on board Aristotle Onassis's yacht, *Christina*.

X
1954

B Y APRIL 1954 Callas weighed only 143 pounds (sixty-five kilos) and she was less than two-thirds the size she had been only a year before. For the first time she was beginning to feel a new security and she turned her attention from her voice to her looks; just as she had triumphed as a singer, so now she would, she reasoned, be able to achieve a similar histrionic supremacy. Her willpower was the basic ingredient in this transformation: 'she got what she wanted, so she stopped overeating',[1] a doctor explains. Roberto Bauer, the Metropolitan representative in Milan, recalls[2] seeing her one day at the beginning of her La Scala reign gorging the contents of a large box of crystallized fruits; but now she followed a rigorous regime and would eat nothing save steak tartare and salad; although when dining out with friends she would pick from their plates! As photographs reveal, in her plump days, although she was never ugly, she had no conception how to dress. When she had originally gone to Biki to ask for advice she was told first of all that it would be necessary for her to lose weight. Now that she had slimmed, she went again to Biki, who remembers[3] how surprised she was at her striking physical metamorphosis. During the next three years, guided implicitly by her, Callas came to accrue a caravan-like wardrobe: twenty-five fur coats, forty suits, 200 dresses, 150 pairs of shoes, at least 300 hats, and innumerable gloves; these she would toss away when she had worn them only a few times. Biki's son-in-law, Alain Reynaud, tells how even her hands had changed: 'They seemed to have grown long and beautiful, one had never noticed them before, it was a kind of miracle.'[4]

On the 4th she sang her third role that season at La Scala, Gluck's Alceste. She undertook this only four times and to judge from the noisy prompt, she had her usual problems remembering the text, though not the music. It was conducted by Giulini and he relates how 'I edited the score carefully, going back to the original edition, but using Gluck's later French musical revision.'[5] We see how significant Callas's repertory was then, at the commencement of the age of revivals, for *Alceste* had never been performed before at La Scala, although it was first staged in 1767, nine years before the theatre was built. The conductor remembers how it was two and a half years since Callas had sang Violetta with him in Bergamo and, at first, she had changed so much that he did not recognize her. He tells of their relationship during the rehearsal period: 'She not only grasped the musical phrases as you demonstrated them to her, but she made them her own ... We looked for the reasons a phrase might go one way rather than another ... I know she loved singing Alceste, and she did it with immense humility, humanity and passion. Offstage Maria is a simple woman of very humble background. Alceste, however, is a great queen, a figure of classic nobility, yet, through some mystic transformation, [she] transmitted all Alceste's royal stature.'[6]

In a recording of a broadcast we hear how she makes an impact by the unaffected simplicity of her delivery. In the opening adagio in Act I, 'O dei, del mio fatto tiranno', it is her freedom of tempo that helps her establish her musical characterization. How responsive her voice is at the commencement of the concluding allegro, 'disparata al mondo Io son', as she surges forward the orchestra follows. The great aria, 'Divinità infernal', she seemed to sculpt as if it were in marble; ably supported by Giulini, her interpretation serves to reveal a veritable monument. Although the aria is shorn of appoggiaturas, she again reveals the classical style through complete musical sympathy as she had in Donna Anna's 'Non mi dir'. At the end of the first part, on 'la vostra pieta crudele', how perfectly poised her tone is as she introduces a ritard and marks the phrase. In the middle section, following Gluck's indication 'un poco andante', she relaxes the tension and draws limpidly the phrase, 'salvar lo sposo mio', revealing the perfection of her portamento. We note how in this classical work she uses this device altogether more chastely than in *I Puritani*. Later in the presto section, beginning 'novella ho forza in core', she sets a prodigious tempo, yet her voice is so limpid that she can still articulate each phrase precisely, and the b'' flats present her with no problem, as they would when she attempts the aria on a recital record.

Callas's third La Scala season finished with a revival of Verdi's *Don Carlo* on April 12th. She sang Elisabetta. Five performances were given but, perhaps because Erhardt's production was only a revival, the opera was not broadcast, so no recording survives. Rossi-Lemeni was Filippo II, and he remembers: 'Everybody was wondering what Callas would do. She sang the last act particularly well. The duet with

Don Carlo, more than her aria, "Tu che la vanità", which was a little too aggressive, but her pianissimi were exquisite. In our scene in Act III we did not need to rehearse; it was natural for us . . . I remember particularly how beautiful she looked.'[7] However, she did not make anything like the impression that she had done as Alceste, Lucia or Medea. The opera is not conceived as a soprano vehicle, though in this century Elisabetta was sung by Farrar, Giannina Russ, Ponselle and Cigna. Malipiero in *Opera* thought, 'Callas's voice was not quite suited to Verdi's music; for this wonderful singer, so confident in difficult passages and powerful in dramatic passages, lacks the sweetness and softness necessary in moments of abandon.'[8]

No sooner had she finished Alceste than she began her first La Scala recording of *Norma*, on April 23rd at the Cinema Metropol, with Stignani, Filippeschi and Rossi-Lemeni. Serafin conducted. This over, on May 3rd she travelled back to Verona. She was then obliged to take to her bed with 'flu. It was not for almost another three weeks that she emerged from her retreat for two Leonoras in *La Forza del Destino* at the Alighieri, Ravenna on 23rd and 26th. Then on June 12th she returned again to La Scala for six consecutive days for a recording of Nedda in *Pagliacci*. She had continued to slim through these months, and with her hair now blonde the dark, dumpy woman of a year before had become virtually unrecognizable.

Legge had tried to lure Karajan into conducting *Pagliacci* but at the last moment he cried off so Serafin undertook it. Nine, very pregnant, months had elapsed since its companion piece *Cavalleria*. And by the time she recorded Nedda her voice, too, has slimmed away. There is little of the limpidity, and consequently of that peculiar vocal responsiveness we noted above in her interpretations. There is a sad irony in the fact that having transformed herself, swan-like, into a beautiful woman, her voice quickly lost the bloom of youth. It is as if a veneer had been wiped off it; it has become not only thinner, but less steady and harder in tone. And Nedda is not a role that could ever have suited her. There is an air of contrivance in her impersonation; she seems to be exaggerating, imposing on the music more than it can bear: shrewishly chiding Tonio, 'Eh! dite, mastro Tonio! La schiena oggi vi prude . . .' ('Eh! tell me, Master Tonio! have you an itching back?') and in practically the next breath bursting with tenderness as she turns to Silvio, 'A quest' ora che imprudenza' ('How rash at this hour'). Altogether her Nedda is far more imposing a characterization than anything Leoncavallo suggests or, indeed, deserves; we feel she would have settled Canio's hash in a jiffy. Although she contrives a particular effect in the Act II *commedia dell'arte* scene, we cannot help noting signs of her taking her voice off the support, a habit which would all too soon prove terminal.

Straight after *Pagliacci*, on 18th June, Legge began another La Scala recording, this time of Verdi's Requiem, with de Sabata conducting what was to be his last recording. Legge had booked di Stefano and Siepi and he had determined that the soprano part would be sung by Schwarzkopf; apart from questions of style inevitably raised by such casting, it surprised those who believed Schwarzkopf's voice was too light for this music. But, as we hear on the records, she reveals a full lyric soprano – at least when she, so to speak, takes the lid off. By 1954 the rapidly expanding sales of the new LPs and the first Callas recordings of *Lucia*, *I Puritani* and *Tosca*, were creating a sensational effect, to which we may be sure that Legge was sensitive: his ears were never far from the ground. He was in a quandary. He felt the need to secure Callas in the Requiem somehow or other, so at the last minute he sent her a cable offering her the mezzo-soprano part. She declined. As Schwarzkopf says,[9] she was not about to play 'seconda donna'.

Callas brought that season's performances to a conclusion at the Verona Arena on July 15th with another role new for her: Margherita in Boito's *Mefistofele*. Rossi-Lemeni sang the title role. He thought it 'was a little heavy ... Nevertheless "L'altra notte in fondo al mare" she sang dramatically, and it was a great interpretation, reminding many of ... Muzio.'[10] This proved to be her last engagement at Verona. She had also been announced for some *Aidas* but at rehearsal she had a contretemps with conductor Fausto Cleva, 'Is that the way you do it? Well, that's not the way I do it',[11] and she quit. During the summer de Hidalgo, who had been teaching in Ankara since the war, moved to Milan and she came out to Verona where they renewed their friendship.

After a three-week vacation, which the Meneghinis spent at Lacco Ameno on Ischia, in the middle of August they were back in Milan for Callas to record two operas at La Scala, the first was *La Forza del Destino*, between the 17th and 27th. The rest of Legge's cast is run-of-the-mill. By comparison his devotion to the German repertory is very obvious: compare the ensemble in *La Forza del Destino* with the excellent casts of sets he also made that year with Schwarzkopf. In Strauss's *Der Zigeunerbaron*, *Wiener Blut* and *Eine Nacht in Venedig* she is joined by a front-ranking roster including Gedda, Köth, Kunz, Prey and Dönch, and the Philharmonia under Ackermann; and with the same orchestra, under Karajan she recorded Fiordiligi in *Così fan tutte* with Merriman, Simoneau, Panerai and Bruscantini and *Ariadne auf Naxos* with Streich, Seefried, Schock and Cuénod.

In *La Forza del Destino* there is a blown-out and strident-toned Preziosilla, Nicolai. Tucker's Alvaro reproduces many of the faults that become so obtrusive on Martinelli's later records: the thin tight tone, and pedantic sounding Italian, not coincidentally, one imagines, for he succeeded to much of Martinelli's repertory at the Met. We may be curious why Legge did not engage Corelli, Callas had already sung with him. Perhaps he had not heard him yet. It was 'German' singers that he knew *au fond*; Nicolai Gedda and Christa Ludwig, for example, whose records did much to establish them internationally. At that stage of Corelli's career he had no exclusive recording contract, he had only recorded some arias for Cetra. The Don Carlo, Tagliabue, was fifty-six and he sounds every day of it – he stepped in as a last-minute replacement for Gobbi. It tells us something about Legge's knowledge of Italian opera, or lack of it, that he should have supposed by that stage of Gobbi's career he would record a role requiring so little histrionic skill and yet be so demanding vocally. Rossi-Lemeni may have looked well as Padre Guardiano, and he makes a gesture or two in the direction of characterization, but his voice is not fully supported and air escapes through his tone like leaking gas. There are a large number of comprimari who are by no means merely confined to a cough and spit, yet that seems more than most of them can manage. Legge must have been banking on Callas to sell the set. At any rate it is a relief to listen to Plinio Clabassi's Marchese di Calatrava and Renato Capecchi's Fra Melitone. Serafin, too, is at his best, conveying much of the grand manner.

Although Callas also casts her Leonora in the grand manner and her breath spans are of a truly prodigious length, she is by this stage no longer able to sustain slow tempi without an intrusive wobble. Her tone, too, often curdles, so vitiating much of the pleasure we might have expected. By the time she came to record Amelia in *Un Ballo in Maschera* in 1956 she had speeded up somewhat and we are not so frequently distracted from her musical skill. Nevertheless her Leonora makes us conscious of every section of her music. She sets off the first scene in Act I with fitting simplicity. As Leonora bids her father good-night knowing it to be farewell, her voice exactly reflects the music's minor tonality, rising on 'Ah! padre mio' with untramelled assurance from *e* to *e'* flat. She reminds us of something written half a century ago by W.J. Henderson, doyen of New York critics, in *The Art of Singing*:

'The vocal music of today is not embroidered with runs, trills, groups and ornaments, as the operas of the late seventeenth century were, but it does contain thousands of progressions which can be executed with perfect smoothness and fluency by the agile voice, but by the singer untrained in coloratura only awkwardly and uncertainly.'[12]

After Leonora's father has retired she sings the aria 'Me pellegrina'. It is as attractive and expressive as either of her two more famous arias yet, as is often the way in middle period Verdi, it calls for a soprano with a more brilliant technique. Whereas two notable Leonoras, Ponselle and Zinka Milanov have both recorded 'Pace, pace mio Dio', and Milanov has also recorded the Act II aria, 'Madre, pietosa vergine', we doubt whether either would have been able to articulate this music with anything approaching the accuracy Callas achieves. Later in Act I, however, when she attacks 'Ah! seguirti fino agl'ultimi confini della terra', it is possible to feel that her voice is no longer sufficiently limpid to shape the phrases with the rhythmic freedom she shows only three years before in *I Vespri Siciliani*. Although in the passage beginning 'Ah no, dividerci il fato', we hear the difference between her fluency, her rhythmically exact and clean execution of dotted quavers (eighth notes) and semiquavers (sixteenth notes), and Tucker's aspirated heffalumping. In Act III, in the duet with Padre Guardiano, 'Piu tranquilla', again she shows her just rendition of note values. Each of them is as Verdi requires: contained within a perfect legato, and yet sung with the subtlest rubato so giving life to the rhythm. Under Serafin's guidance she sings the two famous arias with appropriate grandeur, on a tragic scale, underlining Verdi's indications 'come un lamento' and 'con dolore'. Though she secures from the music the maximum of passion, this is not achieved without her voice becoming unsteady and the tone acidulous, especially on exposed sustained phrases.

Straight after *La Forza del Destino*, between August 31st and September 8th, she took part in another recording: Fiorilla in Rossini's *Il Turco in Italia*. This had had its première at La Scala in 1814. Until comparatively recent times, when the Fondazione Rossini was established and some diligent research undertaken, not only were performances, as they were at this revival, cut wholesale but scores of the opera were often incomplete and differed markedly. Rossini had used several pieces before, after his usual fashion, or would do so again. The Act II duet, 'Per piacere alla signora', he also included in *La Gazzetta*, composed two years afterwards, which was first performed at Naples. The edition of *Il Turco* recorded here and used, presumably, at the Eliseo, Rome in 1950 and La Scala in 1955, is skeletal, with many curious cuts of varying sizes, only a modicum of appoggiaturas and with hardly any embellishments.

From the time Callas has lost weight we note the element of contrivance beginning to obtrude in her characterizations. However, spontaneity is essential to Rossini's style. Although Callas's Fiorilla may be remarkably different from her Leonora, it lacks charm and does not engage the listener's sympathy. It might be argued that the fault is the composer's, even his Rosina often sounds nothing more than a shrew, but if we listen to Tetrazzini's classic rendering of 'Una voce poco fa', we hear how it is possible not only to dazzle but charm too. By so doing she adds another dimension to the characterization: the buffo style. As Zeffirelli tells (he directed *Il Turco in Italia* when it was revived at La Scala, in 1955), inducing from Callas something that could be interpreted as comic was not easy: 'She [was] not a funny lady at all . . . but she was greedy [so] I covered Selim [Rossi-Lemeni] in jewels, and I gave her the right image – I told her to play greedy for jewels, exaggerate, if necessary – and that I knew she would have no difficulty doing!'[13] Exaggerating was the nearest Callas could get to comedy. Whereas the quick juxtaposition of moods she employs as Nedda seems false, in opera buffo it is effective. The exceptionable thing about her singing in *Il Turco in Italia* is that we are too aware of the mechanics. As we saw with her Nedda, she is becoming increasingly self-conscious to the point that in her attempts to refine her characterization she loses sight of the basis of secure vocal emission: a correctly supported voice.

After finishing *Il Turco in Italia* Callas took no summer rest but travelled to London with Meneghini, staying again at the Savoy Hotel. This time she was not to appear at Covent Garden but to record two recital albums for EMI: one devoted to Puccini arias and the other a medley of selections. For these, instead of just crossing the Strand and walking through the flower and vegetable market, it was necessary to journey out of London, some twenty-five miles to Watford, where Legge used the Town Hall as a recording studio. The sessions began on September 15th and lasted six days until the 21st. The accompaniment is provided by Serafin and the Philharmonia. There seems to have been much initial discussion as to what excerpts she was to include. Among those rejected were 'Divinità infernal' from *Alceste*, 'D' amore al dolce impero' from *Armida*, 'Bel raggio' from *Semiramide*, 'Selva opaca' from *Guglielmo Tell*, 'Io son Titania' from *Mignon* and Proch's

Varazioni, over this Serafin was especially dismissive. But how much more we should have preferred any of these to the three sides of verismo she did record. By this time her voice had become manifestly unsuited to much of Puccini's music. On the first record, as well as excerpts, from *Gianni Schicchi* and *Suor Angelica*, there are also excerpts, from *Manon Lescaut, La Bohème, Madama Butterfly* and *Turandot*, all of which, in the next three years, Legge would persuade her to record in full.

The London critics, when the Puccini recital was issued that December, were not slow to note the pronounced wobble. It is more obtrusive in the Puccini, and on the other album in selections from Cilea, Catalani and Giordano, than in those from Boito, Rossini, Meyerbeer, Delibes and Verdi. This is because verismo music calls for her to sing with too much emphasis on a blown-up sound in the upper middle register, especially in passage notes, like f' and f' sharp, whereas in florid arias she employs the head voice on these, which is more under control and does not jeopardize her support. Rudolfo Celletti states, incorrectly, that 'from the beginning of her career . . . [the wobble is] particularly noticeable on . . . d'', e'' and especially e'' flat.'[14] In fact, as can be heard on any of her recordings, her highest notes, the head voice, are unaffected; indeed they never become wobbly, with the passage of time they just collapse altogether. It is not the e''s in the Bell Song (on the *Coloratura Lyric* recital), but the exposed b'' in the vocalise at the end of the phrase 'e alla notte ineggiar' which is very wobbly. In the Puccini album we hear the wobble on the last note of Suor Angelica's 'Senza mamma', a prolonged a'' and again, when she attempts a diminuendo on b'' flat at the end of Liù's 'Signore, ascolta!'—though, as she shades the note from middle into head voice, she does manage to get a better control over it.

In the Puccini arias she executes certain details inimitably. For example, the precision of her attack on the unaccompanied g' flat at the beginning of 'Un bel dì' calls to mind Hanslick's tale of Patti's unerringly precise sense of pitch when encoring the Jewel Song in Vienna in 1877: 'Without giving any signal to the orchestra, she attacked the trill on the B natural. The orchestra entered in the next measures, and all was precisely in tune.'[15] Notwithstanding Callas's lack of sense of humour, in Lauretta's 'O mio babbino caro' from *Gianni Schicchi*, she shows that an ironic effect is well within her means on the phrase 'ma per buttarmi in Arno', in which Lauretta threatens to jump into the Arno if her father will not let her marry Rinuccio. The three excerpts from *Turandot* are managed effectively enough, but other singers have since surpassed her achievements: Caballé's Liù and Nilsson's Turandot, to mention but two. She must have been aware that something was missing from her Madama Butterfly, for though the following year she recorded it complete and undertook it three times in Chicago, these were the only times she sang it. Both her Mimì and Manon Lescaut mistake artfulness for artistry. None of Puccini's roles are sufficiently ambitious or vocally rewarding to justify the attentions of a great Norma: could one imagine, say, Lilli Lehmann or Ponselle,[16] undertaking any of them?

In the *Coloratura Lyric* recital the third versimo side commences with two arias from Cilea's *Adriana Lecouvreur*. Callas does not, like Muzio, begin the first of these with the bit of declamation from Racine, which Adriana is rehearsing; this might only have sounded like those other unfortunate bits of spoken dialogue we have noted above. She starts with the recitative, 'Ecco, respiro ancella'. Her interpretation benefits from her remarkably expansive breath span, and her control of line and moulding of phrases reveals just how musically expressive it can sound. This piece is untypical of verismo, for it makes its effect by being sung simply. If we compare Callas's singing with the expostulatory manner of Olivero, who in the 1960s was still undertaking Adriana, we can hear just how decadent the verismo style had become. On the other hand, in an aria which works up to a dramatic climax, that of Maddalena from *Andrea Chénier*, Callas's voice becomes squally and over-driven. This piece, ill-written for the voice, creates special problems for her. It is a pity that she does not follow convention by snipping out a few measures before the awkwardly placed climactic b''.

She concludes the side with Margherita's 'L'altra notte' from *Mefistofele*. This is not especially taxing in range, rising only to a sustained a'' and a fleeting b'' in the cadenza, but the trills and coloratura make it much more demanding. In this music Callas revolutionizes performance practice by not only correctly singing all the written notes, but she also understands implicitly what the dramatic situation calls for in her treatment of the cadenzas at the end of each verse. She makes something quite extraordinary out of these, not only singing them accurately (we note how she resolves the trills to the upper note as written), but also shaping them with her customary rhythmic freedom. Throughout the remarkable length of her phrases, her choice of vocal colours, her command of rubato and her dynamic range reveal much more than one had thought the music contained. It becomes not just another verismo aria, after the fashion of Muzio or Tebaldi: Callas makes us aware it is one of the last Mad Scenes.

But it is the other side of this record that is more remarkable. Notwithstanding Callas's lack of a sense of humour, her 'Una voce poco fa' ranks second only to Tetrazzini's amongst countless recorded versions. Her florid singing is still remarkable today, but in the 1950s it created a sensation. Although Serafin's slow tempo does not encourage her to produce sparkling vocalism, her coloratura is the very quintessence of the term. In 1954, before the bel canto revival was under way, she sings unwritten fioritura unashamedly, as in Tetrazzini's day. The embellishments she adds are all traditional, and can be found in Ricci's collection. She executes them all accurately and expressively. As we noted above, in her recording of Donna Anna's 'Non mi dir', on the word 'docile', at the beginning of the second verse, so musical is her singing that her voice seems to anticipate the succeeding flute staccato passage. In Janine Reiss' words, she 'sought to match the colours in her voice to the orchestra'.[17] We note also another instrumental effect: the difference between her production of the last note, a b'', at the end of the cadenza in the first verse, which she produces wholly in head voice, from the same note at the end of the aria, in which she mixes middle with head voice. Later recordings of her singing this music survive, but in none of them is she so assured, musically or vocally. Years later, when she talks about interpreting this aria,[18] she attempts to make a virtue out of what for her, as recordings abundantly testify, soon becomes a necessity. She does not recommend some of the ornaments she herself includes in the 1954 recording, excusing herself by clumsily re-telling a story she seems only half to remember, about Rossini reproving a singer: actually Patti. Saint-Saens records precisely what happened.

'When [Patti] had sung "Una voce poco fa" from *Barbiere*, Rossini said to her, after the usual compliments, "Who wrote that aria you just sang?" ... "I am fully aware", he said, "that arias should be embellished. That's what they are there for – but not to leave a note of them even in the recitatives! That is too much!" In his irritation he complained that sopranos persisted in singing this aria which was written for a contralto and did not sing what had been written for sopranos at all. On the other hand the diva was irritated too. She thought the matter over and realised that it would be serious to have Rossini for an enemy. So some days later she went to ask his advice. It was well that she took it, for her talent though brilliant and fascinating [she was then still only in her teens] was not as yet fully formed. Two months after this incident, Patti sang the arias from *La Gazza Ladra* and *Semiramide*, with the maestro as her accompanist. And she combined with her brilliancy the absolute correctness which she always showed thereafter.'[19]

XI

1954–1955

I N THE LAST week of September Callas returned from London to
Verona then, at the beginning of October, she sang a couple of Lucias
at the Donizetti, Bergamo, before departing for the United States. Not
for New York but for Chicago, where she was to have made her U.S.
début seven years before. In recent years performances had been given
there either by touring companies or scratch ensembles, but now a
young trio, Carol Fox, Lawrence Kelly and Nicola Rescigno, had
come forward determined to fill the gap. It was at the end of 1953
that they asked Ettore Verna, an Italian agent, to enquire whether
Callas would be interested in appearing in Chicago. That January he
was able to tell them that she was willing to come, notwithstanding
memories of Bagarozy. In February they founded the Lyric Theater
of Chicago, and gave a couple of curtain-raisers: *Don Giovanni* with
Rossi-Lemeni, John Brownlee, Léopold Simoneau, Eleanor Steber and
Bidú Sayão under Rescigno, just to show they could. After the success
of the initial venture they felt ready to mount an inaugural season and
in May Fox flew off to Europe. She visited Callas at Verona, where she
found her indisposed with 'flu. She persuaded her to sign a contract, for
$2,000 a performance, twice the Metropolitan ceiling, and she would
sing three roles: Norma, Violetta and Lucia. With her Fox secured
a distinguished roster of front-ranking artists led by Simionato, de
Stefano, Gobbi and Rossi-Lemeni.

Kelly remembers the sub-zero temperature at Chicago airport on
that October day when he went to meet Callas. He had organized
a full press delegation who, much to their surprise, or maybe
disappointment, found the arriving prima donna unexpectedly de-
mure. She thanked everyone, introduced her husband, accepted a
bouquet from members of the chorus, checked her luggage and was
escorted to the Ambassador West Hotel. On the way she asked all
manner of questions, about the rehearsal schedule, even about ticket
sales. In spite of her arduous journey she insisted on meeting the

maestro immediately. She had, she said, come early so that she might begin rehearsals at once. Rescigno recalls that first rehearsal: 'I sat down at the piano in front of her and played through the whole of *Norma*. I wasn't a Serafin, or any of those great conductors. It was a test, Maria said she would feel more comfortable. She had such integrity that if I hadn't been up to par then, she wouldn't have made any bones about it. She was by far the easiest singer I have ever conducted because of her musicality. Her sense of everything that makes a performance vital was instinctive.'[1] She went shopping at the local supermarket, bought food and cooked meals. Since Meneghini could not speak English he could not play supporting role, so she had to deal with business affairs herself; and she was ready for almost any number of rehearsals. The impression she made on the fledgling company was certainly at odds with tales of egocentric divas.

The season began on November 1st with *Norma*. On opening night the company backstage were so preoccupied that no one remembered to give Callas her cue before the last act, the protagonist's most taxing act, yet by some musical telepathy, she was on stage and ready to make her entrance at the right moment. It was agreed that 'the Lyric had paid for a star attraction and she gave full measure'.[2] About her performance next day the press was enthusiastic: Cassidy in the *Tribune*, presumably with memories of her Verona Gioconda two summers before, wouldn't have recognized her: 'She is wand slim, beautiful as a tragic mask . . . In the shift towards coloratura roles there is a slight unsteadiness in some sustained upper tones. But to me her voice is more beautiful in colour, more even throughout the range, than it used to be. Her range is formidable, and her technique dazzling.'[3] James Hinton Jnr., in *Opera*, noted how 'she moved with lithe control, never wasted a gesture, and in general, brought to the visual side of her interpretation the same concentration and vitality of purpose that characterized her singing . . . Especially at the outset there was a good deal of . . . cloudy, bottled-up sound . . . particularly on upper tones . . . and some high [notes] . . . were wavery. [But] the amazing thing . . . hearing her for the first time in the theatre was that even the most imperfectly produced tones projected completely.'[4] René Devries, in the *Musical Courier*, thought '[she] guides her voice as a 'cellist uses his instrument to achieve a fine legato'.[5] Irving Kolodin, in the *Saturday Review*, summed up: 'vocally . . . it is substantially an instrumental concept of the human voice she espouses . . . She works on, and with, the voice almost externally. Now shading it to a thine line of filigree . . . later exploding its vengeful power in a denunciation of the perfidious Pollione. It is a measure of [her] increasing command of her remarkable instrument that ... "Casta Diva" was more even, better articulated than the recorded one, that she flung off Cs with abandon, and a climaxing D at the end of Act II with assurance.'[6]

No first performance by a new opera company since the Second World War had received such acclaim. 'There was a good deal that was wrong, and more that was at least debatable, but nobody said so very loudly.'[7] All they noticed was Callas, then at the summit of her career and returning, at last, to the country of her birth. She was quickly becoming the most celebrated opera singer of her day, and her peculiar vocal skills were helping to revive an almost forgotten repertory. Also in the cast were a number of other first-rate singers who, though known from the then rapidly expanding LP market, were not currently on the Met's roster of artists. Chicago could hold its head high. The failure of various attempts to mount opera there on a fitting scale during the previous decade was vindicated. Setting the seal on the new régime in the audience on first night were great names from the city's operatic past: Mary Garden, Raisa, Turner, Edith Mason, Martinelli and conductor Giorgio Polacco. Directly after the performance Angel Records, the Sorias and Legge, played host at a ball for the benefit of the Illinois Opera Guild at the Hilton Hotel. Callas and Meneghini attended in company with her father, Fox, Kelly and Rescigno and the rest of the cast: Simionato, Mirto Picchi and Rossi-Lemeni. Meanwhile, while Chicago was celebrating, Bagarozy, who had been silent during the previous six and a half years, filed suit against Callas claiming that he had spent $85,000 on her career, that she had signed a contract entitling him to receive ten per cent of all her earnings, and that his wife had coached her without being paid. Callas dismissed his claims as risible: he had done nothing to promote her career, and that his wife had coached her was 'an enormous, preposterous, and ridiculous lie'.[8]

Her second role in Chicago was Violetta, on November 8th, and like Norma and Lucia she undertook two performances of it, with Simoneau and Gobbi. Gobbi had only sung with her on one previous occasion, in *La Traviata* in São Paulo three years before; it was not until a decade passed, in 1964, that they would enjoy their great successes in *Tosca* in London, Paris and New York. Gobbi tells[9] how the only disagreement he and Callas ever had took place at one of the Chicago *Traviatas*. Violetta had left the stage before the end of Act II. After Germont's aria 'Di provenza il mar', part of the curtain stuck fast so, in response to the stagehands' request, he went out and took a number of bows while they got it working again. Meneghini saw Gobbi taking what seemed to him endless bows and, not understanding the reason, rushed backstage to tell Callas. The interval had gone on an inordinate length of time when Gobbi received a summons to come immediately to her dressing room. When he arrived she imperiously ordered him to shut the door, as if he were a lackey, he recalls, and told him that if he ever did such a thing again she would ruin his career. He then took a deep breath, calmly explained what had happened, and asked that the performance should continue without further delay, otherwise he would have to go out and tell the audience precisely what had happened. The opera proceeded as usual. But just before the last act was to begin and Gobbi was on stage checking production details, he heard a rueful voice from Violetta's bed asking, in Veronese dialect, whether he was still angry with her. No, he said, biting his tongue; he understood why she had felt aggrieved and they should forget it.

Almost two years had elapsed since Callas had last undertaken Violetta, in January 1953 in Rome, since which time she had lost weight, and to suit her new slim figure she had Biki create her costumes. By all accounts she sang it 'extremely well [and] you never heard a suspicion of wobble',[10] but it was not her singing of this performance, rather the one in São Paulo, that Gobbi remembers for her surpassing vocal prowess. Nor had she yet made out of Violetta a supreme dramatic impersonation, as she would the following season at La Scala under Visconti's direction. As Hinton wrote in *Opera*: 'the idea of Miss Callas mounting a pyre whose construction and lighting she has herself ordered is quite believable. So is the idea of Miss Callas travelling about in a chariot drawn by dragons. But belief in the idea of Miss Callas lying poor and neglected in a furnished room is too much to ask of any audience.'[11] Cassidy tells how after a *Traviata* she went round to the Ambassador Hotel to see her and on the way stopped off at Elizabeth Arden's to get a lipstick to match the bow on her Act III ball gown. When Callas saw it she snatched it 'greedily . . . saying, "I love presents . . . It's the colour of the bow on my dress. How wonderful."'[12]

Her last part in her inaugural Chicago season was Lucia. She sang the first performance on November 15th. Cassidy was quite carried away: 'An innocent bystander wandering in to . . . Lucia . . . might have thought Donizetti had scored the Mad Scene for the audience. [There was] an avalanche of applause . . . roars growing steadily hoarser . . . and a standing ovation . . . To use a voice of that size with such superb technical command, and to subordinate that technique to the mood of the music – that is singing in the grand manner.'[13] Hinton had no reservations this time: 'She was in virtually flawless voice, and her singing throughout was almost unbelievably lovely, with the tone always clean and forward, the phrasing aristocratic, and the execution of colortura phenomenally crisp and well articulated . . . [H]aving heard Miss Callas I cannot imagine why anyone would [prefer the traditional Lucia], except out of sheer perversity. It was not so much the size of the voice that told . . . It was the play of colour and the sense of reserve power that could be brought to bear . . . in climaxes. The effect was far less that of a dramatic soprano with an exceptional top than it was a huge soprano leggero with great variety of colour and practically unlimited dynamics.'[14] If we listen to either the Mexico *Lucia* of 1952 or the EMI recording of 1953 we note how her voice does sound 'a dramatic soprano with an exceptional top'; but by 1954, as we can hear at La Scala, although her technique has become more proficient, the voice has slimmed down so she has become in effect 'a huge soprano leggero'. After the last Chicago *Lucia* on November 17th, Kelly recalls how 'Callas took 22 solo curtain calls and received a seventeen minute standing, screaming ovation.'[15] The next day she flew back to Italy with Meneghini, declining to sign a contract for the next season: 'She wanted to appraise the total picture from her home base, La Scala'.[16] There had, however, been considerable discussion as to her undertaking new roles and she had even taken a score of *Carmen* to look over.[17]

Callas's Lucia in 1954 had not yet lost the vaunting ease of execution that made it so remarkable, but from this time the scale of her singing would diminish rapidly, with the highest notes becoming increasingly difficult for her to execute freely. Inevitably, the more preoccupied she became with them, the more studied-sounding her singing grew. Her drastic regime was a reflection of her preoccupation with becoming a great actress, it was not enough for her being a unique singer. It was at this time that Visconti commenced directing opera, she was the magnet that attracted him, the trail-blazer setting the pace in the revival of early nineteenth-century operas. He tells how he 'had already admired her for many years [even when] . . . she was fat, but beautiful on stage . . . She was already distinctive. Her gestures thrilled you.'[18]

It was on the opening night of the 1954 La Scala season, December 7th, that Visconti came to direct opera for the first time, with Callas in Spontini's *La Vestale*. She had herself asked that *La*

Vestale be revived, her attention having first been drawn to it by
Ponselle's records of Giulia's arias. Although this was the operatic
début of Visconti, a scion of a noble family whose grandfather had
been Sovrintendente at La Scala before the First World War, he
already enjoyed a distinguished career in the Italian theatre, where
he directed plays and dramatic adaptations. In the 1930s he worked
on films with Jean Renoir. After the war he concentrated at first on
modern realist dramas, like *Ossessione* and *La terra trema*, then, in
1953, he directed his first colour film, *Senso*. This has a historical
setting and derives from a novel of Camillo Boito, brother of the
composer. Set during the Italo-Austrian war of 1866, one of its scenes
takes place at the Fenice, Venice during a performance of *Il Trovatore*.
Visconti describes how 'I filmed . . . from a box nearly on the stage,
and the part where Leonora comes out on to the apron was inspired
by Maria. On one occasion I went to see her Leonora at La Scala. I
had not booked, I had just arrived in Milan and I asked Ghiringhelli
to let me sit in his box which is almost on the stage. As Maria sang she
. . . kept moving forward on the apron . . . I had the strange sensation
of being myself on stage and Leonora off-stage.'[19]

It was with Visconti's production of *La Vestale* that it can be
said that stage directors joined conductors and singers: the operatic
trinity. There had been remarkable stage directors before, especially
in Germany, where Reinhardt had been busy since the beginning of
the century; but it was not until 1954 that in Italy a singer as singular
as Callas appeared attracting a director of the calibre of Visconti. The
production of *La Vestale* created a sensation. It was the ultimate in
magnificence and the budget, $140,000, broke all previous records.
The conductor, Votto, recalls how Visconti 'wanted every detail
perfect . . . In the finale there is an allegory where Jove, the god,
comes forth from heaven and sits at table with the principals to bless
them. This was an apparition that lasted two or three minutes – the
music does not last any longer. On the table he placed authentic silver,
not stage props. I don't know where he got them from. Perhaps from
a museum, but it was all real. He was starting something new with this
production.'[20] At the glittering première Toscanini was in a stage-box;
there was talk that he would open the new smaller auditorium, the
Piccola Scala, later that season with *Falstaff*. At one point 'Callas . . .
walked over to the stage-box and graciously handed him a bouquet of
flowers thrown to her . . . the audience went wild.'[21]

With *La Vestale* Visconti ushered in a new style of opera production, although it was not for some while that it was properly

appreciated. In this the work is deliberately alienated from the time indicated in the libretto by the period of its composition. Thus, Malipiero, in *Opera*, failed to appreciate that Zuffi, the set designer, following Visconti, had sought to recreate Classical Rome through Napoleonic France: that the anachronistic costumes were purposefully designed with 'gilded capitals, which reminded one more of the *ottocento* of Piermarini rather than of pre-Christian Rome'; that the 'frightful conglomeration of colours', 'feathered headgear . . . and yards of ribbon',[22] which he complained of were deliberate: Spontini was writing in France in 1807, not in pre-Christian Rome.

A recording made on opening night suggests that though the singers might have looked well they sounded variable. Corelli, making his La Scala début as Licinio, sings somewhat crudely but the voice has an appropriately heroic timbre that is more than acceptable. Though he is guilty of aspirating some of the more exacting intervals, we feel this has to do with lack of practice rather than any throatiness in his tone. Stignani was typecast playing the Gran Vestale, a kind of Mother Superior. She reverses the usual Italian sin of her generation by taking the middle register down too low rather than the chest register up too high. The result is that her tone sounds old, but that is not inappropriate in this role. Enzo Sordello, as Cinna, manages his music adequately, and Rossi-Lemeni's Sommo Sacerdote is after his usual fashion. The dim recording suggests that, save for Callas, it must have been Visconti, and de Jouy's melodrama, rather than Spontini's music that took precedence. Certainly Votto's reading of the score, with a lack of appoggiaturas, rigid and unimaginative tempi, especially in the recitatives, which are much cut about, does not suggest confidence in the music or any knowledge of the authentic style. Although she alone phrases her music expressively, Callas can make nothing special out of her part; perhaps there is nothing special to make. In her Act I aria 'Il vedro fra momenti, a mio bene!' we hear how, by her skilful use of upward portamenti, she does her best to make the music cohere and give it shape. The Act II aria 'Tu che invoco' she executes nimbly and includes a cadenza at the end, which she would not in later years when she sang it in concert. In the same act comes a short andante, 'O nume tutelar', a piece distinguished by her beautifully shaped phrasing with perfect triplets and we note how deftly, after the word 'latona', she marks a comma in the phrasing, interrupting but not breaking the line. But, by this time her voice is no longer of the size or limpidity of only a year before, and her tone has become harder and thinner.

It was during the rehearsals of *La Vestale*, when Callas had become physically, at least, a new woman, that Visconti describes her as having fallen in love with him. 'It was a stupid thing all in her mind. Like so many Greeks she had a possessive streak, and there were many jealous scenes. She hated Corelli because he was handsome. It made her nervous, she was wary of handsome people. She was always watching to see I didn't give him more attention than her.'[23] But just how profound this was we may question. There is nothing very surprising in a chemist's daughter being enthralled by a duke; Visconti was a nobleman, his background worlds away from hers. She was always prepared to sit like Paul at the feet of Gamaliel, as she had been before Serafin and Toscanini. At first she was attracted to Visconti because she thought, rightly, that he would assist her satisfy another of her ambitions; to become as great an actress as she was singer. But his bad language and his affectation of vulgarity, which he deliberately flaunted, came increasingly to affront her *petite bourgeoise* susceptibilities. No doubt partly, at least, this was his intention; it flattered him to project a macho-like image of himself. But he went too far and she tired of him, though not before she had learned from him all she could. Through him she not only metamorphosed her acting technique but she also got him to assist her choosing many of the works of art that the Meneghinis were buying at that time for their new Milan home into which they were moving in the new year. Meneghini reproduces a lot of Visconti's correspondence,[24] the tone of which certainly suggests that he never did more than play the role of *cavaliere servente*. Meneghini dismisses various tales about them: 'that one evening . . . [Callas] was so overcome by the desire to embrace Visconti that she left the theatre during the . . . interval wearing her costume and make-up, and joined [him] . . . nearby at the Biffi Scala.' At that time Callas's life was built about La Scala; while she was its queen she devoted herself solely to it. It was not until after she had lost her voice, and so lost her identity, that she welcomed distraction and ran off with Onassis. But that is another story. As a singer she had placed herself at Serafin's feet and as an actress she did so at Visconti's, but his imputation that she was sexually motivated sounds a typical piece of homosexual self-aggrandisement.

After five performances of Giulia Callas's last engagement in 1954 was on December 27th with a Martini-Rossi broadcast from the Teatro del Casino, San Remo. For this the RAI orchestra was conducted by Simonetto and Gigli joined her, regrettably they did not duet. Her programme was announced to include 'Anch'io dischiuso' from *Nabucco*, but this she seems to have realised she had already included in a RAI concert so she substituted Dinorah's 'Ombra leggera'. A recording reveals a performance very similar to the one she had made for EMI in Watford that September, except that she introduces it with part of the recitative. 'Tutte le torture' from *Il Serraglio*, which is impressive and gives an idea of the effect she must have created at La Scala two and a half years before, although it is possible to feel that she might have made a more telling effect at the bottom of her voice, and in 'D'amore al dolce impero' from *Armida* she not only cuts some of the embellishments she sang in Florence but this is one of the very few occasions when she aspirates an interval. But it is her first surviving performance in any language other than Italian – the air 'Depuis le jour' from Charpentier's *Louise* – which reveals just how profoundly unsuited her voice was to 'modern' opera. She may phrase it expressively, but it requires the absolute mastery of vocal control of a Melba, a Garden or a Caballé, not the wavery dribbling she contrives.

Her next role at La Scala proved another example of her miscalculating the limits of her talent: Maddalena in Giordano's *Andrea Chénier*, of which she undertook six performances beginning on January 8th 1955. Apparently it had originally been the intention of La Scala to offer *Il Trovatore* with del Monaco, but he demurred, 'he said he had had an attack of appendicitis',[25] so he offered *Andrea Chénier* in its place. Although he could have transposed 'Di quella pira' down into B if not B flat, for the last measures of the final duet in *Chénier* are taken down a semitone, it seems likely that there was less effort in his making an impression as Chénier than as Manrico, especially if he had to share it with Callas's Leonora. Although photographs of her Maddalena show her looking a beautiful young débutante in *ancien régime* attire yet, as Malipiero in *Opera* thought 'she was wasted . . . in this part, which she nevertheless sustained with dignity'.[26] Harewood saw her in it. He had not seen her since she lost weight, and he expresses surprise at the change in her appearance. '[Although] this was not . . . the type of role in which she had won fame [yet] by the time I caught it, she was completely assured and what I saw and heard was a revelation.' It was later when she met him again that she told him something she would repeat often: 'If you want to appreciate me, you must hear me often. I know I vary, that the voice varies, but I am always trying to do something and only sometimes will it be successful. If you don't come often you won't catch the good performances.'[27] Nevertheless she did not repeat Maddalena.

She returned to the Rome Opera on January 22nd for four performances of *Medea*. Sets, costumes and Wallmann's production were brought from La Scala to accompany her. It was conducted by Santini, and the rest of the cast included Barbieri, Albanese, Tucci and Christoff. After one of the performances Christoff became furious because of the number of solo bows Callas took: barring her way, he told her, 'either we all go out together, or no one goes out'.[28] Perhaps it was not so surprising she took so many: she needed something to console her. Medea's great cape had rubbed her neck so badly she had developed a painful boil. Back in Milan again, after the final two Maddalenas she was obliged to take to her bed, and the next La Scala production, *La Sonnambula*, announced to open on February 17th, was postponed for two weeks.

It was at this time that Kelly came over to Milan from Chicago to endeavour to persuade her to sign up for another season that autumn. He tells how he was permitted a look at her boil: 'It was the size of a silver dollar and quite horrible.'[29] Meneghini and Callas kept him dallying in Milan throughout the rehearsal period of *La Sonnambula*. At first he passed the days at the Grand Hotel then, when she was well enough, he would accompany them to La Scala for rehearsals, in the evenings they would dine at the Biffi, La Scala's restaurant. Although Kelly remembers he 'ate strictly off the bill of fare . . . when the Meneghini bill was totted up it was always less than mine',[30] presumably he noted this because he always paid for them! At length after satisfying innumerable new demands thought up by Meneghini, and agreeing 'to make a specific guarantee to . . . protect her from any legal harassment Bagarozy might cause her',[31] he persuaded her to sign the contract. 'Then she turned to [him] and . . . said: "You should sign up Renata Tebaldi . . . your audiences will have the opportunity to compare us and your season will be even more successful."'[32] And so he did.

It was on March 5th that Callas sang in the second of Visconti's La Scala productions: Amina in Bellini's *La Sonnambula*. Bernstein and Visconti made a perfect partnership. If, by the beginning of 1955, Callas's voice had become too thin to compete with Tebaldi as Maddalena, it was perfect for Amina. We hear how, reducing it to half-cock, she executes the most intricate coloratura with phenomenal accuracy. She had always wanted to sing Amina. De Hidalgo tells[33] of the effect it had on her as she listened to an excerpt sung by another pupil as long ago as 1940, when she was studying in Athens. Visconti's production was conceived to give an impression of the turning of the leaves in an old album. Callas was arrayed as Malibran or Grisi might have been; her hair was dark again, and she was dressed as a simple village maiden, but with a diva's diamonds – and Bernstein's ornaments reflect these. He builds the musical architecture around Callas, tosses off the choruses at prodigious speeds and encourages her to execute the coda to the Act I cabaletta, 'Sovra il sen', with phenomenal agility and rapidity. In the third verse (more properly the beginning of the second) there is one supremely ambitious passage: upward staccati rise to e'' flat on the phrase 'egli e il cor . . .' then descend more than two octaves to a flat in three bars '. . . che i suoi contenti non ha forza a sostener'. It may be difficult to imagine today the sensation these variants caused, for at that time even the most modest gesture in the direction of interpolated fioritura raised eyebrows. Bernstein's ornaments suggest he was familiar with the legend of Bellini meeting Malibran in London, after her performance of Amina at which the composer had been carried away by her singing in the finale, on the phrase 'ah! m'abbraccia'; here too Callas contrives an effect, deploying her vocal registers differently in each verse. In the second she does not simply embellish the melody but, as she does in the reprise of the Brindisi in *Macbeth* in 1952, she pulls out all the stops, like an organist, to create something unique. At this point Visconti had her, in the style of a diva of Bellini's day, come down to the front of the stage and, with the house lights turned up, give an exhibition of virtuosity. After the opera was over the evening was completed, in early nineteenth-century style, with two short ballets.

It was in April that the Meneghinis changed their abode. During the last three and a half years, though Callas was based at La Scala, they were still living in Verona. By this time their need to find somewhere in Milan and give up rooms at the Grand Hotel led them to purchase a town house, Via Buonarroti 40, 'a little villa with large trees in the front and a garden at the back',[34] which they had furnished throughout in eighteenth-century Venetian style. Here in the mornings Callas would practise at the piano on a glassed-in terrace. Meneghini had it furnished by Tamaglini, a Milanese interior decorator. The rooms had white walls and red and grey marble floors. There was a mixture of antiques, carpets, paintings and statuary: Visconti helped them choose a pair of blackamoors. In juxtaposition were luxurious modern fittings and a kitchen in the American style, of which Callas was inordinately proud. In *Oggi* a photograph of Callas appeared in the kitchen clad in a Biki creation, draped in an apron concentrating attentively, minus her spectacles, on what looks like a measuring cup. Since without them she could see even less than we can here, tales of her culinary disasters do not seem improbable.

The two embellished stanzas of 'Sovra il sen' from *La Sonnambula* with the ornaments Callas sang at La Scala in 1955 (courtesy Aspinall: Roberts).

XII

1955

B Y THE SPRING of 1955 Callas was becoming widely known as a prima donna through her gramophone records and through her new svelte image. Although the conflict between the singer's vaunting ambition and her physical febrility had not yet begun to manifest itself conspicuously, there were already portents in the wind. During the later 1950s the pressures on her would grow increasingly, as we shall see, and she would find herself caught up in a maelstrom, divided between the woman and the singer. The dedication with which she had until this time single-mindedly, almost ruthlessly, applied herself to becoming a great singer, would become more difficult to cope with: not only because her life was beginning to develop other dimensions, each of which demanded a part of the concentration she had been accustomed to reserve solely for her singing, but also because her physical mutation had caused her to lose weight and so, inevitably, her voice began to start to contract, not only in size but also in range. In the next few years it would become less responsive and increasingly less able to contend with the escalating demands she made of it. Throughout the rest of the 1950s it went on steadily shrinking, regardless of whether she was singing frequently, as she was this season, or hardly at all, as in 1960. Although she did not lose her voice through misusing it, she had soon lost sufficient strength to be able to support it. It was her inability, or refusal, to perceive the consequences of the metabolic changes she had wreaked upon herself that led so swiftly to the crises that from this time began rapidly to overtake her.

Ten *La Sonnambula*s were planned and three days after the eighth, on April 15th, she undertook Fiorilla in *Il Turco in Italia*, her fourth opera that season at La Scala. She was joined by substantially the same ensemble she had sung with at the Eliseo, Rome in 1950, except that this time the production was by Zeffirelli. Zeffirelli had worked first in the legitimate theatre with Visconti, but he came to opera on his own before his mentor. This was, in fact, the third production he had worked on at La Scala. He had been engaged first in the 1952/3 season designing sets and costumes for Pavolini's production of Rossini's *L'Italiana in Algeri*. It was as a result of Pavolini's indisposition during rehearsals that Zeffirelli stood in for him so when, at the last minute, Pavolini withdrew, he asked Ghiringhelli if he could direct it, as he tells,[1] and much to his amazement Ghiringhelli assented. With the success of this initial venture he both designed sets and costumes and produced Rossini's *La Cenerentola* with Simionato; and then, four days after the beginning of this season with Visconti's production of Spontini's *La Vestale*, Zeffirelli produced Donizetti's *L'Elisir d'Amore*.

Like Visconti, Zeffirelli had admired Callas since the early 1950s. He tells how she came to one of the performances of *La Cenerentola* and enjoyed it so much that, remembering her success with *Il Turco in Italia*, she suggested he might like to direct her in it. In the wake of Visconti's productions of *La Vestale* and *La Sonnambula* Zeffirelli determined to create a completely different effect, so he went down to Naples, where *Il Turco* is set, to get the feel of 'Neapolitan folk art with its bright peasant scenes and with . . . the traditional Pulcinella shows'.[2] He set the opera in the period of its composition, but when rehearsals started Callas did not care for the costumes. She chided Zeffirelli: 'All that dieting and you give me a waistline up here. No one will see how slim I am.'[3] During rehearsals she would go to the seamstress and secretly get her to lower the waistline but then, just as secretly, Zeffirelli got her to take it back up again. At this time Callas was anxious to reveal just how much weight she had lost and she took as her model Audrey Hepburn, whose success in the film *Roman Holiday* had set a style.

Her next role at La Scala, on May 28th, was Violetta in *La Traviata* with di Stefano and Bastianini, conducted by Giulini. This was another Visconti production, his third that season, and it caused the biggest sensation. After four performances it would be revived the following season. Visconti had been determined to direct Callas in it for some while. In June 1954 he wrote to Meneghini stressing how significant he regarded it: '[it] should represent . . . her aim, her interpretative masterpiece, her artistic culmination, her Ninth Symphony.'[4] The scenery and costumes were by Lila de Nobili. Visconti explains how 'de Nobili and I changed the story to the *fin de siècle* . . . Maria look[ed] wonderful in costumes of that epoch. She was tall and slender, and in a gown with a tight bodice, a bustle and long train . . . I sought to make her a little of Duse, a little of

Rachel and a little of Bernhardt.'[5] Sequi remembers 'it was something unbelievable, I had never seen anything like it before. People said it was extremely realistic, but in fact it was not so much realistic as poetic. A kind of dream of the romantic epoch. Callas's Violetta had completely changed from Rome in 1953, when I first saw it. In those days she sang it with great drama and great power, but at La Scala it was very refined and full of nuance. And there was the marvellous effect of de Nobili's settings. She had the sure touch of the real artist, a capacity for capturing the mood of the period. She could convey the poetic distance – "allontanamento". Everything looked real yet, when you examined closely the oriental vases, screens and marble they were all painted. It was all *trompe l'oeil*.'[6]

Giulini tells how 'Visconti began his staging with the cast [and] we worked alone with Maria over an extended period. We three arrived at her characterization . . . a complete rapport between words, music and action. [He] . . . had incredible sensitivity to romantic opera. Each of Maria's gestures he determined solely on musical values.'[7] Visconti explained: 'I gave Callas a freedom to operate within a general framework . . . I always allowed her to do what she wanted. One example, in Act I, in "Sempre libera", the moment Violetta hears Alfredo's voice I told her, run downstage to the window, but how you run is up to you. And she would find her own way of doing it. Not only that but once she found it, she would always execute each action in exactly the same way. She was one of those artists who, having worked out and perfected a detail, did not keep on changing it.'[8]

Today Visconti's production might seem a modest gesture in the direction of realism, yet its appearance was of a beauty, photographs testify, that had certainly not been equalled until then; and it became the precursor of countless *La Traviatas*. In Act I much of the atmosphere was created by the choice of sombre colours suggestive of death. De Nobili's costumes were black, deep red and gold. Chorus members were all dressed differently, as personalities, and they generated the atmosphere of a real party. After they had gone off everything looked stale, the floral decorations had wilted, the table was a mess, plates heaped on it, fans on the floor, and chairs all over the place. Annina came in, extinguished the candles, and Violetta was left alone. As she sang 'Ah! fors è lui' she took the pins out of her hair and let it fall then, when she began 'Follie' she stood up, leant back against the table and kicked off her shoes. At the time such business seemed revolutionary and outraged many of the critics; but the public was totally enthralled.

Act II represented a complete change of mood. For this de Nobili created a pastoral scene and the predominant colours were pale greens and blues. The background was merely suggestive, an evocation: a country villa draped in a heavy arboreal setting, thick foliage, shutters drawn to keep out the sunlight, and a driveway leading to tall garden gates. As the eye travelled nearer, impressions became more real: a parasol, a wicker table, chairs and cushions. Various pieces of garden bric-à-brac lay around: a watering can, wheelbarrow, fork and hose. The effect was to concentrate attention on the intimate front-stage drama. The costumes too were realistic: for Callas's Violetta an afternoon gown Visconti had had copied from a daguerrotype portraying Sarah Bernhardt as Marguerite Gautier in *La Dame aux camélias*.

In Act III, at Flora's party, Violetta was draped in a fitted gown of red satin, complete with bustle, red camellias and a train. On her dress were rubies and around her neck she wore a choker of them. For the setting de Nobili had contrived a hothouse atmosphere with lush plants. Visconti had the women in the chorus simply dressed and the men in black so making a contrast with the multi-coloured gypsies and florid toreadors. When the curtain went up on Act IV, Violetta's bedroom, the lugubrious atmosphere was reinforced by dim lighting; at the back of the stage removal men could be seen taking away furniture, against a wall was a ladder they were using, perhaps to remove a painting. When the chorus sang, off-stage, shadows played across the walls; 'for Violetta the world had become nothing but shadows'.[9] In the final minutes, after the return of Alfredo, Visconti underlined the drama by getting Violetta to put on the cloak and gloves Annina gave her and then try to fix the bonnet: But her hands had already grown stiff with the imminence of death; she could not manage it and it fell off.

Meneghini relates[10] an incident that took place at the première during the last minutes. As often as not by then he was dozing, but on this occasion he was wide awake. He was sitting in a box with Visconti and they had reached the point in the last act where Callas tries to fix on her bonnet. He tells how exasperated Visconti became when it fell off, apparently accidentally. But Meneghini knew there was nothing accidental about it; Callas had determined it should fall off. She was prepared to go along with a stage director's devices, except when they conflicted with her ability to represent the music fully. But the notion of her having to wear a bonnet at such a critical moment, so obscuring her face to the upper reaches of the house, to

her seemed absurd and so she had no hesitation in ridding herself of
it.

The copious rehearsals for *La Traviata* were not much to di
Stefano's taste: he was invariably unpunctual and uninterested.
Visconti remembers how vexed Callas became, 'It's a lack of respect
for me, a lack of regard and also for you!'[11] But Visconti brushed
di Stefano's behaviour aside, his coming late would prove his own
problem. So it was to prove, for the success of Callas and Visconti
was too much for di Stefano and after she was persuaded to take a solo
bow he rushed back to the dressing room and left that night for his
villa at Ravenna. Giacinto Prandelli sang the remaining performances
that season. Later di Stefano offered an explanation for his behaviour:
'I was having trouble with pitch . . . in *Traviata*. It was originally
announced that de Sabata would conduct and he persuaded me to
sing. But I told him "Maestro, forget about me I'm scared. I don't
want to sing it. I'm afraid I'll go flat in . . . 'Parigi, o cara'." I hated
the rehearsals and I started not going. I was scared and, of course,
the other artists took offence and construed my behaviour as a lack
of respect to them.'[12]

It was at this time at La Scala that Callas and Tebaldi had their last
direct confrontation: Tebaldi sang Leonora in *La Forza del Destino* on
April 26th, 28th, 30th, May 3rd and 5th, and Callas sang Amina on April
24th and 27th, Fiorilla on May 4th and Violetta on May 28th. Callas
tells[13] how she went often to Tebaldi's performances but her attentions
were not reciprocated. After the season was over at La Scala, between
June 9th and 12th, and with the orchestra under Serafin, she recorded
'Dei tuoi figli la madre' from *Medea*, 'Tu che invoco', 'O nume tutelar'
and 'Caro oggetto' from *La Vestale*, and the two big scenas from *La
Sonnambula*. This represented just how far Legge was prepared to go
in 1955 towards making complete recordings of these three operas. For
the *Sonnambula* excerpts, when Callas proposed venturing Bernstein's
ornaments, Serafin, one presumes, turned up his nose; and accordingly
she sings the arias in a naked, prosaic fashion. But she seems not to have
accepted his judgment, for when the record was issued after another
three years, although it contained the arias from *La Vestale* and *Medea*,
those from *La Sonnambula* were not included. Substituted were the
Mad Scene from the complete recording of *I Puritani* and the Act I
scene from a complete recording of *La Sonnambula*, which was not
made until 1957 and is conducted by Votto. The latter does, though,
include some of Bernstein's ornaments, albeit simplified. The two arias
conducted by Serafin were issued on pirate labels in 1966 and 1972,

EMI only seems to have become aware of their existence after Callas's death and they were not officially released until 1978.

On June 29th Callas went down to Rome to undertake Norma for RAI with Stignani, del Monaco and Modesti under Serafin. From a rehearsal there survives a snippet of film of her singing part of 'Casta Diva'. Serafin and Stignani make this performance much in the same mode as the EMI recording, only at the end of Act II are there a few extra bars of music, and Callas caps the trio with a *d''*. When she had finished it Visconti invited Callas and her husband to dine with him at Ostia, a resort on the coast near Rome. Then, straight afterwards, in the summer night, the Meneghinis commenced the drive back north. But they had only reached Siena when Meneghini was stricken with food poisoning. Callas was very upset, she even wrote to Visconti accusing him of 'having made an attempt on [Battista's] life'.[14] Whilst Meneghini was recuperating she received a last-minute invitation to sing Aida at the Verona Festival but she declined, claiming to be too preoccupied by his illness. She did not sing there again.

Back in Milan that summer Callas undertook three recordings at La Scala for EMI. *Madama Butterfly* under Karajan, and *Aida* and *Rigoletto* under Serafin. *Butterfly* she recorded between August 1st and 6th. In view of the fact that she planned to sing it in Chicago that autumn this would seem an obvious selection. If Karajan as conductor seems an unconventional, if not bold, choice the reason would seem to be partly because Serafin was unable to record *Butterfly* again, having already made it the previous year for HMV, and partly because of Karajan's sensational success with *Lucia* at La Scala; Legge was anxious to secure his services in an Italian opera. But the rest of the casting, as in the 1954 *La Forza del Destino*, is scarcely worth perpetuating even for her sake. No doubt Pinkerton would have been sung by di Stefano had he not also been in the Serafin recording, forcing Legge to look elsewhere. He booked Nicolai Gedda, an important discovery of his, a young lyric tenor of refined musicianship, with considerable linguistic skill and a well-blended head voice. Already in three years Legge had recorded him in a catholic repertory running all the way from Mussorgsky's *Boris Godounov* to Bach's *Mass in B Minor*, via Rossini's *Il Turco in Italia*, Lehár's *Die lustige Witwe*, Johann Strauss's *Der Zigeunerbaron*, *Wiener Blut* and *Eine Nacht in Venedig*, and Richard Strauss's *Arabella*! In all of these he gives a good account of himself. Presumably, Legge reasoned, if he were close enough to a microphone he would sound well enough as Pinkerton. Unfortunately

Pinkerton calls for one thing Gedda is unable to simulate: a sensual, Italianate vocal quality.

The star of the set is Karajan. He enables us to admire the beautifully idiomatic playing of the Scala orchestra and, at the same time, reminds us just how eloquent it is in verismo opera under the sway of a front-rank conductor. Alas, the principal singers are not in his league. Not only is Gedda miscast but Callas's Butterfly, notwithstanding many inimitable touches, is unconvincing. From the beginning of Act I she seems intent on contriving a vocal character to suit Butterfly. It is a pity that she did not listen to dal Monte, in the complete recording EMI made with Gigli in 1939. Her voice was a light soprano, a coloratura, and she had appeared as Lucia in Toscanini's La Scala revival, and subsequently on tour in Berlin and Vienna. She was Karajan's model for the role. After one of Callas's Lucias dal Monte came round to congratulate her, assuring her that she herself had not been able to make half the effect in it. Dal Monte undertook Butterfly late in her career, when her voice no longer possessed any altitudinous notes. It suits her perfectly, and she conveys her characterization by means of the type of voice she possessed naturally. She sings it unaffectedly and creates an effect entirely spontaneously.

Callas's interpretation, however, is a product of cerebration. In Act I, instead of just singing she contrives a way of seeming to speak the music, as she fancies, à la japonaise; but she should have remembered that this music is occidental, not oriental. It is not in the pages of quasi-recitative allotted to the child-bride that the music is memorably encapsulated but in the celebrated lyric passages: the Entrance, the Love Duet, 'Un bel dì' and the Flower Duet. In these Puccini drops his japonoiserie. What they need to work effectively is the typical effulgence of a verismo soprano; a singer with her voice fully supported, opening out as she rides the orchestral climaxes. Callas's reading of 'Un bel dì' may be remarkable for the finish of her phrasing but not for the beauty of her singing; and what this music needs above all is a voice to match the fecundity of the melody. In the Love Duet with Gedda or the Flower Duet with Lucia Danieli, the singers' voices do not blend persuasively, and such effect as there is is not made by them but by Karajan's conducting.

Four days after the recording of *Madama Butterfly* was finished, on August 10th, Callas commenced recording *Aida* at La Scala with Barbieri, Tucker, Gobbi, Modesti and Zaccaria under Serafin. Although she had not sung it in the theatre since 1953 at that time it still ranked, after Norma and Violetta, as the role she had sung most times.

Aida is an opera in which many sopranos in the twentieth century have been unequivocally successful, among them Destinn, Rethberg, and Leontyne Price. By the time Verdi wrote it his music had changed in style, it had grown manifestly more instrumental than vocal, though it seems unlikely he was aware of it. For a letter he wrote to Ricordi in 1877 was triggered off at the prospect of Patti singing Aida at La Scala: '[Y]ou may imagine how pleased I should be . . . [Patti] is perfectly organized. Perfect balance between singer and actress, a born artist in every sense of the word'.[15] She did sing Aida but, like Callas, she was not a success in it; the music's style was too modern for her. She had a whole grammar of expression at her disposal (we can hear remains of it in old age on her records) which the part simply does not call for. She could hardly have thought it a compliment that her singing should have excelled in the fashion of an instrumentalist. In her day instrumentalists were busy modelling their legato on singers.

For Callas, however, 'the voice was the first instrument of the orchestra . . . we must treat the voice as a violinist treats the violin'.[16] If we go back to Paganini's and Liszt's time we find the greatest violinists and pianists took vocal music as their model. A remnant of this 'grand tradition' survived until only yesterday in the great tyro Vladimir Horowitz's 'interest . . . near obsession'[17] with a king of bel canto, the baritone Battistini, who came from a generation before Caruso and is one of the oldest great singers who made records while still in the plenitude of his powers. In the last hundred years there has been a gradual, if not precipitate, decline in the finish of singers' techniques, occasioned by changes in musical taste. The voice is altogether narrower in musical range than most instrumentalists. Inevitably the singer has been unable to keep pace with the more sonorous orchestras demanded by successive generations of composers without relinquishing many of his or her peculiar accomplishments. But in the age of bel canto, more than 150 years ago, the voice was the archetypal instrument. It should not be forgotten that song is even older than speech, and is an extension of the cry of man the animal, which is why it is naturally affecting. Until contemporary composers come again to use the voice to enable the singer to reveal his or her unique potency, there are not likely to be any new operas to vie with those of Rossini, Donizetti, Bellini or Verdi.

When Callas came to undertake this recording of *Aida* her execution of the music may be more refined than it is in the early 1950s but it is certainly less sure. By this time the role made demands of her that she would have been unable to manage comfortably in the theatre, the wobbly climax to 'O patria mia' is only the most abrasive. The performance is far less secure a representation of the music than she gives in live performances four or five years before, although she does make an occasional phrase tell: for example, her delivery of the words 'ah! ben rammento' in the Act III duet with Amonasro, when he reminds her of home – though here we note that it is the libretto that she inflects meaningfully, not the music. But her singing does not leave an agreeable impression. It is instructive that by the time she came to Juilliard in the early 1970s, she ventures nothing from Aida with any student, despite the importance it played in her early career.

Too many of Callas's recordings are, by this time, arty and artful rather than artistic. We can hear this clearly enough in the last recording she ventured that summer, Gilda in *Rigoletto*. *Rigoletto* began on September 3rd and includes, for once, an excellent accompanying cast led by di Stefano and Gobbi. Yet, notwithstanding their presence, even Legge does not single out it out for special praise. Gilda was never a favourite role of Callas and we noted even in Mexico City in 1952 the first signs of contrivance in her interpretation. Her interpretation has not radically changed since then though it has not the sweep it once had and it has also fallen prey to her usual vocal failings, being more wobbly and her tone more curdled. This time she does not transpose down 'Caro nome' but neither does she venture the alternate ending to the coda, which would have taken her up to e''. Although she still includes some high notes, like a (screamed) e'' flat at the end of 'Si, vendetta,' she omits a d'' flat at the end of the Quartet. If the 'quiet ending to the Quartet', as Ardoin suggests,[18] is more felicitous than a wavery high note, then we may wonder why, only a month previously, over the chorus at the end of Butterfly's Entrance, she sustains a very wobbly d'' flat when it too is only an optional, yet dal Monte, a coloratura soprano, is content with b'' flat.

She resumed her round of performances at the Städtische Oper, Berlin, on September 29th when she made her first appearance in Germany under Karajan in a couple of *Lucias* with substantially the same ensemble that she had appeared with at La Scala, Milan in January 1954. An excellent-sounding recording of this was eventually issued by EMI in 1991. It is frequently suggested that it is amongst her best surviving performances.[19] However, apart from anything else, the orchestra is not from La Scala but the Berlin radio and its contribution is obtrusive; it plays in an unidiomatic, unstylish fashion. From the beginning we are aware of an atmosphere of excess rehearsal: the crashing chords in the recitatives, the protuberant plucking of the strings in the introduction to the Sextet. It is possible to feel that the recording over emphasizes these. Throughout it is as if Karajan were trying to make something almost Wagnerian out of *Lucia*: indeed, photographs suggest that he succeeded in making the production look like a murky teutonic tragedy. Inevitably he seizes on the basic weakness of Callas's singing we have noted above; her confusion between artistry and artfulness. By this time more than a year and a half has elapsed since she sang Lucia at La Scala, and her voice has aged considerably. It has become thinner and paler. If we compare the conducting of the Berlin performance with that at La Scala we note how much more Karajan indulges in a stylistic solecism: how he fails to make a clear distinction between the tempo of a cavatina and a cabaletta, starting both 'Quando rapito' and 'Spargi d'amaro' at a lethargic tempo and then speeding up as he goes along. Part of the Sextet is encored, but Callas no longer seems able to mark the repeated b'' flats cleanly or firmly, and in the stretta following, in which Karajan restores a few measures then often cut, her voice does not surmount the ensemble as limpidly as it had once done. In the Mad Scene her singing is certainly prodigiously accurate, but it lacks spontaneity, an important prerequisite of florid singing. We get an idea of the rapid rate at which her voice was starting to deteriorate when she brings the cadenza to a lame conclusion without an e'' flat; and, without the climactic resolution, there is no applause despite the audience's disposition elsewhere to give way to unstinting approbation. At La Scala, however, no sooner has she sung e'' flat than pandemonium breaks out and the performance is halted. Di Stefano remembers in Berlin how 'neurotic she was. Afterwards she kept crying, "I was horrible, I was no good"'.[20] She was very anxious about missing the note, so Karajan persuaded her to avoid it.

XIII

1955–1956

F ROM BERLIN CALLAS returned to Milan prior to making her
second visit to the United States, appearing once again with the
Chicago Lyric. This year she came back a 'brunette with curls left
over from the Visconti-directed *Traviatas*',[1] complete with Dior A-
Line and sporting, newspapers claimed,[2] a million dollars' worth of
jewellery. The Meneghinis took rooms in an apartment hotel on the
north side. Before the season began a lengthy story entitled 'Voice of
an Angel' appeared in Life magazine[3] detailing her career so far. A
six-page spread began with a full length photograph of her as a slim
and elegant Elvira in Bellini's *I Puritani*, which she was to sing that
year. It must have specially posed for, for she had not undertaken
the role since she had reduced. The story repeated most of the well
worn tales: of her Met audition in 1946, her first Venice *I Puritani* in
1949, how her fee was going up, details of her stringent regime and the
Callas/Tebaldi feud.

The second Chicago season opened on October 31st with the first
of two performances of *I Puritani* conducted by Rescigno, with di
Stefano, Bastianini and Rossi-Lemeni. This was the last time she
would sing it. Recordings of excerpts in concert in later years, an
ensemble in Act I, 'Oh vieni al tempio' and the Mad Scene, suggest
that the role particularly suited her. Kelly described her interpretation
as 'definitive. She arrived with a smaller voice . . . [but] there wasn't
the slightest wobble . . . there [were] no frailties in it.'[4] Though
Howard Talley in *Musical America* complained that the interpolated
d"'s were 'forced and out of focus'.[5] And Taubman, in the *New York
Times*, after commenting on the ecstatic applause that greeted her first
appearance, noted '[she] is [not] the perfect singer. She reminded one
who had heard her in Italy four years ago [at the Maggio Musicale
in Florence] that she was capable of uneven work, that she could be
strident and off-pitch. But she has gained in authority. And when she
is in the vein, she is an extraordinary vocalist and technician.'[6] Stewart
Manville in *Opera* wrote fulsomely: she sang 'first offstage in a unison
prayer for departing soldiers [her] voice soaring above the others . . .

From the start she was in excellent voice, giving a performance even better than the one she has recorded, with here a bit more intensity, there a phrase more clearly delivered. One deduces that Callas, good as she is, is still improving.'⁷ Although not all the critics cared for the opera, Cassidy thought 'it was fantastic to see Callas make Elvira a totally different creature from her Lucia. Where Lucia was a normal girl gone mad for love, Elvira is a fey, unstable creature who is off and on again like Finnegan. The glint in her eyes, the dark hair, the lovely hands – you can't take your eyes off her. And her singing is magnificent.'⁸ After the performance, as in the previous year Angel Records, with the Sorias and Legge, played hosts at another opera ball at the Hilton. At the height of the proceedings Callas made a spectacular entrance swathed in emerald green and gold.

The next night, November 1st, *Aida* was given with Tebaldi, Astrid Varnay, Doro Antonioli and Gobbi under Serafin. Serafin had not been too pleased to learn that Rescigno was conducting all the Callas performances. So, with her husband, Callas came to *Aida* in a placatory mood. She was seen in the orchestra stalls applauding vigorously. She seemed to be enjoying herself and was overheard telling an acquaintance: 'Renata is in very good voice tonight.'⁹ But in the middle of the Nile Scene, during 'O patria mia', there was a sudden commotion. A torch was switched on, the string of Callas's necklace had broken and stones spewed out underneath the adjoining seats. While the light was flashing around those nearby helped the diva and her husband retrieve them. Afterwards a jeweller expressed surprise that anyone with a million dollars' worth of jewels should have stones not even individually stranded; they could only have been made of paste.

On November 5th and 8th Callas sang Leonora in *Il Trovatore*. Like *I Puritani* she would not sing it again in the theatre. These were also the only occasions that she appeared with the tenor, Jussi Björling. He thought 'her Leonora was perfection, I have heard the role sung often, but never was there a better one than hers'.¹⁰ The cast also included Stignani as Azucena, Bastianini as di Luna and it was conducted by Rescigno. 'Not in many a long year has Chicago had a *Trovatore* to rival [it]', Cassidy averred. 'The applause was roof-shattering . . . and [Callas] is a wonder of the western world.'¹¹ At the second performance Claramae Turner and Weede replaced Stignani and Bastianini. In the audience were Bing, General Manager of the Metropolitan and Assistant Manager, Francis Robinson. Bing had made a feint or two at securing Callas in the past, but he had preferred to be content with Tebaldi and Milanov. By 1954, however, when Callas had lost weight, he deemed 'it . . . urgent for the Metropolitan to have her'.[12] But for all the Met's international reputation and the theatre's having an on-the-spot representative in Milan, Chicago signed her up for her American début, and for appreciably more money than Bing had been talking of. It was not until the spring of 1955 that he managed to persuade her to come to New York. But, in Callas's usual dilatory fashion, she had not signed the contract by the time she returned to Chicago. After Act III Bing went backstage and the memorable moment was sealed with photographs of him kissing her hand. As to the inevitable demands about the size of her fee, he smiled, remarking gallantly: 'Our artists work for the love of art and a few flowers . . . let's just say she'll be getting a few more flowers.'[13]

The third part Callas sang was Butterfly, on November 11th and 14th, conducted by Rescigno, with di Stefano as Pinkerton and Weede as Sharpless. Though no recordings survive from any of the Chicago performances, critics suggest she made the same kind of effect that she does on the commercial recording. Dettmer, of the *Chicago American* describes himself as 'Callas-crazy for more than a year, and none has been more demented than I'.[14] But of her Butterfly he writes temperately. 'The Callas Butterfly . . . is scaled for an intimate house, the Piccola Scala, for example. Such a setting would require a measure of less coyness of expression and deportment in the first act, but it would reward all present with the subtle Callas conception of a beloved but fiendishly difficult role, a potentially great conception, and one that may yet find maturity before another week has passed here.'[15] Cassidy, too, was disappointed: '[the] full-throated, soaring ardour was seldom heard . . . Not even its love duet was the flood of melody to send pulses pounding . . . This was charming make believe, but it was not Cio-Cio-San, nor was it the ultimate Callas.'[16] She went again to the second performance, as if she were anxious to give the diva another try, but this time she began her review unequivocally: 'If [Callas] were anyone else, I would say the music does not lie in her voice.'[17]

By the time of the *Butterflys* Callas's agreement with the Met was common knowledge in Chicago and, as she would not be returning because the seasons clashed, she was entreated to give an additional performance of *Butterfly*. Although she was required back for opening night at La Scala, the reception that she had earned, not to mention the size of her fee, encouraged her to accede. 'The announcement of an extra performance brought a record crowd to the . . . box-office. The line . . . stretched the length of the theatre, around the corner, and over the Washington Street bridge to the *Daily News* building. The 3,600 seat house was sold out ninety-eight minutes after the ticket windows opened.'[18] Chicago opera lovers had gone quite mad. In newspapers, on the arts pages, there were stories about her and the critics went on about her almost every day. Even the news of her defection prompted one outburst of lyricism:

'Oh, Maria Meneghini Callas! Of me myself, I sing.
For I shook the hand that took the kiss from the lips of Rudolf Bing.'[19]

She sang the third Butterfly on November 17th. Doubtless her publicity had kept Bagarozy concentrated on his legal suit. He had been attempting to secure a court order requiring her to pay $300,000, which he calculated equal to ten per cent of her earnings since 1947, but he was frustrated by U.S. law, which insists on a summons only being made legal by bodily contact. For most of the year Callas was outside the U.S. and she had a clause inserted in her contract requiring the Lyric Theater to protect her from any harassment while she was in Chicago. This the theatre management were able to do, though there were several close shaves. On one occasion Fox, Soria and Legge managed to whisk Callas out of the theatre just in time before the Marshal arrived. She went down the freight lift, took the fire exit and proceeded out along the riverside. On another she spent the morning locked up in her apartment and, when she ventured out to the theatre, she must have been very grateful to a crowd of fans who mobbed her, making it impossible for the Marshal to approach before she got away in a car.

In fact all the precautions worked well, until the last performance. That she was not returning to Chicago and would be appearing in New York instead stuck in the gullet of certain members of the Lyric Theater. In particular, Fox was only waiting for an opportunity to get her own back. After the last performance she decided that here was the golden opportunity: to let the Marshal through, and see to it that photographers were present. Di Stefano recalls: 'immediately after Butterfly dies, "con onor muore chi non puo serbar vita con onore", ["Let him die with honour who cannot live honourably"] and Maria had finished taking solo bows, the backstage drama began . . .' A photographer was there and a man came forward. 'Suddenly Butterfly became like one of those Greek furies . . . I had no idea who he was: I thought he was a crazy. It was like cowboys and Indians – what did I know about a Sheriff?'[20]

Few of the onlookers could have had much idea either. Callas herself was bewildered until the Marshal had satisfied legal requirements and 'thrust his document into her kimono'.[21] The next minute she was shrieking after him: 'No man can sue me! I have the voice of an angel! Chicago will be sorry for this!'[22] In the world's press during the next few days a photograph appeared of the Marshal hastening away; and one can well see why, with Callas directly behind him still clad as Butterfly, her mouth in a hyena-like snarl, as a bewildered onlooker gapes over her shoulder. In a trice the camera had translated her from the arts section into a front page personality. After a few minutes she collapsed in tears and then allowed herself to be taken to Kelly's brother's apartment. All that night she spent complaining about the way she had been treated. Meanwhile Meneghini got seats on a plane to return to Italy immediately. Doubtless the Lyric Theater was grateful, for had she stayed, as Kelly states, 'and personal attachment . . . been placed on her, her Scala contract would have been broken'.[23] By the terms of her Chicago contract the Lyric Theater would be held responsible should she return to Milan late for the Scala opening night. Early the next morning the Meneghinis finally embarked on the transatlantic flight for Milan. Back home Callas wrote to Dorle Soria in 'characteristically operatic [vein]: "I couldn't have been betrayed worse. When I write you details you will freeze in horror."'[24]

Why, we may ask, did she go to such trouble to avoid the summons? Surely it would have been easier when she arrived in Chicago to have just accepted it and made an appearance in court denying that Bagarozy had given her any help whatsoever, certainly he had not given her any for the last eight years. When she returned to Milan she made a statement. She claimed she had been tricked into signing the contract before she left New York in 1947, that Bagarozy had embezzled a large part of the thousand dollars which her godfather, Dr Lantzounis, had given her before she departed for Italy and that he had abandoned her. Yet if this were so we may wonder why, when she arrived in Verona, she was travelling with Caselotti, Bagarozy's wife, and because of her agreement with him she paid Caselotti ten per cent of her Gioconda fee. After she had made these claims Bagarozy revealed through his lawyers copies of letters she had written to him after she arrived in Italy. In one of them dated[25] more than two months after she made her first appearance at Verona, when she was already living with Meneghini, she still expresses herself in love with Bagarozy. From her early days she had been preoccupied with her career, and when Bagarozy first tantalized her, we may believe, it was not with him but with what he offered her that she fell in love – at this stage her infatuation was with a career. Judging from the tenor of her letters to Bagarozy, in the course of the interval between her first Italian engagements in 1947 when she was unemployed, it did not take her long to realize that rich Meneghini would make a more reliable manager than poor Bagarozy. By the time she arrived in Chicago more than seven years had passed and she had forgotten Bagarozy completely. Memories he evoked of Callas the unlovely child of Greek immigrants, overweight and gawky, was an image of herself she wished to forget. In October 1956 a clandestine meeting took place in New York at the Sorias' apartment between Meneghini and Callas and the Bagarozy lawyers. Although Bagarozy's demand had been for $300,000, they were prepared to settle for $20,000. Dorle Soria remembers Callas's distress at this: '[t]ears stream[ing] down her face',[26] so the case continued another two years until a settlement was finally reached, when we may believe Callas eventually paid out less than $20,000!

Back in Milan she opened the La Scala season as Norma on December 7th. Her fee had now risen to 900,000 Lire a performance. The production was by Wallmann with sets and costumes by Fiume, and opening night was in the presence of the President of Italy, Luigi Einaudi. The opera was conducted by Votto, and the cast also included Simionato, del Monaco and Zaccaria. A recording of this performance shows her off to the best advantage; and although her voice is smaller it is still steady and she sings suavely. In the following years the number of performances reaching this level would decline dramatically. Maybe it was the Chicago fracas, or perhaps her battle with del Monaco, that was responsible for steaming her up sufficiently to get enough power behind her voice to support it fully. During one of these *Norma*s she accuses him of spreading an incredible story. '[A]ccording to that fantastic account . . . I allegedly gave him such a violent kick in the shins it made him groan and limp, in order to prevent him from taking a curtain call with me!'[27] By this time the number of stories about her had been growing steadily; photographs of her Chicago contretemps encouraged any number. Jacques Bourgeois, the French critic, describes an effect she made at another of these *Norma*s. 'She seemed to sense the public's hostility, and in the last act took a fantastically long silent pause of seven or eight seconds before she removed her crown of laurels and sang "Son io". The public acclamation was sensational and went on seemingly endlessly before the opera could resume.'[28]

The Act II duet, 'Mira, o Norma', she and Simionato now transpose down into E flat, whereas at Covent Garden in 1953 they sang it in the original higher key. Notwithstanding their different vocal methods, it is an outstanding example of duet singing, the passage in thirds particularly. Votto may not be much of a conductor but he gives them their head; both singers are far more secure with him than they were five years previously in Mexico City. The music is taken at an expansive tempo with traditional accelerandi, ritards and expressive shadings, and the singer's tone is properly balanced and equally audible on every note. The whole is more affecting than the sum of the parts: which is as it should be in duet singing. In the last act, especially, she seems by the force of her personality to have metamorphosed Votto. As Norma rages against Pollione, 'Si sovr' essi alzar la punta' through to 'Mi poss' io dimenticar', the rhythm becomes freer until, at the end, the accompaniment almost disappears, and how precisely she realizes Bellini's marking 'a piacere abbandonandosi'. Here she reminds us of the difference between, as Garcia explains, 'accelerando and rallentando which require that the accompaniment and the voice are together and slow down or speed up the music as a unity [and] tempo rubato which, in contrary style, accords this liberty only to the voice'.[29]

The finale, 'Qual cor tradisti', she takes slightly faster than in London in 1952, for she has not as much voice now. Particularly telling is her execution of three groups of semiquavers (sixteenth notes) in the opening andante, on the words 'Tu sei con me', 'In vita e in morte' and 'Saro con te'. After the first word of the final ensemble, 'Deh!', it is the perfection of her legato that enables her to mark the exclamation point, as a slight catch in her breath punctuates the line without disturbing it. On the repeated words 'abbi di lor', she realizes the triplets each time more intensely so that, eventually, they become plaintive devices; and again she accomplishes this wholly musically without disturbing her legato, as do verismo sopranos like Amerighi Rutili and Cigna. It is no exaggeration to describe this scene as a high water-mark in Italian opera, surpassed not even by Verdi. Even as late as 1965 at the Paris Opéra, no matter how debatable the condition of Callas's voice, the effect of her performance was cumulative, one could almost say Wagnerian. Indeed we know that Wagner admired Norma, and at the end of his music dramas, he contrives a similar effect, though in them it is not so wholly dependent on the singers. Here, as Callas proves in any of her Normas, Bellini rises to the greatest heights of musical invention, and makes an effect without parallel. But she is perhaps at her most eloquent in this La Scala performance.

In the 1955/56 season at La Scala Callas appeared in *Norma* nine times after which, between January 19th and May 6th, she undertook Violetta again in the Visconti production of *La Traviata* seventeen times, with a similar cast and conductors except that Raimondi was now the tenor. At the première, as we can hear on a recording of the broadcast, straight after she attacks 'Gioir', before 'Sempre libera', there was a disturbance in the gallery, which so surprised her that she cut the note short. Furious, she determined, after bringing the act to a conclusion with a brilliant *e''* flat, to take a solo bow and test public opinion. She was greeted, in her own words, 'with a generous rain of applause calculated to extinguish my fury'. Notwithstanding her success during the run of *Traviatas* there was a hard core determined to make the atmosphere unpleasant for her. As she tells, 'at the end of another performance I gathered up a bunch . . . of turnips which had fallen from the gallery. I mistook them for flowers because of my nearsightedness . . . Visconti, who was in the prompter's box . . . was dying of laughter. They . . . could not have been purchased during the performance, but must have been brought in [by] . . . prearranged plan. [W]ho goes to the theatre with turnips in his pocket?'[30] Visconti remembers the occasion somewhat differently: 'Maria, who had the hearing of Diogenes, heard that it wasn't only flowers that were falling, she reached out picked them up and sniffed them . . . flowers she showed off to the audience, and as she did so she made a sweeping bow, of course it was a triumph. I couldn't have staged the scene better myself.'[31]

After the sixth *Traviata* on February 5th, Callas was a guest at the Red Cross Ball in Milan, and there was a gap of eleven days before, on the 16th, she sang her first Rosina in Rossini's *Il Barbiere di Siviglia*. During the next month she continued performances of Violetta as well as appearing another four times as Rosina. These were the only occasions she ventured the part. Zeffirelli had been ousted from the production by intrigue, he had wanted to direct *Il Barbiere*, 'I think [I never found out, but I think] she was responsible for my not directing it'.[32] According to Meneghini Visconti, jealous of Zeffirelli's success with *Il Turco*, used his influence with Callas to 'circulate negative observations about Zeffirelli'[33] and so a very routine production was revived instead. As far as Callas was concerned it proved a fiasco. Zeffirelli describes[34] her dramatic conception as being better suited to *The Merry Widow*. It is true that she brays with forced laughter in the recitative before 'Dunque io son', but it is typical of her musical excellence that, like the tears she introduces in her 1950 Mexico City *Norma*, she does not let these interpolations interfere with the vocal line. There is certainly no need today, with only the recording left, to bother ourselves unduly with the theatrical effectiveness of her assumption. Her singing of Rosina certainly sounds less contrived than many of her other interpretations. Indeed, we are tempted to believe that there was more of Rosina's character about her than there was, say, of Amina's or Gilda's. By this time her voice is not notably attractive and an occasional sustained tone, like the *b''* at the end of the Lesson Scene, understandably disturbs certain sections of the audience. Nevertheless she executes the florid music accurately: runs, trills and fioritura of every kind, reminding us what the word coloratura means. Although her voice is not as powerful nor is her singing as limpid as it was when she undertook Armida, and it is not spontaneous in the way of Tetrazzini, it is still remarkably adept.

There are only two satisfactory ways of performing *Il Barbiere*: either by presenting every note of it in an *Urtext* edition with all the latest discoveries as to performance practice, or by a 'traditional' style of performance with cuts, transpositions, embellishments, etc., all of which have been handed down through successive generations of performance in the theatre. Unfortunately, at La Scala they seemed not to know which way to play it. Although Callas sings 'Una voce poco fa' in the original key of E, the rest of her performance is a mere whimsy. She makes a lot of cuts, embroiders the part fairly extensively and transposes some of the lower passages up an octave. The Lesson Scene is up a tone, and at the end she interpolates a lengthy cadenza; who wrote it, one wonders? We know that she wished to substitute an aria out of Jommelli's *Fetonte*, which she had learned with di Hidalgo years before, Giulini dissuaded her, but that was a pity. Since she made so many changes she should have been encouraged to go the whole hog and interpolate whatever she liked. A piano might have been wheeled on, as it was in Patti's day, and she could have sung almost anything from Brunilde's Battle Cry to Proch's Variazione. One should either sing what is written or else follow a century-old tradition; half-way houses, like this performance, satisfy no one.

After Callas's fifth Rosina, on March 15th, she left Rosina to Eugenia Ratti and Victoria de los Angeles. On the 22nd in Naples she appeared as Lucia, the first of the last three performances she sang at the San Carlo. Meneghini describes how, so as to keep her fee within prescribed limits, his name was added to the payroll and he was styled assistant stage director. On April 5th Callas was back at La Scala for Violetta. It was at the end of the run, on May 6th, that the last echo of the erstwhile rivalry between Callas and Tebaldi resounded. On that day Tebaldi began a series of performances of *La Traviata* under Serafin at the Florence Maggio Musicale at the Comunale. The tables were now turned: Ghiringhelli had Callas in Milan and Siciliani had Tebaldi in Florence.

Callas's last appearance at La Scala that season took place on May 21st when she ventured the first of six performances of Giordano's *Fedora*. It had originally been planned to present her as Kundry in *Parsifal* under Kleiber. But he died suddenly, so *Parsifal* was replaced by *Fedora*, 'as odd a change in repertory as any opera house has devised', Legge thought.[35] In *Fedora* the cast also included Corelli and Anselmo Colzani. This was not broadcast and no recording of it survives. Gavazzeni, who conducted, admired her in it. 'For me it was because she did sing it with her qualities that made her so fascinating. She imposed . . . her style on the opera. . . . She gave her special vocal timbre . . . I remember a page in the last act "Tutto tramonta" when Fedora dies, where she found the most untypical sounding tone. She was almost talking. As an actress she was tremendous.'[36] Celli, however, one of her most devoted admirers, did not agree. He was anguished at her decision to sing it: 'Today, alas, she is only a singer with an unpleasant voice, struggling, with varying luck, with the difficulties of her part.' He did not attempt to conjecture why her vocal deterioration should have been so precipitate, but her determination to undertake such unsuitable parts as Fedora, Tosca and Butterfly must, he felt, account for it in some measure. He concluded: 'let us hope she returns to La Scala with her voice in a condition which enables her to do justice to the musical intelligence and sensitivity which made her so great.'[37]

From Milan Callas journeyed to the Vienna Staatsoper for the first time, for a repetition of the Scala *Lucia* under Karajan. She arrived on June 9th at the Hotel Sacher behind the opera. Three performances were given commencing on June 12th with the same ensemble as at Berlin the previous September. No sooner had she arrived than she discovered that she had not brought with her a miniature by Cignarolli. Meneghini had given it to her at the beginning of her career in Verona and she always had it with her, she considered it 'her mascot'.[38] She telephoned Giovanna Lomazzi in Milan who promptly brought it over. The performances were all sold out and many people crowded outside the newly rebuilt Staatsoper for a glimpse of the diva. Vienna opera goers, like those in Berlin, were not assiduously critical where Italian opera is concerned and she received a thunderous ovation, yet by this time her vocal deterioration in the stratospheric passages was obvious enough. As in Berlin she omitted the first *e''* flat in the Mad Scene and Cassidy of the *Chicago Tribune*, a staunch ally, who came there specially to hear her, noted regretfully 'there is little of the spontaneous brilliance, the seemingly effortless incandescence, the exquisite shadow play that made her Lyric Lucia an indelible radiance in history's hall of song ... At one point in the Mad Scene her voice just simply doesn't respond.'[39]

During the next six weeks Callas and Meneghini took a vacation at Lake Garda, then they travelled to Ischia in the Bay of Naples where they visited William Walton at Forio. Later that month they made a secret visit to New York for yet another episode in Callas's legal battle with Bagarozy; then, at the beginning of August, the couple returned to Milan where she took part in another three complete recordings: *Il Trovatore, La Bohème* and *Un Ballo in Maschera*. She commenced with Leonora on August 3rd. Karajan conducts, and his symphonic style in this opera, although carried out with exemplary polish, puts too much emphasis on the orchestra. In addition many of his tempi seem mannered. The other singers include Barbieri, a routine Azucena, di Stefano who sounds very much out of his depth as Manrico (but then he was deputizing for Tucker, who declined to sing under Karajan because of his Nazi associations), and Panerai, who is also overparted, for he was never a heroic baritone.

By this time Callas's Leonora no longer has the steadiness, the limpidity or weight of tone, to rival the effect she had once made on stage. We are not surprised that by 1956 she had given up singing Leonora in the theatre. There are countless examples of her vocal deterioration. If we compare the Act I cabaletta 'Di tale amor' with her first 1950 Mexico City performance it is not so much the *e''* flat at the end that we miss, but the voice is thinner, less responsive, the trills no longer so nimbly responsive on the breath, and as a result her voice cannot render the music as spontaneously as it had done. The Act IV aria, 'D' amor sull'ali rosee', though by general standards a fine performance, hardly has the haunting melismatics, the underlying tension in the phrasing, or the sheer scale of conception she accomplishes in 1950. Just before Manrico's Act III aria, 'Di quella pira', Karajan restores the few measures between Leonora and Manrico then customarily cut, and in Act IV Callas also includes, after the Miserere, one verse of the cabaletta, 'Tu vedrai che amore', which completes the scene. Its inclusion does satisfy our concern for form in operas of this period, yet the music is not up to the exalted level of the rest of the act and even when she sings it she can make little of it. Among all Callas's recordings this represents the only example of the restoration of a traditional cut in mid-period Verdi. We might be inclined to credit this to Legge or Karajan, were it not more indicative that this recording followed, after a few months, the Decca/London set with Tebaldi and del Monaco in which it is first included. The move toward complete *complete* recordings was started by John Culshaw of Decca/London.

Callas's next recording that summer was Mimì in Puccini's *La Bohème*, which she began on August 20th. The wonder of this was not that it was well done but that it was done at all. Votto's conducting is dutiful and dull and the other principals are in variable form. Di Stefano should have made a perfect Rodolfo but at climactic moments he becomes self-indulgent; the effort of singing a role like Manrico has taken its toll and at the top, in 'Che gelida manina' and 'O soave fanciulla', he sounds strained and uncomfortable. Anna Moffo is a characterless Musetta, but better that than the shrill overacting of so many soubrettes in this role. Mimì ranks with Desdemona as the least taxing leading soprano role in the conventional repertory. By Callas's lights there is nothing much for her to do. Mimì calls, basically, for two things: a naturally affecting lyric tone and perfection of execution. The tessitura, range of expression, and dramatic devices, are all modest. But Callas's voice is unsuited to the role and towards the top of the stave becomes unsteady and insecure. She sings with about as much voice as she deploys as Amina, though once or twice the real Maria slips out, or rather dribbles out. It is true that occasionally she manages a refined touch, in Act II, for example, in the ensemble in the Caffè Momus scene, when she sings the phrase 'Amare e dolce ancora più del miele' ('Love is sweeter than honey') there is her rhythmic mastery to admire, Votto notwithstanding. But generally her Mimì ranks with her Nedda as her least convincing undertaking. Still, if her Nedda may be considered negative, then her Mimì is merely neutral, though with an artist of Callas's prodigious gifts that is scarcely a compliment.

For whatever reasons, the recording of *La Bohème* took almost twice as long to accomplish as *Il Trovatore*. Indeed, the last two sessions took place on September 12th, a week after the third complete recording that summer had begun, Verdi's *Un Ballo in Maschera* under Votto. This is by far the best of the three: di Stefano sounds typecast as Riccardo, as is Gobbi as Renato. Ratti's Oscar produces a typical steam-whistle scream: she was one of the last Italian soubrettes whose voices were pinched so as to be able to hold on tightly, literally, in company with the big guns of the generation before Callas, the Caniglias, Cignas and Pacettis. If we compare Ratti with Ribetti, in the 1946 EMI Gigli/Caniglia set, we note how much further soubrette singing has deteriorated, but whereas Ribetti has only to hold her own against the vague imprecise execution of Caniglia's Amelia, Ratti has Callas to stand up to. In the Quintet at the end of Act III, 'Ah! di che fulgor', in which Oscar enters and sings a passage of brilliant music inviting Amelia, Renato, Samuel and Tom to the masked ball, Verdi underlines the ironic effect by having Amelia echo Oscar's fioritura in the minor. Here Callas's echo is clearer than Ratti's original, she executes the florid measures not just accurately but with her characteristic clarity and rhythmic precision.

After the difference between the Scala *Lucias* in Milan and in Berlin, it is interesting how alike Callas's singing is in *Un Ballo in Maschera* in this recording and the one made the following year on the opening night at La Scala. The casts are similar, except that in the recording Renato is Gobbi instead of Bastianini, and Ulrica is Barbieri instead of Simionato. The main difference centres on the conducting: Gavazzeni, at La Scala, gives a more dramatic reading. Callas chooses a plangent tone colour throughout and in Amelia's brief Act I appearance she is in slightly more persuasive voice in the recording. But elsewhere, though her tone has become thinner and more curdled, her performance at La Scala is superior. In the Act II aria 'Ecco l'orrido campo', in either version, her singing shows the kind of detail redolent of her best work: the perfection of the repeated triplets, her shaping and control, and her inimitable way with the cadenza. In this, as in that we have noticed in 'D'amor sull'ali rosee', she goes beyond what is written in the score. Discussing her records she was altogether too modest when she told Ardoin: 'It is all there for anyone who cares to understand or wishes to know what I was about.'[40] Well, the notes may be there, but her rhythmic elasticity and vitality, elegant and expressive phrasing, balancing and weighting of the musical line and subtle breaths, are all things that cannot be notated. In the last bars of this aria there is an ascent to c'' accompanied by the orchestra fortissimo, which she manages surprisingly smoothly. When Verdi writes a similar phrase in Aida's 'O patria mia' the accompaniment is marked pianissimo, and as we saw in her 1955 recording of *Aida*, she seems so preoccupied by the exposure that she does not lift the tone high enough in the head – partly a problem of support. As a result the c'' does not soar so much as see-saw.

Although in the Act II love duet Callas and di Stefano are both in slightly better voice in 1956, there are too many 'Leggisms' in their performances. At the moment when Riccardo protests his love for Amelia, di Stefano takes his voice off support and whispers the first 'M'ami' and Callas, in the passage 'Ahi sul funereo letto', shades off her support too far and the voice does not project forth surely. In either performance, in the Act III Oath Quartet at the end of a phrase, 'ah! qual lampo balena', after a sustained b'' flat, we note how dazzlingly accurate she is as she whips through a passage of triplets descending to d and e flat. It would be hard to imagine them being sung more accurately. Only in the final scene of Act IV do we note a vocal effect that she was always ambiguous about: at the end of the phrase 'e la vittima che muor!' she seems unable to articulate cleanly the tied repeated b'' flats. This would seem to have been a frailty due to her support problem; as we noted above she has the same trouble in Norma's 'Casta Diva' and the *Lucia* Sextet.

Callas brought the 1955/6 season to a conclusion with another Martini-Rossi concert for the RAI on September 27th (although it was not transmitted until December 8th). This was made at their Milan studios with the orchestra under Alfredo Simonetto and the other soloist was Raimondi. She sings 'Tu che invoco' from *La Vestale*, 'Oh vieni al tempio' from *I Puritani*, 'Bel raggio' from Rossini's *Semiramide*, and 'Ai vostri giochi . . . Ed ora a voi canterò', the Scena della follia, from Thomas's *Amleto*. As with her recital at San Remo in 1954, it seems hard to believe that these excerpts were all recorded on the same day, so radically do they differ. The *La Vestale* aria is typical of Callas at this time in the more dramatic repertory. She still includes a c'' at the end, though she omits the cadenza, and her tone is noticeably thinner and less agreeable than it is at La Scala. The *Puritani* excerpt is an odd choice, for it is part of an ensemble at the end of Act I and she is supported by some very routine singers. We notice at once how much more her voice suits Bellini's music (or how much more grateful is Bellini's vocal writing) and she manages even the alternative passage which rises to d'' without any of the disagreeable tone we might have expected by this time. As to 'Bel raggio', she told Kelly that '*Semiramide* is simply not believable [with] its hero a mezzo soprano'.[41] But the credibility of opera does not depend on anything so simplistic. In real life people do not sing, they speak. We should discount Callas's critical cerebrations. Her singing of this aria suggests her conception of Semiramide has not been fully realized. She seems not to have grasped the sense of the very first words 'Bel raggio lusinghier' ('Beauteous ray of flattery'); it is a brilliant showpiece and the vocal line merely a point of departure. It may be taken up a semitone, to make simple embellishments sound more brilliant, or down by the same interval, so that the singer may introduce liberal ornamentation, transpose the lower passages up an octave and finish on e'' flat, which is what Sutherland did. Between verses of the cabaletta Callas interpolates a cadenza: her musical instincts were so much surer than her rationalizations, and showed she realized the piece needed some brilliant effect. In a single gesture from a trill on e she sweeps up to c'' sharp and then cascades down a chromatic run with every note clearly indicated. A veritable *tour de force* which goes some way to relieving her otherwise too literal singing. It is a pity that she never undertook Semiramide on stage.

The most remarkable selection is the Mad Scene from *Amleto*. This is the first time she sings it and, as is so often the way, it is the best of her surviving performances. Here, unlike *Semiramide*, most of the embellishments are written out and there is little need for any spontaneous ornamentation. At this stage of her career her voice is ideally suited to Ofelia's music; in fact, it could be said that the reason she sings it so perfectly is because, like the excerpt from *I Puritani*, it demands of her no more than the natural size of her voice. Since the tessitura extends all the way to e'' it needs full support and she does not meddle with it. Even the subtlest, and seemingly most insignificant markings, like the phrase marked pianissimo, 'ed Ofelia e il mio nome', or the *scoppii di risa* on the repeated f' sharps in the ballad, are persuasively rendered. The latter she enunciates exactly as it is notated, but in later performances she omits it, presumably because she found it difficult technically. She differentiates lucidly between chromatic and diatonic scale passages. The trills are perfectly responsive in tones and semitones, and she assumes appropriate vocal colours without getting too arty. She takes full account of all the dynamic markings and reveals a mastery of rubato, as well as accomplishing the whole scene effortlessly and within the most prodigious breath spans. We can understand Nikolaidi, the *répétiteuse* who knew her in her Athens days, when she states it does not sound the same piece she had heard other sopranos sing.[42]

XIV

1956–1957

CALLAS HAD NOT appeared in the theatre for four months when she arrived in New York on October 15th, exactly two weeks before her Met début. In 1956 the Met may not have enjoyed the artistic renown of La Scala but it was still a great theatre. Save for the Paris Opéra, it was the only one of the world's front-ranking opera houses at which she had still not appeared, and the culmination of her progress. With three-quarters of a century of history behind it, nearly all the most renowned sopranos had sung there, from Patti to Tebaldi. From Callas's arrival she was caught up in a barrage of publicity. The press was preoccupied with her and hardly a day passed without a line or two on her in its columns. The ballyhoo reached its apogee with the publication of *Time* magazine's profile on the day of her début.[1] On the front cover was a reproduction of a painting by Henry Koerner, and inside a leading feature article. In an age as unoperatic as the 1950s, when leading figures in the world of music were Johnny Ray, Bill Haley and Elvis Presley, it was certainly extraordinary for an opera singer to receive this kind of attention. *Time* magazine had gone to considerable lengths ferreting out gossip and tittle-tattle from the diva's friends and enemies. Among the most contentious passages was one detailing her relationship with her mother. This had been written with the complicity of Litza, for it contains excerpts from the last letter her daughter had written her in 1951. The effect of it was to incur the public's indignation. As Kolodin puts it: 'Among Americans conditioned to a belief that motherhood is even more sacred than country, [it] aroused antagonism where nothing else – professional rivalries, personal animosities, artistic differences – would have.'[2] The article had been written by the winner of the 1952 Pulitzer Prize, George de Carvalho, who had gone to Italy to talk to people who knew her, and to meet Callas herself. She seems not to have realized how significant the article was to prove. She kept him dallying round her and even coaxed him into going down to Rome to collect her new baby poodle from the kennel, though on the way back the dog turned out not to be toilet trained and ruined his suit.

By first night curiosity was at fever pitch. The audience included some of the most important figures in New York, and an admixture of musicians and artistic figures. Angel Records took the Trianon Room at the Ambassador Hotel for a reception afterwards. Among those present were the Greek and Italian Ambassadors, Callas's father, a covey from the Metropolitan including Bing, Anthony Bliss, Lauder Greenway, Mrs August Belmont, Walter and Wally Toscanini and Wanda Horowitz, with singers Lucrezia Bori and Martinelli, and composers Samuel Barber and Menotti. Marlene Dietrich had obtained Callas's wig from her Hollywood *perruquière* and had 'spent hours boiling down eight pounds of beef to a quart of purest broth. Maria naïvely said, "It's very good. Tell me, what brand of cubes do you use?"'³ The box-office broke all records and took $75,510.50, yet Callas's fee was modest. She earned only $1,000 a performance, though she did receive an extra $2,000 for transportation and, as Bing tells, 'we added another $3,000 ... for "expenses" for her twelve [appearances]'.⁴ Though this may have been more than any singer had received at the Met for quarter of a century, yet it was substantially less than the $2,500 a performance Caruso earned in his last seven seasons, and the $3,500 Chaliapin commanded on the Met tour during the prosperous pre-depression days.

Callas's New York début took place at the beginning of Bing's seventh season in which he was seeking to metamorphose productions in a fustian repertory. Unlike La Scala, then at the forefront of changes in operatic taste, for Callas Bing was only able to bring out and dust up one unfamiliar work: *Norma*. This was given five New York performances and one at the Academy of Music, Philadelphia, with Barbieri, del Monaco or Baum and Siepi or Moscona. It was conducted by Cleva whom Callas had not wanted at first, remembering their Verona disagreement two years previously; but Bing persuaded her 'to ignore an incident of the past'.⁵ The production was not new but a revamping of a 'frowsy spectacle'⁶ originally mounted in 1943 for Milanov. At this stage of Callas's career the visual aspect was becoming increasingly more important; not only would it serve to reveal her dramatic talents to their best advantage, but it would also help distract attention from her increasing vocal frailty.

After the first night Taubmann, in the *New York Times* wrote: 'She phrased with sensitivity; she coloured her tones to suit the drama; she was telling in the florid passages. [But] it is a puzzling voice. Occasionally it gives an impression of having been formed out of sheer will power rather than natural endowments.'[7] Kolodin noted that '[al]though not a huge or weighty [voice], [it] is so well produced and floated that it is audible at all times, most particularly in the piano and pianissimo effects . . . [She] refuses to force it for volume's sake alone, and it comes clearly to the ear even when she is singing out a top D at the end of the trio.'[8] In the opinion of *Time* magazine, 'her voice has flaws . . . notes became shrill in the upper register. But in the middle and lower registers she sang with . . . purity, tender and yet sharply disciplined, and in the upper reaches – shrill or not – she flashed a sword-like power that is legendary.'[9] Eyer, in *Musical America*, comparing her with her Chicago Norma wrote 'she is treating her voice more kindly now and no longer . . . putting it through the tortuous paces in the interest of emotional expression . . . which made one fear for its safety'.[10]

Even then, in the afternoon of her career her singing was still, recordings testify, consummately executed. Her voice was perfectly placed, the instrument responsive to every musical demand; but inevitably it proved impossible for her new-found figure, with its frailer resources, to sustain her in the wide-ranging repertory she continued to undertake. By this time it was becoming increasingly difficult to determine which came first: her health problems or her vocal problems. Her health had always been variable and throughout the early 1950s she was plagued with one complaint after another: lassitude, boils, skin trouble and so on. But, indicatively, it was not until after she had lost weight that the demands she made of herself came to create vocal problems.

We may imagine how apprehensive she had become by the second *Norma*. This was a Saturday matinée on November 3rd. Bing records how 'she sent word from her dressing-room during the Overture that she would be unable to go on. I literally ran to her room, and found . . . Meneghini and a doctor in solicitous attendance; by the time I got there, I suppose, I looked sicker than she felt, and after a few encouraging words from me she agreed to go on, saving us from what would have been a riot.'[11] Noël Coward was in Bing's box, and he was told of '[her] fighting a bad cold . . . but she completely captured me. True her high notes were a bit scratchy but she is a fine singer, beautifully controlled and in technical command of every phrase. . . . At the very end [she] got an ovation the like of which I have seldom heard.'[12] It was at this performance that she told del Monaco she felt so unwell she was fearful of attempting the climactic B flat at the end and asked him if he would mind if they left it out. He agreed but, by that time, 'she suddenly found the strength to take the note, leaving the celebrated tenor high and dry'.[13] Needless to say he was enraged, for it appeared as if it were he who was having difficulty with the note. In the course of time she found herself increasingly involved in battles, but not so much with other singers as herself. In her youth, she had had the strength to surmount every obstacle effortlessly and the physical tension exacted nothing from her singing. But by this time every occasion was a proving ground.

Her next role, Tosca, she sang on November 15th. Callas did not appear much in this opera in her best days and no doubt she agreed to do so partly because it would not make the same vocal demands of her as Norma and Lucia, and also because Bing's mundane repertory gave her few other opportunities. That season she sang it on two occasions and also appeared in a truncated version of Act II on Ed Sullivan's CBS television show. It was conducted by another Greek, Dimitri Mitropoulos, with Giuseppe Campora as Cavaradossi and George London as Scarpia. When London found himself down to sing with Callas he felt apprehensive but at the first rehearsal, as he tells, he met 'a trouper, a fanatic[al] worker, a stickler for detail'. He recalls an incident at the telecast, how 'at one point, during the dress rehearsal, after she had "murdered" me, I fell too close to [Scarpia's] desk and she couldn't pass to cross the stage and pick up the two candelabras which Tosca places next to the dead Scarpia. [She] laughingly stopped and announced to the director, "There are just too many legs around here." We all had a good laugh. I fell thereafter so that she and her long train could pass, and that was that. Yet, the day after . . . many newspapers reported that Mme Callas and I had had a tiff . . . I tried to tell [them that] this was just not so but, I finally gave up. [I] realized that Callas, the prima donna reincarnate, fires not only the imagination of her audiences but also . . . the press. They want her to be "tempestuous" and "fiery".'[14]

Callas's third role, Lucia, commenced on December 3rd and she was announced to appear in it on five occasions. Lucia seems to have disquieted the New York critics more than either Norma or Tosca. Sabin, in *Musical America*, had 'the impression that Lucia was appearing as Callas, rather than that Callas was appearing as Lucia'. However he commends her 'virtuosic flexibility and smoothness. But no more than "Regnava nel silenzio" in Act I was needed to reveal a disturbing tremolo in her sustained tones, and notes above the stave in climaxes frequently approximated screams.'[15] Kolodin noted '"Ardon gli incensi" [was] sung with steady accuracy, a full-measure of musical meaning and strongly executed embellishments.' But he goes on: '[t]he succeeding "Spargi d' amaro pianto" showed some signs of vocal weariness, and the final top E flat [not in the score] was barely struck before she dropped to the floor ending "life" and all incidental difficulties.'[16]

The second *Lucia*, a Saturday matinée on December 8th, was Callas's only Met broadcast. Hereby hangs a tale. At the end of the Act II duet for Lucia and Enrico, there was an incident between her and baritone Sordello. Various stories survive, most of which seem to have been spawned by Bing's memoirs, *5000 Nights at the Opera*. According to him, '[Sordello] held a high note beyond the value Donizetti had given it, making . . . Callas, who had sung her part . . . correctly, look short of breath. She said "Basta" [which was misinterpreted by the audience in the orchestra rows that heard her]; and so did I: I ordered the balance of the baritone's . . . contract cancelled.'[17] But a recording of the broadcast makes it quite clear that she does not say anything that anyone in the audience could have overheard, and both she and Sordello interpolate high notes. What Bing does not tell is that Callas barely attacks the d'' before attenuating it, whereas Sordello sustains his g through the last measures. This may not be gentlemanly but Bing's use of it as an excuse for firing Sordello is disingenuous. Certainly, five years previously, in Mexico City, Callas herself was not above holding on to tonic or dominant high notes *ad lib*. Nor does it seem likely that at the first Met *Lucia* Sordello had behaved any differently, yet neither Cleva, the conductor, nor Bing issued him with a warning. The decision to dispense with Sordello was the result of Callas's back-stage pressure. After the duet was over she told Sordello, 'you'll never sing with me again',[18] and to Bing she issued an ultimatum: 'it's him or me'.[19] At first he seems not to have believed her but, at what was to have been her third *Lucia*, on the 11th, she withdrew. She was, she claimed indisposed, and 'police had to be called to disperse claimants for refunds when they discovered they were about to hear Dolores Wilson instead'.[20] Bing gave in. After all, throwing out a routine baritone who hung on to high notes did at least portray him as a stringent upholder of musical values.

Newspapers were full of stories about Sordello having been hard done by and pictures of him were published tearing up Callas's photograph. He delayed returning to Milan until the 22nd and booked a seat on the very same flight the Meneghinis were on. When Callas arrived at Idewild airport she found he had arranged a battery of photographers – he had an eye for publicity. He went up to her offering to shake her hand, but she turned her back on him, sniffing: 'I don't like a nasty bit player taking advantage of my publicity.'[21] It was then, as the Meneghinis boarded the plane, that a journalist noted that whereas Callas travelled first-class, Meneghini went tourist. When Legge hinted that that kind of publicity was not the sort she needed, she became very aerated. 'If those stinkers [the Met] won't pay for him to travel first-class. I won't pay either. Anyway I always order a second portion of whatever I eat and drink, put it in a vomit-bag and send a stewardess to take it back to him.'[22]

In spite of the fact that the Meneghinis fortune was growing fast they were disinclined to spend much of it, except when they were shamed into doing so; as they were at the beginning of the new year, back home in Milan, on January 3rd 1957, when Tebaldi gave a UNICEF benefit concert at the Teatro Manzoni. During the next few days Cardinal Montini, later Pope Paul VI, who was present at Tebaldi's concert, suddenly received from Callas 'a million Lire for the poor of the city'.[23] Newspapers were quick to note 'that Maria had made this gift so as not to be shown up'.[24] At the same time, to humanize her image, *Oggi* ran a series of photographs of her, showing her 'posing with her poodle', *à deux* with Meneghini 'in one of their more happy moments', and 'in a relaxed musical moment', although she doesn't look very relaxed. She is holding a score in front of her as if she were reading from a lectern.

On January 12th Callas was back in Chicago to reappear at the Civic Opera House. She was soloist in a gala concert with the Chicago Symphony Orchestra in aid of Hungarian relief after the recent Soviet invasion. Originally it was to have been conducted by Karl Böhm, but some differences arose between them in rehearsal and he withdrew, delivering a parting shot: 'I am a conductor and not an accompanist.'[25] She sang six arias representing one of her most ambitious programmes. Cassidy acclaimed her: 'She began [with "Ah! non credea" from *La Sonnambula*] and . . . sang it superbly [her] voice at its most magical, with the sound of the oboe in it. . . . [T]he shadow song from . . . *Dinorah* . . . was in its fey way gayer than a lark . . . but it didn't rise to heaven's gate. It got there, but the sound was shrill . . . [Then s]he put down her bouquet, rested a foot on the podium, folded her arms, and sang "In questa reggia" from *Turandot* . . . The soprano tessitura is mercilessly high. It got them cheering, but at what cost?'[26] The programme continued with Norma's 'Casta Diva', Leonora's 'D'amor sull'ali rosee' from *Il Trovatore* and finished with the first part of the *Lucia* Mad Scene, 'Il dolce suono'.

It was during her first season at the Met that she became acquainted with Elsa Maxwell. In his memoirs Arthur Rubinstein writes a tribute

to her, '[she was] a remarkable woman who exploited the rich and gave
to the poor . . . physically so completely unattractive, without any
particular gift, but endowed with a powerful vitality which brightened
for half a century the lives of hundreds'.[27] In her autobiography[28] she
details with relish trivial tales of her endless round of party-giving, and
assiduously lists the vast crop of international personalities she came
to know, including Shaw, the Windsors, Marie Curie, Lady Astor,
Hitler, Coward, Dali, Churchill, Diaghilev, Marconi, Mistinguett,
Eisenhower, Cole Porter, Mussolini, Beaverbrook, Queen Mary,
Einstein and Roosevelt – yet she tells us how contemptuous she is
of snobs!

Maxwell was born in San Francisco in 1883 to very ordinary parents,
as she tells. Her profession, if she can be said to have had one, was
party-giver. Unlike any of the names listed above she had but two
modest talents: some skill as a café pianist and song composer, and
a capacity for getting to know everybody she wanted to. It was
her acquaintance with any number of celebrated musicians which
accounts, at least in part, for her relationship with Callas. At first she
was a devoted fan of Tebaldi and, in her Hearst newspaper columns,
she acted to rekindle the old Tebaldi/Callas feud, firing broadsides at
Callas: of her Norma she wrote 'I was disappointed', and her *Lucia*
'Mad Scene left me completely unmoved'. Before Callas departed New
York at the end of her first season she determined to make peace with
Maxwell so she accepted an invitation to a ball in aid of the American
Hellenic Welfare Fund at the Waldorf Astoria by the Greek magnate
Spyros Skouras. She knew she would meet Maxwell there for she lived
at the Waldorf. Skouras introduced them and Maxwell reports their
conversation:

> *Maxwell*: Madame Callas, I would have imagined myself to be the
> last person on earth that you would have wished to meet.
> *Callas*: On the contrary, you are the first one I wished to meet
> because, aside from your opinion of my voice, I esteem you as a
> lady of honesty who is devoted to telling the truth.

This seems to have had the desired effect and Maxwell relates 'when
I looked into her amazing eyes, which are brilliant, beautiful and
hypnotic, I realized she is an extraordinary person. Thus we buried
the hatchet. I was amazed at her lack of animosity towards me.' After
which, according to Meneghini, 'Maxwell [became] infatuated with
[Maria]'.[29] She at once set into reverse everything she had ever written.
'The damaging articles disappeared from . . . [news]papers like magic

. . . [and] Maria was invited to appear on television programmes and to attend balls.'[30] They appeared together at one, five days before the Chicago concert, at the annual costume ball at the Waldorf Astoria. Callas was clad as Empress Hatshepshut, wearing a king's ransom in emeralds hired for the occasion from Harry Winston. Photographs of her appeared in newspapers next day in a sleek gown and looking the picture of soignée elegance with a couple of muscle men carrying her train.

On her way back to Italy from America Callas stopped off in London and, after three and a half years, on February 2nd and 6th, she returned to Covent Garden as Norma, once again with Stignani. Harewood tells how at the dress rehearsal she sang 'Casta Diva' 'much more quietly and in a uniquely imaginative way', and he complimented her but she claimed that she could not sing it in such fashion in performance. 'In Italy, she said, a heroic approach . . . was mandatory.'[31] At the première the Times critic complained that '"Casta Diva" ended very sharp . . . [and] in the middle of her voice the timbres do not mix so much as curdle. [But] her singing is still glorious, at once epic and pathetic in effect. Her breath control is . . . astonishing, enabling her to draw out a legato as suave as that of the finest instrumentalist, subtly shaded but always even in quality. Fioritura never sounds vacuous when she sings it, for she understands and can convey the shades of emotion and temperament that Bellini intended.'[32] On the other hand, Noël Goodwin, in the Daily Express,[33] wrote of the obvious effort that it cost her to produce a d'' at the end of the Act I trio, and he predicted that her career would be over in five years if she went on singing that way – as indeed, it was. I myself can confirm this impression. At the second performance, public acclaim was so great that Callas and Stignani encored 'Mira, o Norma'. Pritchard, the conductor, tells how 'I am the only conductor who gave an encore at the Royal Opera House in an operatic performance since the last war. The house was turbulent with applause, it went on and on. So I gave a signal and we repeated the cabaletta.'[34] Bing sent Callas a cablegram of congratulations on her success and she wired back: 'I am still trying to discover what happened in New York. I am only sorry I couldn't give you personally what other theatres have. I hope next year.'[35]

On February 4th Callas appeared on a BBC Television programme, Meet Jeanne Heal. After Norma was over she stayed on at the Savoy Hotel, London and, in the week beginning the 7th, at the Methodist Hall, Kingsway, she recorded Rosina in Il Barbiere di Siviglia with

Gobbi, Alva and Zaccaria and the Philhamonia Orchestra conducted by Alceo Galliera. This was the first complete opera she had recorded away from Milan since the Cetra *La Traviata*, and it was also the first to be issued in stereo. The vulgarity that she was accused of at certain moments in the Scala *Barbiere* is absent; but if her characterization is more chaste it is also more precious. Legge, not renowned for a sense of humour himself, considers that in this recording 'comedy brush[ed] her with its wings';[36] but we find that Callas mistakes being coy for comic. Rosina is a bravura role and her interpretation is very obviously microphone-orientated, if we play the live recording from La Scala immediately afterwards we have no difficulty in hearing just how muted a performance she gives. Not only has she simplified 'Una voce poco fa' from the Scala production, and from her recording made in 1954, but it is not as musically pointed. In the first measures of the Act II Lesson Scene, 'Contro un cor', most untypically for her, when the music descends to *a*, she introduces an ugly aspirate; perhaps it lay uncomfortably for her, for she is singing it in the original key whereas, at La Scala, she transposes it up a tone. The cadenza, the same she sings at La Scala, although it ends on a wobbly *a''*, is the one brilliant tour de force in the entire recording – indeed the whole point of it is to show off the singer. We might be inclined to blame much of the lack of scintillation on her rather than on Legge, except that Gobbi, in the Act I duet with Rosina, 'Dunque io son', fakes the roulades beginning 'oh che volpe sopraffina'. As with so many of Legge's Callas recordings, one wonders where he unearthed some of the rest of the company: Fritz Ollendorff, for example, the crude Bartolo with his Teutonic-sounding Italian, or Galliera, a mediocre conductor. The edition of *Il Barbiere* used is bland and without taste; better bad taste than none at all.

From London Callas returned to Milan to appear in a revival of Visconti's production of *La Sonnambula* at La Scala on March 2nd. This was her first appearance there that season and Meneghini demanded one and a half million Lire, but no objections were raised. The day after, with the same company, Legge began a recording of *La Sonnambula* at the Basilica of Santa Euphemia. This is conducted by Votto, who lacks sufficient sense of style to manage anything better than a routine revival. He seems unaware of Bernstein's conceits. He irons out the tempi, and transposes the Act I duet, 'Son geloso', down a further semitone. Nicola Monti, who replaces Valletti as Elvino, cuts the cadenza and Callas sings the stretto back as written not, as she had done, up an octave. Votto also dispenses with the third verse

of 'Sovra il sen', or perhaps Callas does, for in the second verse of
'Ah! non giunge', she not only simplifies some of the ornaments but
she no longer has the reserves to amplify her tone. Between verses
she interpolates a cadenza ascending to *e''* flat, which she does not
include under Bernstein. Remarkably, on this stratospheric note, she
contrives to execute a diminuendo, a feat unrivalled in the history of
the gramophone.

On the 8th, the day after the second *La Sonnambula*, the Meneghinis
spent the evening at a reception given by the Milan press club. After
a further four *La Sonnambulas*, on April 14th, Callas undertook
Donizetti's *Anna Bolena*. This was only the second twentieth-century
revival. It had been given once before, in 1956 at the Teatro Donizetti,
Bergamo, the composer's birthplace. Shawe-Taylor, in *Opera*, writes
of the Scala revival: 'In each of his five sets [Nicola] Benois uses to
splendid effect the immense height and depth of the Scala stage; and
the first entry of the afflicted Queen down a long double staircase was
most impressive. Smeaton attempts to raise her spirits by a touching little
romanza, sung with lovely tone by Gabriella Carturan – so well indeed
that we regretted the decision to omit its second and more decorated
stanza. At some artless phrase about "first love", the Queen interrupts
the song, and advancing to the footlights [it is one of the great merits
of Visconti's production that he is never afraid of such simple effects
when they are truly called for] begins to sing a soft cavatina of
recollection ["Come innocente giovane"] which suited Mme Callas
to perfection and provided her with the first of many triumphs during
the evening. . . .

'The last scene of Act I, when Anna is discovered in an apparently
compromising situation with Percy and Smeaton, was notable for the
immense force of outraged dignity which Mme Callas threw into the
words of recitative, "Giudici! Ad Anna! Giudici!" It was doubtless in
such tremendous moments, of which the score gives no hint, that Pasta
[the creatress] too revealed her greatness. . . . The final scene in the
Tower of London is the greatest thing in the opera, and it also showed
Mme Callas at the summit of her powers both as singer and tragic
actress. The scene opens with a beautiful elegiac chorus in two parts for
the Queen's faithful attendants; it is in F minor, with a soft Schubertian
close in the major. Anna enters, vacillating between sanity and a world
of illusions . . . We have here no conventional mad scene with flute
obbligato, but a long chain of arioso, arias and recitatives: the main
feature is a limpid F major evocation of happier days, "Al dolce guidami
castel natio" . . . upon which there breaks the sound of military drums

announcing the Queen's impending execution and restoring her to the realities of her situation. Her companions in misfortune enter: Smeaton is pardoned for his involuntary part in her downfall; then she drifts away once more into forgetfulness of the present, breathing out a prayer to Heaven for release. Another sound is heard from outside; bells and the acclamation of the crowd at the crowning of their new Queen. Finally, regaining her senses, Anna launches into a forceful cabaletta, with sequences of rising trills, in which she arraigns the guilty couple ["Coppia iniqua"], yet magnanimously pardons them as, with dignity and composure, she leads her companions to the block. Interpreted by such an artist as Maria Callas, and directed with perfect taste by Visconti, this was a scene of high tragedy.'[37]*

It is noteworthy that *La Sonnambula*, first produced three months after *Anna Bolena*, which Callas had sung directly before it, had also been written for Pasta. However, just as we were chary of seeking to draw too close a parallel between Colbran and Callas when considering Armida, so too, we are between Pasta and Callas because they both sang Anna Bolena. For the *Medea* Pasta undertook was not by Cherubini but by Mayr, and she ventured a number of 'trouser' roles including Romeo in Bellini's *I Capuleti ed i Montecchi*, Rossini's Tancredi and even Cherubino in *Le Nozze di Figaro*. It would be hard to imagine Callas in any of them. As they were different histrionically so they must have been different vocally. Contemporary opinion suggests that Pasta's voice in its prime never had the limpidity of Callas's. Moscheles relates of Pasta that, in her best days, her voice was 'at first veiled . . . like the sun breaking through the mist',[38] and Lumley remembers how it was 'always thick and husky even in its prime'.[39] Yet Callas's voice was surpassingly responsive, not only in Naples in 1949 and Mexico City in 1950 but even in 1961 when her career was virtually over. As we hear in her EMI recording of the *Mignon* Polonaise, the perfection of her coloratura remains, like the Cheshire cat's smile, when the voice itself has practically disappeared.

If there is not so much in common vocally between Callas and Pasta, their domestic lives had even less in common. A visitor describes meeting Pasta in later life at Como in a small house adjoining her villa. 'Close to the door we stumbled on some prosaic matters, dirty saucepans, kitchen utensils, and the like, not to mention the leavings of an early dinner. Amid the debris sat three unkempt [maids], not one

---

*The author would particularly like to thank Desmond Shawe-Taylor for permitting him to reprint so much of this review.

of them in love with soap and water . . . The great lady soon appeared. We did not see her at her best, for having just risen from her siesta, in which we had disturbed her, she was only half awake. We found her friendly and evidently gratified with our visit. Her mouth and teeth are still lovely, [but] her black hair was in a dishevelled state, and her dress an original medley of oddities.'[40] In fact no one could have looked less like Callas for, with the passage of time, as photographs testify, she became ever more model-like, and Meneghini lists the stringent rules she laid down for her domestic staff at the Via Buonarroti: the washing and ironing of their clothes, their standards of cleanliness, the way they should address the master and mistress of the house, and so on. As Meneghini admits, these read like 'Prussian guidelines', though he is at pains to point out that for all Callas's 'rigid sense of propriety, [she] had wonderful human qualities and she knew how to make herself loved'.[41]

Anna Bolena took place before the age when it was the custom for newspapers to review new opera productions internationally, yet the London *Sunday Times* and the *New York Times* carried not only notices of it but also photographs of her in it. It made an unprecedented effect. With it she came as near as she ever did in making a perfect marriage between her lyric and dramatic gifts. Unfortunately, although a complete recording of a broadcast of *Anna Bolena* survives, there is no film of it; yet photographs convey something of her histrionic skill. When we listen to her we can only marvel at how fitting is her musical characterization. Unlike Nedda, Madama Butterfly or Mimì, Anna Bolena does not encourage her to indulge in studied effects; it was enough that the music should have preoccupied her. Although, as the recording testifies, her voice has begun to age all too obviously its decadence is not yet so obtrusive nor does a work from the age of bel canto tax her unduly. Although by this stage we note how careful she is, before interpolating an occasional ultimate or penultimate c'' or d'', to have other voices support hers she does, once in a while, add a few modest embellishments, as in the last scene in the cantabile, 'Cielo, a' miei lunghi spasimi'; although in the final cabaletta, 'Coppia iniqua', she simplifies the first verse and merely sings what is written in the second. That spring she told the critic Eugenio Gara, 'I'll do everything I can so as not to dismount my tiger'[42] but, as Rossi-Lemeni, the Enrico VIII remembers, 'she was frightened because her voice was no longer responding to her perfectly.'[43]

XV

1957–1958

AFTER SEVEN PERFORMANCES of *Anna Bolena* Callas was to have travelled to Vienna again, this time to sing Violetta on May 4th. Karajan was anxious to secure her for the Staatsoper in another production loaned from La Scala, that of Visconti's *La Traviata*; except, of course, that he would conduct, not Giulini. Visconti wrote to Meneghini expressing his disgust: 'We will soon have an Austrian Scala as in 1848. . . . Does it not seem to you a great slight to [Giulini], unfair and tactless? . . . [He] is a noble, refined man and, as a conductor, dignified, scrupulous, enthusiastic.'[1] Meneghini tells how the subject of Callas's returning to Vienna had first been raised immediately after the *Lucias* the previous year. According to Meneghini she told Karajan she would be pleased to come again, but she expected a higher fee, to which he agreed. It was not until the end of April that the contract arrived but the Meneghinis were surprised to find the fee had not changed. They protested but Karajan declined to offer more. This story was not, however, untrue so much as incomplete, for although Meneghini is usually fulsome with figures he avoids mentioning any in this context. But when Callas had sung Lucia she had earned $1,600, and now he demanded an increase of $500. He was desirous of driving his usual hard bargain but he miscalculated, for less than two years had elapsed since the allied occupation forces had withdrawn and Austria was hardly as prosperous it has since become. Karajan was not of a mind to pay any singer such a fee (it might have drawn too much attention to his own), so Callas did not go to Vienna again.

She continued her Scala season uninterrupted. During rehearsals for the next production, Gluck's *Ifigenia in Tauride*, Maxwell flew in from Paris. Callas went out to Malpensa to greet her and for the next few days Maxwell, in her newspaper column, posed as a custodian of culture dispensing with her usual princely litter. She tells how she spent the time ensconced at Via Buonarroti listening to a tape of Callas's Anna Bolena and hearing her try out Imogene in Bellini's *Il Pirata*, which she was to sing the following year. At other times they would go to La Scala. Doubtless in so unfamiliar an environment Maxwell found it all so elevating. When she was told of an anti-Callas lobby it seemed to her utterly incredible; 'someone somewhere is spreading poison about one of the most touching individuals I have ever known. Nothing can destroy the supreme art of Maria Callas.'

Callas gave only four performances of Ifigenia, commencing on June 1st; it would prove the last new Visconti production she would work on. Although the drama is based on the classical unities of time, place and action, Visconti had Benois model the set after the rococo style of Bibiena. Callas protested: 'Why are you doing it like this? It's a Greek story and I'm a Greek woman, so I want to look Greek on stage.'[2] Visconti endeavoured to reassure her: 'The opera must look like a Tiepolo fresco come to life. The Greece you are talking of is too far off.'[3] Callas allowed herself to be persuaded. As Benois notes, 'the décor may have been parachronistic but it went perfectly with the music'.[4]

The curtain went up during the overture revealing Ifigenia frantically pacing the stage. Visconti recalls the effect Callas created: 'She wore a majestic gown with many folds of rich silk brocade and an enormous train, over which was a large cloak of deep red. On her head was a crown of pearls, and loops of pearls hung from her neck.'[5] 'All I told her was go to the top of the stairs, stand there in the wind and then come down again so that she would be in the right position by the time she was to sing. I gave her no timings but Maria had timing in her blood. Notwithstanding the fact that she was short-sighted and the steps had to be plainly marked so that she would be able to see her way, she needed nothing else. With the wind machine behind her she would run up the staircase and come back down again, trailing twenty-five feet of cloak, and with split second timing and still enough breath to start fortissimo dead on cue. So extraordinarily co-ordinated for her was music and movement that at each performance she would hit her first note in exactly the same position.'[6]

As a recording suggests, the role makes few vocal demands of Callas, the music lying only very occasionally uncomfortably for her. We agree with Lionel Dunlop in *Opera*: 'her singing caused none of that momentary discomfort which has sometimes seemed to go with her slimmer figure'.[7] Nevertheless, her voice has lost much quality, the tone has become thin and horny, as if the stuffing had been knocked out of it. It not only lacks sufficient variety of colour but it is not as smoothly produced as it is, so notably, in the broadcast recording of her other Gluck venture, *Alceste*, three years before, though she can still emit an occasional phrase tellingly, for example 'Ei m'e fratello', when Oreste reveals himself. The rest of the company sound as if they might have made an effect in verismo, but in a classical opera they are stylistically shipwrecked.

On June 19th Callas made her only appearance in Switzerland, at a concert at the Tonhalle, Zurich, where she sang the Act I scena from *La Traviata* and the Mad Scene from *Lucia*. A week later, at the RAI studios, Rome, she undertook Lucia in concert form. It was conducted by Serafin and this was the first time she had appeared with him since the summer of 1955. It was typical of Callas that the temper she had thrown over his recording *La Traviata* for EMI with Stella, when she had vowed never to work with him again, should by this time have spent itself. Save for Eugenio Fernandi, a very routine Edgardo, the cast of *Lucia* is made up of familiar names, including Panerai and Modesti. Her Lucia has now certainly slimmed down vocally, though she does not deliver the music with the compensating accuracy that we associate with the appearance of her new figure, as she had done so notably at La Scala at the beginning of 1954. We hear how much thinner her voice is becoming, how her upper register is growing ever more wavery, and the top notes ever more chancy. She not only has to leave out the first e'' flat in the Mad Scene, as she had done in Berlin, but now she no longer steps up to the final one easily, by kicking off to it from b'' flat, as she had used to do. She just takes a whacking great breath and makes a lunge. Recordings put the best complexion on these notes, but when one saw her live the effort they cost her was all too obvious. Four years have elapsed since the EMI recording, when Serafin had cut Lucia to the absolute minimum; but the example of Karajan, in restoring part of the ensemble at the end of Act II, seems not to have gone unnoticed.

In the last week of June Maxwell was back in the picture again, this time to reciprocate the Meneghinis' hospitality. Playing the role of fairy godmother she spirited them away to Paris on a three day conducted tour. They were actually, *mirabile dictu*, paying their own way and, perhaps, a part of Maxwell's too. This was the first time they had ever been outside Italy on holiday; it was the first crack to appear in the elaborate musical façade which, throughout the last decade, Callas had built up with such concentrated single-mindedness. And there was something cryptic about the visit being to Paris, for here, twenty years later, she would be mewed up in the last days of her life, when she had long ceased to be a singer and, like a recurring character in a Balzac novel who had once been a heroine, she was reduced to looking on. In 1957 Paris glittered with the fashionable and famous. Maxwell took the Meneghinis to 'cocktails at the Rothschilds, dinner at Maxim's, sipping tea with the Windsors [and] going to the races with Aly Khan'.[8] Nevertheless Callas was not yet ready for café society, though she may have been impressed, and Maxwell was bringing the curtain down on her career too soon. When they parted she begged Callas to come to Venice in September for a party she was planning, but Callas left undecided; she was anxious to appear with the La Scala company on tour, for was she not still the greatest opera singer in the world?

On July 4th, with the La Scala troupe, she made her second appearance in Germany at the Grosses Haus, Cologne in two performances of *La Sonnambula*. Recordings survive of the dress rehearsal and the first performance on July 4th and, like the Scala *Norma* of 1955, they reveal her voice still at its best at this stage of her career. It is indicative that in the last three months she had been singing Ifigenia, for her scarcely a taxing role and Anna Bolena, a bel canto role in which, though it may have demanded a lot histrionically, she could at least still cope with vocally. However, on July 9th, she commenced her summer schedule of recordings at La Scala with Turandot. We are amazed to find her agreeing to undertake a role so vocally hazardous. In the days of her youth when she had to pursue her career without vocal compromises it may have been necessary but as soon as she could, wisely, she dropped it from her repertory. Maybe she thought recording it different from singing it in the theatre and it would do her voice no lasting harm. Nevertheless, next March in New York, we may believe she was remembering it and not stage performances years before, when she tells radio interviewer Fleetwood, 'I sang Turandot all over Italy, hoping to God that I wouldn't wreck my voice. Because. . . . It's not really very good for the voice . . . It's ruined quite a few.'[9]

Serafin is again on the podium, as he was when she sang it last in Buenos Aires in 1949. Although she is more restrained before the microphone, the effort it costs her emitting almost every note is all too obvious. We note her facility in contrasting registers and how reponsive her voice is in the execution of wide intervals, though little of the atmosphere that Puccini creates is left principally to the singers, as it is in operas of Rossini, Bellini or Donizetti. Serafin's tempi are slightly faster than in Buenos Aires, so enabling her more quickly to relinquish top notes at the end of phrases which threaten to get out of control. We know that by this stage she was bothered by the problem of keeping her voice steady. Legge tells[10] how one day at the Biffi Scala he and Schwarzkopf, who sings Liù, were lunching with the Meneghinis, when Callas turned to her demanding to know 'how you sing top As and Bs and make a diminuendo on them. Walter says mine make him seasick.' Much to the astonishment, if not fright, of the waiters and the other diners, she and Schwarzkopf, there and then, stood up and began exchanging top notes and feeling each other in turn, their 'diaphragm[s], lower jaw[s], throat[s] and ribs'. After a bit Callas claimed that she had 'got it' but, perhaps because both singers' methods were *sui generis*, she did not effect a cure.

She finished *Turandot* on July 15th and began to record *Manon Lescaut* on July 18th. The programme was undoubtedly much facilitated by her remarkable musical skill, though she may not have known much of *Manon* before, and whatever one can say for or against her undertaking it at this stage of her career, there is not the slightest doubt as to her command of the music. Those pages we are accustomed never to hear accurately sung, for example, 'L'ora, o 'Tirsi', in Act II, she sings with polish, executing the triplets with perfect exactitude – indeed, all the florid figures and trills she turns immaculately, though the effect of Turandot is all too obvious. The c'' at the end she leaves almost as soon as she reaches it. In the preceding duet with Lescaut, 'Per me tu lotti', she may sing every note with rhythmic precision but her voice sounds thin and wavery and her tone, in the climactic passage, 'vieni! vieni!', scarcely has the plenitude to suit Puccini's accompaniment, nor can she make the right effect with the c'' at the end, which yaps away. Whereas the *Turandot* recording was published the following year, *Manon Lescaut* had to wait until 1960, by which time she had run off with Onassis and her La Scala reign was over. The days of her being able to undertake as disparate a repertory as Amina and Turandot in juxtaposition were over; but instead of reconciling herself to the inevitable her programming courted disaster. Nor was Meneghini able to help her, for just as she either could not or would not admit to herself a rapidly approaching vocal crisis, he was solely preoccupied with securing her the highest fees. He saw to it she wore the finest clothes, that she always travelled first-class (even if he didn't!), that their home was decorated to at least the highest *petit bourgeois* standards, and that she had the best medical attention. But that was as much as he did or, indeed, could do; he was not a young man, and he knew next to nothing about the voice or vocal health.

Callas's next engagement was to sing two concerts in Athens at the Herodes Atticus Amphitheatre. According to Meneghini she had wanted to give her services but the 'organizers . . . refused saying that the Festival did not need any subsidy'.[11] He relates how offended she was, and she insisted her fee was $9,000, that is, 270 thousand drachmas, and they were obliged to accept. Details were leaked in Greek newspapers and became the talk of Athens. There was a deal of hostility to her coming back and receiving such a fee when at the time the country was plagued with economic problems. Her appearance became a *casus belli* for the opposition which was intent on causing the Karamanlis government the maximum embarrassment. The first recital had been scheduled for August 1st, but with all the fuss generated, the hot dry weather and her vocal problems, she was unable to muster sufficient strength and, only hours before it was to take place, she cancelled. She was, she claimed, indisposed. She appeared on the second occasion, the 5th. When she came on stage her reception was chilly and reserved, Nikolaidi remembers 'she was so nervous . . . that her foot was shaking. I was sitting up front and could see'.[12] Yet, after her usual fashion, this brought out the spunk in her. The programme was surpassingly difficult, though for her not untypical, including: 'D'amor sull'ali rosee' from *Il Trovatore*, 'Pace, pace mio Dio' from *La Forza del Destino*, 'Regnava nel silenzio' and 'Quando rapito' from *Lucia di Lammermoor*, the Morte d'Isotta from *Tristano e Isotta* and the *Hamlet* Mad Scene. By the time she got to the end of it she had, as it were, stiffened the sinew and summoned up the blood, so managing to support her voice. A recording shows her singing to have been easier and surer than it was in the two Puccini operas she had just recorded, but her voice is no longer what it had been only a year before when she sang the RAI concert. The ovation she earned was overwhelming. But though she consented to encore the second part of the *Hamlet* Mad Scene, when she was asked to give another recital in lieu of the one she had cancelled, she refused.

She returned to Milan to prepare for her next engagement abroad with La Scala, this time at the Edinburgh Festival and again as Amina in *La Sonnambula*. By then she was she claimed, utterly exhausted, certainly her schedule seems exhausting. Meneghini tells how she had 'symptoms of nervous strain . . . caused by overwork and fatigue',[13] yet the number of performances she gave was no more than she had in previous years. Her indifferent health and continued weight-loss was at least in part due to her refusal to accept the fact that, although still a young woman, she no longer had the physical stamina she had possessed only a handful of years before, when she would oscillate between music of the widest diversity in a matter of days. Eventually, however, she was persuaded to leave for Edinburgh, and she managed four Aminas at the King's Theatre from August 19th. Whatever impressions one might draw from Meneghini's account of her being 'vocally . . . in fine form',[14] or from some of the reviews, recordings of broadcasts of the second and third performances on the 21st and 26th reveal that her voice was threadbare. Which may be accounted for partly by the strenuous Puccini recording sessions referred to above, but also because at the same time she was ceaselessly refining her vocal art so as to endeavour to keep pace with her ever-reduced figure. '[Amina] is very difficult because you have to control yourself so much and sing very softly throughout',[15] she admits. In her inner ear she must have heard a sound she was striving for but, inevitably, there came a point beyond which it was just impossible to refine her singing further and manage to keep her throat open. In the second broadcast a vein of weakness begins to appear in her tone; and after Edinburgh she never again ventured Amina.

The programme for the Edinburgh Festival had been available from that spring and it listed a fifth *La Sonnambula* on September 3rd, though Callas was not contracted for this. This was the same night as Maxwell's party, which Maxwell had been entreating her to come to all summer. At first Callas had not wanted to, but by the time she got to Edinburgh the strain of her schedule, plus Maxwell's eloquence, persuaded her she should go. In past years there had been many performances for which La Scala did not have her name on a contract but which they had no difficulty coaxing her into singing. Until only recently she had wanted to undertake anything and everything. Now, however, it was not that she did not wish to; it was simply that she was no longer able. She determined to treat her contract literally and leave after the fourth performance. When Robert Ponsonby, Director of the Festival, learned of her imminent departure he rushed round to her hotel and she showed him her contract. He was, Meneghini reports, amazed.[16] If news had leaked to the press that La Scala had permitted the Edinburgh Festival to announce and sell tickets for a performance by the world's most famous prima donna that she was not contracted for, a major scandal would have resulted. So she was persuaded that she should allow them to announce that her 'precarious health'[17] made her withdrawal necessary and a new young soprano, Renata Scotto, whom La Scala had taken the trouble to bring with them in anticipation of just such an emergency, would appear in her stead. On August 30th Callas returned to Milan: she needed, she said, to take a rest.

There the incident might have rested but for the fact that only a few days later photographs appeared of her in newspapers throughout the world at the party Maxwell gave in Venice and this hardly lent credence to her excuse of 'precarious health'. The party was a marathon and lasted seven days commencing on September 3rd at the ballroom at the Hotel Danieli during the 13th Film Festival, with more than a 170 guests including various multi-millionaires, Rubinstein, Merle Oberon and Henry Fonda. In the daytime guests would collect at Harry's Bar or Florian's, or go out to the Excelsior on the Lido. On one such occasion at lunch Maxwell introduced the Meneghinis to Aristotle Onassis, who had come to Venice especially on his yacht, the *Christina*. On another she got Callas to sing 'Stormy Weather' to her accompaniment. Maxwell was coy about revealing her own gifts as composer: in the 1920s she had written a number of songs, including two, 'I will not grieve' and 'I need no song', to words of Barbara Hutton, the Woolworths' heiress, and another, that Alda and Melba sang, 'The Singer', in which she wrote both music and lyrics:

> Last night I faced the tumultuous throng,
> Waiting and eager for my ev'ry song;
> And I, proud singer in the world's kind heart,
> Felt as I sang, 'How great thou art'!
> Today alone, so worn and spent,
> I wander at last with head low bent,
> A little bird sang ah on a tree close by,
> Dear God, how small a singer am I.

Maxwell was like a parrot in full cry – 'Party, party! Where's the party?' After a week it was over but in her newspaper column she kept it going as long as she could. She proudly trumpeted: 'I have had many presents in my life . . . but I have never had any star give up a performance in an opera house for a friend.'

It was while Callas was in Rome singing Lucia in concert at the end of June that year that the Italian music publishers Ricordi had written to discover whether she would be able to record Cherubini's *Medea* for a new label they were launching. Meneghini contacted Legge who agreed to release her for, characteristically, he had no plans to record it, and by the terms of her contract, in such a case, she would be allowed to record for another company. Ricordi duly made the arrangements and an agreement was reached on July 17th,[18] in spite of the fact that, as Meneghini admits, 'I came up with an amount I assumed they would never be willing to pay.'[19] Like EMI Ricordi proposed using La Scala, and the theatre was booked between September 14th and 21st. Less than a week was left to elapse before the opening night of the San Francisco season, on the 27th, on which Callas was announced to sing Lucia. By this time, it was obvious, her fee was expanding at such a rate that she could now have got far more money from the San Francisco Opera than she had been contracted for eight months before. There was a coincidence between the escalation in her fee, which Meneghini was preoccupied with securing, and escalating vocal problems she was obliged to face up to, so the Meneghinis decided, if for different reasons, that they should endeavour to get her out of at least part of her San Francisco contract. No sooner had she got back to Milan from Edinburgh, on September 1st, immediately before leaving for Venice, than she cabled Kurt Adler, Director of the San Francisco Opera, advising him that he should have another singer ready as her health might not permit her to honour her contract. But only a few days later Adler saw press photographs of her in Venice at Maxwell's party, apparently in the pink. Not surprisingly he was suspicious and he made a number of attempts to get her to come; but still she pleaded lassitude and general weakness. But he did, finally, on September 13th manage to exact a promise from her that she would nevertheless still be able to undertake performances of Lady Macbeth scheduled from October 15th. It was during the period when she should have been rehearsing Lucia, and Adler was finalizing the *Macbeth* schedule, that he telephoned her in Milan, but she was out. Surprised, he asked her maid where she was, and she told him she was out singing. She was, in fact, at a recording session of *Medea* though it was doubtful if he was told that. He was highly indignant and at once cancelled her contract filing a complaint with the American Guild of Musical Artists (AGMA).

So, following the recording of *Medea*, for the next two months, Callas remained silent. At the beginning of November she returned to the United States for the last instalment in her legal wrangle with Bagarozy. On the 21st she proceeded to Dallas to the State Fair Music Hall to sing in a concert to inaugurate the Dallas Opera, for which $17,000 was taken in ticket receipts. The company was launched by two founders of the Chicago Lyric, Kelly and Rescigno. She gave one of her usual concerts: 'Tutte le torture' from Mozart's *Serraglio*, the Mad Scene from *I Puritani*, 'Vieni t' affretta!' from *Macbeth*, 'Ah fors' è lui' and 'Sempre libera' from *La Traviata* and the Final Scene from *Anna Bolena*. For the first part she was clad in a gold silk creation and then, for the *Anna Bolena* scena, she changed into 'a black lace sheath with a blazing diamond necklace',[20] both outfits were by Biki. A recording made at the dress rehearsal seems to be the first extant live recording of Callas that does not derive from a broadcast. Although copies were in circulation on tape within a few years it was not until the 1960s, when Callas's career had petered out, that small record companies began to publish many different broadcast performances she gave. Today, reminted on CDs these offerings have become as familiar as those of the big companies. Indeed, EMI now seems to have realized that with Callas the best way to beat the pirates is by joining them; they have issued the (1955) La Scala Violetta, the (1955) Berlin Karajan Lucia, an extract from one of the RAI concerts and the Amsterdam recital. A CD of this Dallas rehearsal, complete with repetitions and talk by Rescigno and Callas, is an obvious candidate for future issue.

The Dallas rehearsal shows her off at her best, for the microphone seems to have been at some distance from her, putting the best complexion on her voice: We might remember that an opera singer is judged on how he or she sounds in a theatre not on how a microphone up close inflates the noise he or she makes, warts and all. Although the *Serraglio* aria may have some typically wobbly high notes, the concluding passage of ascending and descending fioritura is sung to perfection. When Rescigno, the conductor, gets her to repeat it she does so using practically no voice at all, yet she still sings every note accurately. By so doing she reveals the perfect placement of her instrument, the kind of felicity that disguises art. We have noted before how the *Puritani* Mad Scene suits her; the tessitura of 'Vien diletto' enables her voice still to rise easily to a ringing e'' flat. Here once again she demonstrates how a responsive voice makes its best effect in the music of a composer, like Bellini, concerned to show the singer off to advantage. Afterwards she sings Lady Macbeth's entrance aria and it is indicative that even in rehearsal she has to give her all. At the end of Violetta's scena, in 'Sempre libera', she is content to mark c' for c'' and e' flat for e'' flat it was, after all, only a rehearsal. She finishes with the Final Scene from *Anna Bolena* which she manages more easily and effortlessly than she would in the EMI recording the following summer, although her singing of the passage 'Cielo, a miei lunghi spasimi' is neither as refined nor as eloquent.

Meanwhile another episode of the Maxwell drama had been going on. Callas's naïvety in her relations with La Scala was paralleled in her relations with Maxwell. If it had taken her a while to accept male homosexuals, like Visconti, we may imagine how much ruder was her awakening to the nature of Maxwell's affection. It was only finally, during her Dallas stay, where Maxwell had followed her, that she understood; and on the plane back to New York she expressed herself unambiguously. Maxwell got the message. Years later Meneghini published parts of some of Maxwell's letters. She had written to Callas: 'I must write to you and thank you for being the innocent victim of the greatest love one human being can have for another.'[21]

Back in Milan Callas had been vainly trying to get Ghiringhelli to accept responsibility for her failure to sing the fifth La Sonnambula in Edinburgh. But Ghiringhelli's concern was the reputation of La Scala, and he looked down his nose at her precipitate exit for Venice and Maxwell's party; it was, he felt, not becoming of La Scala. With characteristic skill he resisted her attempts to get him to clear the air with a press conference. She insisted, and countered with threats to leave La Scala if he refused; but he judged this was mere braggadocio. Eventually she became so exasperated that she told him it would be necessary for her to give her own statement to the press, to make her position clear; but this was just what he intended! He left her to it. He may have been in the wrong, but he judged that nobody would believe her; and subsequent events would all too soon prove how right he was.

Meanwhile Callas opened the season at La Scala again, on December 7th, this time as Amelia in Verdi's Un Ballo in Maschera. Amelia, like Elisabetta in Don Carlo and Leonora in La Forza del Destino, is not the protagonist and her music does not call for the technical skill or dramatic range of other Verdi heroines like Lady Macbeth or Violetta. The ensemble also included di Stefano, the last time they would appear in opera together, Simionato and Bastianini, and it was conducted by Gavazzeni. He remembers '[Callas] had this strange, burning, singular talent; she was always herself and yet always different in every role. A voice of more even quality could not have imparted the tension, or Amelia's desperation so effectively. Had she sought less wide a range, fewer colours then perhaps she may have achieved a more homogeneous sound, but she preferred richness of colour and to make a play of light and shade in recreating the character.'[22]

After five performances Callas went down to Rome on December 27th to make her first appearance for three years at the Teatro dell'

Opera, where she was to undertake Norma. She had sung it there in two previous seasons: the first time when she was still plump, in February 1950, and then again when she had begun to slim, in April 1953. On the second occasion the cast was identical with the one announced this time, not only the same singers, Barbieri, Corelli and Neri, but also the same conductor, Santini. However, before the first rehearsal Barbieri became unwell and was replaced by Pirazzini. Callas commenced rehearsals on the 28th and Jellinek tells of 'a slight pain developing in her throat'[23] but, the next day, after resting at her hotel, she felt better, and on New Year's Eve she was well enough to sing the dress rehearsal. Santini even had to 'ask her to conserve her powers'.[24] At nine o'clock the same night she appeared in a RAI television transmission from the Rome studios singing 'Casta Diva', which was transmitted throughout western Europe, after which she and Meneghini joined friends dining at the Circolo degli Scacchi, and it was noticed that they did not leave until after 1 in the morning.

This was New Year's Day 1958, a public holiday in Italy. When Callas woke she found herself voiceless. Meneghini tells of her having 'caught a cold and being obliged to take to her bed',[25] she had been incessantly complaining about the theatre's lack of heating. He called the Sovrintendente who was summoned to their suite. When he arrived she began to talk about having to get a substitute, but he cut her short, such a thing was impossible. It was the opening night of the season and the audience was to include the President of Italy, Giovanni Gronchi, and his wife, as well as other state dignitaries: 'The house is sold out, and the public paid to see and hear [you],'[26] he said, 'you must get better, you absolutely must sing.'[27] In any case, he went on rather lamely, there was not sufficient time to find anyone else. So an anxious period passed while doctors looked down her throat and prescribed all manner of medications. At length, in response to persistent entreaties, she agreed to see how she felt the next day. When she awoke the following morning, she did feel a good deal better, 'her voice seemed to be returning [and] she was filled with optimism';[28] she would, she said, be able to sing. A doctor examined her an hour before curtain-up and confirmed she was well enough.

Nevertheless, whilst singing 'Casta diva', so she afterwards claimed, she felt her voice leaving her and she had no alternative but to withdraw after the end of the act; in such fashion the performance came to an abrupt halt. But she did not sing so poorly as to invite public condemnation, as can be easily checked by listening to a recording of the broadcast, although one biographer states that '[t]he audience sat in amazed silence' during 'Casta Diva' and that there were 'loud shouts' of 'Go back to Milan' and 'You've cost us a million Lire!' and another tells how she barely 'got through . . . "Casta Diva". The rousing cabaletta . . . sounded tired and uninspiring. There was mild applause, all but lost in mounting noises of displeasure.' Here again, as with Bing's recollections of the Met *Lucia*, it would have been more convenient for such storytellers had it not been possible for us to hear a recording. In fact Callas sings with her customary skill. Occasionally, perhaps, at the top of her voice her tone, particularly in the cabaletta, which rises to c'', does sound thin, and her singing generally is not as effortless as it once was; but to what extent that is a reflection of indisposition, or merely a comment on the condition of her voice at this stage of her career, it would take a bold man to guess. Certainly she sounded no different to the telecast of two nights earlier.[29] In any case 'Casta Diva' was never the high point of Callas's Norma. It is at the beginning of the opera, not at the end and for her Norma was always a cumulative experience; nor is it possible for an audience to receive the aria with 'mounting . . . displeasure', for Norma has left the stage long before the orchestral postlude has finished. In Rome, as usual, the scene ends without an ovation, and there is certainly no point at which 'loud shouts' of the kind quoted above can be heard: in fact, it is not until long after the end of Act I during the extended interval, when an announcement is made 'the performance has been cancelled', that one hears anyone in the audience expressing any kind of displeasure whatsoever.

It is curious that her biographers should have accepted her claim of voicelessness without questioning it. Indeed, they have gone on to embellish her story, describing her voice gradually leaving her during the scene. Yet, the c'' at the end of cabaletta sounds much the same as the one she emits in the *Serraglio* aria in the Dallas rehearsal two months earlier. For an unthroaty voice, as Callas's unquestionably was, it should be possible to sing above almost any cold: singing correctly is a natural business, which is why a great singer's voice will not be troubled unduly by a cold. I remember Sutherland singing Semiramide in concert in London[30] when she was suffering from very obvious catarrh, yet none of the critics guessed. To sing with influenza or a more severe virus would be unwise, not for vocal so much as physical reasons. It is significant that in her youth Callas suffered from all types of malady, yet she rarely cancelled performances, it is only by 1958, when her vocal problems start to escalate, that she persuades herself, or allows herself to be persuaded, that she has lost her voice.

Meneghini admits that although 'Maria was certainly not well, she would have continued the performance had I urged her to'.[31] We may be sure that Callas was bolstered in her decision not to sing not only by Meneghini's counsel but also Maxwell's, who had made a reappearance after Christmas spent in Paris with the Windsors. In spite of concerted supplications from Rome Opera officials, Wallmann, the stage director and Santini, the conductor, Callas refused to continue; they tried to get her on to the stage even if it meant her just walking through the part miming, 'You can go on even without a voice,'[32] they pleaded. Needless to say, in an opera as quintessentially vocal as *Norma*, she did not even bother to answer. The interval had gone on for what seemed an interminable length, even for a first night, when President Gronchi and his wife finally quit their box and an announcement came from the stage that the performance was cancelled. It was only then that voices can be heard expressing displeasure. It took time for the reason for the cancellation to become known upstairs, and it was not until the house lights were finally lowered that those still left in the theatre emerged whistling and shouting into the street. Meanwhile Callas, Meneghini and Maxwell had made their way through an underground passageway to the Quirinale Hotel, backing on to the Opera in Via Nazionale.

Upon re-entering her suite Callas at once despatched a letter tendering her apologies to the President and Signora Gronchi. Under her windows the noise continued unabated through the early hours, but it was not the audience reaction so much as the media's that in the next few days turned the incident into a *cause célèbre*. Rome journalists, few of whom had been anywhere near the Opera, were principally concerned with using Callas as a weapon against the Milanese, for was she not a *creatura della Scala*? No one was at all bothered by the fact that the Rome Opera had no understudy ready. Maxwell lost no time rushing into the fray, hurling abuse at the press and calling them names: a case, if ever there was one, of the pot calling the kettle black. In Milan, at the Biffi Scala, an argument between pro- and anti-Callas supporters threatened to degenerate into a brawl. In the Italian parliament the Callas walkout became a cue for a heated debate on the (mis)management of opera houses, all of which enjoy considerable government subvention. While the floor-show was going on Callas was inundated with sympathetic messages from fans and admirers. Colleagues, including Visconti, came to visit her at the hotel to express their solicitude personally. Later, on television, she related how 'I had such a reaction from the public . . . I never had so many flowers and so many letters . . . I know that I am really loved, it gives me great courage to go on'.[33]

For the second performance of *Norma*, on the 4th, the Opera had, at last, found a singer to deputize for Callas, a young Italian soprano, Anita Cerquetti, who was currently appearing in the same role at the San Carlo, Naples. She was brought in and another opening night gala rustled up, though without the President. However, notwithstanding a dozen curtain calls for Cerquetti, it proved anti-climactic. After which Callas, who was still in Rome, declared herself restored to health and well enough to sing the two remaining performances. But this she was not permitted to do for the Sovrintendente, determining to show he was in charge, ruled it impossible for her to return: the opera house could not be held responsible for 'possible disturbances which might damage the theatre, as well as law and order'.[34] Needless to say, as soon as the dust had settled the Meneghinis were not slow to sue the Rome Opera for four million Lire, Callas's fee for three performances. Although the case went on for thirteen years eventually, as Meneghini tells, 'the Supreme Court ... not only found Maria innocent of responsibility for what had happened, but it ordered the Rome Opera to pay damages'[35] On January 7th Callas, clad in navy blue with a Persian lamb shoulder cape and hat with veil, left the Quirinale Hotel in Rome bound for Milan. A crowd of newspaper photographers were waiting for her in the lobby. She posed for them but gave no interviews.

The final two *Normas*, on the 8th and 11th, were also sung by Cerquetti, who continued to flit between Rome and Naples. It may be wondered what part this frenetic activity played in the twenty-six-year-old soprano's premature retirement only three years later. For when it became known that Cerquetti had given up singing, there were those who crossed themselves, sure that Callas had put the evil eye on her; but the fact is that Norma, although perhaps the most rewarding of all soprano roles in Italian opera, is also too demanding even for a singer seasoned in experience to undertake lightly.

XVI

1958–1959

ON JANUARY 16TH 1958 Callas plus Meneghini and a caravan made up of her maid, her poodle, a couple of mink coats and seven items of baggage left Milan by air for Chicago. The trip involved two stop-overs in Paris and Montreal. In Paris, though she had not yet sung there, her arrival was greeted with a fanfare of journalists and well-wishers, and she was required to go through what for her was becoming the typical question-and-answer session. In the six hours before she reembarked she managed to find time for a change at the Hotel Crillon before being taken out to dine at Maxim's by a contingent from EMI/Pathé and she also signed a contract to make her Paris Opéra début that December in a special gala concert. This was the last of the world's great opera houses at which she would appear. In those days there was some truth in Bing's tart riposte to a French critic, after the Met came on a visit to Paris and there were complaints: 'Miss Peters [may have] had a bad night but the Paris Opéra [has] had a bad century.'[1] Like Covent Garden, the Opéra was going through a drab patch with works mostly given in the vernacular. Callas was not the first internationally-known opera singer in recent times to appear in London or in Paris, but in both cities the enthusiasm she engendered confirmed that for the public, now that the dramas had become old hat, the language of the libretto was irrelevant and eventually both houses came to abandon so dated a policy.

Her engagement in Chicago, for another concert on the 22nd, was for the Allied Française, as had been the one she had given there the previous January. In view of the success of that occasion Meneghini, when the charity organizers came to know if she would sing for them again, decided to ask what seemed to him a fabulous sum and, off the top of his head, he demanded $10,000. When they agreed at once his jaw no doubt dropped blocks, but for the event the box-office took $22,000, which shows how her reputation was starting to roller-skate. This was to be her last appearance in her great days in the city of her

American début and, after only a little more than three years, reviews leave little doubt how much her voice had deteriorated. Dettmer of the *Chicago American*, who in the past had been ecstatic in her praises, wrote '[she] sounds to be in big vocal trouble, how serious only she is equipped to measure. But last night . . . her voice was recurrently strident, unsteady and out-of-tune. It seems to have aged ten years in one . . . there were sounds fearfully uncontrolled, forced beyond the too-slim singer's capacity to support or sustain.'[2] Even Cassidy in the *Tribune*, though warming to Callas the interpreter, could not forebear from finishing: 'Was everything perfection? Of course not. Great things seldom are perfection.'[3]

On the next day, the 23rd, the Meneghinis flew to New York and took rooms at Maxwell's Keep, the Waldorf Astoria. On the 24th Callas appeared on Ed Murrow's nationwide television chat show, *Person to Person*. A recording shows this not to have been very revealing. Her accent certainly does not sound foreign, but it is as if she spoke English so infrequently she was unable to construct it spontaneously. We get an idea of her sense of humour, or lack of it, when she retells the story of how, although she also speaks fluent Italian, French and Greek: 'I always count in English.'[4] Presumably she had not thought it funny in the first place, and it was only when someone overheard her and was amused that she makes a point of regaling Murrow with it.

On the 27th she went up to AGMA's offices at Broadway and 60th Street to defend her failure to appear in San Francisco the previous September. She arrived with a stack of medical evidence and in a session lasting two hours twenty judges cross-questioned her. By all accounts she made a considerable impression, 'it [was] not altogether surprising that they were moved by her persuasive statement'.[5] But the notion that her argument was so cogent as to convince such naturally sceptical cynics, as one assumes AGMA's judges necessarily to be, seems extraordinary in the light of her lack of eloquence in English, testified to in Murrow's show. One would scarcely have believed that she would have made any effect, yet she got out of the fix with no more than a reprimand. 'It was . . . established, [on her] behalf, that she did not appear anywhere else while she was contractually bound to San Francisco',[6] though she had in fact finished recording *Medea* at La Scala only six days before she was to sing there. Presumably she was able to satisfy her interrogators that her maid had been mistaken in telling Adler that she was out singing. It would have been easy to have established she was not singing in public and, luckily for her, the recording of *Medea* was as yet unpublished. Since the rest of the cast is made up of Italians it seems unlikely that anyone at AGMA would have known about it either.

Ten days later, on February 6th, Callas began her second season at the Metropolitan with Violetta in *La Traviata* in a benefit for free milk for babies. With her was baritone Mario Zanasi and tenor Daniele Barioni. Her reception was altogether warmer than it had been in her début season. Sargeant in *The New Yorker*[7] and Kastendieck in *New York Journal-American*[8] all acclaimed it her best performance hitherto and the best Violetta heard at the Met in years. To an extent this was due to the fact that she had now made her Met début and it was known how she sounded, so there were no vocal shocks. Taubman, in the *New York Times*, went so far as to claim that '[she] sang better than at any time last season',[9] Kolodin was of the opinion that though '[she] does not command the beauty of sound to be ideal in any part [yet] hers is the best rounded Violetta offered here in years'.[10] The effect of Visconti's production at La Scala had inevitably caused her, as she herself tells,[11] to refine her characterization. Not that the New York press was unanimous. Paul Henry Lang, in the *Tribune*, also praised her 'brilliant acting', but went on to lament her 'lack of a true and beautiful voice'.[12] Interestingly, Lang complains that Callas and Barioni both sang flat in the Act I duet, 'Un dì felice'; however, Bernstein, who had also been present, wrote to the *Tribune* contradicting Lang: Barioni had sung sharp whereas Callas sang in tune.

Four nights later Callas sang another Violetta, this time with tenor Giuseppe Campora, followed by three Lucias from the 13th, and finally two Toscas from the 28th. These were her first appearances in the role since her last Met season and it is indicative that her performance was more praised this year: '[last year] it was comparatively underplayed and pallid [whereas now] it grew out of an inner flame. Not that Callas exaggerated, but she performed as if every faculty was alert and engaged.'[13] The critical enthusiasm had a dual effect; she herself became more fond of New York, while Bing became more anxious for her to return. He had her sign a contract for the 1958/9 season before she left town: twenty-six appearances in New York and on tour. Meanwhile, when she had arrived in New York in January from Paris, her mother who had come across from Greece the previous May was anxious to make contact, but Callas refused to talk to her, memories of Litza's attempts to put pressure on her by permitting *Time* magazine to publish her letters were too fresh. She and her father frequently saw each other. When she visited New York photographs of them together were often taken, yet Litza was not interested in seeking a reconciliation with him. After Callas's final appearance in New York she journeyed back to Europe stopping in Madrid for a concert, on March 24th, at Cinema Monumental. From this time concerts in cities where she never appeared in opera, or had not yet appeared, like Zurich and Dallas came to occupy an increasing part of her schedule, affording her a way of satisfying the ever-increasing demand to see her, and at the same time making it possible for her to earn a greater sum than she ever did in opera. At these concerts she would manage a characteristically wide range of arias, without having to undertake the rigours of complete performances. In Madrid, she sang four arias no other soprano ever programmed: 'Casta Diva' from *Norma*, 'D'amor sull'ali rosee' from *Il Trovatore*, 'L'altra notte' from *Mefistofele* and the *Hamlet* Mad Scene.

From Madrid Callas proceeded to Lisbon to the São Carlos to sing Violetta in *La Traviata*. She gave two performances, making her bow on March 27th. This was broadcast and a recording of it was published by EMI three years after her death – in such fashion did they seek to make good Legge's lacunae in their catalogue. The Lisbon cast of *La Traviata* includes Alfredo Kraus, then at the beginning of his career. His Alfredo is securely if a little stiffly sung when compared with the persuasive singer we know from a quarter of a century later, but the rest of the performance is routine. Callas returned to Milan via Brussels, where she confirmed concert appearances the following year in Amsterdam and at the Monnaie. There had been some anxiety in Brussels when La Scala announced a visit that summer to coincide with the International Exhibition, but with *Il Matrimonio Segreto* and *Tosca*, neither of them with Callas. Before proceeding back to Milan she was inveigled out to Château Ixelles, once home of Malibran's husband, the violinist, Charles de Bériot; and while there she was photographed with flowers next to a bust of Malibran.

Callas was to reappear in Milan as Anna Bolena in a revival of the previous year's production. In spite of jealousy between the vying opera houses the Milanese showed themselves no more sympathetic to Callas than did the Romans. Ghiringhelli no longer needed to regard her with any special favour. He realized, maybe more acutely than she, though without having any notion of the reason why, how she was gradually beginning to distance herself from opera; her sacrificing the Edinburgh *La Sonnambula* for Maxwell's party in Venice and the Roman defection were but the first steps. His concern was solely the well-being of La Scala. Years before he had ignored her, and when he came to realize just how important she was, he did an about turn. It was he who enabled her to show off her skills, for he not only accepted her repertory but also engaged Visconti and Zeffirelli to work with her. But now he was becoming apprehensive. Feeling her career was taking her away from La Scala, he was prepared to shrug her off: 'Prima donnas come and prima donnas go, but La Scala remains.'[14]

On April 9th 1958 Callas made her return to La Scala as Anna Bolena. The cast was the same as the previous year, except that Siepi replaced Rossi-Lemeni as Enrico VIII, and the opera was again conducted by Gavazzeni. Gavazzeni remembers how 'all the public could think about was her cancellation in Rome. I went to her dressing room before the performance. She was there alone and in the costume of Anna Bolena; she looked ready to go to the block, for she knew the public was there to get her. I took her hand and it was icy cold. I looked at her and said, "Now let's raise the temperature". But Act I ended coldly and it was not until the great ensemble at the end of Act II, when the guards went to arrest her, that she swept them aside, and turned to the audience in a fury of singing beyond anything she had ever done the year before. I was amazed at how much she gave. She at once proved who she was and the public went wild in delirium.'[15] The Roman crisis was forgotten in an instant and from that moment her success was complete. After the performance, when she emerged from the theatre Harewood, who was there, remembers how 'the drama was not yet over. I was going to have dinner with her ... [and] we found ... the streets ... lined with hundreds of enthusiastic Milanese ... [It] had really been a battle won.'[16] The police had been called out in anticipation of a disturbance and they must have wondered what was going on; when she entered the theatre she was the devil incarnate and, when she came out, an angel. But all she needed was precisely this kind of provocation.

Nevertheless, in spite of her overwhelming success, a contingent was at work determined to make her life in Milan as unpleasant as possible. Meneghini tells[17] after each of the remaining performances at curtain-calls, she was taunted with radishes and tomatoes, and even an old shoe was thrown at her. Throughout Ghiringhelli imperturbably adopted a pose of indifference: when the Meneghinis dined at the Biffi he would pass their table feigning not to notice them. One night when they arrived home in Via Buonarroti they found the garden gate smeared with excrement, the pathway befouled and the walls and front-door defaced with graffiti. They had hardly got inside when the telephone started to ring with obscene calls, and in the succeeding days the mail contained a selection of anonymous letters. Complaints to the police went unheeded, and at length they determined to leave for their new retreat on Lake Garda.

On May 19th Callas undertook her last new role at La Scala for more than two years, in fact, the last new role of her halcyon days, Imogene in Bellini's *Il Pirata*. The cast also included Corelli and Bastianini and the opera was conducted by Votto. The production was by Franco Enriquez and settings were by Zuffi. Although Zuffi had also provided those for *La Vestale*, in *Il Pirata*, photographs suggest, he showed no more feeling for the age of bel canto than he had for a classical work like *Alceste* four years before; it is as if he had gone back to the days before Visconti arrived at La Scala. Nevertheless Dragadze, in *Musical America* describes how 'Callas had a triumph second only to her unforgettable Medea. In the first two acts, the soprano's voice was sometimes harsh and forced, but her remarkable musicality, style, vocal agility and personality combined with a warmed-up voice in the last act to give us as much pleasure and excitement as of old.'[18] Though she sang four more performances by now it had become common knowledge that she would not be returning the following season. It was at this time that she was obliged to undergo a painful operation for haemorrhoids. She went into hospital on May 24th, the day before the third performance. Nevertheless she sang again on the 28th as scheduled.

It was at the fifth and last *Il Pirata*, on May 31st, that a great mass of flowers had arrived at the opera house for her; however, they were not allowed to be brought backstage. During the performance Ghiringhelli sat in the Sovrintendente's stage box. In the final scene Imogene, realizing that her lover, Gualtiero, is to be executed, imagines she sees him mounting steps to the scaffold, at which point Callas customarily commenced the cabaletta facing the audience. But that night, she whirled round in the direction of the stage box and, though her acute myopia prevented her seeing Ghiringhelli, she delivered the line 'La vedete il palco funesto' ('There, behold, the fatal scaffold' [theatre box]) directly at him. The allusion was not lost on the audience: the atmosphere could have been cut with a knife, and Ghiringhelli at once withdrew. However, he affected a speedy revenge. After the opera had ended and a mass of Callas fans stayed behind to acclaim her, he had the fire curtain abruptly lowered and the lights dimmed, so obliging the fans to take to the streets. The police outside made an attempt to disperse them but they stayed on, and when Callas finally emerged followed her and her entourage across the piazza to Savini's restaurant in the Galleria.

Except perhaps to Milanese idolaters, her departure from La Scala did not at the time seem so final, for her reputation was such as to carry her name to every opera house, and there were plenty of others anxious to secure her services. Yet she would fail to add any new roles to her repertory until she made peace with La Scala again, at the end of 1960, when she ventured just one more: Paolina in Donizetti's *Poliuto*. Her records now enable us to understand that the scandals she became involved in arose from her rapidly failing vocal powers, not from opera house politics, as was claimed on her behalf in the case of Rome, nor out of any prima donna antics, as was implied by much of the press at the time. She had been singing professionally since she was a mere seventeen, and when she arrived at La Scala she was still only twenty-eight. Her days there mark the great years of the career of Maria Meneghini Callas. By the end of her reign she had changed so completely as to be almost unidentifiable, as her husband confirms: 'She seemed to be another woman with a different personality.'[19] She was rapidly becoming front-page news. Yet, all too soon she would be obliged to face up to the fact that her career was over.

At the beginning of June Callas proceeded to London. Although, as Harewood remembers, 'we failed to persuade her to sing two operas at Covent Garden',[20] yet she did undertake five Violettas in *La Traviata* and she made her Covent Garden bow that year at a gala in front of the Queen on the occasion of the centenary of the theatre. The evening also included contributions from Margot Fonteyn and Sutherland, who sang 'I dreamt that I dwelt in marble halls' from Balfe's *The Bohemian Girl*. Harewood tells of his taking Callas through the theatre whilst Sutherland was rehearsing. 'Maria instantly stopped to listen, raised her eyebrows quite high as she remembered the beginner who had sung Clotilde . . . "She has learnt very well to copy from me." It was neither unkind nor untrue, and Joan was delighted when I told her.'[21] Callas sang the Mad Scene from *I Puritani* with John Shaw and Forbes Robinson, though she was clad, so to speak, in mufti. A photograph shows her after the performance, back to the camera, curtseying or, should one rather say, bowing to the Queen; for her dress, a black lace creation by Biki, looks too tight to have permitted so condescending a gesture. Afterwards, when she dined with the Harewoods,[22] she asked why the Queen, who had said something to other members of the cast, had merely smiled at her. Harewood explained that the Queen probably could not think of anything to ask or say to her.

Her next engagement was on Granada television in a programme entitled *Chelsea at Eight* from the Chelsea Empire Theatre on June 17th. She sang 'Vissi d'arte' and 'Una voce poco fa'. Three days later she returned to Covent Garden as Violetta. The London critics were generally enthusiastic, though they did not fail to notice the decay in her voice since her Norma the previous year. Nevertheless her Violetta wrought a profound effect, a bigger one, in my opinion, than Norma. In 1958 her voice was certainly not the same instrument it had been six years previously in Mexico City, yet, as we can hear from a live recording, her Violetta is refined to an extent that makes it musically, at any rate, one of her most telling interpretations. As we noted years before in *I Vespri Siciliani*, she makes the subtlest rubato without needing any accommodation from the accompaniment. But whereas her Elena was vocally responsive to a degree that few of her later interpretations are, because she then had ample support to sustain so powerful an instrument, her Violetta manages to respond as readily to the music only because she contrives to fine her voice down to the merest pencil point of sound, so keeping it within her means.

It is in Act I that she reveals the greatest refinement. Indeed, one feels safe in saying that this had never before been sung with such seemingly infinite variety of detail. Consider subtleties that go beyond the printed notation, such as the way she seems to mark the pitch of the music with her restrained laughs, or the rhythmic precision with which she snaps her fan shut, like a percussionist. Years later at Juilliard, though she shows how assiduous a musician she was, she does not draw her pupils' attention to such subtleties, for with her they were completely instinctive. Her talent was not intellectual, which is why, despite so many extant recordings and so many would-be imitators, no soprano has managed to approach her achievement. Perhaps some of the intricate variety of dynamics in her singing of Violetta could be reproduced; but it would not, I think, be possible to relate this to her spontaneous use of rubato as, for example: the way she sustains the last note before the Brindisi just a shade longer than the rest of the company, an effect she repeats at the end of other ensembles. In the theatre we were not aware of this, merely of her voice dominating as, of course, it should. She achieves this exquisitely not, as she had done years before in the Mexico City *Norma*, by loudly outsinging the rest of the company.

At Flora's party, when the company has gone off-stage and Violetta hurries back on to persuade Alfredo to leave, I remember how even her quick movements were a response to the music, like a ballerina's, perfectly matched to the rushing semiquavers (sixteenth notes) in the strings. Her singing echoed other aspects of bel canto. I vividly recall the hush she created as she commenced the ensemble 'Alfredo, di questo core'. One could have heard a pin drop, so 'perfectly produced and controlled [was her voice], that its most delicate pianissimo reached the remotest listener'.[23] The quotation is from Shaw on Patti: it was this same third dimension, which the gramophone keeps no record of, that made Callas's singing memorable.

In the last act a problem arose, as the conductor, Rescigno, remembers. 'At the end of "Addio del passato" the high A she would shade away to the point that the note began to crack. I kept on telling her to sing it just that little bit louder, then she could diminish it. She said yes, but she never did, still she cracked, she just wouldn't compromise.'[24] This was not simply a problem of support, more one of ambition. A voice cracks because something prevents the throat remaining open. With Callas, it was simply that in fining her voice down, there inevitably came a point beyond which there was insufficient air to set the vocal cords vibrating. This was characteristic of her mania for striving always to refine her art, even beyond the limits of the possible. In *La Traviata* she contrived to produce a tone with as little breath as possible, and yet still keep the throat open. That she was able to attempt anything so rigorous was a testament to her remarkable vocal fluency, the result of assiduous early training. At the close of the opera we note in Violetta's death scene, 'Se una pudica vergine', at the end of the phrase, 'fra gli angeli', portamento is marked from a'' flat down an octave and this grace, if the voice is perfectly poised, will be sung proportionately softer than the notes it joins. At this stage, as Violetta is dying, Callas fines her voice down to the merest thread of tone; and consequently, though she sings the notes, she does not actually join them with portamento, but she implies the portamento, so perfect is her legato. She shows us again how instrumentally conceived her singing is, for we must go to the piano to find a parallel. Although on the piano portamento cannot be produced, a great pianist will suggest it in the fashion Callas does.

On the final phrase of the opera there is another felicity, one that she had been working on instinctively for years and which she manages most expertly in this performance. As Violetta dies on b'' the note does not end in an ugly yelp or for a moment sag below pitch: so perfectly placed and supported is it that we hear it simply disappear as she takes the breath away, which parallels precisely the way the spoken voice leaves the body at the moment of death. In my opinion Violetta was her greatest role; and across the years, between performances in Mexico City and London, recordings demonstrate the innumerable refinements she brought to her interpretation. Even in 1958 it suited her because it does not require the sheer vocal resources of Norma nor, except in 'Sempre libera', the stratospheric heights demanded of Amina or Lucia.

After her Violetta Callas undertook no further engagements, in marked contrast to the previous year. In July the Meneghinis returned to their lakeside villa at Sirmione. One day they greeted Zeffirelli and Rescigno when they came to discuss a projected *La Traviata* for Dallas that autumn. 'The villa had a wonderful location,' Zeffirelli recalls, 'but [it] was decked out in Maria's usual dubious taste: she had a passion for what can only be described as chic hotel lounge décor.'[25] On another occasion, at the Lido, Venice, where the couple often spent some time, a young man happened by while Meneghini was asleep in a deckchair. In the course of typical beach banter he invited her to a party, without having any idea who she was. She affected to be flattered but, indicating the sleeping Meneghini, claimed she couldn't give an answer until her father woke. Afterwards she couldn't get it out of her head that she had been invited to a party 'because I'm attractive, not because I'm La Callas'.[26]

In September the Meneghinis came to London again. In a period of six days between September 19th and 26th, with the Philharmonia Orchestra under Rescigno, Callas recorded two recitals at EMI's Abbey Road studios and the Kingsway Hall. The first, entitled *Callas Portrays Verdi Heroines*, includes arias from *Nabucco*, *Ernani* and *Don Carlo* coupled with three scenes from *Macbeth*. Abigaille's scena begins with the recitative and includes not only the aria, 'Anch' io dischiuso', but also the cabaletta. However, about that the less said the better. As we have seen, by 1958 she had succeeded in scaling her Violetta down to reconcile it with what remained of her voice; but inevitably, by that stage of her career it proved utterly impossible for her to go the other way about and inflate her tone to encompass music as fulsomely dramatic as Abigaille's. In this excerpt her voice is thin and wobbly when singing piano, while in the dramatic expostulations it becomes ugly and raucous, especially in the cabaletta.

Elviva's 'Ernani! Ernani, involami' is the only aria from this not very rewarding role that Callas ever sang. (The question of her undertaking it at La Scala was raised, but nothing ever came of it.) At the beginning of this century *Ernani* was one of the first early Verdi operas to be revived at the Met; and Elvira was sung on that occasion by Sembrich, a noted Amina, Lucia and Rosina. The music is not gratefully written for a high lightweight voice, and at the next Met revival, in 1921, it was undertaken by a more dramatic soprano, Ponselle. We have noted before a superficial similarity between Callas and Ponselle; and in this aria, no doubt, Callas had Ponselle in her inner ear, for she recorded it several times. Yet whereas Ponselle's singing is admirably secure, smooth, neat and with a good trill, it lacks grace and brilliance, especially in the cabaletta. Unlike Abigaille, Elvira was still within Callas's means in 1958. The recitative, 'Surta e la notte' is typical. We note how tellingly she expresses her loathing for Silva and she makes the phrase 'Questo odiato veglio' ('This hated dotard') stand out vividly with her instantaneous change of vocal colour. Though by 1958 her voice is scarcely as agreeable as Ponselle's in 1927, her interpretation is notable for a wealth of subtlety. In the cabaletta she seems to falter for a moment on the phrase after the trill on f'. Nevertheless, it is sung with remarkable accuracy and delicacy, and her finished technique is apparent in her execution of the wide intervals which cross back and forth into chest register.

Elisabetta's 'Tu che la vanità' from *Don Carlo* is also, deservedly, a much admired interpretation. Although her voice may lack the ideal weight of tone, Callas shows how in this piece, with its rather fragmentary structure, the onus is on the singer's musicianship to reconcile the detail within an overall conception. But it is the scenes from *Macbeth* that created the greatest sensation when this record was issued in 1959. Until that time the *Macbeth* recordings were those of 'La luce langue' and the Sleepwalking Scene with Margherita Grandi and Beecham; but these were immediately swept aside. However, since then a pirate recording of Callas's 1952 La Scala Lady Macbeth has surfaced, and we cannot help noticing yet again how much her voice has deteriorated in the intervening six years. Although she still sings the music accurately, since the Scala *Macbeth* her timbre has become thinner and less limpid, and the ornaments are not so nimbly turned. Perhaps more surprising, however, is that at La Scala she is also more assured musically: there is a breadth of phrasing, a sense of command made possible by the ease of her vocalism that creates a grandeur that eludes her in 1958.

The other record she made that September, entitled *Callas sings Mad Scenes*, includes her first recording in French, the Mad Scene from *Hamlet*, which is rather better than the Athens performance, but by no means as faultless vocally or as assured as the RAI performance of 1956. The recording of the Final Scene from *Anna Bolena* shows her interpretation to have developed even further from the Dallas rehearsal and the Scala performance. As in her Violetta three months previously at Covent Garden she works a number of refinements, particularly on the phrases beginning 'Cielo, a miei lunghi spasimi'. During these sessions, on the 23rd, she made another appearance on Granada Television, again at the Chelsea Empire, singing Norma's 'Casta Diva' (the aria only) and Butterfly's 'Un bel dì'. The Meneghinis returned to Milan on the 26th.

Callas was to spend much of the following season in the United States. On October 7th with Meneghini she arrived in New York and next day lunched with Bing to discuss her third Met season to begin the following January. She would sing Tosca, Violetta and Lady Macbeth opposite Warren in a new production by Carl Ebert under Mitropoulos. Bing detailed the arrangements: he had, he said 'allowed her no fewer than eight days to lighten her voice down from Lady Macbeth to Violetta, and four days after . . . Violetta . . . to prepare for Lady Macbeth'.²⁷ Although she seems to have made no objections yet she complained at length about the production of *La Traviata* and 'about the tour . . . the hotels would be inadequate, the planes wouldn't take [her] poodle . . . the trains were smelly, the schedule was too strenuous'.²⁸ When Bing left, so he later claims, he felt apprehensive.

Three days later she was to start her first American concert tour under the aegis of Sol Hurok, doyen of impresarios who had organized similar peripatetic undertakings with Chaliapin more than thirty years before. In each of ten cities she would sing five arias: 'Tu che invoco' from *La Vestale*, 'Vieni! t' affretta!' from *Macbeth*, 'Una voce poco fa' from *Il Barbiere di Siviglia*, Musetta's Waltz Song from *La Bohème*, and the Mad Scene from *Hamlet*. She began the series at Birmingham, from there went to Atlanta, and then travelled north to Canada for appearances in Montreal and Toronto. At this point the tour was interrupted while she went to sing with the Dallas Opera. She was to appear there in two performances of *La Traviata*, in a new production by Zeffirelli, and in two performances of Cherubini's *Medea*, in another new production by Alexis Minotis, Director of the Greek National Theatre, Athens and husband of the distinguished *tragédienne* Katina Paxinou.

The season opened on October 31st with Violetta. 'My plan', Zeffirelli had explained to Callas, when he came to visit her at Sirmione that summer, '[is] to begin at the end, for the curtain to go up on the first note and for us to find . . . Violetta dying. She will simply lie there until [the Prelude ends] . . . The entire opera will thus [be] seen in flashback.'[29] When Callas objected at having to be on stage all evening, Zeffirelli assured her she would be able to do it. 'Oh, well', she said, 'it's only Dallas.'[30] She did not like running risks, 'if it had been La Scala', Zeffirelli remarked, 'then things might have been different'.[31] But just as she had always appreciated her London public, so she felt the public in Dallas would be her ally, and the production was made expressly to suit her. On the first night she left the stage during the curtain calls, so that Zeffirelli might enjoy some of the success – at first she even declined to take a solo bow. This impression of almost girlish modesty created a great effect. Right through to the curtain calls Callas had gone along with Zeffirelli's notion of emphasizing Violetta's youth; and her appearance at this stage of her career certainly fitted such an interpretation. But her voice did not. Although it was becoming lighter, it was far from becoming younger-sounding. Askew, critic of the *Dallas Morning News*, could not help noticing how, in 'Sempre libera', 'the ear was ready with a tense concern'.[32] In fact Callas never sang Violetta again.

Meanwhile, after *La Traviata* Bing had wired Callas congratulating her on her success and then added, 'but why in Dallas?'.[33] What none of Callas's disputants, in Rome, San Francisco or Milan, took into account was that she may well have been greedy, even capricious, but these factors were less significant than her fast-fading vocal powers and consequently her lack of nerve. Her powers were slipping steadily from her, tempting her to endless procrastination over her contracts. It was in Dallas that Meneghini spoke 'with some promoters of concerts [and] saw an opportunity to make a major tour of the United States, with fabulous financial returns and the involvement of television'.[34] The problem was getting Callas out of her Met contract without becoming involved with AGMA again. '"If you can manage that, you're good," she . . . laughed.'[35] So while Bing insisted on her confirming the Met schedule, Meneghini kept up a series of endless prevarications; these would, he judged, be sure 'to exasperate [Bing] to the point where he would lose his temper and cancel the contract himself'.[36]

When, as the Meneghinis hoped, Bing did finally, issue a proclamation firing her, the news reached Dallas six hours before the curtain was to go up on the first *Medea* on November 6th. Callas commenced her dramatic portrayal immediately, at a hastily summoned press conference. Beginning in a hushed pianissimo she detailed her case gradually working up to a furious fortissimo: 'My voice is not like an elevator, going up and down . . . All those lousy *Traviatas*

[Bing] made me sing, without rehearsals, without even knowing my partners ... Is that art?'[37] She had barely stopped to draw breath before going on stage as Medea. She must have been pleased that Bing fired her for it provided the perfect excuse for working herself into a Medea-like fury. In such fashion she recharged her vocal batteries, so enabling her to give a performance showing her talent off at its most exultant – she would, she reasoned, let New York know what it was missing! After a six-hour tirade, by some *léger de voix*, a recording shows her singing returned to the excellence of her Norma at La Scala in 1955. By the time Medea was over and she arrived at a party she had got over her simulated indignation and, as Mrs Mead Carter, a close friend tells, '[she] seemed quite undisturbed by [her] dismissal. She wasn't really upset. She had a wonderful time [and] danced and partied until dawn.'[38]

Callas resumed her concert tour at Cleveland on November 15th, and in the next two weeks she proceeded via Detroit on the 18th, Washington on the 22nd, San Francisco on the 26th, to Los Angeles on the 29th. In between in New York she was a guest at Maxwell's party for Karajan. On another night she was at the Waldorf again with Maxwell, Aly Khan and Noël Coward, at a dinner dance given by the U.S. Ambassador to Cuba. On the 30th she left for Europe, and spent the next two weeks at Sirmione.

On December 19th she proceeded with Meneghini to Paris to make her début at the Opéra at a Légion d'Honneur gala. The occasion was the last state appearance of René Coty before de Gaulle became President. Numerous government ministers and diplomatic plenipotentiaries were present, as well as General Norstad, Paul Henri Spaak, the Begum Aga Khan, Ali Khan, the Windsors, the Rothschilds, Marquis de Cuevas, Jean Cocteau, Charlie Chaplin, Brigitte Bardot, Juliette Greco, Gerard Philipe, Michele Morgan, Martine Carol, Sacha Distel and Aristotle Onassis! Television audiences watched the performance throughout north-west Europe, the house was completely sold out and the box-office broke all records. Callas's fee, $10,000, she gave to the Légion d'Honneur. Ticket prices were as much as $85 for a box. The special programme was priced at $20. With it was a new gramophone record, *Callas sings Mad Scenes*, a ticket for a fund-raising lottery and a sachet of perfume. After the performance supper was served to 450 guests in one of the grand salles in the Opéra.

Not only has a recording been preserved of the occasion but a film survives of it. It begins with the Overture to Verdi's *La Forza del Destino*, after which the curtain rises and Callas comes out on

From left to right: Milton Embericos, Jackie, Evangelia, and friend, and Callas in Athens, 1940.

With Evangelia and George in New York in 1945.

A moment of relaxation during rehearsals of *I Vespri Siciliani* at La Scala, 1951.

Dinner with Mascherini after the première of *I Vespri*.

At La Scala, Milan, in 1953. Medea takes a cup of tea!

Elena Nicolai regaling Callas with a tale at the Verdi, Trieste, before a rehearsal for *Norma* in 1953. Callas is evidently unimpressed.

Signora di Stefano, the tenor's mother, at her fabric shop in Milan with assistant (in background), Callas and di Stefano in the summer of 1954.

Before opening night: Visconti, Callas and Meneghini, with Corelli after rehearsal for Spontini's *La Vestale* at La Scala, 1954.

Callas, del Monaco and Simionato in a photocall during rehearsals for *Norma* at La Scala, 1955.

Luis de Hidalgo (brother of Elvira, Callas's teacher) and Callas, plus her baby poodle, Toy, with couturière Biki.

Painting of Callas, with the diva gazing into a mirror. The influence of Visconti, perhaps?
Or, maybe, even Dali – is she about to disrobe?

Callas seated at the piano, 1956.

The Meneghinis outside their house in Via Buonarroti in 1957.

Sordello tearing up Callas's photograph after his dismissal from the Met in 1956.

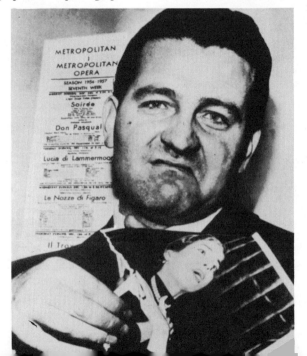

The diva surprised, 1959.

stage in evening dress with her familiar stole and, around her neck, a million-dollar necklace from Van Cleef and Arpels. She sings, in concert with the chorus layed out in serried rows, 'Sediziose voce . . . Casta Diva' and 'Ah! bello a me ritorna' from *Norma*, 'D'amor sull'ali rosee' and the Miserere from *Il Trovatore*, with Albert Lance; she then finishes the first half with 'Una voce poco fa' from *Il Barbiere di Siviglia*. The second half is devoted to a staging of Act II of *Tosca*, in which she is joined by Lance and Gobbi. One can only lament that of the 1958 performances which might have been filmed, it should be this and not *Anna Bolena* from La Scala, *La Traviata* from Covent Garden or *Medea* from Dallas. It is an inadequate document: the first half shows an obtrusive looking check floor like a monster chess board; and Georges Sebastian's routine stick-waving. The two *Il Trovatore* excerpts are the best and reveal something of what made her Leonora a great assumption. After the interval the curtain goes up on the dim remains of a setting of *Tosca*. And it is by a bizarre fate that nothing should survive of any of her stage performances other than *Tosca* – there is another film of the same act from *Tosca*, again with Gobbi, made at Covent Garden in 1964. She is not in particularly good voice; had Bing waited until then before sacking her, she might perhaps have summoned up more. Still, we agree with Ardoin, 'seeing her makes her more exciting',[39] or at any rate distracts us sufficiently for us not to notice how her voice is nothing like as responsive as it was only a few years previously.

After spending Christmas in Italy, in January 1959 Callas returned once more to the United States; and on the 11th, in Saint Louis, she undertook the twelfth and last concert in her Hurok tour. On the 24th she appeared at another gala benefit, this time in Philadelphia to commemorate the 102nd birthday of the Academy of Music. The Philadelphia Orchestra was conducted by Eugene Ormandy and she sang 'L'altra notte' from *Mefistofele*, 'Una voce poco fa' from *Il Barbiere* and the *Hamlet* Mad Scene; with her on the programme was Van Cilburn, the young American virtuoso, who played Rachmaninoff's Third Piano Concerto with the same orchestra and conductor who join the composer on the RCA Victor recording made 19 years before.

On the 27th Callas returned to New York, not to the Met, but uptown to Carnegie Hall where she appeared in one of the concert evenings of the American Opera Society. She sang Imogene in Bellini's *Il Pirata*; and it was, of course, sold out, even with ticket prices as much as $25 for orchestra stalls. We may imagine how surprised, indeed amazed, Bing must have been at the success of this performance, although, no doubt, he was prepared to shrug it off as part of the Callas mania. Like the Dallas rehearsal in November 1957 *Il Pirata* was not broadcast but recorded in the hall. Certainly, on this occasion, mania or familiarity with earlier offerings could alone account for the diva's adulatory reception. Carnegie Hall had, at least in 1959, perfect acoustics, as the recording reveals. The opera is much cut about and chunks are missing. This was due in part, probably, to the rest of the ensemble, which includes a very second-rate tenor, Ferraro. Rescigno seems principally concerned with Callas. He conducts the Final Scene at a speed noticeably faster than on the EMI recording made the previous year. By this time it is obvious how much disparity exists between fat Callas of the early 1950s, the incomparable singer, and the sleek, *soignée* Callas on this occasion. Photographs show how she used her stole, as one critic quipped, like the Indian rope trick; but stage illusions are for the eye not for the ear. Though she accomplishes fluently a prodigiously difficult four-bar passage of fioritura in the Act II stretta, even at Rescigno's brisk tempo, her voice has become thin and raw. It has lost so much quality that the only analogy this feat conjures up is that of a turkey gobbling.

After a repeat *Il Pirata* two nights later at Constitution Hall, Washington, Callas left for Europe. In Milan Harewood again came over to talk her into singing another role that summer at Covent Garden, as well as Medea. The production of *Medea* was to be borrowed from Dallas, and Covent Garden would in exchange send them a new Zeffirelli production of *Lucia* that they would be mounting. Since Callas was to sing this in Dallas would it not be an excellent idea, Harewood suggested, that she sing it in London also? But when she heard Covent Garden were planning to inaugurate the new production the following month with Sutherland she made 'it quite clear . . .' as Harewood remembers, 'that [the theatre] had been treacherous in arranging to mount [it for someone else]'.[40] Harewood had to return to London without getting her to agree to anything else. But she flew over herself so as to be at the dress rehearsal of Sutherland's Lucia on the 15th. The opera had Serafin conducting and was produced by Zeffirelli, who remembers Callas's reaction when she went round to see Sutherland after the performance. 'You are a great artist. I would have been jealous of anyone singing so well, but not of you. Of course, you owe a lot to others, and you might include me among them, but we all owe somebody something.'[41]

On March 16th, after returning briefly to Milan, Callas did come to London again to sing Lucia, not at Covent Garden but at Kingsway Hall, where she recorded it a second time. The excuse for so doing was that it would be in stereo, and at that time there was only one other EMI recording with Callas, that of *Il Barbiere di Siviglia*. Legge had been outmanoeuvred by Decca/London who had been taking the trouble to record in stereo for some years, even though they had had to wait before issuing them until reproducing equipment could be marketed at a price accessible to all. Now everyone wanted stereo recordings. For the second *Lucia* Legge produced an uneven ensemble, once again showing himself out of touch with Italian opera. Instead of engaging Kraus as Edgardo, whom Callas had sung with the previous year in Lisbon, he dug up Tagliavini. He had not sung on stage with Callas for five years, and this is the last complete recording he was to make. Conversely, the rest of the cast includes young and mostly inexperienced singers: the baritone Piero Cappucilli, and the Polish bass, Bern(h)ard Ladysz, whom Legge dropped as quickly as he had discovered him. But the nub of the matter is Callas. Her mono Lucia is one of her finest recordings; six years later, her voice has aged alarmingly, and the musical felicities that formerly made her singing so memorable are now barely suggested.

By this time gaps in Callas's schedule were starting to open up, even at the height of the opera season. One would have to go back a decade, to the beginning of her Italian career, to find an April in which she was not singing. On the 21st, she and Meneghini journeyed to Paris, to Maxim's, to celebrate their tenth wedding anniversary, after which they went on to the Lido where they stayed until four in the morning. It was during this visit that she talked, to almost anyone who would listen, of her husband's unique place in her life: 'I could not sing without him present. If I am the voice, he is the soul'.[42] But, even then, when she and Onassis were no more than casually acquainted, her marriage was rapidly fading. So long as her career was her life Meneghini may have been all-important to her; but now it was coming to a summary conclusion. It was not a coincidence, therefore, that she was setting out for new pastures. In the previous two years she had been several times to Paris; and sooner than she could have realized that city would become her home.

On May 2nd she returned to Madrid for a concert, this time to the Teatro Zarzuela. She sang a typical parade of pieces, including 'Bel raggio' from *Semiramide*. Between verses of the cabaletta, Fernandez-Çid in *ABC* tells how, she interpolated a cadenza, presumably the same which she recorded in the RAI broadcast two and a half years before. 'Without a doubt, [it showed] the best and worst of her art: an uneven, very unpleasant and hard upper register, followed by a chromatic descending scale right out of the textbook.'[43] In August 1960 I remember going to Watford Town Hall where she was recording 'Bel raggio' and several times she had a shot at this cadenza, screeching the c'' sharp and then indeed following it with 'a chromatic descending scale right out of the textbook'. However the record was not issued until 1987, and on it she not only omits the cadenza but does not even venture the b'' at the end.

After another recital, on May 5th in Barcelona, Callas undertook a quartet of concerts in Germany, beginning on the 15th, in Hamburg. Of this a film exists of a television broadcast. 'We [can] watch . . . the constantly sinking, depressed chest and hear the resulting deterioration'[44] as she desperately tries to find some support for her voice. But her singing method was instinctive, acquired in her youth, and no amount of latter-day cerebration would reveal to her its secrets, no matter how often '[she endeavoured to] play and study [her early] records . . . and try to get back to the vocal positions [she] used then'.[45] It is only with the diaphragm fully supporting the tone, projecting it as far from the throat as possible, that a singer keeps control over the voice. By this time the increasingly obtrusive wobble was an indication that the demands she made of herself were proving impossible to contain. She does not seem to have realized that she was trying to put the cart before the horse. As with a brass or wind instrumentalist, a singer's virtuosity can only be sustained by complete mastery of breath control.

Afterwards she sang at Stuttgart on the 19th, Munich on the 21st and Wiesbaden on the 24th. At the beginning of this tour she is described as having a cold and it had not left her by the time of the Stuttgart concert, which is also recorded. At all four German recitals the programme was identical: 'Tu che invoco' from *La Vestale*, now minus cadenza and the ultimate c'', 'Vieni! t'affretta' from *Macbeth*, minus cabaletta, and 'Una voce poco fa' which is, at this stage, a barometer of her vocal state. In it we note how she no longer has the same power at either end of her range as she had in 1954. Much of the elaborate fioritura she can barely get through, some of it she cuts and some she simplifies. She changes staccato ornaments into legato, wisely, for her voice is no longer sufficiently responsive for her to dare risk opening, closing and reopening it again without its collapsing. After the interval she sings 'Tu che la vanità' from *Don Carlo* and the Final Scene from *Il Pirata*, at the end of which she does not venture the c''.

On June 17th she began a series of five performances of *Medea* at Covent Garden. Save for two *Traviatas* and two *Medeas* she had performed in Dallas last autumn, this was the first time she had appeared in opera since her Covent Garden performances the previous June. First night was attended by an audience as stellar as Callas herself had by then become, and included Gary Cooper, Douglas Fairbanks Jnr., the Duchess of Kent and her daughter Princess Alexandra, Lady Churchill, Margot Fonteyn, Cecil Beaton and Onassis. Inevitably she was praised ecstatically by the critics; but Medea had last been sung at Covent Garden by Tietjens eighty-eight years earlier, so no one knew how it should sound. I remember how diminished her voice was. Her one high c'', which she interpolated at the end of the second act, was a shred of a note. And it was impossible to ignore how her voice was reducing in size, how its range was contracting, not only at the top but at the bottom too – on phrase endings low notes would frequently become occluded. It was supremely ironic that at the moment she had become world famous, to an extent matched by no other opera singer since the days of Caruso and Chaliapin, her career was in rapid decline.

But this was not the result of her relationship with Onassis, as has been too frequently stated. It was not until the summer of 1959 that she left Meneghini for him. Yet severe vocal problems had begun to affect her even in 1956, during her first season at the Metropolitan, and by this time she was in dispute with opera companies in San Francisco, Vienna, Rome, Milan and New York. Ironically, these scandals and disputes and the consequent publicity that they created, led to her being inundated with offers to appear at hotels and night clubs in Hollywood, Las Vegas and Miami. As we can see when we examine details of her career, in the five years between 1951 and 1955 she made between forty-four and fifty-five operatic appearances each year; but in the next four years the figure dropped precipitately: from forty-nine in 1956, thirty in 1957, twenty-eight in 1958 to only five in 1959. It might be argued that in the 1960s it was her relationship with Onassis that explains why she made only as many operatic appearances in a decade as she had made in just one year in the early 1950s. But since she did not leave Meneghini until the summer of 1959, another explanation must be sought for the falling-off in her schedule before then. This is all too eloquently furnished by her recordings.

XVII

POST MENEGHINI

AFTER FIVE MEDEAS in London Callas proceeded to Amsterdam and Brussels to sing concerts. I went to them both. In Amsterdam she was in much better voice than she had been in London; Harewood thought the 'arias from *La Vestale, Ernani, Don Carlo* and the great scene from Bellini's *Il Pirata* sounded with the . . . full expressive panoply'.[1] The instrument had become steadier, less acidulous in quality, though it had not become any bigger, nor had its range extended; and if the lower notes had become clearer-sounding, the c'' she ventured at the end of the *Pirata* excerpt was worn thin. The Concertgebouw was full to the eaves, yet there were more people afterwards in the streets than there had been in the hall. I remember waiting to see Callas and, as she was leaving, she dropped something. While smiling round she rudely hissed at sixty-three-year-old Meneghini to bend down and retrieve it. In view of later events this image stayed in my memory. Three days later she sang the same programme at the Monnaie, Brussels, where she was in similar voice and her reception no less rapturous. Maxwell was present and afterwards, when she was accosted and asked what she had thought of it, she drew herself up, all five feet of her, before delivering her ultimate accolade: 'Callas,' she squawked, 'is the greatest singer – now and forever!' This was the last appearance of Maria Meneghini Callas.

According to Meneghini, Onassis had not made a particular fuss of Callas when they first met during Maxwell's Venetian romp in September 1957 at the Excelsior Hotel on the Lido. It was not until the Paris Opéra Gala in December 1958 that he believed '[Onassis] was so impressed by what he saw . . . [that the thought came to him] and set in his mind the devilish project: "if I take this woman myself, I shall impress everyone".'[2] Later, in April 1959, at a party given by Wally Toscanini in Venice at which the Meneghinis and Onassis were present, he first invited them to join him and his wife Tina for a cruise on his yacht, *Christina*. Callas told him she would be singing in London in June but she would think about it. He immediately promised to be there to greet her and, after the première of *Medea*, he threw a party at the Dorchester Hotel in honour of Callas, at which he reiterated his invitation. A photograph of her being received by Onassis, with Meneghini behind her, appeared throughout the world's press the next day: it could be seen as a symbol of her sloughing off the old and putting on the new.

On July 15th, after the Brussels concert, the Meneghinis returned to Sirmione. The next day Onassis phoned and arrangements were finalized for the cruise. It was agreed that they would meet in Monte Carlo on the 22nd. On the 20th the Meneghinis left for Milan. Here, Biki remembers, Meneghini came and asked her 'to dress Maria for the occasion, something to stun these people who don't know her'.[3] She then spent several million Lire on her cruising wardrobe. On the 21st they arrived in Nice and took a taxi to Monte Carlo. There Maxwell reappeared, she was staying at the Hôtel de Paris, and a letter from her was waiting for Callas when she arrived. She wished them both a 'splendid voyage' with 'Ari and the ex-man-of-state [Churchill]', finishing off: 'Take everything. Give all that you can bring yourself to give: this is the way to true happiness which you will have to discover ... I no longer want even to see you. The world will say – in fact, already is saying – that you only wished to use me.'[4] Notwithstanding the valedictory tone of her peroration, the very next day, July 22nd, Onassis and his wife the Meneghinis and Maxwell dined together at the Hôtel de Paris.

The cruise began on the 23rd and lasted until August 13th. It was during this that Onassis and Callas became lovers. If we believe a story cited by Stassinopoulos,[5] and originally told by Peter Diamand, Director of the Holland Festival, Callas had urged Diamand on the day after the Amsterdam concert not to pay her fee to Meneghini, but to keep it until she contacted him: she may have been toying with the idea of leaving Meneghini even then. It is certain that she could not expect any guidance from him in the critical situation her career was facing. She was forced to look around for something different or someone new, endeavouring to find a way out of a situation she was having to confront; but her conservative and narrow-minded attitude depended upon an occurrence outside her own volition. Perhaps an inkling of this had crossed her mind.

Onassis wanted Callas on the *Christina* not because of her talent but because of the reputation she had created; she had become a star even though the fashionable word had long ceased to be preoccupied with opera. Her looks, or Greek origins, could have had little to do with it; after all, he could have had any number of lovely young Greek girls. But the Grimaldis and other noble families did not care to accept his hospitality, and in order to boost his social morale he needed on board the *Christina* company that would not be out of place with his other guests: Churchill, Gianni Agnelli and Lord Moran. It was just when her career had descended to a level she herself would have scarcely credited only a few years previously that her need to cut a fine figure in her new milieu forced her to seek her identity through her singing. So during the next decade she continued to make a feint or two at her career. Although Onassis did not like opera, he appreciated its social significance; he had had an affair years before with Muzio, and perhaps his preoccupation with Callas began amidst the splendours of the Paris Opéra gala. From the beginning there was some mutual deception in their relationship: she believed him to be the great man he wanted to appear, and he believed her still to be a great singer. But they were both egocentric to an exceptional degree, and neither belief was more than superficial. Both of them were essentially preoccupied with themselves and their own careers.

A week had passed from the time that Callas and Meneghini had returned to Italy, she to Milan and he to Sirmione, when news first appeared in the press there was some dissension between them. By September 7th newspaper headlines, all the way from Los Angeles to Rome, were full of Onassis and Callas. Meanwhile, a couple of days previously at La Scala, she had begun to record *La Gioconda* for EMI. Though it has been suggested that she made the recording only because of Meneghini's withdrawal from the scene, it had in fact been planned for months. We may imagine how pleased Ghiringhelli was at the prospect of patching up his relationship with Callas, for this was the first recording she had made at La Scala for two years. She manages to sing better than she would in any other post-Meneghini recordings, despite the fact that she was in the first flush of the scandal that put the ultimate seal on her tabloid reputation.

A week after the recording, Callas rejoined Onassis on the *Christina*, this time with only two other guests: his brother and sister. On September 17th she flew to Bilbāo for a concert, her first public appearance without Meneghini, though it had been arranged by him, which perhaps accounts for her cavalier attitude when she told a reporter it was 'a silly little engagement'. Since this remark was printed in Spanish newspapers next day, we are not surprised the public's reception was noticeably cool. She sang 'Tu che la vanità' from

Don Carlo, the *Hamlet* Mad Scene, 'Ernani involami' from *Ernani* and the Final Scene from *Il Pirata*. The concert was conducted by Rescigno. Within a few days she was back on the *Christina*, then on the 23rd she sang in London again at the Festival Hall. The programme began with the *Don Carlo* aria, continued with the Sleepwalking Scene from *Macbeth* then, after the interval, she sang the *Hamlet* Mad Scene and the Final Scene from *Il Pirata*. During the lengthy orchestral introductions she suggested the characterization before she had begun singing. I took a large, cumbersome tape recorder into the auditorium and managed to get it to work uninterruptedly in the Sleepwalking Scene, one of the first pirate live recordings made in Europe. Compared with her performance the previous year for EMI it was more broadly interpreted and her chest register had become markedly darker-sounding. Towards the end she turned and walked off through the orchestra. The lights had been lowered and, as she was unable to see very clearly without spectacles, her skirt toppled one of the orchestra' music stands. We may imagine how concerned she was to get off-stage before having to emit the final d'' flat.

Off-stage the drama was still going on; and the press was more preoccupied by her wearing the minimum of jewellery, a ring and modest pearl necklace, than with how she was singing. A week later, on the 29th, a recording of a television programme in London in front of an audience at the Wood Green Empire Theatre had to be postponed at the last minute, for she was in Milan with Meneghini attempting to make a settlement of their property. The previous day he had filed a petition for separation, and she was only free to come to London on October 3rd. On this occasion, with no time to book an audience, applause was dubbed in. Perhaps that was as well, for the programme was, by her standards at any rate, unrevealing: 'Sì, mi chiamano Mimì' from *La Bohème* and L'altra notte' from *Mefistofele*, conducted by Sir Malcolm Sargent. The only thing memorable about it was that she had had her hair completely restyled for the first time since she arrived in Italy. Irrespective of various shades of colour she wore, she had always kept a chignon as a base for use in her many operatic characterizations. But now, significantly, having largely dispensed with those characterizations she dispensed with the chignon too.

Meanwhile on both sides of the Atlantic the popular press rushed in to take sides and hastily express their opinions on her love life. During the remainder of October she made two more concert appearances, one in Berlin, on the 23rd, at Titania Palast, at which she sang 'Non mi dir' from *Don Giovanni* and then proceeded with excerpts from, *Ernani, Don Carlo* and *Hamlet*. Her next engagement, in Kansas City on October 28th, involved a particularly long journey. A couple of days after her return to the United States Maxwell, who had been silent on the subject of Callas in her column for more than three months, related a conversation she had with Bernstein. She told how he pressed her to say whether she took any stand, musically or morally, about Callas. We can almost hear her purse her lips before making one of her portentous-sounding judgments: 'Musically, I can only say she is the greatest artist in the world.' Immediately after the Meneghinis had returned to Italy from the *Christina* and first separated, Callas telephoned Meneghini to ask him to send her all the letters Maxwell had written, 'so that this episode could be terminated definitively'.[6] But he could not have done for he quotes from some of them more than twenty years later when Maxwell and Callas were both dead.

Callas had no sooner arrived at Idewild to change planes than a bevy of photographers and journalists descended upon her. For a while she kept her cool, but eventually ended up yelling at them 'Lay off me, will you!'.[7] Generally her English was more redolent of Bond Street, but on this occasion at least the Bronx slipped out. In Kansas City the concert had scarcely begun when a man telephoned the theatre saying that a bomb had been planted in the orchestra pit. So, after she had sung her first aria, Donna Anna's 'Non mi dir', the audience were obliged to leave the auditorium while a search was made; but nothing was found. Whether the object of the spoof was Callas or ex-President Truman, who came to the concert, was never made clear. After the audience was reseated she proceeded with 'Regnava nel silenzio' and 'Quando rapito' from *Lucia*, and finished the programme with excerpts from *Ernani* and *Il Pirata*.

From Kansas City Callas travelled to Dallas where she undertook *Lucia* in the Covent Garden production originally staged for Sutherland; Lucia's costumes had failed to arrive, so Callas wore Alisa's, which Zeffirelli did his best to resuit, and as her hair was now cut short she wore a blonde wig. When the music rose above the stave she no longer had sufficient strength to support her voice; inevitably she forced and her tone became strident. I remember particularly the effort the c''s and d''s cost her, alternatives in the second verse of 'Quando rapito' and the sustained d'' at the end which, unlike in Kansas City, she did venture, though her throat muscles stood out as if she were weight-lifting. In the Mad Scene she did not, as Sutherland had in London, rush round the stage in a state of dementia. Zeffirelli explained[8] he had Sutherland do it like that because she would look better; but for Callas too, by that time, it would have been more tactful if she had not been made to stand still, so enabling the audience to concentrate on her every vocal malaise. At the end of the cadenza which, as in the second EMI recording, she abbreviated, she made an attempt to reach e'' flat; but she missed it and had to content herself slithering down to mark the resolution an octave lower. She had not ventured this note in the first part of the Mad Scene since her Lucia at La Scala more than five years before, so it is hard to understand why she did so on this occasion. At the end of the cabaletta, 'Spargi d'amaro', she did at least manage to sustain the e'' flat, but it was very obviously flat. Many are the tales of her off-stage immediately afterwards, incessantly repeating the note, shaking her head, loudly telling all those within earshot that she just could not understand it. But later she confided to Giovanna Lomazzi 'I gambled my career tonight, my career ends here'.[9] At the second performance, on the 8th, she did not attempt either e'' flat.

Straight after the Lucias she had to interrupt her Dallas stay and fly back to Italy for a court hearing on the division of the Meneghinis' property, so she was unable to appear for the scheduled Rosinas, – the date for the court hearing had already been postponed once and it was impossible to change it again. Zeffirelli also directed the production of *Il Barbiere* and might have elicited more of the buffo style from her than she had managed at La Scala. Rosina's music is generally lower than Lucia's and it could only have lain more comfortably for her. On her way back to Milan she had to change planes in New York and it was then that she made the first moves in a rapprochement with Bing, though it would take another five years before she returned to the Met. Back in Italy on the 14th she drove to Brescia for court proceedings. Surprisingly, an agreement was quickly reached. The estate was divided equally: Callas kept the Milan property at Via Buonarroti and Meneghini the villa at Sirmione; she kept her jewellery and he the real estate. Of the paintings and *objets d'art* each was granted a share; only the poodles were left undivided. At this stage Meneghini must have felt sufficiently pacified for he withdrew a separation order he had made against his wife and agreed to one instead by mutual consent. She went straight back to Dallas for *Medea* on November 19th and 21st; the production was repeated from last year but performances were not on that level, though there were no spectacular misses in the fashion of Lucia.

Callas had hardly boarded *Christina* again when, in New York, an action for divorce was made against Onassis by Tina. However, for some reason, she preferred to cite one of Onassis's old flames. Although there was talk of a production of *Medea* at the Paris Opéra in December it did not take place. Freed at last from engagements Meneghini had planned, she was operatically silent until the summer of 1960. With him gone there was no inducement for her to continue singing, and during the next eight months she was content to be Onassis's moll. In July she did, though, agree to reappear in recital at the Kursaal, Ostend. This was no longer a familiar stopping-off place for famous singers, as it had been at the beginning of this century, when Casino audiences went to the opera and Caruso sang there on several occasions. Callas chose it because, we presume, it was now off the operatic mainstream and would not attract more than token attention. She was announced to sing arias from *Don Carlo*, *Il Barbiere di Siviglia*, *Ernani* and *Il Pirata* but, at the last moment, because of a cold, as she claimed or, more likely, cold feet, she cancelled. At the beginning of August she came to London and with Legge drove to Watford to record a recital with the Philharmonia under Tonini. But her voice proved no more responsive here. She attempted 'Bel raggio' from *Semiramide*, 'D'amore al dolce impero' from *Armida* and 'Arrigo! ah parli a un core' from *I Vespri Siciliani*, but none of the arias was issued in her lifetime.

It was not until August 24th 1960 that she made her first appearance of the year. She sang Norma at the Epidavros Amphitheatre, her first operatic engagement in Greece for fifteen years. The première was originally to have been given on the 21st but there was a violent thunderstorm and at the last minute, when coachloads had journeyed out sixty miles from Athens, it had to be postponed. The amphitheatre dates from ancient times and is one of the largest, as well as oldest, in the world. It seats some 18,000 and, considering how much smaller the population was in Classical Greece, we can understand how important it was. On this occasion opera was given there for the first time ever, and since there is no orchestra pit it was necessary to raise the stage. Nevertheless the acoustics proved perfect. The seats were all sold and the usual international coterie was present, plus Onassis in company with Callas's father. Situated in the country, the theatre is surrounded by hills. The performance began after sunset and the rapidly darkening azure sky, with the stars coming out, made it an idyllic setting. I remember sitting next to some people who had never seen Callas before and they were worried lest they should not recognize her. As the chorus ladies came on they leaned across to ask me which was her; but when at last she did appear, they had no need to ask. She certainly looked well and, as she had done in Lucia in Dallas, she wore a blonde wig. But it was strange, and sad, that although she had not sung in public since then, her voice had continued to thin out at the same rate as if she had still been working to the kind of exhaustive schedule of former years.

I remember her finishing the recitative before 'Casta Diva' without the alternative a'' flat, nor did she interpolate c'' at the end of the cabaletta. Yet like so many Callas performances at this stage it was a triumph, and she completed her success by giving her fee of $10,000 towards the creation of a Scholarship Fund for Young Musicians. Before the second performance, on the 26th, it was announced that she was unwell, but the third, scheduled for the 28th, was cancelled. On September 5th she returned to La Scala, Milan to record Norma a second time. On this occasion, although she does not sing d'' at the end of the trio in Act I, she does sing the other notes she had not included at Epidavros. Corelli makes a lusty Pollione and a mezzo-soprano Adalgisa, Christa Ludwig, sings in conventional style. Zaccaria's Oroveso, although more assured vocally than Rossi-Lemeni, sounds hoarse.

After another three months spent on board the Christina, on December 7th Callas reappeared at La Scala to open the season, the first time she had done so for three years. In the summer of 1959 she had been toying with the idea of undertaking Alaide in Bellini's La Straniera; she had taken a score on board the Christina, but she decided instead to appear as Paolina in Donizetti's Poliuto. It was her least important undertaking in years. Poliuto is a tenor vehicle and with Corelli, a first-class tenor and handsome man, it suited her to take second-place. The production was to have been by Visconti but his film Rocco e suoi fratelli had been censored by the Italian authorities and in protest he withdrew, to be replaced by Graf. In the event the staging was grandiose and splendid, and if one did not miss Visconti too greatly that was because Benois's settings à la Gonzaga went some way in compensation; Act II, I recall particularly, looked like the interior of the Pantheon in Rome. Poliuto had last been in the Scala repertory twenty years before with a cast including Gigli and Caniglia, on which occasion it had been conducted by Gino Marinuzzi; and his version, a mixture of the Italian and French editions, was used on this occasion.

On the first night the auditorium was elaborately decked out with carnations and a notable stream of celebrities: the Prince and Princess of Monaco, the Begum Aga Khan, Onassis and countless others. I remember the novelist, Erich Maria Remarque, and his wife Paulette Godard sitting near me. Certainly it was one of the best-dressed audiences I have ever seen; it was one of the many ironies of Callas's career that as soon as her voice had begun obviously to deteriorate, audiences became more star-studded and theatre prices rocketed – at this stage it was her appearance as much as her singing that made the effect. Benois had her swathed in classical garb and her wig was elaborately permed and piled up high in the form of a diadem, styled after a bust of Julia, daughter of Emperor Titus, displayed in Rome's Capitoline museum.

After Paolina Callas never risked another new role, although, as the years passed, she seemed to become younger-looking so, by a kind of reverse logic, her voice became markedly older sounding – she was, one could say, a kind of vocal Dorian Grey. But even in *Poliuto* we hear the responsiveness of what remains of her voice when she launches into the Act I cabaletta, 'Perche di stolto giubilo'. She has problems at the top, and at the bottom she has to tread carefully. Like a tight-rope walker her vocal cords wobble under the slightest pressure; but her technical, as well as musical, skill remains on a virtuoso level. Even at this stage of her career we can still hear precisely what Donizetti writes. Even in 1960 she could still execute the most intricate and demanding music with her familiar accuracy. It is customary to talk of singers losing their voices; but it would be more precise to discriminate between losing their voices and losing the ability to sing. For most it is the latter but, even with only a whisper of tone, which was all Callas had left by this time, she could still sing. The French critic Bourgeois remembers her saying: '"I still have my voice, it's my technique that's gone: I've no control any longer." But that was not true; it was her voice that was gone; she still had her technique.'[9]

After *Poliuto* Callas did not sing again at La Scala that season; and in the meantime she moved to Paris. At first she resided at the Hotel Lancaster, Rue Berri, in the eighth arrondissement. It was at the Salle Wagram, between March 28th and April 5th, that she recorded her first French recital, with Georges Prêtre and the Orchestre National de la RTF. For this she sings a strangely diverse repertory: a mélange of contralto, mezzo-soprano, coloratura and lyric soprano arias 'J'ai perdu mon Eurydice' from *Orphée*; 'Divinités du Styx' from *Alceste*; the Habañera and the Séguedille from *Carmen*; 'Printemps qui commence' and 'Amour! viens aider ma faiblesse!' from *Samson et Dalila*; Juliette's Valse from *Roméo et Juliette*;

Philine's Polonaise from *Mignon*; 'Pleurez mes yeux' from Massenet's *Le Cid*; and 'Depuis le jour' from *Louise*. Three other titles were recorded but not issued; the Scène des Cartes from *Carmen*, the Air du Miroir from *Thaïs* and 'Mon coeur s'ouvre à ta voix' from *Samson et Dalila*, though this last was issued in 1982. Perhaps we might have believed she was toying with the idea of taking up another career singing Orphée, Dalila and Carmen, except that Juliette and Philine suggest that she had not completely cut herself off from high parts.

We can only lament that she did not make this record years earlier. Although a RAI broadcast of 1954 confirms 'Depuis le jour' from *Louise* was always beyond her, it is a pity that she did not record the aria from *Alceste* the year she sang it at La Scala. Then her delivery had a vocal surety (she emitted the b''s without any problems), a dynamic range and rhythmic certainty that we do not hear on this recording. After she had ventured Orphée's aria Kelly invited her to sing it in Dallas, but she did not accept; not so much because, as was said at the time, she would not admit to herself that her upper register had collapsed, as because the range of her voice had become restricted at both ends. Legge remembers, 'the lower register needed more consistent power than she could sustain'.[10] We hear how, in Dalila's music, she does not make the mezzo-soprano effect that Ponselle does when she recorded Dalila's arias in 1953. Whereas Callas has difficulty sustaining the tessitura, Ponselle sounds as though this is where she should always have been.

By 1961, doubtless, there was a part of Callas that would have liked to give up even thinking about singing. But she was the most famous opera singer in the world, and without her career she was nobody. As far as the general public was concerned she had given up singing for the sake of Onassis; but that was not quite true, though she preferred him to believe it. She knew him well enough to know that it was better he should think her capable of going back to sing whenever she chose. Her problem was how much longer he could be fooled. She was desperately concerned to keep him, because she knew her voice was unable to keep her any longer. Not that she needed his money: indeed, though she was hardly singing during these years, her record royalties continued to rise prodigiously.

On May 30th 1961 Callas took part in a concert given in aid of the Edwina Mountbatten Fund at St James's Palace, London. This was held in a L-shaped hall in the Palace, in which half the audience faced her and half were off to one side in an annexe. In the main hall were seated the Queen Mother, the Earl and Countess of Harewood,

Lord Monkton and members of the diplomatic corps. Callas looked, as she often did at this time, nervous and chic, wearing a slinky black dress attached to her right shoulder – Onassis liked her in black. The hall was so small that when she emerged one could clearly see how ill at ease she was. She must have known that this kind of exposure, in a confined ambiance, with piano accompaniment, showed her off to less advantage than did her usual concerts with orchestra. Yehudi Menuhin shared the evening, and with Sir Malcolm Sargent began the concert with violin sonatas by Beethoven and Franck. Then, after a brief interval, Callas, with Sargent at the piano and Ivor Newton turning the pages, sang four arias: 'Casta Diva', Chimène's 'Pleurez mes yeux' from *Le Cid*, 'Tu che la vanità' from *Don Carlo* and 'L'altra notte' from *Mefistofele*. When Newton asked her why she had not included any songs she told him she did not know any.[11]

Since Onassis had become free, Callas was anxious to secure a divorce and marry him. But Italian law made this impossible. She was the guilty partner and though Meneghini claimed he had had propositions made him by other would-be divas, he refused to give her any opportunity to secure her freedom. For him newspaper stories on the Callas/Onassis relationship were a continual slap in the face – not infrequently they were photographed together, on some occasions even kissing! Eventually Meneghini went to the Civil Tribunal at Milan determined to annul the agreement that they should live apart by mutual consent, and have it replaced by a separation order which would lay the blame squarely on Callas. But just how significant the Callas/Onassis relationship really was we may question. By this stage it is doubtful whether Onassis envisaged his affair with Callas as more than transitory: two professionals who were not averse to a little fun on the side. It was not till he went to *Poliuto*, we may believe, that the thought crossed his mind that Callas had not abandoned her career for his sake, but rather that her voice had abandoned her. After the first flush of the affair he must have been very relieved that her equivocal matrimonial situation had prevented a rush to the registry office.

In the summer of 1961 she appeared in Epidavros again, on August 6th and 13th, this time as Medea and, once again, in the Minotis production, although with different scenery. Again she gave her fee to the Scholarship Fund for Young Musicians. It was on this occasion, after years of being out of touch, that she invited her sister Jackie. Jackie was swept away: 'I needed', she writes, 'only to see that one great performance to understand everything she had achieved. She acted with her whole being, even the sandals on her feet seemed to project the role.'[12] Legge, too, was there; but he had had the advantage of seeing her many times through the years, and though for him 'there were occasional flashes of the "real" Callas, her career as an important artist [had] hardly lasted thirteen years'.[13]

After another three months' silence she returned to London for a recording session at Kingsway Hall with the Philharmonia Orchestra under Tonini, lasting four days from November 13th. She sang the Act I scena from *Il Pirata*, 'Sorgete . . . Lo segnai ferito . . . Sventurata anch' io deliro,' in company with tenor Alexander Young and contralto Monica Sinclair. This was not issued until March 1972, when she was giving master-classes in New York at the Juilliard School of Music. Legge wrote to Callas, on November 7th 1971, insisting '[it] should have been published sooner'.[14] No doubt by her standards at the time it does not seem too bad. But if we compare her in the same scene at Carnegie Hall in 1959 (a performance that is certainly not notable for lovely tone), we cannot help noticing how her voice has not only lost range, at the bottom as well as the top, but her singing throughout has lost much of its fluency. This session also included 'Come, innocente giovane' from *Anna Bolena*, 'Selva opaca' from *Guglielmo Tell*, 'Com' e bello!' from *Lucrezia Borgia*, the Rondo finale from *Cenerentola* and 'Bel raggio' from *Semiramide*, none of which was published in her lifetime. It was not until a decade after her death, in 1987, that the modestly written 'Selva opaca' was issued.

Callas returned again to La Scala at the beginning of the 1961/2 season for *Medea*, but not until four days after opening night; the production once again was by Minotis, with Simionato, Vickers and Nicolai Ghiaurov, conducted by Thomas Schippers. She sang three performances before Christmas and then commenced a concert tour at the Festival Hall, London, on February 26th 1962, with the Philharmonia Orchestra conducted by Georges Prêtre. I recorded five of the six arias she sang, beginning with 'Ocean! Thou mighty monster' from Weber's *Oberon*, in largely incomprehensible English; by this stage she was obliged to modify so many of her vowels that her diction was clouded. She continued with Chimène's air from *Le Cid*, the Rondo Finale from *Cenerentola*, which had a few modest embellishments, 'La luce langue' from *Macbeth*, shorn of the coda, 'O don fatale' from *Don Carlo* and a truncated account of the Final Scene from *Anna Bolena*. From London she proceeded to Munich on March 12th, Hamburg on the 16th, Essen on the 19th and Bonn on the 23rd. In all of these, with various orchestras under Prêtre, she sang Chimène's air, the Habañera and Séguedille from

Carmen, the recitative and aria 'Ernani, involami' but without the cabaletta, and 'O don fatale'. On April 9th she returned to Kingsway Hall, London and with the Philharmonia orchestra under Tonini, recorded Cenerentola's Rondo, 'Ocean, thou mighty monster' and 'O don fatale'. Only the first of these was issued, and again not until 1987. In New York that month Litza made a suicide attempt. But if it was designed to have any effect on her daughter it failed, for Callas did not rush over to see her mother.

Although she did come to New York this was only to a Madison Square rout to celebrate the birthday of President Kennedy on May 19th, when she sang the Habañera and Séguedille from *Carmen*. Then, back at La Scala, she gave her last two performances of Medea on the 29th and June 3rd. I was at both of these, which were put on the same week that Meyerbeer's *Gli Ugonotti* was revived in a grandiose production with sumptuous sets and costumes by Benois. The role of Valentina had been offered her but, by that stage, it would have been altogether beyond her. Simionato sang it instead, with Sutherland, Cossotto, Corelli, Vladimiro Ganzarolli, Tozzi and Ghiaurov conducted by Gavazzeni. The casting was by Siciliani, who had moved to La Scala as Artistic Director. Callas sang on only one other occasion in 1962, in London, on November 4th in an ITV *Golden Hour* from Covent Garden: 'Tu che la vanità' from *Don Carlo* and the Habañera and Séguedille from *Carmen*. The memorable thing about it was when a pendant fell from her dress whilst she was singing. There was not even an involuntary inflection of her eyes to suggest that she realized it. At the end, when the applause had ceased, she bent down and recovered it; though, of course, she did not attempt to put it back on while she was on stage. Also on the bill was the violinist Mischa Elman; forty-five years before, on December 27th 1917, he had provided Caruso's obbligato when he sang Bizet's 'Agnus Dei' in a Musical Matinée at the Waldorf Astoria, New York.

It was at the end of 1962 that Callas received a letter from the New York Welfare Department informing her that her mother had applied for public assistance. They had not been in direct contact for more than a decade, though Litza had written a book about her daughter, and when this failed to make her rich she took to producing dolls representing various Callas roles. Litza's friends had telephoned Callas when she was in New York and attempted to make peace between them, but they were rebuffed and eventually Dr Lantzounis was left as go-between. At length, through him, Callas agreed to pay Litza $70 a month towards her living expenses, plus her rent, $130 a month but, on condition that she would grant no more press interviews. At that time she lived in the Upper West side, a Puerto Rican neighbourhood, and though she was prepared to accept the money and make the most abject promises she still could not resist talking to journalists. Stassinopoulos quotes from a letter Callas wrote Dr Lantzounis, after reading a story that Litza had given an Italian magazine: 'You've got to help me put some sense into her head and make her realize her position and shut her lovely mouth. Anyway that's like cancer. I'll never get rid of her.'[15]

For the first time since 1946, Callas did not appear in opera in 1963; and she sang only six concerts: at Berlin, Düsseldorf, Stuttgart, London, Paris and Copenhagen. She also recorded another album of French arias: 'O malheureuse Iphigénie' from *Iphigénie en Tauride*, 'D'amour l'ardente flamme' from *La Damnation de Faust*, the Cavatine de Leïla from *Les Pêcheurs de perles*, the Adieux and Cours la Reine scene from *Manon*, the Air des Lettres from *Werther* and the Ballad of the King of Thulé and Jewel Song from *Faust*. This was made at the Salle Wagram in Paris in the first week of May with the Orchestre de la Société des Concerts du Conservatoire under Prêtre. It was the last record that she made with Legge. Although he did not retire until the end of June the following year, in September 1963 he produced another recording of Verdi's Requiem Mass, this time with the Philharmonia under Giulini, with Schwarzkopf, Ludwig, Gedda and Ghiaurov as soloists. As Glotz relates, 'Callas had always wanted to record this. She was furious she was not invited and severed her relationship with Legge, so I became her record producer thereafter.'[16] This was the third and final time she nearly sang in the Requiem.

It was in 1963 that Onassis was introduced by an old friend, Lee Radziwill, to her sister Jackie Kennedy. At the beginning of August, when she gave birth prematurely to a third son, who died within twenty-four hours, Onassis offered Jackie the *Christina* for a convalescence cruise; he would not, he said, be coming on it himself. Perhaps the memory of his being indicted for conspiracy to defraud the American government and $7 million dollars he had to pay, persuaded him that his presence would have been *de trop* and President Kennedy would have found it embarrassing that his wife was in such company. Nevertheless she was pleased to accept his offer, insisting he must come too; and so he did, escorting her and her party through the Greek islands. Needless to say, representatives of the press were omnipresent. Callas, though, was not. She had been ordered off, for it would hardly have been in Onassis's interests to have had his 'concubine on board'.[17] When the cruise was over Onassis presented Jackie Kennedy with a number of magnificent gifts. Then, less than six weeks later, on November 22nd, President Kennedy was assassinated in Dallas. Onassis immediately rushed to Washington. William Manchester describes him with the Kennedy clan at the White House on the night of the funeral.

Coincidentally or not, it was at this time that Callas decided to concentrate once again on her career. Her name was still often in the newspapers, though generally in the gossip columns, and it was difficult to realize that she had not sung on stage for a year and a half; nor, in the last six months, had she even made any records. She determined to start recording again, so that December, in Paris, she commenced three new albums at the Salle Wagram. The first is devoted to classical music, including Beethoven's 'Ah, perfido', 'Ocean! Thou mighty monster' from Weber's *Oberon* (the only music in English she ever recorded), and several Mozart items, three from *Don Giovanni*, two arias of Anna and one of Elvira, and the Countess's 'Porgi amor' from *Figaro*. The second record is of Verdi arias: two of Mina from *Aroldo*, Elisabetta's 'Non pianger, mia compagna' and Eboli's 'O don fatale' from *Don Carlo*, and the Willow Song and Ave Maria from *Otello*. The third is of Rossini and Donizetti arias: the Rondo Finale from *La Cenerentola*, 'Selva opaca' from *Guglielmo Tell*, 'Convien partir' from *La Figlia del Reggimento*, 'Bel raggio' from *Semiramide*, 'Com'e bello!' from *Lucrezia Borgia* and 'Prendi, per me sei libero' from *L'Elisir d'Amore*. All three are conducted by Rescigno with the Orchestre de la Société des Concerts du Conservatoire.

One item, inevitably among the most modest vocally, stands out: the Willow Song and Ave Maria from *Otello*. One can hardly imagine her bothering with it in her halcyon days, but in 1963 she contrives a haunting effect in it, despite her modifying the vowels – when she repeats 'Salce' it sounds more like 'Sulce'. This is the result of an attempt to keep what little of her voice is left forward on the breath. She tries other devices: we note, for instance, how she introduces a sudden diminuendo, shutting the voice off the support – whether to prevent the note developing a pronounced wobble or because of physical weakness is difficult to say, for the wobble was a result of physical febrility. In the Ave Maria she shows how simple yet effective Verdi's writing is, and how much can be made of it when the singer's legato is a model. How musically she utters the text: the relationship between vowels and consonants, the perfect double consonants. At the beginning of her career she had been able to embark on the most extended flights but now, with a mere remnant of a voice, she can only work effectively in music of a narrow range. She hones her voice down so as to reveal a myriad details, and she does not have to make the compromises we hear on most of the other arias included in these albums.

Callas returned to opera on January 21st 1964 when she reappeared at Covent Garden in Zeffirelli's production of *Tosca*. The company included Renato Cioni, Gobbi and the conductor Cillario. By this time her Tosca had a much lighter voice than ten years previously. Her histronic skill had grown considerably since the early 1950s and this enabled her to give a fuller dramatic realization of Tosca than she had done before, even if this could hardly compensate for her vocal weakness. In these late performances her portrayal was still musically memorable, though perhaps most obviously when she was not required to sing. I recall the moment at the end of the Act I duet with Cavaradossi, when Tosca was about to leave the church, how she turned back to gather up the silk stole she had put down, and then left hurriedly – as it floated out behind her it seemed perfectly to mirror the orchestral reprise of the melody.

After six *Tosca*s, on February 9th there was a special telecast of Act II from Covent Garden. In those days for television the stage had to be vividly lit. I remember being almost roasted by the heat coming off the powerful lights; yet, looking at a film of it today, it is as if there were hardly any lights at all; the stage is so dark and Callas looks so ghoulish one can understand her reluctance to commit her Tosca to film. Opera is not a realistic art form. It is not concerned with verisimilitude as the cinema and television are. As Visconti states 'opera must be staged in an opera house . . . one needs an audience, the distance, the orchestra, the curtain'.[18] The cinema can only follow one thing at a time and it is incapable of holding the disparate elements of opera, staging, singers and orchestra, in balance; just as a snapshot from a box camera cannot convey the majesty of an Alpine vista. No medium is less suited to Grand Opera. Early nineteenth-century opera, with its set pieces and textual repetitions, is not merely the anithesis of reality, it also requires highly stylized acting. Callas had the perfect face for it. Her big features matched its grandiloquence and spoke volumes from a distance whereas up close, after a performance, all I can remember is how much acne and dandruff her Violetta had.

After *Tosca* Callas revived *Norma*, which opened at the Paris Opéra on May 22nd. Eight performances were given. It was a stunning-looking production by Zeffirelli with costumes by Marcel Escoffier. Before reading reviews of her performance today it is as well to remember how much her reputation had grown by then. But in choosing the role of Norma all attempts at the kind of self-deception so many well wishers had been indulging in up to that time had to be abandoned, for it took her very obviously to the limit and beyond. At the second performance, in the last act, she collapsed on a c''. Bing was present and he relates how, 'the house fell into an uproar ... She raised her hand, and there was silence. She motioned to the conductor to start ... again, and this time [all went well].'[19] She was richly costumed, certainly a little too opulently for a Druid priestess; but at this stage Callas was more significant than Norma. Like Marilyn Monroe and Judy Garland she had become a cult figure; most of the audience came to gape at her rather than be concerned with her art.

On July 6th Callas commenced a complete recording of *Carmen*. Over the years there were many attempts to persuade her to sing it in the theatre. Zeffirelli tried to in Paris at this time but she resisted, possibly, he surmises, because she was ashamed of her legs. But then she could have worn a long dress. She was in fact, just looking for excuses; though she could not easily articulate her musical instincts, they were impeccable. The secret of a successful Carmen does not lie in the music the way it does with Norma, Lucia or Violetta. With only modest transpositions it can be sung by almost any female singer. Galli-Marié (the role's creator), Calvé, Garden, Supervia to Migenes (in the movie) were all actresses first, singers second whereas Callas was always a singer first and actress second, which is why she was content to sing Carmen on record, yet never interpret it on stage.

Between December 3rd and 19th she made her second recording of Tosca at the Salle Wagram, with Bergonzi and Gobbi, conducted by Prêtre. Then, on February 19th 1965, she began the first of nine performances at the Paris Opéra with the Covent Garden production and principals. This time the first three were conducted by Prêtre and the remainder by Rescigno. On March 19th, having buried the hatchet with Bing, she reappeared at the Met and sang Tosca, at a fee of $14,000, in the shabby remains of an old production, though she and Gobbi wore the Covent Garden costumes. Back in Paris again, on May 14th, she returned to the Opéra as Norma. On the 18th she sang on television in *Les Grands interprètes*: 'Adieu, notre petite table' from Massenet's *Manon*, 'Ah! non credea' from *La Sonnambula* (but without 'Ah! non giunge'), and 'O mio babbino caro' from *Gianni Schicchi* with the Orchestre National de la RTF under Prêtre. Although Duparc's 'L'Invitation au voyage' appeared on the announced programme it was never transmitted. When Réal la Rochelle asked Glotz about it[20] he denied that she had sung it. He was always trying to inveigle Callas into recording the song repertory – not only Duparc, but Fauré, and Ravel and even popular Greek songs, yet she always declined.

In the spring of 1965 Callas sang five *Normas* at the Opéra but all the medicines in the world could not give her strength to sustain the run. The fifth performance came to a summary end after Act II and this time, indicatively, there was none of the fuss she had created when she attenuated *Norma* in Rome seven years previously. Afterwards she was due to come to Covent Garden for another five *Toscas*, beginning at the end of June; but the prospect filled her with apprehension. She telephoned Webster only days before to tell him her health did not permit her to undertake them. But hers was not basically a health problem, as was apparent when she was seen at the Rothschilds' ball only days before she was due in London. Webster flew to Paris and coaxed her into undertaking one of the performances, the charity gala in front of the Queen on July 5th. During the performance a man sitting in front of me complained loudly that he could not hear her; but although Callas's voice was only a shadow of what it had once been, every note was clearly audible even in the gallery. Her voice had hardly any support left, yet she still somehow mustered sufficient strength to project all the notes tellingly. With this performance she appeared on the operatic stage for the last time. She was forty-one.

During the next twelve years Callas was offered an amazing number and variety of roles. At Covent Garden John Tooley, successor to Webster, invited her to sing Santuzza with Plácido Domingo in Zeffirelli's production, but she refused; although Zeffirelli had dressed her Norma in the fashion of a goddess rather than a priestess, even he might have drawn the line at turning a Sicilian peasant into fashion-plate beauty. He suggested instead Monteverdi's *L'Incoronazione di Poppea*, outdoors at the Campidoglio, Rome; '"but Poppea doesn't have the biggest part," she protested'.[21] Visconti and the Paris Opéra tried talking her into *La Traviata*. She didn't exactly refuse but demanded so much rehearsal time, '20 to 30 days for the orchestra and chorus'[22] that it would have been exorbitant. At the Met Bing proposed a double-bill: the mute role of Potiphar's wife in Strauss's melodrama *Josephslegende*, and with it another 'really good idea'[23] (his words), Poulenc's *La Voix humaine*. And there were all manner of attempts to get her to sing modern works, notwithstanding the fact that she had always been vociferously against them. In London in 1954 she was asked to undertake Lady Hamilton in Berkeley's *Nelson*; in New York in 1957 Barber tried to interest her in *Vanessa*. An echo of nearly twenty years before took place when, in 1969, an attempt was made to coax her into singing Magda in Menotti's *Consul* at the Théâtre du Champs-Elysée, Paris; but, by that time, when she was all looks and no voice, one wonders where the idea came from that she should emerge from retirement to sing a role requiring her to be so plain and prosaically clad!

In the summer of 1965 Zeffirelli wanted to make a film of Callas in *Tosca*, the second time he had tried to make a film with her. In Dallas in 1958, after the success of his staging of *La Traviata*, 'there were some millionaires ready to put money into a film, but Maria was very uncertain switching mediums'.[24] Now, however, he was determined. So he was invited on the *Christina*, as he tells, to 'discuss the proposal with the great man himself'.[25] As well as Onassis, Callas and Zeffirelli, two directors of British Home Entertainment were also present. The discussion went on some days. 'The main difficulty . . . was that . . . Karajan . . . had acquired the film rights to the opera and insisted on producing it with his company',[26] but it was thought a way could be found to accommodate him. Zeffirelli stated he needed an advance. Callas was reluctant to sign. She prevaricated; she must, she said, first see the designs, his preparatory work, etc. She must have known them well enough from Zeffirelli's stage production, for he proposed booking Mongiardino for sets and Escoffier for costumes, as he had at Covent Garden. Her prevarication stemmed from her fear of venturing into a new medium. Nevertheless Onassis announced 'that the project must go ahead'. Perhaps he was tired of discussing it, so he agreed to give $10,000 'development money'.[27] But to Zeffirelli this seemed a derisory sum from a man of Onassis's worth: 'it was a sign of how he viewed the project'.[28] However, from other accounts it was not so much Onassis but Callas who was unenthusiastic. Film producer Franco Rossellini maintains that, '[Callas] didn't believe opera should be filmed . . . [but Zeffirelli] pushed and pushed'.[29] According to Rossellini, Zeffirelli asked for $30,000, and Onassis put the money up. But when Karajan declined to co-operate, it was Callas, not Onassis, who insisted on Zeffirelli returning his advance. '[Zeffirelli] refused . . . He said, "Onassis is rich enough, he can afford it."'[30] The upshot was that Callas and Zeffirelli did not speak for some years.

In April 1966 Callas found a way to get out of her marriage with Meneghini. Since an Italian divorce had proved impossible she decided to relinquish her American citizenship and take Greek nationality; for a Greek marriage is not valid unless it takes place in a Greek Orthodox church. In such fashion, therefore, she would only be Signora Meneghini in Italy. But by this time Onassis had realized that not only was she no longer Signora Meneghini, she was no longer a prima donna either. Inevitably journalists quizzed him, but he dismissed the obvious implication: 'We are close friends [but] this new event changes nothing.'[31] As Stancioff observes 'his investment in Callas ended'.[32] Henceforth he kept her dangling.

Later that year Callas became pregnant, or so she told Stancioff. When Onassis learnt of her condition he immediately threatened that if she had the baby he would never see her again. Faced with that, she said, 'I had to make a choice',[33] so she had an abortion. But it does seem somewhat coincidental that she should have claimed to have got pregnant precisely at the time she was trying inveigle Onassis into marrying her, though she had not done so throughout the years when their relationship was much closer. She was now nearly forty-three, not beyond the age of child-bearing but certainly near to it. In the days of her marriage, Meneghini asserts,[34] she had always wanted a child; but since she never became pregnant eventually, in 1957, she underwent a variety of tests. At first the gynaecologist ascribed her infertility to being 'always tired . . . and a serious loss of strength in general',[35] then he 'found symptoms of a rather early menopause, and he prescribed a series of injections'.[36] Eventually, however, he discovered that 'a malformation of her uterus'[37] made child-bearing impossible. Meneghini may have been lying. But by 1966 she was so desperate to hold on to Onassis that any story might serve her purpose. Stancioff says[38] that in 1972, when Onassis was no longer the man in her life and she was working with di Stefano, she came to Rome and asked to see a doctor, thinking that she was pregnant again. But he assured her she definitely was not. By then she was forty-eight and the idea must have seemed very flattering.

On May 31st 1967 Callas appeared at the first night of a visit of an ensemble from the Metropolitan, New York to the Théâtre Odéon, Paris. The company had been invited by Jean-Louis Barrault to perform *Il Barbiere di Siviglia*. She, needless to say, was not there to sing, but only in the audience, yet her reception was clamorous. Truth to tell, much of her ovation was the result of the low standard of performance; even Bing was obliged to admit the visit 'was not a success'.[39] The audience wanted to vent its wrath, so when Callas came down an aisle prominent figures led by Madame Pompidou, wife of the President of the French republic, got to their feet cheering loudly. If that was all she needed to do, she reasoned, what point was there in her attempting to sing again?

The previous month Callas had made a reappearance in London, this time neither on stage nor in the audience, but in court. She and Onassis were there in an action against Panaghis Vergottis, sometime friend of Onassis and shipping magnate. Onassis claimed that in the summer of 1964 the three of them had set up a company to buy a 27,000 ton tanker, which cost $3.9 million: they divided the share capital: Callas twenty-five per cent, Vergottis twenty-five per cent and Onassis fifty per cent. Vergottis disputed their claim: Callas, he said, had only loaned money to the company and she was not entitled to a share. The court ruled in favour of Callas. Vergottis went to the Court of Appeals and won round two. Finally the case went to the House of Lords, who passed judgement in favour of Callas and Onassis. Vergottis's costs alone amounted to £25,000. From the sums mentioned, the often repeated notion that Callas was like an orphan-in-the-storm, virtually penniless, seems hard to believe. For it was at the time she became involved in this multi-million dollar litigation, that she bought an apartment in Paris, in the sixteenth arrondissement; at 36 Avenue Georges-Mandel. She had it decorated with Louis Quinze furniture, Renaissance paintings, chinoiserie, a pair of dogs, an elephant and pagoda, a Regency inlaid rosewood and violet wood commode, a jonquil-yellow lacquered commode, an eighteenth-century Italian double bed complete with flower-painted and carved headpiece, a silk carpet in petit point, and paintings by Bassano, Sebastiano del Piombo and Fragonard. She was no longer singing, yet she still had her record royalties – these were, indeed, still are, considerable. But she was always pleading poverty; and perhaps by Onassis's standards she was poor.

By this stage Callas was obliged to ignore Onassis's passing back-stage amours. But in 1968 rumours commenced of his being one of the contenders for Jackie Kennedy's hand. At first, no doubt, she dismissed them as gossip columnists' lore. For eight years she had been hostess on the *Christina* and in the summer of that year Lawrence Kelly was on board. They were cruising around when Onassis suddenly appeared and ordered her to go to Paris. She refused, and a row followed. He insisted. He told her he was having special company and it was impossible for her to be there. Thereupon Kelly invited her to return with him to America. So, in company with Kelly, Mrs Carter and other friends, she mooched round America for the next month able neither to stay in one place nor to keep her mind off Onassis. At length she returned to Paris where she received a call from his butler to tell her, just before the story was to appear in the world's press, that Onassis and Jackie Kennedy were to be married on October 20th.

In the face of this she was once again thrown on her own resources. EMI proposed that she record *La Traviata* in Rome at the Accademia Santa Cecilia with Luciano Pavarotti, conducted by Giulini. But by now her voice was so run down she could not contemplate trying to make it work again. She had to do something, so she decided on attempting another career, this time in the movies. However, whereas her decisions in opera had been guided by her unimpeachable musical instincts, she had little conception of what was required in the very different medium of the cinema. Years before, Foreman had offered her a part in *The Guns of Navarone*, but she had not accepted (Irene Papas played it instead), nor did she when Visconti attempted to get her to play Jeritza in a life of Puccini. Losey tried to cast her in Tennessee Williams's *Boom* but the part, that of 'an aging figure in the entertainment world making a comeback',[40] had too many overtones of her own predicament. Elizabeth Taylor took it. Onassis became indignant when she refused to play Sarah in Houston's *The Bible*, and the part went to Ava Gardner. Eventually, in the summer of 1969, she agreed to make a film of *Medea*, not of the opera but of the drama. For this, Pasolini, the director, ignored Euripides, turning to the myth to prepare his own version. Perhaps the fact that it was a Greek story made her feel she was on safe ground. Looking at it now we can only marvel that she should have made it; it is as revelatory of Callas as a couple of silent movies are of Caruso.

If Callas's activities in recent years had made plain the futility of her life, Onassis's was hardly any different – indeed, one could say they were related by futility. By the end of the first year of his marriage to Jackie even he was beginning to feel that it was costing a great deal. Quite apart from jewellery he had lavished on her (a pair of earrings alone cost $300,000!) she is reputed to have spent $1.5 million during that first year. It is perhaps not surprising that Callas's parsimony should have seemed more attractive; and in the first months of 1970, he returned to Paris, where Callas had been living since the première of the film *Medea*. He had no difficulty persuading her to resume their 'close friendship'. Photographs appeared in the press of them dining at Maxim's again; but then, a few days later, when Jackie flew in, husband and wife dined there *à deux*. It seems that Callas had little idea what was going on: indeed, it's doubtful if Onassis did either. One evening at Avenue Georges-Mandel she entertained Giulini and his wife to dinner. They found her in low spirits. The next morning she was rushed to the American Hospital at Neuilly. On Radio Luxembourg it was announced she was admitted having taken an overdose of barbiturates. She issued a statement denying it, but when a weekly magazine repeated it she lost no time suing both radio station and weekly, eventually she was awarded 20,000 Francs damages. She admits, 'I was depressed, but you know as well as I do, that I would never do anything stupid like that'.[41] Perhaps she would not premeditate an overdose; but by this time she had begun to indulge ever more frequently in sleeping pills.

In fact without her husband, Onassis or her voice, her life was coming apart at the seams. Since she was afraid to sing, and the film *Medea* had been at best only a *succès d'estime*, her area of manoeuvre was becoming ever more restricted. It was not until 1971 that a new lifeline presented itself. She was invited by Max Rudolf of the Curtis Institute of Music, Philadelphia to give a course of Master Classes. She went but 'dismissed herself after two or three days [perhaps, as Kelly suggests], because she did not have the opportunity of being prima donna assoluta'.[42] However Peter Menin, President of the Juilliard School of Music, hastily stepped in, and she agreed to come instead to Juilliard. Menin introduced her on February 3rd, and she gave twenty-three classes between October 11th and March 16th 1972 for twenty-six students. At first audiences were only a few hundred, but the public's appetite was so whetted that by the end classes were invariably full and numbers had increased to more than 1000. Callas then recommended that Menin charge admission, though she did not ask for payment herself – it was enough that she should have 'a suite at the Plaza, a limousine at the door, first-class travel arrangements, food, and fresh flowers in her room'.[43] Against the background noise, as it almost invariably was, of the students' voices, she would occasionally sing a phrase herself as she was guiding them. In fact, while in New York she had been practising regularly with a pianist; and so it was that at the Master Classes she came to sing once again for a fee-paying audience after a gap of more than six years.

Much of what Callas tells the students, or the audience, is derived from her pedagogues, and can be found easily enough elsewhere. Though it may seem selfish, Kelly observes, 'she thought of [the classes] in terms of herself and not in terms of the students'.[44] It is a pity that she does not tell how she managed to tune her voice up to such an extent that it was more responsive than that of almost any other singer. What we should like to know is which came first, her technique or her musicianship, or were they the chicken and the egg? Her motivation, we know, was wholly musical: as Ardoin notes 'many of Callas's most penetrating "remarks" were sung rather than spoken'.[45] We have seen so often how she was unable to communicate in words, so it is not surprising that she proves unable to explain what sets her performances off from others. The kind of analysis she indulges in is second-hand, or even third-hand. It is true that she may have derived a lot from de Hidalgo and Serafin, but not what makes her unique; they guided many other singers, but there was only one Callas. Although an assiduous learner, she knew by instinct what to accept and what to ignore. It was her instincts that made her art *sui generis*. As we hear, even in Rigoletto's 'Cortigiani', she communicates more surely in her singing than in all her verbal analysis.

It was after one of the master-classes that Callas met di Stefano again. Although they had known each other for more than twenty years, singing together in São Paolo, Mexico City, Chicago, Milan, Verona and Berlin, as well as making many recordings together, yet there had not been any intimacy between them until this time. Many years previously she had hoped he would make a fuss of her. He was very much a ladies' man, but at that time he was too much preoccupied with his own career. By this time, however, things were different. His voice was gone. He was in his usual financial difficulties and he made her appreciate how much in life she still had. Would she not be helping him, she reasoned, if she commenced recording again? At least that was how she saw it, but he saw it differently: 'She was very depressed. At the time my daughter, who was only a teenager, was dying of cancer. We talked of this and then of the years of fun and all that was behind us.'[46] His daughter's imminent death did bring them closer together, but two people of such utterly disparate characters would be hard to imagine. After spending the summer of 1972 together at San Remo, in the autumn they came over to London to make a duet recording for Philips in St Giles, Cripplegate. But the venture was not a success and the record was never published. During three-hour recording sessions, as a member of the orchestra remembers, they would sing only for the last twenty minutes, spending the rest of the time arguing in the control room. The conductor, de Almeida, blames Callas: 'she was artistically egotistical. She used the recording as a warm-up for a farewell tour'.[47]

The next episode in the Callas/di Stefano partnership took place the following spring at the Regio, Turin. This was burnt down in 1936 and was to reopen on April 10th 1973 with a new production of *I Vespri Siciliani* – by Callas. The cast included Raina Kabaivanska, Raimondi,

Licinio Montefusco and Bonaldo Giaiotti with Gavazzeni conducting. Callas persuaded Vernizzi, the Artistic Director, to appoint di Stefano co-producer. Gavazzeni, thereupon, withdrew and Gui, then eighty-eight, replaced him. But he collapsed on the podium. So eventually Vernizzi had to conduct. Neither di Stefano nor Callas had much idea what to do. It was a case of the blind being led by the blind: for her, literally, for on stage in her great days she had not bothered with contact lenses. 'She never knew what was going [on around her] . . . she was too involved with what she herself was doing.'[48]

In this period she was wholly under di Stefano's influence. She had forgotten, if she ever knew, how she had learned to sing. According to Kabaivanska, she was prepared to accept di Stefano's vocal philosophy, which shows how desperate she must have been. From the beginning of his career he sought to amplify his lyric tenor, which caused him to blow out his tone in more senses then one, and at a prodigiously rapid rate. We can understand that Callas and Kabaivanska, two divas, would not have got on too well. At first some criticism Callas made of Kabaivanska's singing, based not so much on her own but on di Stefano's methodology, resulted 'in a 24-hour silence'[49] between them. But they soon became friends and Kabaivanska recalls how much 'invaluable musical advice'[50] Callas gave her.

The next stage in her involvement with di Stefano was a Master Class with him in Osaka for winners of the Madama Butterfly competition on May 20th 1973. Then, that autumn, he coaxed her into undertaking a concert tour with him; so as to assist him meet the costs of his daughter's medication. At first they toyed with the idea of beginning this in Japan, but thought better of it – it may have been on the other side of the world but that would not prevent American critics being present. It was therefore decided that London would be more fitting. But at the last moment, no doubt because she felt it safer not to risk it in such an international city, her first concert took place, after more than eight years, in Hamburg on October 25th. Others followed in Berlin, Düsseldorf, Munich, Frankfurt and Mannheim; then one in Madrid, two in London, one in Paris and another in Amsterdam. A concert announced for Stuttgart did not take place; di Stefano was indisposed. Callas sang 'O mio babbino caro' and the public got their money back. In January 1974 the tour ended with their only appearance in Italy, at a hospital in Milan. I went to the two London concerts. The show began before the music, as soon as di Stefano and Callas had emerged from the green room and came out on the platform. He was in tails, she in a Biki creation, the Empress's new clothes, perhaps? Slowly, ever-so-slowly, waving and smiling first one way then the other, they perambulated about the piano, seducing from an all-too-willing audience an ovation before singing a note. Since her last appearance in 1965 Callas's glamour had taken on a celluloid look. And every time she opened her mouth what one noticed first was not her voice, or its remains, but two rows of orthodontistry – it was as if she had too many teeth.

On each occasion she would muster at most three arias: 'Voi lo sapete' from *Cavalleria Rusticana*, 'Suicidio' from *La Gioconda* and 'O mio babbino' from *Gianni Schicchi*. There were six duets, but often only four; from *L'Elisir d'Amore*, *Faust*, *I Vespri Siciliani*, *Carmen*, *Cavalleria Rusticana*, *La Forza del Destino* or *Don Carlo*, and a similar number of solos by di Stefano. There were perhaps twenty minutes of music in the entire evening. It was the audience who had to do the work; the applause was interrupted, as a critic quipped, 'by two dogs . . . barking at one another'. An interesting comment on the first concerts was the presence of Ivor Newton at the piano, then in his eighties. One would have liked to know what he was thinking. In his distinguished career he had accompanied many great singers, including Melba, Chaliapin, Butt, Tetrazzini, Gigli, McCormack, Tauber and Björling.

After a short adjournment there followed an American tour. The first concert took place on February 11th in Philadelphia, others followed in Toronto, Washington, Boston, Chicago, New York, Detroit, Dallas, Miami, Columbus, Brookville L.I., New York again, Cincinnati, Seattle, Portland, Vancouver, San Francisco and Montreal, where the tour ended on May 13th. The programme was similar to that in Europe, but in Boston, where she sang alone, she included six arias, adding 'Vissi d'arte', 'Sola, perduta, abbandonata,' from *Manon Lescaut* and 'Tu che le vanità' from *Don Carlo*. In Detroit, when di Stefano was again indisposed, she repeated the Boston programme, and in Dallas, once again without di Stefano, she increased the total to seven by including the Habañera from *Carmen*. At the second New York recital she did manage to change the programme, for although she repeated 'Suicidio' and 'Voi lo sapete', she added the Habañera, Charlotte's Air des lettres from *Werther* and Manon's 'Adieu notre petite table'. Meanwhile, behind the scenes, there were many occasions when di Stefano could hardly decide whether to sing or not. He broke off half-way through in Chicago, and in Vancouver, although announced as indisposed, he eventually did appear. But the only time a concert was postponed was when Callas was unwell; without her it would have been impossible.

The strain the tour put on Callas was obvious. Her first New York appearance had to be postponed because 'she took enough sleeping pills to knock her out for forty-eight hours'.[51] The concert was rescheduled, but on the same day impresario Hurok died. Although he was over eighty Callas became so distressed that she was only with difficulty persuaded to go on. She began the evening with an address to his memory, then at the end she launched off into a disjointed, incoherent ramble about theatres, management, conditions of performance – in fact, almost anything that came into her head. The audience was reduced to silence. Sheila Porter told Stancioff[52] how much she had changed from the Callas of the Covent Garden *Toscas* nine years before; though she had no difficulty remembering the music, for the words she needed cue cards, and even the order of the programme confused her. Di Stefano recalls the effort it cost her to sing at all. 'She was in very bad shape, she started to shake as she approached the piano. She began the last act aria from *Manon Lescaut*, and tears were coming down.'[53] Nevertheless she continued with the American tour, and that autumn they began another of the Far East. Though di Stefano remembers[54] an occasion when she took so many pills she collapsed before one concert yet neither cancelled any: they gave two in Korea and seven in Japan. She sang the same arias she had in America, except at some she replaced 'Suicidio' with 'Sì, mi chiamano Mimì'. Her last appearance took place on November 11th 1974 at Sapporo. This was, in fact, her last public appearance anywhere.

She returned to Europe with di Stefano, to a friend's villa on the Riviera. Then after a little while, she went back alone to Paris. Meanwhile Onassis had become involved with his largest scheme ever; *Project Omega*, worth $400 million. Then in January 1973, he had been stricken by the death of his son in a plane accident, after which his career plummeted. In January 1975 financial difficulties obliged him to surrender Olympic Airlines to the Greek government, and the following month he was flown to Paris for an operation for a gall bladder complaint. Callas endeavoured to escape from the memory of him by taking off for Palm Beach, where she rented a house. While she was there, on March 15th 1975, he died.

Back in Paris she toyed with the idea of singing Tosca in Japan with di Stefano that November. But although she did start practising again, whilst she was rehearsing at the Théâtre du Champs-Elysées, which a friend had given her the use of, a journalist slipped in secretly and an article appeared in *France Dimanche* detailing her vocal collapse. Again she sued and won. But without anyone to lean on she wrote to Dr Lantzounis at the end of June: 'I have come to a big decision. I am stopping singing'.[55] And so Caballé undertook Tosca instead. During the last two years of her life, she was still constantly pestered to make the most improbable appearances; but she shut the door firmly on her career. Her death, on September 16th 1977, was the final curtain.

In the last days of her life she was resorting to drugs to sleep and drugs to wake, so whether she may have committed suicide is a technicality. It is doubtful though if her death was the result of a conscious decision at a particular moment. More likely it was the inevitable result of her ceasing to see any reason for living. She did not leave a will, and left nothing at all to her long-time faithful maid and chauffeur – in fact, at the time she died she owed them money. Nor does it seem likely, bearing in mind her attitude, that she would have died intestate without at least making sure that her husband and her mother were not her sole legatees. They came to a speedy settlement, dividing the estate in two without legal dispute. At the time of her death it was worth $12 million, though her records will continue to earn royalties into the next century.

Those who look for meanings in death as in life will see something cryptic in the various posthumous happenings involving her estate. There is the story of the pianist Devetzi swindling Litza and Jackie of a substantial amount of their half. Jackie even throws doubt on whether Meneghini, who outside Italy was divorced from Callas, had any legal claim to his half. Callas's ashes were stolen from their bier in Père Lachaise cemetery in Paris. After they were recovered and being scattered over the Aegean, Jackie relates how 'a gust of wind . . . blew in from the sea and just as Maria's fluffy grey ashes left the receptacle they were instantly blown back over us . . . we all got some in the face and mouth and were forced to spit and cough it up'.[56] Ardoin remembers, while the sale of her possessions was going on at Avenue Georges-Mandel, 'one of the locked glass doors leading out to the garden patio burst open with immense force. It knocked over a chest of drawers, broke its marble top and caused a painting to crash to the floor.'[57] A mirror, he relates, split from side to side. The Meneghinis' house in Milan was demolished, and even their Sirmione property became overgrown and neglected: 'By some mysterious fate,' as Meneghini puts it, 'that which belonged to this great woman has crumbled'.[58] Well, not everything. Her records survive, and that is enough.

CHRONOLOGY OF PERFORMANCES AND RECORDINGS

* Complete recording available in good or satisfactory sound.
† Part of recording exists in good or variable sound.
R Recording of rehearsal available.
f Film available on video.
Film of part of a rehearsal.

Part 1: 1938–1945

Sung in Greek, unless otherwise noted

a) Student performances while studying with Maria Trivella at the National Conservatory.

1938

ATHENS – Parnassos Hall

Apr. 11th
An aria of Agathe from Weber's *Der Freischütz* (probably 'Leise, leise'); 'Plus grand dans son obscurité' Gounod's *La Reine de Saba*; Psaroudas's 'Two nights'; duet from Puccini's *Tosca* w. Kambanis t: piano Valtetsiotis.

1939

Olympia Theatre

Apr. 2nd
Santuzza in Mascagni's CAVALLERIA RUSTICANA w. Euthimiadou ms; Simiriotis t; Athineos b: piano Bourtsis p. Mordo.

Parnassos Hall

May 22nd
'Belle nuit, o nuit d'amour' Offenbach's *Les Contes d'Hoffmann* w. Bourdakou ms; 'Ocean! Thou mighty monster' Weber's *Oberon*; 'Ritorna vincitor' Verdi's *Aida*; Psaroudas's 'I will not forget you'; 'O terra addio' *Aida* w. Kambanis t: piano Valtetsiotis.

May 23rd
'Ocean Thou mighty monster' *Oberon*; 'Dis-moi que je suis belle' Massenet's *Thaïs*: piano?

	Olympia Theatre
Jun. 25th	In concert-form: Act III Verdi's UN BALLO IN MASCHERA w. Athineos b; Koidas bs; Aliprandis bs: Sc. II CAVALLERIA RUSTICANA w. Sakellariou ms; Koronis t: piano Nikolaidi p. Karakandas.

b) Student performances while studying with Elvira de Hidalgo at the Athens Conservatory.

1940

	Odeon Concert Hall
Feb. 23rd	'Mira o Norma . . . Sì, fino all'ore estremo' Bellini's *Norma* w. Mandikian ms: piano Koundouris.

	Radio station
Apr. 3rd	Duets from *Norma*, *Aida* and Ponchielli's *La Gioconda* w. Mandikian ms: ?

	Odeon Concert Hall
Jun. 16th	Suor Angelica in Puccini's SUOR ANGELICA w. Zografou s. Efstratiadu ms. Mandikian ms: ?

c) Performances whilst under contract to the Lyric Theater.

	Royal Theatre
Oct. 21st	Songs (composer not specified) in Shakespeare's *Merchant of Venice* w. Papadaki (Portia), Minotis (Shylock) (22nd, 23rd, 24th and 27th).

1941

	Palas Cinema
Jan. 21st–Mar. 9th	Beatrice in performances of von Suppé's BOCCACCIO, shared by Galanou w. Vlakopoulou/Remoundou s. Mustaka/Kolassi ms; Koronis/Glinos t: Kalogheras/Xirelles b. Horn b: c. Pfeffer/ Zoras p. Mordo.

	Park Summer Theatre
Jul. 3rd–15th	Repeat performances of BOCCACCIO w. cast as above, except Stilianopoulos for Horn.

1942

	Summer Theatre, Klafthmonos Square
Aug. 27th	Tosca in Puccini's TOSCA w. Delendas t. Kalogheras/Xirellis b: c. Vassiliadis p. Yannopoulos (28th, 30th, 2nd, 4th and 6th – though it is doubtful if Callas sang them all).
Sep. 8th	TOSCA (in Italian) w. Kourousopolis t: Vasilakis b: c. Vasiliadis p. Yannopoulos (Sep. 10th, 12th, 13th?, 14th?, 16th, 18th?, 20th?, 22th?, 24th, 26th?, 27th and 30th?).

Oct. ?
SALONIKA – Palas Cinema
Concert: 'Bel raggio' Rossini's *Semiramide*?; 'Selva opaca'
Rossini's *Guglielmo Tell*?: piano Paradis.

1943

Feb. 21st
ATHENS – National Theatre
A singer in the Intermezzo in Kalomiras's *'O PROTOMAS-
TORAS* w. Remoundou s. Galanou s; Delendas t: c. Zoras
p. Mikailidis (Feb. 23rd, 26th, 27th, Mar. 2nd, 5th, 6th, 11th,
13th, 16th and 20th).

Feb. 28th
Sporting Cinema, New Smyrna
Concert: ??

Apr. 22nd
Italian Institute
Pergolesi's *STABAT MATER* w. Mandikian ms: c. Likoudis.

Jul. 17th
Summer Theatre, Klafthmonos Square
TOSCA w. Delendas t. Xirellis b: c. Vasiliadis (Jul. 21st? and
31st).

Jul. 21st
Summer Theatre, Kosta Mousouri
'Care selve' Handel's *Atlanta*; Rondo Finale Rossini's *La
Cenerentola*; 'Io sono l'umile ancella' *Adriana Lecouvreur*;
an aria from Verdi's *Il Trovatore*; Lavda's 'They are marrying
off my love'; Palandios's 'Kimitiri': pianist Paradis.

Aug. ?
SALONIKA – White Tower Theatre
Concert: Lieder of Schubert and Brahms.

Sep. 26th
ATHENS – Olympia Theatre
'Abscheulicher' Beethoven's *Fidelio*; 'Et incarnatus est'
Mozart's *Mass in C Minor*; 'Dis-moi que je suis belle'
Thaïs; 'Ritorna vincitor' *Aida*; Turina's Canciones espagnol
'Tamare'?; Lavda's 'They are marrying off my love': pianist
Kidoniatis.

Dec. 12th
Kotopouli-Rex Theatre
'Abscheulicher' *Fidelio*; 'Bel raggio lusinghier' *Semiramide*;
an aria from *Il Trovatore*; Turina's Canciones espagnol
'Tamare': pianist Androutsopoulos.

1944

Apr. 22nd
Olympia Theatre
Martha in d'Albert's *TIEFLAND* w. Vlakopoulou s; Delendas
t: Mangliveras b: c. Zoras p. Mordo (23rd, 25th, 27th, 30th,
May 4th, 7th and 10th).

May 6th
CAVALLERIA RUSTICANA w. Kourakani ms; Delendas t;
Tsoumbris b: c. Karalivanos p. Mordo (and 9th).

May 21st
'Casta Diva' *Norma*: c. Zoras.

	Herodes Atticus

Aug. 5th   Herodes Atticus
Smaragda in *'O PROTOMASTORAS* w. Galanou s. Bourdakou ms. Delendas t; Mangliveras b: c. Kalomiras p. Karandinos.

Aug. 14th   Leonore in Beethoven's *FIDELIO* w. Vlakopoulou s; Delendas t; Kokolios t; Mangliveras b. Moulas bs: c. Hoerner/Zoras p. Walleck. (Callas sang only some of the performances announced for the 15th, 17th, 22nd, 25th, 31st, Sep. 1st, 3rd, 6th and 7th.)

1945

Mar.14th–24th   Olympia
Martha in *TIEFLAND* (probably the same cast as above).

Mar. 20th   (in English) Trad. air 'Willow, willow'; Ronald's 'Love, I have won you'; Vaughan Williams's 'On Wenlock Edge' (w. quintet): c. Karalivanos.

Aug. 3rd   Kotopouli-Rex
An aria of Zerlina from Mozart's *Don Giovanni*; 'Bel raggio lusinghier' *Semiramide*; 'Ritorna vincitor' *Aida*; an aria of Leonora from *Il Trovatore*; 'Ocean! Thou mighty monster' *Oberon*; two Spanish songs; Greek songs by Kariotakis and Poniridis: piano Likoudis.

Sep. 5th–13th   Summer Theatre, Avenue Alexander
Laura in Millocker's *DER BETTELSTUDENT* w. Papadopoulou s. Damasioti ms; Koronis t; Kasantzis t; Kourakani b. Eptropakis bs: c. Evanghelatos p. Mordo (Callas sang in the first of two casts. Performances were given almost nightly – on the 7th, 8th, 10th, 11th, 12th and 13th – and she would probably have appeared on four occasions in all).

Part 2: 1947–1959

1947

Aug. 2nd   VERONA – Arena
Gioconda in Ponchielli's *LA GIOCONDA* w. Nicolai ms. Canali ms; Tucker t; Tagliabue b. Rossi-Lemeni bs: c. Serafin p. Cardi (5th, 10th, 14th and 17th).

Dec. 30th   VENICE – La Fenice
Isotta in Wagner's *TRISTANO E ISOTTA* w. Barbieri ms; Tasso t; Torres b. Christoff bs: c. Serafin p. Frigerio (Jan. 3rd, 8th and 11th).

1948

Jan. 29th   Turandot in Puccini's *TURANDOT* w. Rizzieri s; Soler t, Carmassi bs: c. Sanzogno p. Frigerio (31st, Feb. 3rd, 8th and 10th).

                 UDINE – Puccini
Mar. 11th   *TURANDOT* w. Ottani s; Soler t; Maionica bs: c. de Fabritiis p. Cardi (and 14th).

                 TRIESTE – Rossetti
Apr. 17th   Leonora in Verdi's *LA FORZA DEL DESTINO* w. Canali ms; Vertecchi t; Franci b. Siepi bs. Serpo bs: c. Parenti (20th, 21st and 25th).

                 GENOA – Grattacielo
May 12th   *TRISTANO E ISOTTA* w. Nicolai ms; Lorenz t; Torres b. Rossi-Lemeni bs: c. Serafin p. Cardi (14th and 16th).

                 ROME – Caracalla
Jul. 4th   *TURANDOT* w. Montanari s; Masini t; Flamini bs: c. de Fabritiis p. Frigerio (6th and 11th).

                 VERONA – Arena
Jul. 27th   *TURANDOT* w. Rizzieri s; Salvarezza t; Rossi-Lemeni bs: c. Votto p. Salvini (Aug. 1st [except Tognoli s], 5th [except de Cecco s] and 9th [de Cecco]).

                 GENOA – Carlo Felice
Aug. 11th   *TURANDOT* w. Montanari s; del Monaco t; Maionica bs: c. Questa (and 14th [except Salvarezza t]).

                 TURIN – Lirico
Sep. 18th   Aida in Verdi's *AIDA* w. Nicolai ms; Turrini t; de Falchi b. Stefanoni bs: c. Serafin p. Cardi (19th [except Colasanti ms]), 23rd and 25th [Colasanti]).

                 ROVIGO – Sociale
Oct. 19th   *AIDA* w. Pirazzini ms; Turrini t; Viaro b. Mongelli bs: c. Berrettoni p. Cardi (21st and 24th).

                 FLORENCE – Comunale
Nov. 30th   Norma in Bellini's *NORMA* w. Barbieri ms; Picchi t; Siepi bs: c. Serafin (and Dec. 5th).

1949

                 VENICE – La Fenice
Jan. 8th   Brunilde in Wagner's *LA VALCHIRIA* w. Magnoni s. Pini ms; Voyer t; Torres bs. Dominici bs: c. Serafin p. Cardi (12th, 14th and 16th).

Jan. 19th   Elvira in Bellini's *I PURITANI* w. Pirino t; Savarese b. Christoff bs: w. Serafin (22nd and 23rd).

Jan. 28th	PALERMO – Massimo *LA VALCHIRIA* w. Magnoni s. Cabrera ms; Voyer t; Neri bs. Carmassi bs: c. Molinari Pradelli (and Feb. 10th).
Feb. 12th	NAPLES – San Carlo *TURANDOT* w. Montanari s; Laczò t; (from Act II R. Gigli t). Petri bs: c. Perlea p. Scafa (16th [except Salvarezza t], 18th [Salvarezza], 20th [Salvarezza]).
Feb. 26th	ROME – Opera Kundry in Wagner's *PARSIFAL* w. Beirer t; Cortis b. Dado b. Siepi bs: c. Serafin p. Duhan (Mar. 2nd, 5th and 8th).
Mar. 7th	TURIN – RAI Auditorium Broadcast Concert: Mad Scene *I Puritani*; 'O Patria mia' *Aida*; 'Casta Diva . . . Ah! bello a me ritorna' *Norma*; 'Morte di Isotta' *Tristano e Isotta*: RAI Orchestra c. Molinari Pradelli.
May 20th†	BUENOS AIRES – Colón *TURANDOT* w. Arizmendi s; del Monaco t; Zanin bs: c. Serafin p. Erhardt (29th [except Rossi-Lemeni bs]), June 11th and 22nd).
June 17th	*NORMA* w. Barbieri ms; Vela t; Rossi-Lemeni bs: c. Serafin p. Piccinato (19th, 25th and 29th).
July 2nd	*AIDA* w. Barbieri ms; Vela t; Rossi-Lemeni bs: c. Serafin p. Piccinato.
July 9th	Concert: 'Casta Diva . . . Ah! bello a me ritorna' *Norma* (with Rossi-Lemeni bs); Act III *Turandot* (cast as above except Rossi-Lemeni bs).
Sep. 18th	PERUGIA – Chiesa di San Pietro Erodiade in Stradella's oratorio *SAN GIOVANNI BATTISTA* w. Corsi ms, Pirazzini ms; Berdini t; Siepi bs: c. Santini.
Oct. 31st	VERONA – Nuovo Concert: 'Casta Diva' *Norma*; 'Morte di Isotta' *Tristano e Isotta*; 'O patria mia' *Aida*; Mad Scene *I Puritani*; 'Ombra leggera' Meyerbeer's *Dinorah*; 'Ah! fors' è lui . . . Sempre libera' Verdi's *La Traviata*: c. Berrettoni.
Nov. 8th–10th	TURIN – RAI Auditorium COMMERCIAL RECORDINGS (Cetra) 1st pub. 5/50. 'Morte di Isotta' *Tristano e Isotta*; 'Casta Diva . . . Ah! bello a me ritorna' *Norma*; Mad Scene *I Puritani*: RAI Orchestra c. Basile.

Dec. 20th*

NAPLES – San Carlo
Abigaille in Verdi's *NABUCCO* w. Pini ms; Sinimberghi t;
Bechi b; Neroni bs: c. Gui p. Brissoni (22nd and 27th).

1950

Jan. 13th

VENICE – La Fenice
NORMA w. Nicolai ms; Penno t; Pasero bs: c. Votto p. Cardi
(15th and 19th).

Feb. 2nd

BRESCIA – Grande
AIDA w. Pini ms; del Monaco t; Protti b; Feliciati bs: c. Erede
p. Luzzato (and 7th).

Feb. 6th

ROME – Opera
TRISTANO E ISOTTA w. Nicolai ms; Seider t; Franci b. Neri
bs: c. Serafin p. Frigerio (9th, 19th, 25th and 28th [except
Neroni bs]).

Feb. 23rd

NORMA w. Stignani ms; Masini t; Neri bs: c. Serafin p.
Sanine (26th, March 2nd [except Cassinelli bs], 4th [Cassi-
nelli], 7th [Cassinelli]).

Mar. 13th

TURIN – RAI Auditorium
Concert Broadcast: 'Ocean! Thou mighty monster', *Oberon*;
'Ah, fors è lui . . . Sempre libera' *La Traviata*; 'D' amor
sull'ali rosee' Verdi's *Il Trovatore*; 'Ombra leggera' *Dinorah*:
RAI Orchestra c. Simonetto.

Mar. 16th

CATANIA – Massimo Bellini
NORMA w. Gardino ms; Picchi t; Stefanoni bs: c. Berrettoni
p. Cardi (19th, 22nd and 25th).

Apr. 12th

MILAN—La Scala
AIDA w. Barbieri ms; del Monaco t; de Falchi b. Siepi bs:
c. Capuana p. Frigerio (15th and 18th [except Protti b.]).

Apr. 27th

NAPLES – San Carlo
AIDA w. Stignani ms; Picchi t; Savarese b. Siepi bs: c. Serafin
p. Scafa (30th, May 2nd and 4th).

May 23rd*

MEXICO CITY – Palacio de Bellas Artes
NORMA w. Simionato ms; Baum t; Moscona bs: c. Picco p.
Tibón (and 27th).

May 30th*

AIDA w. Simionato ms; Baum t; Weede b. Moscona bs:
c. Picco p. Tibón (June 3rd† and 15th [except Filippeschi
t]).

June 8th*

TOSCA w. Filippeschi t; Weede b: c. Mugnai p. Defrères (and
10th).

June 20th*	Leonora in Verdi's *IL TROVATORE* w. Simionato ms; Baum t; Warren b. Moscona bs: c. Picco p. Defrères (24th and 27th† [except Petroff b.]).
Sep. 22nd	SALSOMAGGIORE – Nuovo *TOSCA* w. Pelizzoni t; Inghilleri b: c. Questa.
Sep. 24th	BOLOGNA – Duse *TOSCA* w. Turrini t; Azzolini b: c. Questa.
Oct. 2nd†	ROME – Opera *AIDA* w. Stignani ms; Picchi t; de Falchi b; Neri bs: c. Bellezza p. Azzolini.
Oct. 7th	PISA – Verdi *TOSCA* w. Masini t; Poli b: c. Santarelli p. B. Pizzi (and 8th).
Oct. 19th†	ROME – Eliseo Fiorilla in Rossini's *IL TURCO IN ITALIA* w. Canali ms; Valletti t; Bruscantini bs. Calabrese bs. Stabile b: c. Gavazzeni p. Guerrieri (22nd, 25th and 29th).
Nov. 20/21st*	RAI Studios *PARSIFAL* (in concert) w. Pagliughi s. Baldelli t; Panerai b; Modesti bs. Christoff bs: c. Gui (20th Act I, 21st Acts II and III).

1951

Jan. 14th	FLORENCE – Comunale Violetta in Verdi's *LA TRAVIATA* w. Albanese t; Mascherini b: c. Serafin p. Bassi (16th and 20th).
Jan. 27th*	NAPLES – San Carlo *IL TROVATORE* w. Elmo ms; Lauri Volpi t; Silveri b. Tajo bs: c. Serafin p. Forzano (30th and 1st [except Vertecchi t]).
Feb. 9th	PALERMO – Massimo *NORMA* w. Nicolai ms; Gavarrini t; Neri bs: c. Ghione (15th and 20th).
Feb. 28th	REGGIO CALABRIA – Cilea *AIDA* w. Pirazzini ms; Soler t; Manca-Serra b. Morisani bs: c. del Cupolo.
Mar. 12th	TURIN – RAI Auditorium Concert Broadcast: 'Preghiera d'Agata' Weber's *Il Franco Cacciatore (Der Freischütz)*; 'Polacca' Thomas's *Mignon*†; 'Ecco l'orrido campo . . . Ma dall'arido stelo divulsa' Verdi's *Un Ballo in Maschera**; Proch's 'Variazioni'†: RAI Orchestra c. Wolf Ferrari.

Mar. 14th

CAGLIARI – Massimo
LA TRAVIATA w. Campora t; Poli b: c. Molinari Pradelli (and 18th).

Apr. 21st

TRIESTE – Verdi
Concert: 'Casta Diva' *Norma*; Mad Scene *I Puritani*; 'O patria mia' *Aida*; 'Ah! fors' è lui . . . Sempre libera' *La Traviata*: Orchestra Filharmonica Triestina c. la Rosa Parodi.

May 26th

FLORENCE – Comunale
Elena in Verdi's *I VESPRI SICILIANI* w. Kokolios t; Mascherini b. Christoff bs: c. Kleiber p. Graf (30th*, June 2nd and 5th).

June 9th

Pergola
Euridice in Haydn's *ORFEO ED EURIDICE* w. Farkas s; Tygeson t; Christoff bs: c. Kleiber p. Salvini (and 10th).

June 11th

Grand Hotel
Concert: 'Casta diva' *Norma*; 'Ombra leggera' *Dinorah*; 'O patria mia' *Aida*; Proch's Variazioni; 'Polacca' *Mignon*; 'Ah! fors' è lui . . . Sempre libera' *La Traviata*: piano Bartoletti.

July 3rd*

MEXICO CITY – Palacio de Bellas Artes
AIDA w. Dominguez ms; del Monaco t; Taddei b; Silva bs: c. de Fabritiis (7th and 10th).

July 15th

Radio XEW studios
Concert Broadcast: 'Pace, pace, mio Dio!' *La Forza del Destino*; 'Morrò, ma prima in grazia' *Un Ballo in Maschera*: Orchestra c. de Fabritiis.

July 17th*

Palacio de Bellas Artes
LA TRAVIATA w. Valletti t; Taddei b: c. de Fabritiis (19th, 21st and 22nd [except Morelli b.]).

Sep. 7th

SÃO PAULO – Municipal
NORMA w. Barbieri ms; Picchi t; Rossi-Lemeni bs: c. Serafin.

Sep. 9th

LA TRAVIATA w. di Stefano t; Gobbi b: c. Serafin.

Sep. 12th

RIO DE JANEIRO – Municipal
NORMA w. Nicolai ms; Picchi t; Christoff bs: c. Votto (and 16th).

Sep. 14th

Concert: 'Ah! fors' è lui . . . Sempre libera' *La Traviata*; 'O patria mia' *Aida*: piano Gaioni.

Sep. 24th*

TOSCA w. Poggi t; Silveri b: c. Votto.

Sep. 28th

LA TRAVIATA w. Poggi t; Salsedo b: c. Gaioni (and 30th).

BERGAMO – Donizetti

Oct. 20th   *LA TRAVIATA* w. Prandelli t; Fabbri b: Giulini (and 23rd).

CATANIA – Massimo Bellini

Nov. 3rd   *NORMA* w. Simionato ms: Penno t; Christoff bs: c. Ghione
p. Piccinato (6th, 17th and 20th [except Wolowski bs]).

Nov. 8th   *I PURITANI* w. Wenkow t; Tagliabue b. Christoff bs: c.
Wolf-Ferrari p. Piccinato (11th, 13th and 16th).

MILAN – La Scala

Dec. 7th*   *I VESPRI SICILIANI* w. Conley t; Mascherini b. Christoff
bs: c. de Sabata p. Graf (9th, 12th, 16th, 19th, 27th [except
c. Quadri] and Jan. 3rd [except Modesti bs. Quadri]).

PARMA – Regio

Dec. 29th   *LA TRAVIATA* w. Pola t; Savarese b: c. de Fabritiis.

1952

FLORENCE – Comunale

Jan. 9th   *I PURITANI* w. Conley t; Tagliabue b. Rossi-Lemeni bs: c.
Serafin (and 11th).

MILAN – La Scala

Jan. 16th   *NORMA* w. Stignani ms; Penno t; Rossi-Lemeni bs: c.
Ghione p. Frigerio (19th, 23rd, 27th, 29th, Feb. 2nd, 7th,
10th and Apr. 14th).

Circolo della Stampa

Feb. 8th   Concert: 'Ah! fors' è lui . . . Sempre libera' *La Traviata*; Mad
Scene *I Puritani*: piano Tonini.

TURIN – RAI Studios

Feb. 18th*   Concert Broadcast: 'Vieni! t'affretta . . . Or tutti sorgete'
Verdi's *Macbeth*; 'Il dolce suono' Donizetti's *Lucia di Lammermoor*; 'Ben io t'invenni . . . Anch'io dischiuso . . . Salgo
già' *Nabucco*; 'Aria delle campanelle' Delibes's *Lakmé*: RAI
Orchestra c. de Fabritiis.

CATANIA – Massimo Bellini

Mar. 12th   *LA TRAVIATA* w. Campora t; Mascherini b: c. Molinari
Pradelli p. Moresco (14th and 16th).

MILAN – La Scala

Apr. 2nd   Constanza in Mozart's *IL RATTO DAL SERRAGLIO* w.
Menotti s; Prandelli t; Munteanu t; Baccaloni bs: c. Perlea p.
Giannini (5th, 7th [except Duval s.] and 9th [Duval]).

Apr. 26th*
FLORENCE – Comunale
Armida in Rossini's *ARMIDA* w. Albanese t; Filippeschi t; Raimondi t; Salvarezza t; Ziliani t: c. Serafin p. Savinio (29th and May 4th).

May 2nd
ROME – Opera
I PURITANI w. Lauri Volpi t; Silveri b. Neri bs: c. Santini p. Frigerio (6th and 11th [except Pirino t]).

May 29th*
MEXICO CITY – Palacio de Bellas Artes
I PURITANI w. di Stefano t; Campolonghi b. Silva bs: c. Picco (and 31st).

June 3rd*
LA TRAVIATA w. di Stefano t; Campolonghi b: c. Mugnai (and 7th).

June 10th*
Lucia in Donizetti's *LUCIA DI LAMMERMOOR* w. di Stefano t; Campolonghi b; Silva bs: c. Picco (14th† and 26th).

June 17th*
Gilda in Verdi's *RIGOLETTO* w. Garcia ms; di Stefano t; Campolonghi b. Ruffino bs: c. Mugnai (and 21st).

June 28th
TOSCA w. di Stefano t: Campolonghi b: c. Picco (and July 1st*).

July 19th
VERONA – Arena
LA GIOCONDA w. Nicolai ms. Canali ms; Poggi t; Inghilleri b. Tajo bs: c. Votto p. Moresco (and 23rd).

Aug. 2nd
LA TRAVIATA w. Campora t; Mascherini b: c. Molinari Pradelli (5th, 10th and 14th).

Sep.
TURIN – RAI Auditorium
COMMERCIAL RECORDING (Cetra) 1st publ. 3/53. Gioconda in Ponchielli's *LA GIOCONDA* w. Barbieri ms. Amadini ms; Poggi t; Silveri b; Neri bs: RAI Orchestra and Chorus c. Votto.

Nov. 8th
LONDON – Covent Garden
NORMA w. Stignani ms. Picchi t; Vaghi bs: c. Gui p. Enriquez (10th, 13th [except c. Pritchard], 18th* and 20th).

Nov. 17th
Italian Embassy
Concert: 'Ah! fors è lui . . . Sempre libera' *La Traviata*: piano Count Saffi.

Dec. 7th*
MILAN – La Scala
Lady Macbeth in Verdi's *MACBETH* w. Penno t; Mascherini b; Tajo bs: c. de Sabata p. Ebert (9th, 11th [except Modesti bs], 14th and 17th).

Dec. 26th	*LA GIOCONDA* w. Stignani ms. Danieli ms; di Stefano t; Tagliabue b. Tajo bs: c. Votto p. Frigerio (28th, 30th, Jan. 1st, 3rd, Feb. 19th (except Modesti bs).

1953

VENICE – La Fenice

Jan. 8th   *LA TRAVIATA* w. Albanese t; Savarese b: c. Questa p. Marchioro (and 10th [except Tagliabue b]).

ROME – Opera

Jan. 15th   *LA TRAVIATA* w. Albanese t; Savarese b: c. Santini p. Nofri (18th and 21st).

FLORENCE – Comunale

Jan. 17th   COMMERCIAL RECORDING (EMI) 1st publ. /85. 'Non mi dir' Mozart's *Don Giovanni*: c. Serafin.

Jan. 25th   *LUCIA DI LAMMERMOOR* w. Lauri Volpi t; Bastianini b; Arié bs: c. Ghione (28th, 5th [except di Stefano t] and Feb. 8th [di Stefano]).

Jan. 29th and 30th,   COMMERCIAL RECORDING (EMI) 1st publ. 1/54 Lucia
Feb. 3rd, 4th and 6th.   in Donizetti's *LUCIA DI LAMMERMOOR* w. di Stefano t; Gobbi b; Arié bs: c. Serafin.

MILAN – La Scala

Feb. 23rd*   *IL TROVATORE* w. Stignani ms; Penno t; Tagliabue b; Modesti bs: c. Votto p. Frigerio (26th, 28th, March 24th and 29th).

GENOA – Carlo Felice

Mar. 14th   *LUCIA DI LAMMERMOOR* w. di Stefano t; Mascherini b; Algorta bs: c. Ghione p. Marchioro (and 17th).

MILAN – Basilica of Santa Euphemia

Mar. 24th, 26th, 27th,   COMMERCIAL RECORDING (EMI) 1st publ. 11/53
29th, 30th and 31st.   Elvira in Bellini's *I PURITANI* w. di Stefano t; Panerai b. Rossi-Lemeni bs: La Scala Orchestra and Chorus c. Serafin.

ROME – Opera

Apr. 9th   *NORMA* w. Barbieri ms; Corelli t; Neri bs: c. Santini p. Piccinato (12th, 15th and 18th).

CATANIA – Massimo Bellini

Apr. 21st   *LUCIA DI LAMMERMOOR* w. Turrini t; Taddei b; Arié bs: c. de Fabritiis (and 23rd).

FLORENCE – Comunale

May 7th*   Medea in Cherubini's *MEDEA* w. Tucci s. Barbieri ms; Guichandut t; Petri bs: c. Gui p. Bersacq (10th and 12th).

May 16th

ROME – Auditorium of Palazzo Pio
Concert: 'D'amor sull'ali rosee' *Il Trovatore*; 'Pace, pace, mio Dio!' *La Forza del Destino*; Ombra leggera' *Dinorah*: Orchestra c. de Fabritiis.

May 19th

ROME – Opera
LUCIA DI LAMMERMOOR w. Poggi t; Guelfi b. Cassinelli bs: c. Gavazzeni p. Frigerio (21st and 24th).

Jun. 4th†

LONDON – Covent Garden
AIDA w. Simionato ms: Baum t; Walters b. Neri bs. Langdon bs: c. Barbirolli p. Benthall (6th [except Nowakowski bs in lieu of Neri] and 10th).

Jun. 15th

NORMA w. Simionato ms: Picchi t; Neri bs: c. Pritchard p. Enriquez (17th, 20th and 23rd).

Jun. 26th

IL TROVATORE w. Simionato ms: Johnston t; Walters b. Langdon bs: c. Erede p. Gellner (29th and Jul. 1st [except Modesti bs]).

Jul. 23rd

VERONA – Arena
AIDA w. Nicolai ms; del Monaco t; Protti b. Neri bs: c. Serafin p. G.W. Pabst (25th, 28th [except Filippeschi t], 30th and Aug. 8th [except Pirazzini ms; Zambruno t; Malaspina b: c. Ghione]).

Aug. 3rd and 4th.

MILAN – Basilica of Santa Euphemia
COMMERCIAL RECORDING (EMI) 1st publ. 4/54. Santuzza in Mascagni's *CAVALLERIA RUSTICANA* w. Canali ms; di Stefano t; Panerai b: La Scala Orchestra and Chorus c. Serafin.

Aug. 10th–13th, 16th, 18th–21st.

La Scala
COMMERCIAL RECORDING (EMI) 1st publ. 11/53. Tosca in Puccini's *TOSCA* w. di Stefano t; Gobbi b: c. de Sabata.

Aug. 15th

VERONA – Arena
IL TROVATORE w. Danieli ms; Zambruno t; Protti b. Maionica bs: c. Molinari Pradelli.

Sep.

TURIN – RAI Auditorium
COMMERCIAL RECORDING (Cetra) 1st publ. 9/54. Violetta in Verdi's *LA TRAVIATA* w. Albanese t; Savarese b: RAI Orchestra and Chorus c. Santini.

Nov. 19th*

TRIESTE – Verdi
NORMA w. Nicolai ms; Corelli t; Christoff bs: c. Votto (22nd, 23rd and 29th).

Dec. 10th*
MILAN – La Scala
MEDEA w. Nache s. Barbieri ms; Penno t; Modesti:
Bernstein p. Wallmann (12th, 29th, Jan. 2nd and 6th).

Dec. 16th
ROME – Opera
IL TROVATORE w. Pirazzini ms: Lauri Volpi t; Silveri b;
Neri bs: c. Santini p. Frigerio (19th [except Barbieri ms. but
replaced in Act II by Pirazzini] and 23rd).

1954

Jan. 10th
MILAN – Famiglia Meneghina (Milanese Club)
Concert: 'Tacea la notte' *Il Trovatore*: piano?

Jan. 18th†
La Scala
LUCIA DI LAMMERMOOR w. di Stefano t; Panerai b. Modesti bs: c. Karajan p. Karajan (21st, 24th, 27th, 31st, Feb. 5th
and 7th [except Poggi t]).

Feb. 13th
VENICE – Fenice
LUCIA DI LAMMERMOOR w. Infantino t; Bastianini b;
Tozzi bs: c. Questa p. Cardi (16th and 21st).

Mar. 2nd
MEDEA w. Tucci s. Pirazzini ms: Gavarini t; Tozzi bs: c. Gui
p. Bersacq (4th and 7th).

Mar. 10th
GENOA – Carlo Felice
TOSCA w. Ortica t; Guelfi b: c. Ghione (15th and 17th).

Apr. 4th*
MILAN – La Scala
Alceste in Gluck's *ALCESTE* w. Gavarini t; Silveri b; Panerai
b: c. Giulini p. Wallmann (6th, 15th and 20th).

Apr. 12th
Elisabetta in Verdi's *DON CARLO* w. Stignani ms; Ortica t;
Mascherini b; Rossi-Lemeni bs: c. Votto p. Erhardt (17th,
23rd, 25th and 27th).

Apr. 23th–May 3rd.
Cinema Metropol
COMMERCIAL RECORDING (EMI) 1st publ. 11/54.
Norma in Bellini's *NORMA* w. Stignani ms; Filippeschi
t; Rossi-Lemeni bs: La Scala Orchestra and Chorus c.
Serafin.

May 23rd
RAVENNA – Alighieri
LA FORZA DEL DESTINO w. Gardino ms; del Monaco t; Protti
b; Modesti bs. Capecchi bs: c. Ghione (and 26th).

Jun. 12th–17th
MILAN – La Scala
COMMERCIAL RECORDING (EMI) 1st publ. 4/55.
Nedda in Leoncavallo's *I PAGLIACCI* w. di Stefano t; Monti
t; Gobbi b. Panerai b: c. Serafin.

Jul. 15th
VERONA – Arena
Margherita in Boito's *MEFISTOFELE* w. de Cecco s; Tagliavini t; Rossi-Lemeni bs: c. Votto p. Graf ([performance ended after Act II], 20th [except de Cavalieri s. di Stefano t]) and 25th [de Cavalieri]).

Aug. 17th–21st,
MILAN – La Scala
COMMERCIAL RECORDING (EMI) 1st publ. 4/55. Leonora in Verdi's *LA FORZA DEL DESTINO* w. Nicolai ms; Tucker t; Tagliabue b; Rossi-Lemeni bs. Capecchi bs: c. Serafin.

Aug. 31st,
Sep. 1st, 3rd–8th.
COMMERCIAL RECORDING (EMI) 1st publ. 9/55. Fiorilla in Rossini's *IL TURCO IN ITALIA* w. Gardino ms; Gedda t; Rossi-Lemeni bs. Calabrese bs, Stabile b: c. Gavazzeni.

Sep. 15th–18th, 20th and 21st.
WATFORD – Town Hall
COMMERCIAL RECORDINGS (EMI) 1st publ. Puccini arias 12/54, Coloratura Lyric Arias 9/55. 'In quelle trine morbide', 'Sola, perduta, abbandonata' Puccini's *Manon Lescaut*; 'Signore ascolta', 'Tu che di gel sei cinta' *Turandot*; 'O mio babbino caro' Puccini's *Gianni Schicchi*; 'Sì, mi chiamano Mimì' Puccini's *La Bohème*; 'Un bel dì' Puccini's *Madama Butterfly*; 'Senza mamma' Puccini's *Suor Angelica*; 'Tu, tu, piccolo Iddio!' *Butterfly*; 'L'altra notte' Boito's *Mefistofele*; 'In questa reggia' *Turandot*: 'La mamma morta' Giordano's *Andrea Chénier*; 'Io sono l'umile ancella', 'Poveri fiori' Cilea's *Adriana Lecouvreur*; 'Ebben? Ne andrò lontana' Catalani's *La Wally*; 'Donde lieta usci' *La Bohème*; Bolero *I Vespri Siciliani*; 'Una voce poco fa' Rossini's *Il Barbiere di Siviglia*; 'Aria delle campanelle' *Lakmé*; 'Ombra leggera' *Dinorah*: Philharmonia Orchestra c. Serafin.

Oct. 6th
BERGAMO – Donizetti
LUCIA DI LAMMERMOOR w. Tagliavini t; Savarese b; Maionica bs: c. Molinari Pradelli (and 9th).

Nov. 1st
CHICAGO – Lyric
NORMA w. Simionato ms; Picchi t; Rossi-Lemeni bs: c. Rescigno p. Wymetal (and 5th).

Nov. 8th
LA TRAVIATA w. Simoneau t; Gobbi b: c. Rescigno p. Wymetal (and 12th).

Nov. 15th
LUCIA DI LAMMERMOOR w. di Stefano t; Guelfi b. Stewart bs: c. Rescigno p. Wymetal (and 17th).

Dec. 7th*
MILAN—La Scala
Giulia in Spontini's *LA VESTALE* w. Stignani ms; Corelli t; Sordello b. Rossi-Lemeni bs: c. Votto p. Visconti (9th, 12th, 16th and 18th).

SAN REMO – Casinò

Dec. 27th* Concert broadcast: 'Tutte le torture' Mozart's *Il Ratto dal Serraglio*; 'Ahmè! che notte oscura. . . Ombra leggera' *Dinorah*; 'Depuis le jour' Charpentier's *Louise*; 'D'amore al dolce impero' *Armida*: RAI Orchestra c. Simonetto.

1955

MILAN – La Scala

Jan. 8th* Maddalena in Giordano's ANDREA CHÉNIER w. del Monaco t; Protti b: c. Votto p. Frigerio (10th, 13th, 16th, Feb. 3rd [except Ortica t; Taddei b] and 6th [Ortica. Taddei]).

ROME – Opera

Jan. 22nd MEDEA w. Tucci s. Barbieri ms; Albanese t; Christoff bs: c. Santini p. Wallmann (25th, 27th and 30th).

MILAN – La Scala

Mar. 5th* Amina in Bellini's LA SONNAMBULA w. Ratti s. Carturan ms; Valletti t; Modesti bs: c. Bernstein p. Visconti (8th, 13th, 16th, 19th, 24th [except Zaccaria bs], 30th [Zaccaria], Apr. 12th, 24th and 27th).

Apr. 15th IL TURCO IN ITALIA w. Gardino ms; Valletti t; Rossi-Lemeni bs. Calabrese bs. Stabile b: c. Gavazzeni p. Zeffirelli (18th, 21st, 23rd and May 4th).

May 28th* LA TRAVIATA w. di Stefano t; Bastianini b: c. Giulini p. Visconti (31st [except Prandelli t], Jun. 5th [Prandelli] and 7th [Prandelli]).

Jun. 9th–12th COMMERCIAL RECORDINGS (EMI): 'Dei tuoi figli' *Medea*; 'Tu che invoco', 'O nume tutelar', 'Caro oggetto' *La Vestale* (1st Publ. 2/58); 'Campagne, teneri amici . . . Come per me sereno . . . Sovra il sen' (1st Publ. FWR records 3/69: EMI 10/78); 'Oh, se una volta sola . . . Ah, non credea . . . Ah! non giunge' *La Sonnambula* (1st Publ. FWR records 11/66: EMI 10/78): c. Serafin.

ROME – RAI Auditorium

Jun. 29th*# NORMA (in concert) w. Stignani ms; del Monaco t; Modesti bs: RAI Orchestra and Chorus c. Serafin.

MILAN – La Scala

Aug. 1st–6th COMMERCIAL RECORDING (EMI) 1st Publ. 11/55. Madama Butterfly in Puccini's MADAMA BUTTERFLY w. Danieli ms: Gedda t; Borriello b: c. Karajan.

Aug. 10th–12th, COMMERCIAL RECORDING (EMI) 1st Publ. 12/55.
16th–20th, 23rd, Aida in Verdi's AIDA w. Barbieri ms; Tucker t; Gobbi b.
and 24th Modesti bs: c. Serafin.

Sep. 3rd, 5th, COMMERCIAL RECORDING (EMI) 1st Publ. 2/56. Gilda
8th–14th and 16th in RIGOLETTO w. Lazzarini ms: di Stefano t; Gobbi b. Zaccaria bs: c. Serafin.

BERLIN – Städtische Oper
Sep. 29th* *LUCIA DI LAMMERMOOR* w. di Stefano t; Panerai b. Zaccaria bs: RIAS Orchestra and La Scala Chorus: c. Karajan p. Karajan (and Oct. 2nd [Zampieri, who had been singing Arturo, deputized for di Stefano in the last act]).

CHICAGO – Lyric
Oct. 31st *I PURITANI* w. di Stefano t; Bastianini b. Rossi-Lemeni bs: c. Rescigno p. Mirabella Vassallo (and Nov. 2nd).

Nov. 5th *Il TROVATORE* w. Stignani ms; Björling t; Bastianini b. Wildermann bs: c. Rescigno p. Mirabella Vassallo (and 8th [except Turner ms. Weede b]).

Nov. 11th *MADAMA BUTTERFLY* w. Alberts ms; di Stefano t; Weede b: c. Rescigno p. Koyke (14th and 17th).

MILAN – La Scala
Dec. 7th* *NORMA* w. Simionato ms; del Monaco t; Zaccaria b: c. Votto p. Wallmann (11th, 14th, 17th, 21st, 29th [except Nicolai ms], Jan. 1st, 5th and 8th [Nicolai]).

1956

Jan. 19th* *LA TRAVIATA* w. Raimondi t; Bastianini b: c. Giulini p. Visconti (23rd [except Protti b], 26th, 29th, Feb. 2nd, 5th, 18th, 26th, Mar. 9th [except Tagliabue b: c. Tonini], April 5th, 14th, 18th [except Colzani b], 21st, 25th, 27th, 29th [Tonini] and May 6th [Tonini]).

Feb. 16th* Rosina in Rossini's *IL BARBIERE DI SIVIGLIA* w. Alva t; Gobbi b. Rossi-Lemeni bs. Luise bs: c. Guilini p. Piccinato (21st, Mar. 3rd, 6th [except Monti t; Badioli bs]) and 15th [Monti, Badioli]).

NAPLES – San Carlo
Mar. 22nd* *LUCIA DI LAMMERMOOR* w. Raimondi t; Panerai b. Zerbini bs: c. Molianri Pradelli p. Brissoni (24th and 27th).

MILAN – La Scala
May 21st Fedora in Giordano's *FEDORA* w. Zanolli s; Corelli t; Colzani b: c. Gavazzeni p. Pavlova (23rd, 27th, 30th, Jun. 1st and 3rd).

VIENNA – Staatsoper
Jun. 12th *LUCIA DI LAMMERMOOR* w. di Stefano t; Panerai b. Zaccaria bs: c. Karajan p. Karajan (14th and 16th).

MILAN – La Scala
Aug. 3rd, 4th, 6th–9th COMMERCIAL RECORDING (EMI) 1st Publ. 3/57. Leonora in Verdi's *IL TROVATORE* w. Barbieri ms; di Stefano t; Panerai b. Zaccaria bs: c. Karajan.

Aug. 20th–25th, Sep. 3rd, 4th and 12th.	COMMERCIAL RECORDING (EMI) 1st Publ. 9/57. Mimi in Puccini's *LA BOHÈME* w. Moffo s; di Stefano t; Panerai b. Zaccaria bs: c. Votto.
Sep. 4th–12th.	COMMERCIAL RECORDING (EMI) 1st Publ. 4/57. Amelia in Verdi's *UN BALLO IN MASCHERA* w. Ratti s. Barbieri ms; di Stefano t; Gobbi b. Zaccaria bs. Maionica bs: c. Votto.
Sep. 27th*	RAI Studios Concert Broadcast: 'Tu che invoco' *La Vestale*; 'La dama d'Arturo ... Ah, vieni al tempio' *I Puritani*; 'Bel raggio' Rossini's *Semiramide*; 'Ai vostri giochi' Thomas's *Amleto*: RAI Orchestra and Chorus c. Simonetto.
Oct. 29th	NEW YORK – Metropolitan *NORMA* w. Barbieri ms; del Monaco t; Siepi bs: c. Cleva p. Yannopoulos (Nov. 3rd, 7th, 10th and 22nd [except Baum t; Moscona bs]).
Nov. 15th	*TOSCA* w. Campora t; London b: c. Mitropoulos p. Yannopoulos (and 19th).
Nov. 25th*	CBS Studios Television Broadcast: *Tosca* Act II w. cuts, begins Tosca's 'Salvatelo' w. London b: Met. Orchestra c. Mitropoulos.
Nov. 27th	PHILADELPHIA – Academy of Music *NORMA* w. Met. Orchestra, Chorus and Cast as above Oct. 29th.
Dec. 3rd	NEW YORK – Metropolitan *LUCIA DI LAMMERMOOR* w. Campora t; Sordello b. Moscona bs: c. Cleva p. Defrère (8th*, 14th [except Valentino b] and 19th [except Tucker t; Valentino]).
Dec. 17th	WASHINGTON – Italian Embassy Concert: 'Casta Diva' *Norma*; 'Regnava nel silenzio' *Lucia*; 'D'amor sull'ali rosee' *Il Trovatore*;? 'Vissi d'arte' *Tosca*: piano Schaefer.
1957	
Jan. 15th	CHICAGO – Lyric Concert: 'Ah, non credea' *La Sonnambula*; 'Ombra leggera' *Dinorah*; 'In questa reggia' *Turandot*; 'Casta Diva' *Norma*; 'D'amor sull'ali rosee' *Il Trovatore*; 'Il dolce suono' *Lucia*: Chicago Symphony Orchestra c. Cleva.
Feb. 2nd	LONDON – Covent Garden *NORMA* w. Stignani ms; Vertecchi t; Zaccaria bs.: c. Pritchard p. Enriquez (and 6th).

Feb. 7th–9th, 11th–14th	Kingsway Hall COMMERCIAL RECORDING (EMI) 1st Publ. 2/58 (Mono & Stereo). Rosina in *IL BARBIERE DI SIVIGLIA* w. Alva t; Gobbi b. Zaccaria bs. Ollendorff bs: Philharmonia Orchestra and Chorus c. Galliera.
Mar. 2nd	MILAN – La Scala *LA SONNAMBULA* w. Ratti s. Cossotto ms; Monti t; Zaccaria bs: c. Votto p. Visconti (7th, 10th, 12th, 17th and 20th [except Spina t]).
Mar. 3rd–6th, 8th and 9th.	Basilica of Santa Euphemia COMMERCIAL RECORDING (EMI) 1st Publ. 10/57. Amina in *LA SONNAMBULA* w. Ratti s. Cossotto ms; Monti t; Zaccaria bs: La Scala Orchestra and Chorus c. Votto.
Apr. 14th	La Scala Anna Bolena in Donizetti's *ANNA BOLENA* w. Simionato ms. Carturan ms; Raimondi t; Rossi-Lemeni bs. Clabassi bs: c. Gavazzeni p. Visconti (17th*, 20th, 24th, 27th, 30th and May 5th).
Jun. 1st*	Ifigenia in Gluck's *IFIGENIA IN TAURIDE* w. Cossotto ms; Albanese t; Colzani b. Dondi b: c. Sanzogno p. Visconti (3rd, 5th and 10th).
Jun. 19th	ZURICH – Tonhalle Concert: 'Ah fors'è lui . . . Sempre libera' *La Traviata*; 'Il dolce suono . . . Spargi d'amaro pianto' *Lucia*: Winterthurer Stadtorchester c. Moralt.
Jun. 26th*	ROME – RAI Studios *LUCIA DI LAMMERMOOR* (in concert) w. Fernandi t; Panerai b. Modesti bs: RAI Orchestra and Chorus. c. Serafin.
July. 4thR*	COLOGNE – Grosses Haus *LA SONNAMBULA* w. Angioletti s. Cossotto ms; Monti t; Zaccaria bs: La Scala Orchestra and Chorus c. Votto p. Visconti (and 6th).
Jul. 9th–13th and 15th.	MILAN – La Scala COMMERCIAL RECORDING (EMI) 1st Publ. 1/58. Turandot in Puccini's *TURANDOT* w. Schwarzkopf s; Fernandi t; Zaccaria bs: c. Serafin.
Jul.18th–20th, 21st, 25th–27th.	COMMERCIAL RECORDING (EMI) 1st Publ. 12/59. Manon Lescaut in Puccini's *MANON LESCAUT* w. Cossotto ms; di Stefano t; Fioravanti b. Calabrese bs: c. Serafin.

Aug. 5th*	ATHENS – Herodes Atticus Concert: 'D'amor sull'ali rosee' *Il Trovatore*; 'Pace, pace mio Dio!' *La Forza del Destino*; 'Regnava nel silenzio . . . Quando rapito in estasi' *Lucia*; 'Morte d'Isotta' *Tristano*; 'A vos jeux, mes amis' *Hamlet*: the second part, beginning 'Pâle et blonde', she encored: Athens Festival Orchestra c. Votto.
Aug. 19th	EDINBURGH – King's LA SONNAMBULA w. Martelli s. Cossotto ms; Monti t; Zaccaria bs: La Scala Orchestra and Chorus c. Votto p. Visconti (21st*, 26th* and 29th).
Sep. 14th–21st	MILAN – La Scala COMMERCIAL RECORDING (Ricordi) 1st Publ. 6/58 (M&S). Medea in Cherubini's MEDEA w. Scotto s. Pirazzini ms; Picchi t; Modesti b: c. Serafin.
Nov. 21st R	DALLAS—State Fair Music Hall Concert: 'Tutte le torture' *Serraglio*; Mad Scene *I Puritani*; 'Vieni t'affretta' *Macbeth*; 'Ah fors'è lui . . . Sempre libera' *La Traviata*; 'Piangete voi? . . . Al dolce guidami . . . Coppia iniquia' *Anna Bolena:* Dallas Symphony Orchestra and Chorus c. Rescigno.
Dec. 7th*	MILAN – La Scala Amelia in Verdi's UN BALLO IN MASCHERA w. Ratti s. Simionato ms; di Stefano t; Bastianini b. Stefanoni bs. Cassinelli bs: c. Gavazzeni p. Wallmann (10th, 16th, 19th and 22nd [except Roma b. replaced Bastianini in Act III]).
Dec. 31st*	ROME – RAI studios Television broadcast: 'Casta Diva' *Norma*: RAI Orchestra and Chorus c. Santini?
1958	
Jan. 2nd*	ROME – Opera NORMA w. Pirazzini ms; Corelli t; Neri bs: c. Santini p. Wallmann (Act I only).
Jan. 22nd	CHICAGO – Lyric Concert: 'Non mi dir' *Don Giovanni*; 'Nel dì della vittoria . . . Vieni t'affretta' *Macbeth*; 'Una voce poco fa' *Il Barbiere*; 'L'altra notte' *Mefistofele*; 'Ben io t'invenni . . . Anch'io dischiuso' *Nabucco*; 'A vos jeux' *Hamlet*: Chicago Symphony Orchestra c. Rescigno.
Feb. 6th	NEW YORK – Metropolitan LA TRAVIATA w. Barioni t; Zanasi b: c. Cleva p. Guthrie (and 10th [except Campora t]).

Feb. 13th

LUCIA DI LAMMERMOOR w. Bergonzi t; Sereni b. Moscona bs: c. Cleva p. Defrère (20th [except Scott bs] and 25th [except Fernandi t; Tozzi bs]).

Feb. 28th

TOSCA w. Tucker t; Cassel b: c. Mitropoulos p. Yanno-poulos (and Mar. 5 [except London b]).

Mar. 24th

MADRID – Cinema Monumental
Concert: 'Casta Diva' *Norma*; 'D'amor sull'ali rosee' *Il Trovatore*; 'L'altra notte' *Mefistofele*; 'A vos jeux' *Hamlet*: Orquesta de Camera c. Morelli.

Mar. 27th*

LISBON – São Carlos
LA TRAVIATA w. Kraus t; Sereni b: c. Ghione (and 30th).

Apr. 9th

MILAN – La Scala
ANNA BOLENA w. Simionato ms. Carturan ms; Raimondi t; Siepi bs. Maionica bs: c. Gavazzeni p. Visconti (13th, 16th, 19th and 23rd).

May 19th

Imogene in Bellini's *IL PIRATA* w. Vercelli ms; Corelli t; Bastianini b: c. Votto p. Enriquez (22nd, 25th, 28th and 31st).

Jun. 10th

LONDON – Covent Garden
Mad Scene *I Puritani* w. Shaw b. Robinson bs: c. Pritchard.

Jun. 17th*

Chelsea Empire
Television Concert: 'Vissi d'arte' *Tosca*; 'Una voce poco fa' *Il Barbiere*: Orchestra c. Pritchard.

Jun. 20th*

Covent Garden
LA TRAVIATA w. Valletti t; Zanasi b: c. Rescigno p. Guthrie (23rd, 26th, 28th and 30th).

Sep. 19th–21st
and 24th

EMI Studio 1, Abbey Road
COMMERCIAL RECORDINGS (EMI) 1st Publ. 3/59 (M&S). 'Nel dì della vittoria . . . Vieni t'affretta . . . Or tutti sorgete'; 'La luce langue'; Sleepwalking scene *Macbeth*; 'Surta è la notte . . . Ernani, Ernani, involami . . . Tutto sprezzo' Verdi's *Ernani*; 'Ben io t'invenni . . . Anch'io dischiuso . . . Salgo già' *Nabucco*; 'Tu che la vanità' *Don Carlo*: Philharmonia Orchestra c. Rescigno.

Sep. 23rd*

Chelsea Empire
Television Concert: 'Casta Diva' *Norma*; 'Un bel dì' *Madama Butterfly*: Orchestra c. Pritchard.

Sep. 24th–26th

Kingsway Hall
COMMERCIAL RECORDINGS (EMI) 1st Publ. 5/59 (M&S). 'Piangete voi?.. Al dolce guidami . . . Coppia iniquia' *Anna Bolena* (with Sinclair ms. Robertson t; Lanigan t; Rouleau bs); 'Oh, s'io potessi . . . Col sorriso d' innocenza . . . O sole, ti vela' *Il Pirata*; 'A vos jeux' *Hamlet*: Philhar-monia Orchestra and Chorus (only in *Il Pirata*) c. Rescigno.

Oct. 11th	BIRMINGHAM (Alabama) – Municipal Auditorium Concert: 'Tu che invoco' *La Vestale*; 'Ambizioso spirto . . . Vieni, t'affretta' *Macbeth*; 'Una voce poco fa' *Il Barbiere*; L'altra notte' *Mefistofele*; Musetta's Waltz Song *La Bohème*; 'A vos jeux' *Hamlet*: Orchestra c. Rescigno.
Oct. 14th	ATLANTA – Municipal Auditorium Programme and Conductor as above.
Oct. 17th	MONTREAL – Forum Programme and Conductor as above.
Oct. 21st	TORONTO – Maple Leaf Gardens Programme and Conductor as above.
Oct. 31st	DALLAS – State Fair Music Hall *LA TRAVIATA* w. Filacuridi t; Taddei b: c. Rescigno p. Zeffirelli (and Nov. 2nd).
Nov. 6th*	*MEDEA* w. Carron s. Berganza ms; Vickers t; Zaccaria bs: c. Rescigno p. Minotis (and 8th).
Nov. 15th	CLEVELAND – Public Music House Concert: Programme and Conductor as Birmingham.
Nov. 18th	DETROIT – Masonic Auditorium Concert: Programme and Conductor as Birmingham.
Nov. 22nd	WASHINGTON – Constitution Hall Concert: Programme and Conductor as Birmingham.
Nov. 26th	SAN FRANCISCO – Civic Auditorium Concert: Programme and Conductor as Birmingham.
Nov. 29th	LOS ANGELES – Shrine Auditorium Concert: Programme and Conductor as Birmingham.
Dec. 19th*f	PARIS – Opéra Concert: 'Sediziose voci . . . Casta Diva . . . Ah, bello a me ritorna' *Norma*; 'D'amor sull'ali rosee', 'Miserere' *Il Trovatore* w. Lance; 'Una voce poco fa' *Il Barbiere*; Act II *Tosca* w. Lance t. Gobbi b. Rialland t; Hurteau bs: c. Sebastian.
1959	
Jan. 11th	ST. LOUIS – Kiel Auditorium Concert: Programme and Conductor as Birmingham.

Jan. 24th

PHILADELPHIA – Academy of Music
Concert: 'L'altra notte' *Mefistofele*; 'Una voce poco fa' *Il Barbiere*; 'A vos jeux' *Hamlet*: Philadelphia Orchestra c. Ormandy.

Jan. 27th*

NEW YORK – Carnegie Hall
IL PIRATA (in concert) w. Sarfaty ms; Ferraro t. Ego b: American Opera Society Orchestra and Chorus c. Rescigno.

Jan. 29th

WASHINGTON – Constitution Hall
As above.

Mar. 16th–21st

LONDON – Kingsway Hall
COMMERCIAL RECORDING (EMI) 1st Publ. 12/59 (M&S). *LUCIA DI LAMMERMOOR* w. Elkins ms; Tagliavini t. Casellato t; Cappuccilli b. Ladysz bs: Philharmonia Orchestra and Chorus c. Serafin.

May 2nd

MADRID – Zarzuela
Concert: 'Non mi dir' *Don Giovanni*; 'Nel dì della vittoria . . . Vieni, t'affretta' *Macbeth*; 'Bel raggio' *Semiramide*; 'Suicidio' *La Gioconda*; Final Scene *Il Pirata*: Orquestra Sinfonica de Madrid c. Rescigno.

May 5th

BARCELONA – Liceo
Concert: 'Tu che la vanità' *Don Carlo*; 'L'altra notte' *Mefistofele*; 'Una voce poco fa' *Il Barbiere*; 'Vissi d'arte' *Tosca*; Musetta's Waltz Song *La Bohème*; Final Scene *Il Pirata*: Orquesta Sinfonica del Liceo c. Rescigno.

May 15th*f

HAMBURG – Musikhalle
Concert: 'Tu che invoco' *La Vestale*; 'Nel dì della vittoria . . . Vieni, t'affretta' *Macbeth*; 'Una voce poco fa' *Il Barbiere*; 'Tu che la vanità' *Don Carlo*; Final Scene *Il Pirata*: Sinfonieorchester des Norddeutschen Rundfunks c. Rescigno.

May 19th*

STUTTGART – Liederhalle
Concert: Programme and Conductor as above but with Sudfunk Sinfonieorchester.

May 21st

MUNICH – Kongress-Saal
Concert: Programme and Conductor as above but with Bayerisches Staatsorchester.

May 24th

WIESBADEN – Kursaal
Concert: Programme and Conductor as above but with Pfalz-Orchester.

Jun. 17th

LONDON – Covent Garden
MEDEA w. Carlyle s. Cossotto ms; Vickers t; Zaccaria bs: c. Rescigno p. Minotis (22nd, 24th, 27th, 30th*).

Jul. 11th*   AMSTERDAM – Concertgebouw
                Concert: 'Tu che invoco' *La Vestale*; 'Surta e la notte . . .
                Ernani, Ernani, involami . . . Tutto sprezzo' *Ernani*; 'Tu che
                la vanità' *Don Carlo*; Final Scene *Il Pirata*: Concertgebouw
                Orchestra c. Rescigno.

Jul. 14th   BRUSSELS – de la Monnaie
                Concert: Programme and Conductor as above but with
                Orchestre de la Monnaie.

Part 3: 1959–1974

Sep. 4th–11th   MILAN – La Scala
                COMMERCIAL RECORDING: (EMI) 1st Publ. 8/60
                (M&S). *LA GIOCONDA* w. Cossotto ms, Companeez ms;
                Ferraro t; Cappuccilli b. Vinco bs: c. Votto.

Sep. 17th   BILBÃO – Coliseo Albia
                Concert: 'Tu che la vanità' *Don Carlo*; 'A vos jeux' Hamlet;
                'Surta e la notte . . . Ernani, Ernani, involami . . . Tutto
                sprezzo' *Ernani*; Final Scene *Il Pirata*: Orquesta Sinfonica
                del Liceo, Barcelona c. Rescigno.

Sep. 23rd   LONDON – Royal Festival Hall
                Concert: 'Tu che la vanità' *Don Carlo*; Sleepwalking Scene
                Macbeth†; 'A vos jeux' *Hamlet*; Final Scene *Pirata*†: London
                Symphony Orchestra c. Rescigno.

Oct. 7th*   Wood Green Empire
                Television Broadcast: 'Sì, mi chiamano Mimì' *La Bohème*;
                'L'altra notte' *Mefistofele*: Royal Philharmonic Orchestra c.
                Sargent.

Oct. 23rd   BERLIN – Titania Palast
                Concert: 'Non mi dir' *Don Giovanni*; 'Surta e la notte . . .
                Ernani, Ernani, involami . . . Tutto sprezzo' *Ernani*; 'Tu che
                la vanità' *Don Carlo*; 'A vos jeux' *Hamlet*: Berlin Radio
                Symphony Orchestra c. Rescigno.

Oct. 28th   KANSAS CITY – Midland
                Concert: 'Non mi dir' *Don Giovanni*; 'Regnava nel silenzio
                . . . Quando rapito in estasi' *Lucia*; 'Surta e la notte . . .
                Ernani, Ernani, involami . . . Tutto sprezzo' *Ernani*; Final
                Scene *Il Pirata*: Orchestra c. Rescigno.

Nov. 6th   DALLAS – State Fair Music Hall
                LUCIA DI LAMMERMOOR w. Kobart s; Raimondi t;
                Bastianini b. Zaccaria bs: c. Rescigno p. Zeffirelli (and 8th).

Nov. 19th   *MEDEA* w. Williams s. Merriman ms; Vickers t; Zaccaria bs:
                c. Rescigno p. Minotis (and 21st*).

1960

Jul. 13th–15th

WATFORD – Town Hall
COMMERCIAL RECORDINGS (EMI) 1st Publ. '87 (M&S). 'Bel raggio' *Semiramide*. Unpublished: 'D'amore al dolce impero' *Armida*; 'Arrigo! ah parli a un core' *I Vespri Siciliani*: Philharmonia Orchestra c. Tonini.

Aug. 24th

EPIDAVROS – Ancient Auditorium
NORMA w. Morfoniou ms; Picchi t; Mazzoli bs: Greek National Opera Orchestra and Chorus c. Serafin p. Minotis (and 26th).

Sep. 5th–12th

MILAN – La Scala
COMMERCIAL RECORDING (EMI) 1st Publ. 10/61 (M&S). *NORMA* w. Ludwig ms; Corelli t; Zaccaria bs: c.Serafin.

Dec. 7th*

Paolina in Donizetti's *POLIUTO* w. Corelli t; Bastianini b. Zaccaria bs: c. Votto p. Graf (10th, 14th, 18th and 21st [except c. Tonini]).

1961

Mar. 28th–31st,
Apr. 4th and 5th

PARIS – Salle Wagram
COMMERCIAL RECORDINGS (EMI) 1st Publ. 10/61. 'J'ai perdu mon Eurydice' Gluck's *Orphée*; 'Divinités du Styx' *Alceste*; Habañera, Séguedille Bizet's *Carmen*; 'Printemps qui commence', 'Amours! viens aider' Saint-Saëns's *Samson et Dalila*; 'Valse' Gounod's *Roméo et Juliette*; 'Polonaise' *Mignon*; 'Pleurez mes yeux' Massenet's *Le Cid*; 'Depuis le jour' *Louise*: 1st Publ 82: 'Mon coeur s'ouvre à ta voix' *Samson*. Unpublished: 'Air des Cartes' *Carmen*; 'Air du Miroir' *Thaïs*: Orchestre National de la RTF c. Prêtre.

May 30th

LONDON – St. James's Palace
Concert: 'Casta Diva' *Norma*; 'Pleurez mes yeux' *Le Cid*†; 'Tu che la vanità' *Don Carlo*†; 'L'altra notte' *Mefistofele*: piano Sargent.

Aug. 6th

EPIDAVROS – Ancient Auditorium
MEDEA w. Glantzi s. Morfoniou ms; Vickers t; Modesti bs: Greek National Opera Orchestra and Chorus c. Rescigno p. Minotis (and 13th).

Nov. 13th–16th

LONDON – Kingsway Hall
COMMERCIAL RECORDINGS (EMI) 1st Publ. 3/72 (M&S). 'Sorgete, è in me dover ... Lo segnai ferito ... Sventurata anch'io deliro' *Il Pirata* w. Sinclair ms. Young t; 1st publ. /87 (M&S). 'Selva opaca' Rossini's *Guglielmo Tell*. Unpublished: 'Com'è bello' Donizetti's *Lucrezia Borgia*; 'Rondo Finale' Rossini's *La Cenerentola*; 'Come, innocente

giovane' *Anna Bolena*; 'Bel raggio' *Semiramide*: Philharmonia Orchestra and Chorus c. Tonini.

MILAN – La Scala

Dec. 11th — *MEDEA* w. Tosini s. Simionato ms; Vickers t; Ghiaurov bs: c. Schippers p. Minotis (14th, 20th [except Rizzoli s], May 29th [Rizzoli] and June 3rd [Rizzoli].

1962

Feb. 27th

LONDON – Royal Festival Hall
Concert: 'Ocean! Thou mighty monster' *Oberon*†; 'Pleurez mes yeux' *Le Cid*†; 'Rondo Finale' *La Cenerentola*†; 'La luce langue' *Macbeth*; 'O don fatale' *Don Carlo*†; Final Scene *Anna Bolena*†; Philharmonia Orchestra c. Prêtre.

Mar. 12th

MUNICH – Kongress-Saal
Concert: 'Pleurez mes yeux' *Le Cid*; Habañera, Séguedille *Carmen*; 'Surta e la notte . . . Ernani, Ernani, involami' *Ernani*; 'Rondo Finale' *La Cenerentola*; 'O don fatale' *Don Carlo*: Bayerisches Staatsorchester c. Prêtre.

Mar. 16th*f

HAMBURG – Musikhalle
As above but with Sinfonieorchester des Norddeutschen Rundfunks.

Mar. 19th

ESSEN – Städtischer Saalbau
As above but with Orchester der Stadt Essen.

Mar. 23rd

BONN – Beethovenhalle
As above but with Niedersächsisches Symphonieorchester.

Apr 9th and 13th

LONDON – Kingsway Hall
COMMERCIAL RECORDINGS (EMI) 1st Publ. /87 (M&S). 'Rondo Finale' *La Cenerentola*. Unpublished: 'O don fatale' *Don Carlo*; 'Ocean thou mighty monster' *Oberon*: Philharmonia Orchestra c. Tonini.

May 19th*

NEW YORK – Madison Square Garden
Concert: Habañera, Séguedille *Carmen*: piano Wilson.

Nov. 4th*f

LONDON – Covent Garden
Television Broadcast: 'Tu che la vanità' *Don Carlo*; Habañera, Séguedille *Carmen*: c. Prêtre.

1963

May 2nd–7th

PARIS – Salle Wagram
COMMERCIAL RECORDINGS (EMI) 1st Publ. 9/63 (M&S). 'Suis-je gentille ainsi? . . . Je marche sur tous les chemins' Massenet's *Manon*; 'Je ne suis que faiblesse . . . Adieu, notre petite table' *Manon*: 'Me voilà seule . . . Comme autrefois' Bizet's *Les Pêcheurs de perles*; 'D'amour l'ardente

flamme' Berlioz's *La Damnation de Faust*; 'Air des lettres' Massenet's *Werther*; 'La Ballade du Roi de Thulé' 'Air des bijoux' Gounod's *Faust*; 'O malheureuse Iphigénie' *Iphigénie en Tauride*: Orchestre de la Société des Concerts du Conservatoire c. Prêtre.

BERLIN – Deutsche Oper

May 17th* Concert: 'Bel raggio' *Semiramide*; 'Casta Diva . . . Ah! bello a me ritorna' *Norma*; 'Ben io t'invenni . . . 'Anch'io dischiuso' *Nabucco*; Musetta's Waltz Song *La Bohème*; 'Con onor muore . . . Tu? tu? piccolo Iddio!' *Madama Butterfly*: Orchester der Deutschen Oper c. Prêtre.

DÜSSELDORF – Rheinhalle

May 20th Concert: as above but with Niedersachsisches Sinfonie-orchester.

STUTTGART – Liederhalle

May 23rd* Concert: as above but with Südfunk Sinfonieorchester.

LONDON – Royal Festival Hall

May 31st* Concert: as above plus 'O mio babbino caro' *Gianni Schicchi* but with Philharmonia Orchestra.

PARIS – Théâtre des Champs-Elysées

Jun. 5th* Concert: 'Bel raggio' *Semiramide*; 'Rondo Finale' *La Cene-rentola*; 'Adieu, notre petite table' *Manon*; 'Air des lettres' *Werther*; 'Ben io t'invenni . . . Anch' io dischiuso' *Nabucco*; Musetta's Waltz Song *La Bohème*; 'Tu? tu? piccolo Iddio' *Madama Butterfly*; (encore) 'O mio babbino caro' *Gianni Schicchi*: Orchestre Philharmonique de la RTF c. Prêtre.

COPENHAGEN – Falkoner Centret

June 9th Concert: as Berlin May 17th but with Danmarks Radio-symfoni Orkester.

PARIS – Salle Wagram

Dec. 6th–23rd, COMMERCIAL RECORDINGS (EMI) 1st Publ. 8/64
Jan. 8th 1964 (M&S). Beethoven's 'Ah perfido'; 'Or sai chi l'onore', 'Crudele? . . . Non mi dir', 'In quali eccessi . . . Mi tradi' *Don Giovanni*; 'Porgi amor' *Le Nozze di Figaro*; 'Ocean! Thou mighty monster' *Oberon*: Orchestre de la Société des Concerts du Conservatoire c. Rescigno.

Dec. 17th–27th, COMMERCIAL RECORDINGS (EMI) 1st Publ. 8/64
Feb. 20th and (M&S). Willow Song and Ave Maria Verdi's *Otello*; 'Ciel
21st 1964 ch'io respiri . . . Salvami, salvami' 'O Cielo! Dove son io' Verdi's *Aroldo*; 'O don fatale' 'Non pianger, mia compagna' *Don Carlo*: Orchestra and Conductor as above.

Dec. 4th–23rd, Apr. 13th–24th 1964	COMMERCIAL RECORDINGS (EMI) 1st Publ. 3/65 (M&S). 'Rondo Finale' *La Cenerentola*; 'S'allontanano alfine ... Selva opaca' *Guglielmo Tell*; 'Bel raggio lusinghier' Rossini's *Semiramide*; 'Convien partir' *La Figlia del Reggimento*; 'Tranquillo ei posa ... Com'e bello' *Lucrezia Borgia*; 'Prendi, per me sei sei libero' Donizetti's *L'Elisir d'Amore*: Orch. and Cond. as above.

1964

Jan. 21st*	LONDON – Covent Garden *TOSCA* w. Cioni t; Gobbi b: c. Cillario p. Zeffirelli (24th*, 27th, 30th*, Feb 1st and 5th).
Feb. 9th*f	Television Concert: *TOSCA* – Act II cast as above.
Feb. 21st, Apr. 7th–22nd	PARIS – Salle Wagram COMMERCIAL RECORDINGS (EMI) 1st Publ. 6/72 (M&S). 'Liberamente or piangi ... Oh! nel fuggente nuvolo' Verdi's *Attila*; 'Arrigo! ah parli a un core' *I Vespri Siciliani*; 'Ecco l'orrido campo ... Ma dall'arido stelo divulsa' *Un Ballo in Maschera*; 'O madre dal cielo ... Se vano è il pregare' Verdi's *I Lombardi*; 'Ritorna vincitor' *Aida*: 1st Publ. /78 (M&S): 'Tacea la notte ... Di tale amor' *Il Trovatore*; 'Morrò, ma prima in grazia' *Un Ballo*: Unpublished: 'Salve Maria, di grazie il petto'; *I Lombardi*; 'D'amor sull'ali rosee' *Il Trovatore*: Orchestre de la Société des Concerts du Conservatoire c. Rescigno.
May 22nd	PARIS – Opéra *NORMA* w. Cossotto ms; Craig t; Vinco bs: c. Pretre p. Zeffirelli (25th, 31st, Jun. 6th [except Corelli t], 10th [Corelli], 14th, 19th and 24th).
Jun. 7th–9th	Salle Wagram COMMERCIAL RECORDING (EMI) 1st Publ. /90 (M&S). 'Pur ti riveggo' Aida w. Corelli: Orchestre de la Société des Concerts du Conservatoire c. Prêtre.
Jul. 6th–11th, 15th–18th and 20th	COMMERCIAL RECORDING (EMI) 1st Publ. 12/64 (M&S). Carmen in Bizet's *CARMEN* w. Guiot. s; Gedda t. Massard b: Orchestre de l'Opéra and the Choeurs Duclos c. Prêtre.
Aug. 30th	LEVKAS (Greece) – Folk Festival 'Voi lo sapete' *Cavalleria Rusticana*: piano?
Dec. 3rd–4th, 7th–12th and 14th.	PARIS – Salle Wagram COMMERCIAL RECORDING (EMI) 1st Publ. 4/65 (M&S). *TOSCA* w. Bergonzi t; Gobbi b: Orchestre de la Société des Concerts du Conservatoire and Choeurs de l'Opéra c. Prêtre.

1965

Feb. 19th
PARIS – Opéra
TOSCA w. Cioni t; Gobbi b: c. Prêtre p. Zeffirelli
(22nd†, 26th, Mar. 1 [except c. Rescigno]†, 3rd [Rescigno]†,
5th [Rescigno], 8th [Rescigno], 10th [Rescigno] and 13th
[Rescigno]†).

Mar. 19th*
NEW YORK – Metropolitan
TOSCA w. Corelli t; Gobbi b: c. Cleva p. Yannopoulos
(Callas and Gobbi wore the Covent Garden costumes) (and
25th [except Tucker t]*).

May 14th*
PARIS – Opéra
NORMA w. Simionato ms; Cecchele t; Vinco bs: c. Prêtre p.
Zeffirelli (17th†, 21st [except Cossotto ms]*, 24th [Cossotto]
and 29th [Cossotto] performance cancelled after Act III]†).

May 18th*f
RTF Studios
Television Broadcast: 'Adieu notre petite table' *Manon*; 'Ah!
non credea' *La Sonnambula*; 'O mio babbino caro' *Gianni
Schicchi*: Orchestre National de la RTF c. Prêtre.

Jul. 5th*
LONDON – Covent Garden
TOSCA w. Cioni t; Gobbi b: c. Prêtre.

1969

Feb. Mar.
PARIS – Salle Wagram
COMMERCIAL RECORDINGS (EMI) 1st Publ. /78. 'Egli
non riede ancor . . . Non so le tetre immagini', 'Ne sulla terra
. . . Vola talor dal carcere' Verdi's *Il Corsaro*. Publ. TIMA
CLUB: 'Arrigo! ah parli a un cor' *I Vespri Siciliani*; 'Te,
vergin santa' *I Lombardi*; 'Liberamente or piangi . . . Oh! nel
fuggente nuvolo' *Attila*: Orchestre de la Société des Concerts
c. Rescigno.

1972

Nov. 30th–Dec. 20th
LONDON – St Giles's Cripplegate
COMMERCIAL RECORDINGS (Philips) Unpublished.
With de Stefano t: 'Una parola, o Adina' Donizetti's *L'Elisir
d'Amore* (unfinished); 'Ah! per sempre' *La Forza del Destino*;
'Quale o prode' *I Vespri Siciliani*; 'Io vengo a domandar' *Don
Carlo*; 'Pur ti riveggo' *Aida*; 'Già nella notte densa' *Otello*;
London Symphony Orchestra c. de Almeida.

1973/4

Concert Tour EUROPE, NORTH AMERICA and the FAR
EAST.
Duets: w. di Stefano: 'Una parola, o Adina' *L'Elisir d'Amore*;
'O silence! O bonheur! . . . O nuit d'amour!' *Faust*; 'C'est
toi, c'est moi!' *Carmen*; 'Quale, o prode' *I Vespri Siciliani*;
'Tu qui, Santuzza?' *Cavalleria Rusticana*; 'Ah! per sempre'
La Forza del Destino; 'Io vengo a domandar' *Don Carlo*.
Arias: 'Suicidio' *La Gioconda*; 'Voi lo sapete' *Cavalleria
Rusticana*; 'Vissi d'arte' *Tosca*; 'Sola, perduta, abbandonata'
Manon Lescaut; 'Tu che la vanità' *Don Carlo*; 'O mio
babbino caro' *Gianni Schicchi*; Habañera *Carmen*; Air des
lettres *Werther*; 'Adieu, notre petite table' *Manon*; 'Sì, mi
chiamano Mimì' *La Bohème*: piano acc. by Newton or R.
Sutherland.
Recordings or films were made of a number of these, either
complete or in part.

25/10/73 HAMBURG; 29/10 BERLIN; 2/11 DÜSSELDORF; 6/11 MUNICH; 9/11
FRANKFURT; 12/11 MANNHEIM; 20/11 MADRID; 26/11 & 2/12 LONDON;
7/12 PARIS; 11/12 AMSTERDAM; 20/1 MILAN; 23/1 STUTTGART:

11/2 74 PHILADELPHIA; 21/2 TORONTO; 24/2 WASHINGTON; 27/2
BOSTON; 2/3 CHICAGO; 5/3 & 15/4 NEW YORK; 9/3 DETROIT; 12/3
DALLAS; 21/3 MIAMI BEACH; 4/4 COLUMBUS; 9/4 BROOKVILLE L.I.;
18/4 CINCINNATI; 24/4 SEATTLE; 27/4 PORTLAND; 1/5 VANCOUVER;
5/5 LOS ANGELES; 9/5 SAN FRANCISCO; 13/5 MONTREAL:

5/10 & 8/10 SEOUL; 12/10, 19/10 & 27/10 TOKYO; 24/10 FUKUOKA; 2/11
OSAKA; 7/11 HIROSHIMA; 11/11 SAPPORO.

NOTES

PRELUDE

1 Tebaldi created one role, Salammbò in Casavola's opera at the Rome Opera on April 27th 1948. After her début in Zagreb in 1927 Milanov undertook a number of roles in then new and now long-forgotten Croatian operas. Schwarzkopf created Anne Trulove in Stravinsky's *The Rake's Progress* at the Fenice, Venice on September 11th 1952. At the beginning of her career even Sutherland created Jenifer in Michael Tippett's *The Midsummer Marriage* at Covent Garden on January 27th 1955, while Caballé has appeared in a number of world premières.
2 *Opera*, February 1961.

CHAPTER I BEFORE CALLAS

1 Evangelia Callas, *My daughter – Maria Callas*, page 9.
2 *Oggi*, 'For the first time Maria Meneghini Callas tells of her life' as related by Anita Pensotti, part 1, January 10th 1957.
3 E. Callas, *My daughter*, 10/1.
4 Jackie Callas, *Sisters*, 33/4.
5 *Ibid.*, 35.
6 Certificate and Record of Birth: State of New York, No. 49149, dated December 10th 1923.
7 John Ardoin ed., *Callas at Juilliard – The Master Classes*, 4.
8 J. Callas, *Sisters*, 36.
9 *Ibid.*, 45.
10 *Ibid.*, 40.
11 *Ibid.*, 43.
12 Nadia Stancioff, *Maria – Callas remembered*, 52.
13 Letter from Marvin Goodman, Assistant Director, Board of Education of the City of New York, to Joel Honig, January 16th 1979.
14 J. Callas, *Sisters*, 43.
15 Letter from Goodman, Board of Education, to Honig as above.
16 (Chicago) Broadcast Callas interview w. Norman Ross, November 17th 1957.
17 J. Callas, *Sisters*, 44.
18 *Ibid.*, 51.
19 *Ibid.*, 48.
20 E. Callas, *My daughter*, 18.
21 J. Callas, *Sisters*, 47.

22 (CBS) 'Person to Person' w. Ed. Murrow, January 24th 1958.
23 E. Callas, *My daughter*, 18.
24 In November 1966 a record was published (FWR-656) of an item broadcast on the *Major Bowes Amateur Hour* of April 7th 1935. It consists of a brief interview between Bowes and a soprano styling herself Nina Foresti who then sings a truncated account of 'Un bel dì'. It is suggested that this is Callas. But we agree with Ardoin, in *The Callas Legacy*, page 2, when he states that Foresti's 'singing voice [is] weak and quite unlike anything known to be Callas['s].' A voice is as peculiar as finger-prints, it may develop but it does not change its character any more than do a leopard's spots. Even Björling's alto at 9, records reveal, is recognizably the same voice as Björling's tenor at 40, although puberty causes a more dramatic shift in pitch in the male voice.
25 J. Callas, *Sisters*, 48.
26 *Ibid.*
27 E. Callas, *My daughter*, 22.
28 *Ibid.*, 24.
29 J. Callas, *Sisters*, 58.
30 E. Callas, *My daughter*, 33.
31 J. Callas, *Sisters*, 59.
32 *Ibid.*
33 *Oggi*, C's memoirs, pt. 1.
34 E. Callas, *My daughter*, 33.
35 Interview w. Zoras.
36 E. Callas, *My daughter*, 34.
37 J. Callas, *Sisters*, 69.
38 E. Callas, *My daughter*, 35.
39 Ardoin ed., *Callas at Juilliard*, 4.
40 E. Callas, *My daughter*, 34.
41 J. Callas, *Sisters*, 70.
42 E. Callas, *My daughter*, 141.
43 *Elefteron Vima*, May 27th 1939.
44 *Oggi*, C's memoirs, pt. 2, January 17th 1957.
45 Stancioff, *Maria*, 57.
46 *The* (New York) *Sun*, March 8th 1910.
47 *Oggi*, Callas's memoirs, pt. 1.
48 E. Callas, *My daughter*, 35.
49 Ardoin ed., *Callas at Juilliard*, 5.
50 Stancioff, *Callas*, 58.
51 Interview w. Mandikian.
52 *Ibid.*
53 *The Sunday Times*, 'Maria Callas speaks' by Derek Prouse, April 2nd 1961.
54 J. Callas, *Sisters*, 73.
55 Ardoin ed., *Callas at Juilliard*, 4.
56 E. Callas, *My daughter*, 40.
57 *Oggi*, C's memoirs, pt. 1.
58 *The Times*, August 29th 1960.
59 Stancioff, *Maria*, 60.
60 *Ibid.*, 59.
61 *Giornale di Roma*, August 28th 1942.
62 *Oggi*, C's memoirs, pt. 1.
63 *Ibid.*

64 E. Callas, *My daughter*, 56.
65 *Ibid*.
66 *Ibid*., 57.
67 *Ibid*., 46.
68 Rossini was born on February 29th, not in October.
69 J. Callas, *Sisters*, 88.
70 *Opera News*, 'Augusta Oltrabella' by Lanfranco Rasponi, December 5th 1981.
71 J. Callas, *Sisters*, 90.
72 *Ibid*., 90/1.
73 *Opera News*, 'We introduce Maria Meneghini Callas' by Mary Jane Matz, December 3rd 1956.
74 *Deutsche Nachrichten in Greichenland*, April 23rd 1944.
75 From *Atinaika Nea, I Vradini, I proia, I Kathimerini, Elephtheron Vima, Deutsche Nachricten in den Niederlanden* and *Wiener Illustrierte*.
76 *Oggi*, C's memoirs, pt 2.
77 Interview w. Zoras.
78 Stancioff, *Maria*, 66.
79 Interview w. Nikolaidi.
80 Stancioff, *Maria*, 66.
81 *Ibid*.
82 *Deutsche Nachrichten in Griechenland*, May 9th 1944.
83 Interview w. Nikolaidi.
84 E. Callas, *My daughter*, 58.
85 *Oggi*, C's memoirs, pt. 1.
86 Interview w. Nikolaidi.
87 *Nea Estia*, August 15th 1944.
88 *Atineika*, August 17th 1944.
89 *Deutsche Nachrichten in Griechenland*, August 19th 1944.
90 *I Vradini*, August 17th 1944.
91 Interview w. Nikolaidi.
92 E. Callas, *My daughter*, 58 and 57.
93 J. Callas, *Sisters*, 95.
94 *Oggi*, C's memoirs, pt. 1.
95 *Ibid*., pt. 2, January 17th 1957.
96 *Ibid*.
97 *Ibid*., pt. 1.
98 E. Callas, *My daughter*, 82.
99 *Oggi*, C's memoirs, pt. 1.
100 E. Callas, *My daughter*, 85.
101 *Oggi*, C's memoirs, pt. 2.
102 *Ibid*.
103 Stancioff, *Maria*, 69.
104 *Ibid*., 69/70.
105 *Oggi*, C's memoirs, pt. 2.
106 *Ibid*.,
    E. Callas, *My daughter*, 88.
    Arianna Stassinopoulos, *Maria – Beyond the Callas Legend*, 45.
    George Jellinek, *Callas – Portrait of a Prima Donna*, 31.
    Newsweek, 'At La Scala, the Triumph of U.S.-Born Maria Callas', January 10th 1955.
    Life, 'Voice of an Angel' by Robert Neville, October 31st 1955,

Time, 'The Prima Donna' October 29th 1956,
and many other books and articles.
107 Metropolitan Opera archives.
108 Stancioff, *Maria*, 70/1.
109 *Ibid.*, 71.
110 Stassinopolous, *Maria*, 46.
111 E. Callas, *My daughter*, 85.
112 Interview w. Rossi-Lemeni.
113 Stassinopoulos, *Maria*, 50.
114 Giovanni Battista Meneghini, *Maria Callas mia moglie*, 23.
115 Irving Kolodin, *The Metropolitan Opera, 1883–1966*, 356.

CHAPTER II 1947–1948

 1 It took some while for the spelling of Callas's name to be standardized: sometimes
    it appears with a 'C', sometimes with a 'K', sometimes with one 'l', and sometimes
    with two. These aberrations are the result of (mis)transliteration from Greek.
 2 Stancioff, *Maria*, 75.
 3 Meneghini, *Maria Callas*, 16.
 4 *Ibid.*, 18.
 5 *Ibid.*
 6 Stancioff, *Maria*, 77.
 7 Meneghini, *Callas*, 19.
 8 *Ibid.*, 20.
 9 *Ibid.*
10 *Ibid.*, 21.
11 E. Callas, *My daughter*, 94.
12 Meneghini, *Callas*, 25.
13 *Ibid.*, 30.
14 *Oggi*, C's memoirs, pt. 2.
15 Meneghini, *Callas*, 30.
16 *Oggi*, C's memoirs, pt. 2.
17 *Ibid.*
18 *The Sunday Times*, 'The Voice that Launched a Thousand Discs' by Desmond
    Shawe-Taylor, September 19th 1987.
19 Interview w. Harewood.
20 Lanfranco Rasponi, *The Last Prima Donnas*, 47.
21 Meneghini, *Callas*, 32.
22 *Ibid.*
23 *Oggi*, C's memoirs, pt. 2.
24 Meneghini, *Callas*, 246.
25 *Ibid.* 38.
26 Rudolf Bing, *5000 Nights at the Opera*, 119.
27 Meneghini, *Callas*, 45.
28 *Ibid.*, 46.
29 *Ibid.*
30 *Oggi*, C's memoirs, pt. 3, January 24th 1957.
31 *Ibid.*
32 Meneghini, *Callas*, 49.
33 *Ibid.*, 48.

34 Interview w. Barbieri.
35 *Il Gazzettino*, December 31st 1947.
36 *Il Gazzettino-Sera*, December 31st 1947.
37 Meneghini, *Callas*, 55.
38 *Ibid.*, 241.
39 Stancioff, *Maria*, 79.
40 (N.Y.) Broadcast, Callas interview w. Fleetwood, March 1958.
41 (London) BBC TV, Callas interview w. Harewood, April 1968.
42 *Oggi*, C's memoirs, pt. 3.
43 *Ibid.*
44 Harewood, *The Tongs and the Bones*, 225.
45 Meneghini, *Callas*, 59.
46 *Il Lavoratore*, April 19th 1948.
47 Meneghini, *Callas*, 59/60.
48 *Oggi*, C's memoirs, pt. 3.
49 *Corriere del Popolo*, May 13th 1948.
50 Interview w. Rossi-Lemeni.
51 Interview w. Votto.

CHAPTER III 1948–1949

1 *La Stampa*, September 19th 1948.
2 *L'Unità di Torino*, September 19th 1948.
3 *Il Gazzettino*, October 20th 1948.
4 *Oggi*, C's memoirs, pt. 3.
5 Meneghini, *Callas*, 65.
6 *Ibid.*, 66.
7 Interview w. Siciliani.
8 *La Nazione*, October 1st 1948.
9 *Il Pomeriggio*, October 1st 1948.
10 *Oggi*, C's memoirs, pt. 3.
11 Meneghini, *Callas*, 70/1.
12 *Ibid.*, 71.
13 *Il Gazzettino*, January 20th 1949.
14 Meneghini, *Callas*, 72/3.
15 *Ibid.*, 73.
16 *L'Ora*, January 30th 1949.
17 Meneghini, *Callas*, 74.
18 *Il Quotidiano*, February 28th 1949.
19 (Paris) RTF TV, 'L'Invitée du dimanche' w. Visconti, April 20th 1969.
20 *Ibid.*
21 *Saturday Review*, 'Callas, Serafin and the Art of Bel Canto' by Jan Maguire, March 30th 1968.
22 J. Callas, *Sisters*, 122.
23 *Ibid.*, 123.
24 *Ibid.*, 125/6.
25 Meneghini, *Callas*, 75.
26 *Oggi*, C's memoirs, pt. 3.
27 Interview w. Rossi-Lemeni.
28 Meneghini, *Callas*, 82.

29 Interview w. Rossi-Lemeni.
30 *Saturday Review*, March 30th 1968.
31 Meneghini, *Callas*, 104.
32 *Ibid.*, 85.
33 *Ibid.*, 105.
34 *Ibid.*, 98.
35 *Ibid.*, 90.
36 *Ibid.*
37 E. Callas, *My daughter*, 103.
38 *El Mundo*, May 21st 1949.
39 *Ibid.*, June 18th 1949.
40 *Opera News*, October 1949.
41 *Oggi*, C's memoirs, pt. 4, January 31st 1957.
42 Meneghini, *Callas*, 106.
43 Stassinopoulos, *Maria*, 66.
44 Meneghini, *Callas*, 108.
45 J. Callas, *Sisters*, 123/4.
46 Meneghini, *Callas*, 112.
47 *Ibid.*, 118.
48 This recording was advertised on more than one occasion but was never transmitted.
49 Meneghini, *Callas*, 114.
50 Stancioff, *Maria*, 82.
51 Elisabeth Schwarzkopf (ed.), *On and Off the Record*, 198.

CHAPTER IV 1950

 1 *Il Gazzettino*, January 14th 1950.
 2 *Oggi*, C's memoirs, pt. 4.
 3 *Ibid.*
 4 (Paris) RTF TV, 'L'Invitée du dimanche' w. Visconti, April 20th 1969.
 5 *Il Giornale d'Italia*, February 23rd 1950.
 6 Franco Zeffirelli, *The Autobiography of Franco Zeffirelli*, 123.
 7 *Il Corriere Lombardo*, April 13th 1950.
 8 Interview w. Sciutti.
 9 *Time*, 'The Prima Donna', October 29th 1956.
10 Meneghini, *Callas*, 126.
11 *Ibid.*, 124.
12 *Ibid.*
13 *Ibid.*, 127.
14 *Ibid.*
15 Carlos Diaz Du-Pond, *50 Years of Opera in Mexico*.
16 *Opera*, 'Callas in Mexico' by Diaz Du-Pond, April 1973.
17 *Ibid.*
18 Meneghini, *Callas*, 127.
19 *Opera*, April 1973.
20 *Ibid.*
21 Meneghini, *Callas*, 131.
22 Ardoin (ed.), *Callas at Juilliard*, 115.
23 Diaz Du-Pond, *50 Years of Opera in Mexico*.

24 (London) BBC TV, Callas interview w. Harewood, April 1968.
25 Eduard Hanslick (ed. & trans. Pleasants), *Music Criticisms 1846/99*, 179.
26 *L'Avant-scène*, 'At the Source of Singing' ed. Alain Duault, October 1982.
27 Schwarzkopf (ed.), *On and Off the Record*, 199
28 *Ibid.* 193 *et seq.*
29 Meneghini, *Callas*, 126.
30 *Ibid.*
31 *Ibid.*, 128.
32 Meneghini, 136 *et seq.*
33 Joseph Horowitz, *Toscanini*, 224 *et seq.*
34 Meneghini, *Callas*, 147.
35 *Time*, 'The Prima Donna', October 29th 1956, E. Callas, *My daughter*, 119.
36 Interview w. Gavazzeni.
37 Interview w. Menotti.
38 Meneghini, *Callas*, 144.
39 *The Anglo-Saxon Review*, 'A word more about Verdi' by G.B. Shaw, March 1901.
40 (London) BBC TV Callas interview w. Harewood, April 1968.
41 R & H 100: 'The Mapleson Cylinders 1900–1904' Complete Edition.

CHAPTER V 1951

1 *Oggi*, C's memoirs, pt. 4.
2 *Ibid.*
3 Interview w. Zeffirelli.
4 *Ibid.*
5 *La Nazione*, January 16th 1951.
6 Luisa Tetrazzini, *My Life of Song*, 21. What Tetrazzini means by 'Isolde's songs' is more likely to have been the Wesendonck Lieder. Patti often sang 'Sogno' in concert.
7 Meneghini, *Callas*, 149.
8 (London) BBC TV Callas interview w. Harewood, April 1968.
9 *Opera*, August 1951.
10 Manuel Garcia II, *L'Art du chant*, pt. 2.
11 Meneghini, *Callas*, 151.
12 *Musical America*, August 1951.
13 *The New York Times*, June 28th 1951.
14 *The Musical Courier*, August 1951.
15 Bing, *5000 Nights at the Opera*, 180.
16 Du-Pond, *50 Years of Opera in Mexico City*.
17 David A.Lowe, *Callas – As They Saw Her*, 142.
18 *Ibid.*
19 *Oggi*, C's memoirs, pt. 4.
20 Tito Gobbi, *My Life*, 96.
21 Meneghini, *Callas*, 184.
22 *Ibid.*, 152.
23 *Ibid.*
24 *Ibid.*, 154 *et seq.*
25 *Oggi*, C's memoirs, pt. 4.
26 *Ibid.*
27 *Oggi*, C's memoirs, February 7th 1957, pt. 5.

28 *Ibid.*
29 *Ibid.*
30 *Ibid.*
31 Casanova, *Renata Tebaldi*, 220.
32 Meneghini, *Callas*, 155.
33 *Ibid.*, 152.
34 Meneghini, *Callas*, 166.
35 Interview w. Giulini.

CHAPTER VI 1951–1952

1 *Oggi*, C's memoirs, pt. 5.
2 In 1953 Tebaldi sang the title-role in Catalani's *La Wally*. That so unfamiliar an opera was chosen for opening night was the result of the precedent created in 1951 by Callas with Elena in *I Vespri Siciliani* and in 1952 with Lady Macbeth.
3 Meneghini, *Callas*, 176.
4 *Gazzetta di Parma*, January 1st 1952.
5 Schwarzkopf (ed.), *On and Off the Record*, 192.
6 Rosenthal, *Two Centuries of Opera*, 579.
7 Meneghini, *Callas*, 167.
8 *Ibid.*, 168.
9 *Ibid.*, 169.
10 *Musical America*, March 1952.
11 *Ibid.*
12 Schwarzkopf (ed.), *On and Off the Record*, 196.
13 Interview w. Rossi-Lemeni.
14 *Il Giornale di Sicilia*, March 13th 1952.
15 Meneghini, *Callas*, 134.
16 Bing, *5000 Nights at the Opera*, 182.
17 *Giornale delle Due Sicilie*, December 3rd 1817.
18 *Opera*, August 1952.
19 *Oggi*, C's memoirs, pt. 5.
20 *Opera*, July 1952.
21 Interview w. di Stefano.
22 *Opera*, April 1973.
23 Ardoin ed., *Callas at Juilliard*, 163.
24 Interview w. di Stefano.
25 Chorley (ed. & intr. Newman), *Thirty Years' Musical Recollections*, 354 & 368.
26 *Oggi*, C's memoirs, pt. 5.
27 *Opera*, April 1973.
28 *Ibid.*
29 Ardoin & Fitzgerald, *Callas*, 89.
30 (London) BBC TV, Callas interview w. Harewood, April 1968.
31 Interview w. di Stefano.
32 *Opera News*, October 27th 1952.
33 *Opera*, April 1973.
34 Diaz Du-Pond, *Fifty Years of Opera in Mexico City*.
35 *Opera*, November 1952.
36 *Chicago Tribune*, August 4th 1952.

CHAPTER VII 1952

1 Harewood, *The Tongs and the Bones*, 225.
2 *Opera*, April 1972.
3 Garcia II, *L'Art du chant*, pt. 2.
4 Herman Klein, *The Golden Age of Opera*, 245.
5 *The* (New York) *Sun*, November 21st 1907.
6 *Manchester Guardian*, November 10th 1952.
7 *Sunday Times*, November 16th 1952,
8 Lilli Lehmann, *How to Sing*, 282.
9 Rosenthal, *Two Centuries of Opera at Covent Garden*, 625.
10 *Oggi*, C's memoirs, pt. 5.
11 Interview w. Pritchard
12 Harewood, *The Tongs and the Bones*, 226.
13 *Ibid.*
14 Luigi Arditi, *My Reminiscences*, 50 *et seq.*
15 Bing, *5000 Nights at the Opera*, 31.
16 *Les Temps modernes*, 'The Secret of Callas' by René Liebowitz, July 1959.
17 *Oggi*, C's memoirs, pt. 5.
18 Garcia II, *L'Art du chant*, pt. 2.
19 Ardoin, *The Callas Legacy*, 64.
20 Schwarzkopf (ed.), *On and Off the Record*, 194.

CHAPTER VIII 1953

1 *Corriere della Sera*, December 27th 1952.
2 *Opera*, February 1953.
3 Interview w. di Stefano.
4 Interview w. Biki.
5 Schwarzkopf ed., *On and Off the Record*, 195.
6 Ardoin ed., *Callas at Juilliard*, 15.
7 Schwarzkopf ed., *On and Off the Record*, 57.
8 *Ibid.*, 194.
9 *Ibid.*, 193.
10 *Ibid.*, 200.
11 Gobbi, *My Life*, 98.
12 Chorley (ed. & intr. by Newman), *Thirty Years' Musical Recollections*, xvii.
13 *Opera News*, April 4th 1970.
14 Interview w. Rescigno.
15 *Opera*, May 1953.
16 Bing, *5000 Nights at the Opera*, 180.
17 (London) BBC TV, Callas interview w. Harewood, April 1968.
18 Ardoin ed., *Callas at Juilliard*, 5.
19 *News of the World*, June 21st 1953.
20 *Opera*, July 1953.
21 Interview w. Siciliani.
22 Meneghini, *Callas*, 172.
23 Interview w. Menotti.

24 *Il Gazzettino-Sera*, May 10th 1953.
25 *Opera*, June 1953.
26 *Corriere Lombardo*, May 8th 1953.
27 *La Patria*, May 8th 1953.

CHAPTER IX 1953–1954

1 *Opera*, July 1953.
2 *Radiocorriere TV*, No. 48, November 30th 1969.
3 *The New Statesman and Nation*, July 4th 1953.
4 *Opera*, August 1953.
5 *Ibid.*
6 *The Times*, June 27th 1953.
7 Interview w. Copley.
8 Meneghini, *Callas*, 178.
9 Schwarzkopf (ed.), *On and Off the Record*, 198.
10 *Ibid.*, 197.
11 Interview w. Menotti.
12 Interview w. Sequi.
13 Lanfranco Rasponi, *The Last Prima Donnas*, 584.
14 Interview w. di Stefano.
15 Meneghini, *Callas*, 175.
16 *Oggi*, C's memoirs, pt. 5.
17 Interview w. Tebaldi.
18 *Oggi*, C's memoirs, pt. 5.
19 Ardoin & Fitzgerald, *Callas*, 64.
20 Ardoin ed., *Callas at Juilliard*, 39.
21 *Opera*, February 15th 1954.
22 Interview w. Zeffirelli.
23 *Oggi*, C's memoirs, pt. 5.
24 Meneghini, *Callas*, 222 *et seq.*

CHAPTER X 1954

1 *Time*, 'The Prima Donna', October 29th 1956.
2 Interview w. Bauer.
3 Interview w. Biki.
4 Interview w. Reynaud.
5 Ardoin & Fitzgerald, *Callas*, 71.
6 *Ibid.*, 71/2.
7 Interview w. Rossi-Lemeni.
8 *Opera*, July 1954.
9 Schwarzkopf (ed.), *On and Off the Record*, 164.
10 Interview w. Rossi-Lemeni.
11 Lawrence Kelly interview w. Ardoin, January 29th 1973.
12 William James Henderson, *The Art of Singing*, 90/1.
13 Interview w. Zeffirelli.
14 *Radiocorriere TV, No. 48*, November 30th 1969.
15 Hanslick (ed. and trans. Pleasants), *Music Criticisms 1846–99*, 168.

16 Although Ponselle never sang any Puccini role in the theatre, for American Columbia she recorded arias from *Manon Lescaut, La Bohème, Tosca* and *Madama Butterfly*.
17 *L'Avant-scène*, 'At the source of singing', October 1982.
18 Ardoin (ed.), *Callas at Juilliard*, 53.
19 Saint-Saëns, *Ecole buissonière*, 265.

CHAPTER XI 1954–1955

1 Interview w. Rescigno.
2 *Newsweek*, 'At La Scala, Triumph of U.S.-Born Maria Callas', January 10th 1955.
3 *Chicago Tribune*, November 2nd 1954.
4 *Opera*, February 1955.
5 *The Musical Courier*, January 1955.
6 *Saturday Review*, November 13th 1954
7 *Opera*, February 1955.
8 Davis, *Opera in Chicago*, 234.
9 Gobbi, *My Life*, 97/8.
10 Kelly interview w. Ardoin, January 29th 1973.
11 *Opera*, March 1955.
12 *Opera News*, 'Splendor in the Night' by Claudia Cassidy, November 1977.
13 *Chicago Tribune*, November 2nd 1954.
14 *Opera*, March 1955.
15 *Gentry*, 'Music in America: Callas' by Lawrence Kelly, Spring 1957.
16 *Ibid.*
17 Kelly interview w. Ardoin, January 29th 1973.
18 Ardoin & Fitzgerald, *Callas*, 90.
19 (Paris) RTF, 'L'Invitée du dimanche' w. Visconti, April 20th 1969.
20 Interview w. Votto.
21 *Newsweek*, 'At La Scala, the Triumph of U.S.-Born Maria Callas', January 10th 1955.
22 *Opera*, March 1955.
23 Ardoin & Fitzgerald, *Callas*, 90.
24 Meneghini, *Callas*, 176 *et seq.*
25 *Oggi*, C's Memoirs, pt.5.
26 *Opera*, April 1955.
27 Harewood, *The Tongs and the Bones*, 227.
28 *Time*, 'The Prima Donna', October 29th 1956.
29 *Gentry*, Spring 1957.
30 *Ibid.*, 118.
31 *Ibid.*, 119.
32 Davis, *Opera in Chicago*, 237.
33 Ardoin ed., *Callas at Juilliard*, 81.
34 Meneghini, *Callas*, 214.

CHAPTER XII 1955

1 Zeffirelli, *An Autobiography*, 125.
2 Interview w. Zeffirelli.
3 Zeffirelli, *An Autobiography*, 131.
4 Meneghini, *Callas*, 182.
5 Ardoin & Fitzgerald, *Callas*, 115.
6 Interview w. Sequi.
7 Ardoin & Fitzgerald, *Callas*, 117.
8 *Radiocorriere TV No.48*, November 30th 1969.
9 Interview w. Sequi.
10 Meneghini, *Callas*, 166.
11 *Radiocorriere TV No.48*, November 30th 1969.
12 Interview w. di Stefano.
13 *Oggi*, C's Memoirs, pt. 5.
14 Meneghini, *Callas*, 189.
15 Cesari & Luzio (eds.), *I Copialettere di Verdi*, October 6th 1877.
16 (London) BBC TV, Callas interview w. Harewood, April 1968.
17 Glenn Plaskin, *Horowitz*, 283.
18 Ardoin, *The Callas Legacy*, 105/6.
19 *Ibid.*, 106.
   Lowe, *Callas*, 237.
   Wisneski, *Callas*, 121.
20 Interview w. di Stefano.

CHAPTER XIII 1955–1956

1 *Opera News*, 'Greek Sorceress' by Dorle Soria, November 1977.
2 Davis, *Opera in Chicago*, 237.
3 *Life*, 'Voice of an Angel' by Robert Neville, October 31st 1955.
4 Kelly interview w. Ardoin, January 29th 1973.
5 *Musical America*, January 1956.
6 *The New York Times*, November 3rd 1955.
7 *Opera*, January 1956.
8 *Chicago Tribune*, November 1st 1955.
9 Davis, *Opera in Chicago*, 238.
10 *Ibid.*, 238/9.
11 *Chicago Tribune*, November 6th 1955.
12 Bing, *5000 Nights at the Opera*, 181.
13 *Time*, 'The Prima Donna' October 29th 1956.
14 *The Chicago American*, November 16th 1955.
15 *Ibid.*, November 12th 1955.
16 *Chicago Tribune*, November 12th 1955.
17 *Ibid.*, November 15th 1955.
18 Henry Wisneski, *Maria Callas – The Art Beyond the Legend*, 181.
19 Davis, *Opera in Chicago*, 240.
20 Interview w. di Stefano.
21 *Gentry*, Spring 1957.
22 *Opera News*, November 1977.
23 *Gentry*, Spring 1957.

24 *Opera News*, November 1977.
25 Meneghini, *Callas*, 243 et seq.
26 *Opera News*, November 1977.
27 *Oggi*, C's memoirs, pt. 5.
28 Interview w. Bourgeois.
29 Garcia II, *Art du chant*, pt. 2.
30 *Oggi*, C's memoirs, pt. 5.
31 (Paris) RTF, 'L'Invitée du dimanche' w. Visconti, April 20th 1969.
32 Interview w. Zeffirelli.
33 Meneghini, *Callas*, 200.
34 Interview w. Zeffirelli
35 Legge's unpublished text of *Opera News* Callas obituary.
36 Interview w. Gavazzeni.
37 *Corriere Lombardo*, May 22nd/23rd 1956.
38 Meneghini, *Callas*, 213.
39 *Chicago Tribune*, July 9th 1956.
40 Callas interview w. Ardoin.
41 *Gentry*, Spring 1957.
42 Interview w. Nikolaidi.

CHAPTER XIV 1956–1957

1 *Time*, 'The Prima Donna', October 29th 1956.
2 Kolodin, *The Metropolitan Opera*, 576.
3 *Opera News*, November 1977.
4 Bing, *5000 Nights at the Opera*, 182.
5 Ibid.
6 Kolodin, *The Metropolitan Opera*, 575.
7 *The New York Times*, October 30th 1956.
8 *Saturday Review*, November 10th 1956.
9 *Time*, November 26th 1956.
10 *Musical America*, December 1956.
11 Bing, *5000 Nights at the Opera*, 184.
12 Graham Payne and Sheridan Morley ed., *The Noel Coward Diaries*, 399.
13 Lanfranco Rasponi, *The Last Prima Donnas*, 581.
14 *High Fidelity*, March 1957.
15 *Musical America*, January 1957.
16 *Saturday Review*, December 15th 1956.
17 Bing, *5000 Nights at the Opera*, 184.
18 Meneghini, *Callas*, 250.
19 *Ibid.*
20 Kolodin, *The Metropolitan Opera*, 578.
21 Davis, *Opera in Chicago*, 240.
22 Legge's unpublished text of *Opera News* Callas obituary.
23 Meneghini, *Callas*, 251.
24 *Ibid.*
25 *Ibid.*
26 *Chicago Tribune*, January 16th 1957.
27 Arthur Rubinstein, *My Many Years*, 130.

28 Elsa Maxwell, *I Married the World.*
29 Meneghini, *Callas*, 231.
30 *Ibid.*
31 Harewood, *The Tongs and the Bones*, 229.
32 *The Times*, February 4th 1957.
33 *Daily Express*, February 4th 1957.
34 Interview w. Pritchard.
35 Bing, *5000 Nights at the Opera*, 183/4.
36 Schwarzkopf (ed.), *On and Off the Record*, 201.
37 *Opera*, July 1957.
38 Henry Sutherland Edwards, *The Prima Donna*, Vol. 1, 211.
39 Benjamin Lumley, *Reminiscences of the Opera*, 284.
40 Sutherland Edwards, *The Prima Donna*, Vol. 1, 211.
41 Meneghini, *Callas*, 215.
42 *Oggi*, C's memoirs, pt. 5.
43 Interview w. Rossi-Lemeni.

CHAPTER XV 1957–1958

1 Meneghini, *Callas*, 194.
2 Ardoin & Fitzgerald, *Callas*, 162.
3 *Ibid.*
4 Interview w. Benois.
5 Ardoin & Fitzgerald, *Callas*, 162.
6 *Radiocorriere TV No. 48*, November 30th 1969.
7 *Opera*, August 1957.
8 George Jellinek, *Callas – Portrait of a Prima Donna*, 187.
9 (N.Y.) Broadcast w. Harry Fleetwood, 1958.
10 Schwarzkopf (ed.), *On and Off the Record*, 201.
11 Meneghini, *Callas*, 255.
12 Interview w. Nikolaidi.
13 Meneghini, *Callas*, 256.
14 *Ibid.*, 257.
15 Bing, *5000 Nights at the Opera*, 271.
16 Meneghini, *Callas*, 257.
17 *Ibid.*
18 Réal la Rochelle, *Callas – La Diva et le vinyle*, 321.
19 Meneghini, *Callas*, 276.
20 Jellinek, *Callas*, 199/200.
21 Meneghini, *Callas*, 233.
22 Interview w. Gavazzeni.
23 Jellinek, *Callas*, 204,
24 *Ibid.*
25 Meneghini, *Callas*, 264.
26 *Ibid.*, 265.
27 *Ibid.*
28 Jellinek, *Callas*, 205.
29 I watched this in London. It was one of the first Eurovision Telecasts. Callas sang the aria 'Casta Diva' with chorus but without the cabaletta.

30 This was on February 9th 1969, when I was Artistic Director of the London Opera Society. We presented a concert performance of Rossini's *Semiramide* w. Sutherland and Marilyn Horne at the Theatre Royal, Drury Lane.
31 Meneghini, *Callas*, 9.
32 *Ibid*, 263.
33 (N.Y.) CBS Telecast, 'Person to Person', Callas w. Ed Murrow, January 29th 1958.
34 Jellinek, *Callas*, 211.
35 Meneghini, *Callas*, 265.

CHAPTER XVI 1958–1959

1 Bing, *5000 Nights at the Opera*, 198.
2 *Chicago American*, March 1958.
3 *Chicago Tribune*, January 23rd 1958.
4 (N.Y.) CBS Telecast, 'Person to Person', Callas w. Ed Murrow, January 29th 1958.
5 Jellinek, *Callas*, 219.
6 *Ibid.*, 218.
7 *The New Yorker*, February 14th 1958.
8 *New York Journal-American*, February 7th 1958.
9 *The New York Times*, February 7th 1958.
10 *Saturday Review*, February 22nd 1958.
11 (London) BBC TV, Callas interview w. Harewood, April 1968.
12 *New York Herald Tribune*, February 7th 1958.
13 *The New York Times*, March 1st 1958.
14 Jellinek, *Callas*, 232.
15 Interview w. Gavazzeni.
16 Harewood, *The Tongs and the Bones*, 230.
17 Meneghini, *Callas*, 267/8.
18 *Musical America*, September 1958.
19 Meneghini, *Callas*, 206.
20 Harewood, *The Tongs and the Bones*, 232.
21 *Ibid.*, 231.
22 *Ibid.*, 232.
23 *The* (London) *Star*, January 23rd 1889.
24 Interview w. Rescigno.
25 Zeffirelli, *An Autobiography*, 141.
26 Stancioff, *Callas*, 122.
27 Bing, *5000 Nights at the Opera*, 186.
28 *Ibid.*, 187.
29 Zeffirelli, *An Autobiography*, 142.
30 *Ibid*.
31 Interview w. Zeffirelli.
32 *Dallas Morning News*, November 1st 1958.
33 Bing, *5000 Nights at the Opera*, 177.
34 Meneghini, *Callas*, 275.
35 *Ibid*.
36 *Ibid.*, 276.
37 Jellinek, *Callas*, 246.

38 Stancioff, *Maria*, 131.
39 Ardoin, *The Callas Legacy*, 150.
40 Harewood, *The Tongs and the Bones*, 232.
41 Zeffirelli, *An autobiography*, 149.
42 Stassinopoulos, *Callas*, 167.
43 Lowe, *Callas*, 205.
44 *The Opera Quarterly*, Vol.4, No. 4.
45 Schwarzkopf (ed.), *On and Off the Record*, 199.

CHAPTER XVII POST MENEGHINI

1 Harewood, *The Tongs and the Bones*, 233.
2 Meneghini, *Callas*, 283.
3 Interview w. Biki.
4 Meneghini, *Callas*, 286.
5 Stassinopoulos, *Callas*, 170.
6 Meneghini, *Callas*, 301.
7 Jellinek, *Callas*, 283.
8 Interview w. Zeffirelli.
9 Interview w. Bourgeois.
10 Schwarzkopf (ed.), *On and Off the Record*, 198.
11 Ivor Newton, *At the Piano*, 196.
12 J. Callas, *Sisters*, 161.
13 Schwarzkopf (ed.), *On and Off the Record*, 203.
14 Letter from Legge to Callas, November 7th 1971.
15 Stassinopoulos, *Callas*, 214.
16 Interview w. Glotz.
17 Stancioff, *Maria*, 162.
18 (Paris) RTF, 'L'Invitée du dimanche' w. Visconti.
19 Bing, *5000 Nights at the Opera*, 158/9.
20 La Rochelle, *Callas la diva et le vinyle*, 189.
21 Zeffirelli, *An Autobiography*, 297.
22 (N.Y.) *International Herald Tribune*, June 30th 1971.
23 Bing, *A Knight at the Opera*, 101.
24 Interview w. Zeffirelli.
25 Zeffirelli, *An Autobiography*, 207/8.
26 *Ibid.*, 209.
27 *Ibid.*, 210.
28 *Ibid.*
29 Stancioff, *Maria*, 170.
30 *Ibid.*, 171.
31 *Ibid.*, 172.
32 *Ibid.*, 163.
33 *Ibid.*, 161.
34 Meneghini, *Callas*, 7/8.
35 *Ibid.*, 7.
36 *Ibid.*, 7/8.
37 *Ibid.*, 8.
38 Stancioff, *Maria*, 217/8.
39 Bing, *5000 Nights at the Opera*, 198.

40 Stancioff, *Maria*, 192.
41 *Ibid.*, 165.
42 Kelly interview w. Ardoin, January 29th 1973.
43 Stancioff, *Maria*, 208.
44 Kelly interview w. Ardoin, January 29th 1973.
45 Stancioff, *Maria*, 209.
46 Interview w. di Stefano.
47 Stancioff, *Maria*, 219.
48 Interview w. Zeffirelli.
49 Stancioff, *Maria*, 225.
50 *Ibid.*
51 *Ibid.*
52 *Ibid.*, 230.
53 Interview w. di Stefano.
54 *Ibid.*
55 Stassinopoulos, *Maria*, 292.
56 J. Callas, *Sisters*, 209.
57 Stancioff, *Maria*, 250.
58 *Ibid.*, 253.

BIBLIOGRAPHY

Arditi, Luigi. *My Reminiscences*. New York: Dodd, Mead and Co., 1896.
Ardoin, John. *The Callas Legacy*. New York: Charles Scribner's Sons, 1982.
—— ed. *Callas at Juilliard: The Master Classes*. New York: Alfred A. Knopf, 1987.
—— and Gerald Fitzgerald. *Callas*. London: Thames and Hudson, 1974.
Bing, (Sir) Rudolf. *A Knight at the Opera*. New York: G.P. Putnam Sons, 1981.
—— *5000 Nights at the Opera*. London: Hamish Hamilton, 1972.
Bloomfield, Arthur J. *San Francisco Opera: 1923–1961*. New York: Appleton-Century, 1961.
Caamaño, Roberto. *La historia del Teatro Colón 1908–1968* (2 Vols.). Buenos Aires: Editorial Cinetea, 1969.
Callas, Evangelia (ed. Blochman). *My daughter – Maria Callas*. London: Leslie Frewin, 1967.
Callas, Jackie. *Sisters*. London: Macmillan, 1989.
Casanova, Carlamaria. *Renata Tebaldi: La Voce d'angelo*. Milan: Electa, 1981.
Cesari, Gaetano & Alessandro Luzio. *I Copialettere di Giuseppe Verdi*. Milan: 1911.
Celletti, Rodolfo. *Le Grandi Voci*. Rome: Istituto per la collaborazione culturale, 1964.
Chorley, Henry F (ed. and intr. Newman). *Thirty Years' Musical Recollections*. New York: Alfred A. Knopf, 1926.
Coward, Noël (ed. Payne and Morley). *The Noël Coward Diaries*. Boston: Little Brown, 1982.
Davis, Ronald L. *Opera in Chicago*. New York: Appleton-Century, 1966.
Faure, Jean. *La Voix et le chant*. Paris: Heugel et Cie, 1887.
Gara, Eugenio. *Die grossen Interpreten: Maria Callas*. Geneva: Kister, 1957.
Garcia II, Manuel. *L'Art du chant*. Paris: Heugel et Cie, 1847.
Gatti, Carlo. *Il Teatro alla Scala* (2 Vols.). Milan: Ricordi, 1964.
Glotz, Michel. *Revèler les dieux*. Paris: Editions Robert Lafont, 1975.
Gobbi, Tito (ed. I. Cook). *My Life*. London: Hamish Hamilton, 1984.
Guandalini, Gina. *Callas – L'ultima diva*. Turin: Edizione Eda, 1987.
Haltrecht, Montague. *The Quiet Showman*. London: Collins, 1975.
Hanslick, Eduard (trans. and ed. Pleasants). *Music Criticisms 1846–99*. London: Gollancz, 1951.
Harewood, the Earl of. *The Tongs and the Bones*. London: Weidenfeld & Nicolson, 1981.
Henderson, W.J. *The Art of Singing*. New York: The Dial Press, 1938.
Horowitz, Joseph. *Understanding Toscanini*. New York: Alfred A. Knopf, 1987.
Jellinek, George. *Callas, Portrait of a Prima Donna* (with new Preface and Epilogue). New York: Dover Publications, 1986.
Kellogg, Clara Louise. *Memoirs of an American Prima Donna*. New York: G.P. Putnam

Sons, 1913.

Klein, Herman. *The Golden Age of Opera*. London: George Routledge & Sons, 1933.
—— *Great Women-Singers of My Time*. London: George Routledge & Sons, 1931.
—— *The Reign of Patti*. London: T. Fisher Unwin, 1920.

Kolodin, Irving. *The Metropolitan Opera 1883–1966*. New York: Alfred A. Knopf, 1966.

Kutsch, K.J and Leo Riemens. *Unvergängliche Stimmen: Sängerlexicon*. Berne: Francke, 1982.

Lehmann, Lilli (trans. Aldrich). *How to Sing*. New York: Macmillan, 1924.

Lowe, David A. ed. *Callas – As They Saw Her*. London: Robson Books, 1987.

Lumley, Benjamin. *Reminiscences of the Opera*. London: Hurst & Blackett, 1864.

Mackenzie, Barbara and Findlay. *Singers of Australia from Melba to Sutherland*. London: Newnes Books, 1968.

Marchand, Polyvios. *Maria Callas*. Athens: Gnosi Publications, 1983.

Maxwell, Elsa. *I Married the World*. London: William Heinemann, 1955.

Meneghini, Giovanni Battista (ed. Allegri). *Maria Callas mia moglie*. Milan: Rusconi, 1981.

Michotte, Edmond (trans. Weinstock). *Richard Wagner's Visit to Rossini and An Evening at Rossini's in Beau-Sejour*. Chicago: The University of Chicago Press, 1968.

Newton, Ivor. *At the Piano*. London: Hamish Hamilton, 1966.

Ponselle Rosa and James A. Drake. *Ponselle – A Singer's Life*. New York: Doubleday, 1982.

Rasponi, Lanfranco. *The Last Prima Donnas*. New York: Alfred A. Knopf, 1982.

Rochelle, Réal la. *Callas, la diva et le vinyle*. Montreal: Les éditions Triptyque, 1987.

Rosenthal, Harold. *Two Centuries of Opera at Covent Garden*. London: Putnam, 1958.

Sachs, Harvey. *Toscanini*. London: Weidenfeld & Nicolson, 1978.

Saint-Saëns, Charles-Camille. *Ecole buissonnière*. Paris, 1913.

Schwarzkopf, Elisabeth. *On and Off the Record*. New York: Charles Scribner's Sons, 1982.

Scott, Michael. *The Record of Singing – Volume II: 1914–1925*. London: Gerald Duckworth, 1979.
—— *The Great Caruso*. London: Hamish Hamilton, 1988.

Shaw, George Bernard. *Shaw's Music 1876–1950* (3 Vols.). London: Bodley Head, 1981.

Spohr, Louis (trans. and ed. Pleasants). *The Musical Journeys of Louis Spohr*. Norman: University of Oklahoma Press, 1961.

Stancioff, Nadia. *Maria – Callas Remembered*. London: Sidgwick & Jackson, 1988.

Stassinopoulos, Arianna. *Maria – Beyond the Callas Legend*. London: Weidenfeld & Nicolson, 1980.

Sutherland Edwards, H. *The Prima Donna*. London: Remington, 1888.

Tetrazzini, Luisa. *My Life of Song*. London: Cassell, 1921.

Weinstock, Herbert. *Bellini: His Life and His Operas*. London: Weidenfeld & Nicolson, 1972.
—— *Donizetti and the World of Opera*. London: Methuen, 1964.
—— *Rossini: A Biography*. New York: Alfred A. Knopf, 1968.

Wisneski, Henry and Arthur Germond. *Maria Callas: The Art Behind the Legend*. London: Robert Hale, 1976.

Wolff, Stéphane. *L'Opéra au Palais Garnier (1875–1962)*. Paris: L'Entracte, 1965.

Zeffirelli, Franco. *The Autobiography of Franco Zeffirelli*. London: Weidenfeld & Nicolson, 1986.

INDEX

Moffo, Anna (1933–   ), lyric soprano, 172

Monaco, Mario del (1915–1982), tenor, 42, 49, 50, 60, 76, 147, 156, 166, 172, 177, 178

Mongiardino, Renzo, set designer, 240

Monkton, Lord, 232

Montefusco, Licinio, baritone, 246

Montemezzi, Italo, composer, 116

Monti, Nicola (1920–   ), tenor, 184

Montini, Cardinal, later Paul VI, 181

Moran, Lord, Churchill's doctor, 224

Morelli, Carlo (1897–1970), baritone, 77

Morgan, Michele, film actress, 216

Moscheles Ignaz, composer/pianist, 186

Moscona, Nicola (1907–1975), bass, 27, 177

Mundo El, 49, 50

Murrow, Ed, radio compère, 8, 204

Musical America, 75, 83, 84, 161, 178, 179, 208

Musical Courier, 75, 140

Mussolini, Benito, 12, 14, 19, 182

Muzio, Claudia (1889–1936), lyric soprano, 28, 136, 137, 224

Nazione La, 43, 69

Nelli, Herva (1923–   ), soprano, 29

Neri, Giulio (1909–1958), basso profundo, 199

Newman, Ernest, critic, 99, 100, 112

Newton, Ivor, accompanist, 232, 247

(The) New Statesman & Nation, 118

(The) New Y rker, 205

(The) New York Times, 75, 161, 177, 205

New York Herald Tribune, 205

Nicolai, Elena (1912–1985), mezzo soprano, 34, 39, 78, 122, 132

Nikolaidi, Elli, accompanist and répétiteuse, 12, 21, 22, 23, 175, 193

Nilsson, Birgit (1918–   ), Wagnerian soprano, 136

Nilsson, Christine (1843–1921), soprano, 93

Nobili, Lila di, set designer, 152, 153, 154

Nordica, Lilian (1857–1914), dramatic soprano, 67, 93

Norstad, General, 216

Nozzari, Andrea (1775–1832), tenor, 86

Oberon, Merle, film actress, 195

Olivero, Magda (1912–   ), verismo soprano, 124, 136

Ollendorff, Fritz (1912–1977), bass-baritone, 184

Oltrabella, Augusta (1897–1981), lyric dramatic soprano, 19, 122

Onassis, Aristotle, shipping tycoon, 104, 127, 146, 192, 195, 216, 219, 221, 222, 223, 224, 228, 230, 231, 232, 235, 236, 240, 241, 242, 243, 244, 248

Onassis, Tina, wife of above, 222, 223, 228

Onegin, Sigrid (1889–1943), contralto, 103

Opera, 92, 106, 113, 116, 118, 125, 130, 140, 142, 143, 147, 161

Opera News, 50

Ora, L', 46

Orlandi, Mario, 46

Ormandy, Eugene, conductor, 217

Ortica, Mario (1924–   ), tenor, 126

Pabst, G.W., film and stage director/producer, 119

Pacetti, Iva (1898–1981), lyric dramatic soprano, 55, 120

Paderewski, Ignace, pianist, 73

Paganini, Niccolo, violinist, 104, 158

Pagliughi, Lina (1907–1980), coloratura soprano, 112

Panerai, Rolando (1924–   ), lyric baritone, 114, 132, 171, 190

Papajohn, Alexandra, second wife of George Kalogeropoulos (Callas), 26

Papas, Irene, actress, 243

Parepa, Euphrosyne (1836–1874), soprano, 95

Pareto, Graziella (1889–1973), coloratura soprano, 12

Pasero, Tancredi (1892–1983), bass, 67